introduction to

LINEAR MODELS

introduction to

LINEAR MODELS

GEORGE H. DUNTEMAN

SAGE PUBLICATIONS
The Publishers of Professional Social Science
Beverly Hills London New Delhi

For information address:

SAGE Publications, Inc.
275 South Beverly Drive
Beverly Hills, California 90212

SAGE Publications India Pvt. Ltd.
C-236 Defence Colony
New Delhi 110 024, India

SAGE Publications Ltd
28 Banner Street
London EC1Y 8QE, England

Printed in the United States of America

Library of Congress Cataloging in Publication Data

Dunteman, George H. (George Henry), 1935-
Introduction to linear models.

Bibliography: p.
Includes index.
1. Linear models (Statistics) 2. Regression analysis.
I. Title.
QA276.D86 1984 519.5′3 83-19623
ISBN 0-8039-2175-6

FIRST PRINTING

Contents

Preface

This book was designed to address the following question: If one were beginning the study of statistical modeling, what primary concepts and tools would be necessary for a basic understanding of the subject matter? To put it another way, the material presented in this book is the material that I would have liked to have known when I first embarked upon the study of statistical analysis. I assume that my case is not unique and that others have the same needs. The book serves as a linkage between introductory statistics and the more advanced study of linear statistical models. It presents a broad coverage of the basic concepts, tools, and techniques needed for further specialized advanced study. A companion volume, *Introduction to Multivariate Analysis,* picks up where this book leaves off. It extends the models of this book to the case of multiple dependent variables.

The suggested audience for this book is that of advanced undergraduate and graduate students in the behavioral and social sciences, as well as social science researchers and research administrators in both the government and applied research organizations. It should also be useful for broad survey courses taught in departments of statistics. Although the examples are set in a behavioral and social science framework, this book should be useful in other disciplines as well.

In order to cover this type of material, many books assume a rather sophisticated mathematical and statistical background. The present book assumes that the reader has had only a course or two of noncalculus introductory statistics. The book is virtually self-contained. It covers basic statistics, matrix algebra, and linear models at an introductory level. The coverage is broad, and a penetrating discussion of advanced topics is provided in an intuitive and nonrigorous manner. In addition, an appendix presents a subset of data on a sample of 300 high school seniors from the rich data base of a large national survey sponsored by the federal government. This offers an opportunity for the reader to apply various statistical models covered in this book on "real-life" data through the use of "canned" computer packages. Computer packages and considerations are discussed where appropriate.

The reader who diligently works his or her way through this book, and its companion volume, will have a basic understanding of statistical model building that can be used as a stepping-stone to advanced study. Furthermore, the reader should be able to carry out statistical analyses and comprehend statistically oriented articles in his or her discipline.

This book was made possible through the generous support of the Research Triangle Institute. Special thanks are due to George R. Herbert, President, and Dr. William C. Eckerman (now deceased), former Vice President for Social Sciences, for creating the atmosphere conducive to this difficult undertaking. Secretarial support over the years was provided by Nita Blake, "Pete" Pender, Linda Hoffman, and Frances Heald. Nita Blake played a key role in the preparation of both books.

I would like to apologize to my wife, Rosarie, and our two children, George and Elizabeth, for the hardships I put them through over the past several years while working on this book and its companion volume.

1 Introduction

This book is designed to give the reader the basic skills needed to understand and use linear statistical models. Chapters 2 and 3 include a review of basic statistical concepts and a sufficient amount of matrix algebra to enable the reader to understand the remaining six chapters, which develop linear models in a logical sequence.

It is assumed that the reader has had one or two courses in elementary statistics, so that Chapter 2 will serve primarily as a review. However, there may be some material in Chapter 2 that has not been covered or emphasized in the course(s) completed by the reader; for this reason it should be studied carefully. In particular, the concept of the statistical relationship between two variables is especially important. The subject matter covered in Chapter 3, matrix algebra, will be new to many readers and will serve as a review for those who have had an undergraduate course in matrix algebra or linear algebra. The tool of matrix algebra is indispensable for studying most of the models presented in the remainder of this book. When statistical systems with many variables are considered, the reader will learn that the complex relationships can best be summarized in terms of matrices, which represent sets of numbers or unknowns, rather than by the single numbers or unknowns to which we are accustomed from our study of high school algebra.

Chapters 4 through 8 constitute the core of this book, linear models. These models all have a common set of characteristics. They all concern one continuous dependent variable and one or more independent variables. ("Dependent" variable refers to the variable whose behavior we are attempting to explain in terms of other variables, the "independent" variables. For example, the dependent variable might be intelligence and the independent variables various genetic and environmental factors.)

Multiple regression, discussed in Chapter 4, involves a single continuous dependent variable and two or more continuous independent variables. (Examples of continuous variables are height, weight, and intelligence, which are characterized by a continuum of numbers that satisfy certain order and distance properties with which we are all familiar.) Multiple regression is one of the most basic statistical models in use today. In a sense, all the models of the book can be considered to be generalizations of one kind or another of this basic model. Therefore, it is important to study this model carefully. The idea behind multiple regression is to model the continuous dependent variable y as a linear combination of a set of independent variables—$x_1, x_2, \ldots, x_p$. In the case of three independent variables, we would have $y = \beta_0+\beta_1 x_1+\beta_2 x_2+\beta_3 x_3+\epsilon$, where β_0 is the intercept of the regression plane; β_1, β_2, β_3 are the regression coefficients associated with independent variables x_1, x_2, and x_3, respectively; and ϵ is an error term that represents all other influences on y not explained by the three independent variables. The basic idea is to estimate the population parameters β_0, β_1, β_2, and β_3 from a simple random sample and test various statistical hypotheses about them.

The size and direction of the regression coefficients indicate the relative importance of the associated variables in explaining the dependent variable, y. The addition of an error term, ϵ, reflects the fact that we cannot usually explain all of the variation in the dependent variable by any finite set of independent variables. Unlike the physical sciences, where the behavior of the phenomenon can virtually be explained by a few key constructs, variables in the social and behavioral sciences are influenced by myriad factors, including measurement error. The incorporation of an error term representing other unknown influences makes the model a statistical one. Models in the physical sciences, where there typically is no error, are called deterministic models. If we dropped ϵ from the above equation, then we would have a deterministic equation.

Chapters 5 and 6 extend the multiple regression model to the case of one and two categorical independent variables, respectively. (Examples of categorical variables are sex, race, and religion, which have categories that cannot be represented by numbers that have any meaningful order or distance properties.) As in the case of multiple regression, there are regression coefficients attached to each category of each categorical variable and the goal is to estimate them from a random sample and test various hypotheses about them. The model can be extended easily to three or more categorical independent variables. Chapter 7 extends the previous main effect models to include interaction parameters. As we shall see, interaction parameters reflect the extent to which the relationship of one independent variable to the dependent variable depends upon the level of one or more of the remaining independent variables. For example, the relationship between intelligence (independent variable) and school achievement (dependent variable) might depend upon the level of achievement motivation (another independent variable). The coefficient or parameter reflecting the relationship between intelligence and school achievement might be larger for students with high levels of achievement motivation than for students with low levels of achievement motivation. Chapter 8 covers the most general model, which includes both categorical and continuous independent variables as well as variables reflecting interactions among the independent variables. All of these models are linear additive models.

The final chapter outlines the problems of applying the models discussed in this book to real-world data. For example, how does one analyze data from a complex probability sample where the assumptions of simple random sampling are violated? Chapter 9 also discusses logistic regression analysis, which is a procedure developed specifically for modeling a two-level categorical dependent variable rather than a continuous dependent variable. The independent variables can be continuous, categorical, or a mixture of both.

The reader should not be disturbed if this brief summarization of linear models is not clear at this point. The purpose of this introduction has been simply to sketch a broad picture of what is to follow. As the reader studies the book and works the problems, everything should eventually fall into place.

2 Basic Statistical Concepts

2.1 INTRODUCTION

As mentioned earlier, it is assumed that the reader has had an undergraduate course in introductory statistics. This chapter will review the basic statistical concepts that will be helpful in reading the remainder of this book.

Section 2.2 discusses the concept of probability through the use of some simple examples. The reader shall see that probability plays a key role in statistical inference. From section 2.2 it will be clear that possible outcomes of an experiment have probabilities attached to them. Furthermore, a number can be assigned to each outcome and therefore a probability can be associated with each number. This leads to the notion of random variables which are discussed in section 2.3. Univariate frequency distributions are discussed in section 2.4. It will be seen that, under certain conditions, the distribution of a random variable can be summarized by measures of location (that is, mean) and dispersion (that is, variance). The joint distribution of two random variables is characterized in section 2.5. This leads naturally to the notions of marginal (section 2.6) and conditional distributions (section 2.7). The concept of conditional distribution in turn leads naturally to regression and correlation, both of which are discussed in section 2.8. Regression and correlation are ways of describing how two variables are related to one another. Most of the models in this book are extensions of these simple relational models. The normal distribution (section 2.9) is a specific density function of a random variable that plays a critical role in statistical inference. Basically, a density function summarizes the relationship between a random variable and its probability of occurrence. Any statistic that is computed on the basis of a sample from a population can be characterized by a sampling distribution (section 2.10). The sampling distribution plays a key role in estimating the precision of a population parameter estimate through the use of confidence intervals, as discussed in section 2.11. The related procedures of testing statistical hypotheses are then discussed. Tests of hypotheses concerning the mean are discussed in section 2.12. Section 2.13 illustrates how hypothesis testing procedures can be extended to testing hypotheses concerning the regression parameter of the simple regression model discussed in section 2.8. The statistical models presented in this book rely heavily on testing hypotheses concerning the regression parameters of more complex models.

2.2 PROBABILITY

The concept of probability can be understood through an example. Suppose we have three colored chips—red, white, and blue. Suppose further that we put these in a hat and shake them up and then reach in and select a chip without looking in the hat. There are three possible outcomes; any one of the chips could be selected. Because of the nature of the experiment, we could argue that each chip would be selected one out of three times on the average, or that each chip has a probability of 1 / 3 or .333 of being selected. This argument follows from the fact that the chips are thoroughly mixed before one is drawn; consequently, each one should have the same probability of being selected. We could test this assumption empirically by replicating this experiment a large number of times and determining if the estimated probabilities of selecting each chip are consistent with a probability of .333. We cannot, in the real world, replicate this experiment an infinite number of times, but we can test whether or not the results of a large number of replications give us probabilities "close" to .333. Note that from this model we cannot predict with much reliability the outcome of any particular drawing of a chip; it is just as likely to be one color as another. Over the long run, however, we know that we would be right one out of three times.

Using this example as the background, we will talk about some laws of probability. First, we can consider the drawing of a chip as the outcome of an experiment, and the set of all possible outcomes for this experiment can be called the outcome space. The outcome space can be denoted as follows:

{red; white; blue}

In any one experiment any one of these outcomes is possible, and each has the same probability of .333. If we add up the probabilities of all the outcomes, we see that they equal 1. That is .333 + .333 + .333 or

$$\sum_{i=1}^{k} p_i = 1$$

where p_i is the probability associated with the ith outcome and k is the total number of outcomes in the sample space. The symbol Σ is a summation sign and

$$\sum_{i=1}^{k}$$

tells us to add the probabilities associated with the events 1 through k. We also see that each probability lies between 0 and 1 or $0 \leq p_i \leq 1$. These observations reflect three laws of probability:

(1) The probability of an outcome (0_i) is a nonnegative number and lies between 0 and 1.
(2) The probability of any one of a number of mutually exclusive outcomes occurring is the sum of their probabilities. ("Mutually exclusive" means that only one outcome can occur.) For example, the probability of drawing either a red or a white chip is .333 + .333, or .666.
(3) The sum of the probabilities of all mutually exclusive outcomes equals 1. This is the certain event that one of the mutually exclusive outcomes from the sample space must occur with probability one.

Let us now repeat the experiment two times. We first draw a chip after a thorough mixing (that is a random draw), and then replace the chip and repeat the procedure for drawing a second chip. In this experiment, the outcomes are represented by pairs of chips. Each chip can be paired with itself or any other chip. For example, we can draw a pair of red chips, a red and a white chip, and so on. The set of outcomes in this experiment is presented in Figure 2.1.

The first element in each outcome pair represents the chip drawn on the first draw and the second element represents the chip drawn on the second draw. For example, {red, white} indicates that the red chip was drawn on the first draw and the white chip was drawn on the second draw, while {white, red} indicates that the white chip was drawn on the first draw and the red chip was drawn on the second draw. In other words, we can draw both a white and a red chip in two ways, and these two ways are distinguished in the set of outcomes.

Because of the randomness of the experiment, the probability of any one of these nine outcomes is assumed to be equal to 1/9, or .111. The probability of drawing at least one red chip is the sum of the probabilities of the mutually exclusive outcomes 1, 2, 3, 4, and 5 in the sample space shown in Figure 2.1, or .111 + .111 + .111 + .111 + .111 = .555. An event is a collection of outcomes from the set of outcomes in the sample space. The event that at least one red chip is drawn is the union of the mutually exclusive outcomes 1, 2, 3, 4, and 5

(1)	(2)	(3)	(4)	(5)
{red, red}	{red, white}	{white, red}	{red, blue}	{blue, red}
{white, white}	{white, blue}	{blue, white}	{blue, blue}	
(6)	(7)	(8)	(9)	

Figure 2.1 Outcome Space for Drawing Pairs of Chips

($O_1UO_2UO_3UO_4UO_5$ in set theory language) and the probability of the event is the sum of the probabilities of the mutually exclusive outcomes defining the event. The reader can easily verify that the probability of drawing at least one blue chip is .555. The probability of the event—both red chips—contains the single outcome (red, red) and therefore has a probability of 1/9, or .111. The reader should generate the probability of other events, such as the probability of selecting at least one white or red chip, and so on.

The above discussion indicates that in calculating probabilities we create the outcome space, assign probabilities to the outcomes, and then calculate the probability of any event of interest by summing up the probabilities of the mutually exclusive individual outcomes associated with the event. In doing this, we make certain assumptions, such as the assumption that any outcome has an equal probability of being realized. We could, of course, test the assumption by replicating our experiment a large number of times, but from the nature of the experiment this seems like a reasonable assumption to make.

When the outcomes are mutually exclusive, as in the above example, the probability of an event occurring is simply the sum of the probabilities of the individual outcomes. If the outcomes or events are not mutually exclusive, then it is not legitimate to sum the individual probabilities. We must subtract from this sum of individual probabilities certain probabilities of joint occurrence. For example, what is the probability of drawing a football player or a baseball player from a school roster if the probability of being a football player is .03, the probability of being a baseball player is .02, and the probability of one person being both football and baseball player is .01? We notice that, in this situation, the events selecting a football player and a baseball player are not mutually exclusive, but rather the two events can occur together (that is, some students are both football and baseball players), as diagrammed in Figure 2.2

This Venn diagram shows that if we added the probability of selecting a football player and the probability of selecting a baseball player, we would be adding in twice the probability of selecting a student who is both a baseball and football player. Consequently, we must subtract the probability of being both a football and baseball player from the sum of the probabilities of the two events. If P(F) is the probability of selecting a football player, P(B) the

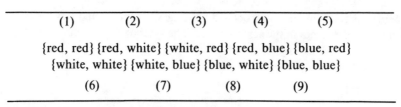

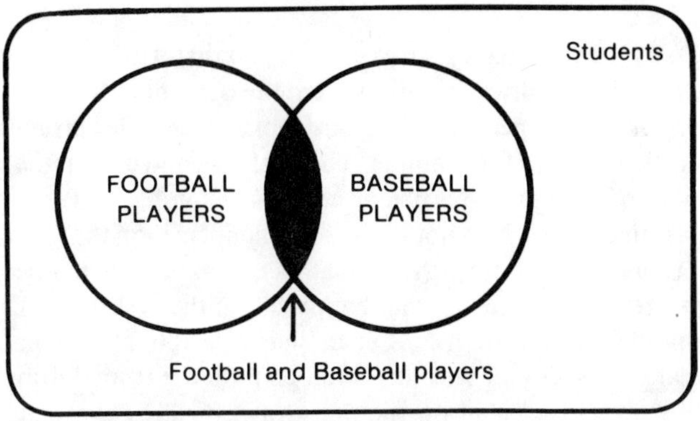

Figure 2.2 Venn Diagram Illustrating the Joint Occurrence of Two Events

probability of selecting a baseball player, and P(FB) the probability of selecting a student who plays both football and baseball, then the probability of selecting a football or baseball player is P(F) + P(B) – P(FB), which in this example is .03 + .02 – .01, or .04.

We can examine the chip-drawing experiment from another point of view if we use another probability law, which states that the probability of two independent events occurring is equal to the product of their individual probabilities. This can be written as P(AB) = P(A)P(B), where P(AB) is the probability of the joint event of both A and B and P(A) and P(B) are the probabilities of the events A and B occurring individually. "Independence" in a probability sense means that the occurrence of one event has no effect on the probability of the other event occurring. For example, if a coin is tossed and comes up heads, this occurrence has no effect on the probability of heads coming up on the next toss. The two events (heads on toss 1 and heads on toss 2) are independent, and the probability of both of them occurring is the product of their individual probabilities. This can be stated as $P(H_1H_2) = P(H_1)P(H_2) = (.50)(.50) = .25$.

We can regard our chip-drawing experiment as two independent draws of a chip. The chip first drawn has no effect on which chip is drawn on the second draw. The probability of any one chip being drawn on the first draw is .333, and this is also true of the second draw, regardless of which chip was drawn on the first draw. The probability of drawing two red chips is P(RR) = P(R)P(R) = (.333)(.333) = .111. The probability of drawing a red chip on the first draw and a white chip on the second draw is P(RW) = P(R)P(W) = (.333)(.333) = .111. Note that these probabilities derived under this law of independence correspond exactly to the probabilities that are assigned to the outcomes on the basis of the random characteristics and symmetrical nature of the experiment.

Suppose now that we modify the experiment so that we do not replace the chip selected on the first draw, but draw from the remaining two chips on the second draw. In this experiment without replacement, the probability of drawing a particular chip (for example, red) on the second draw is the same as the probability of drawing a particular chip (for example, red) on the first draw. This assumes that we do not know what happened on the first draw. If we make this assumption, then the probability of various outcomes on the second draw are not affected by what happened on the first draw. These are called unconditional probabilities. Let us illustrate this by calculating the unconditional probability of selecting a red chip on the second draw. (If we knew which chip was selected on the first draw, then, as we shall see, the probability of various outcomes on the second draw would be affected by the outcome of the first draw. The probabilities are conditional.) The unconditional probability of a red chip being selected on the second draw is the sum of the probabilities of the three mutually exclusive events {red, red; blue, red; white, red}. Under the new "without replacement" sampling scheme, the probability of the event red, red is $P(R_1)P(R_2|R_1)$, where $P(R_2|R_1)$ is the conditional probability of drawing a red chip on the second draw given that a red chip was drawn on the first draw and $P(R_1)$ is the probability of drawing a red chip on the first draw. The conditional probability $P(R_2|R_1)$ is zero since no red chip is available for the second draw since it was selected on the first draw, and $P(R_1)$ is $1/3$, so that $P(R_1R_2)$ equals $P(R_1)P(R_2|R_1)$, which is $(1/3)$ times 0 or 0. The probability of the event blue, red equals $P(B_1)P(R_2|B_1)$ or $(1/3)(1/2)$, which equals $1/6$. Note that $P(R_2|B_1)$ is $1/2$ because only a red and a white chip are present for the second draw and each has an equal probability of being selected. Finally, the probability of the event white, red equals $P(W_1)P(R_2|W_1)$ or $(1/3)(1/2)$, which equals $1/6$. The sum of the probabilities for these three mutually exclusive events is $P(R_1)P(R_2|R_1) + P(B_1)P(R_2|B_1) + P(W_1)P(R_2|W_1)$, which equals $0 + 1/6 + 1/6$ or $1/3$. This is the same probability that was observed under the with replacement sampling scheme.

However, if we know that a particular chip was drawn on the first draw, then the probability of various chips being drawn on the second draw is altered. The probabilities become conditional. They are conditioned by what happened on the first draw. Since there is only one red chip, if this chip is selected on the first draw the probability of a red chip being selected on the second draw is, of course, zero; and the probability of selecting either a white or a blue chip becomes .50. This is in contrast to the equal probabilities of .333 for selecting each of the three chips if we did know that the event red occurred on the first draw or if we replaced the red chip as we did in the previous experiment. If we look at the outcome space, we can calculate the probabilities of drawing a red, white, or blue chip given that a red chip was selected on the first draw. The outcomes of interest are red, white; red, blue; and red, red. In sampling without replacement, the third outcome (red, red) cannot occur, so that our revised outcome space has the remaining two outcomes—red, white and red, blue. From logical considerations, each of these outcomes is equally likely to occur, with probabilities of .50.

When outcomes or events are not independent, as in the above example, then the multiplicative law of probability for two independent events does not hold true and must be modified. Fot two nonindependent events, A and B, the probability of their joint occurrence, $P(AB)$, is $P(B)P(A|B)$ or $P(A)P(B|A)$, which states that the probability of the joint occurrence of the events A and B is equal to the product of the probability of the event B occurring times the probability of the event A occurring, given that the event B has occurred, or is equal to the product of the probability of the event A occurring times the event B occurring, given that A has occurred. In our example of selecting a chip without replacement, we saw that $P(RW) = P(R)P(W|R) = (1/3)(1/2) = 1/6$. Putting it another way, we could say that the conditional probability of selecting a white chip given that a red chip was drawn, $P(W|R)$, is $[P(RW)/P(R)]$, or, in this case, $1/6 \div 1/3$, or $1/2$.

In summary, there are two basic laws concerning the probability of joint events occurring. One applies to the case of independent events and the other applies to the case of nonindependent events:

(1) If n independent events occur with probabilities $P(1), P(2), \ldots, P(n)$, respectively, then the probability of n events occurring jointly or together is the product of the separate probabilities—$P(1)P(2) \ldots P(n)$.

(2) The probability of the n nonindependent events occurring jointly or together is

$$P(1)P(2|1)P(3|1, 2)P(4|1, 2, 3) \ldots P(n|1, 2, 3, 4 \ldots n-1)$$

where $P(1)$ is the probability of the event 1 occurring, $P(2|1)$ is the conditional probability of event 2 occurring given that event 1 occurred, $P(3|1, 2)$ is the conditional probability of event 3 occurring given that events 1 and 2 have occurred, $P(4|1, 2, 3)$ is the conditional probability of event 4 occurring given that events 1, 2, and 3 have occurred, and $P(n|1, 2, 3, 4 \ldots, n-1)$ is the conditional probability of event n occurring given that events 1 through $n-1$ have occurred. It should be noted that there are a number of equivalent expressions for this joint probability. For example, $P(ABC)$ can be expressed as $P(A)P(B|A)P(C|AB)$, $P(B)P(A|B)P(C|AB)$, $P(C)P(B|C)P(A|BC)$, and so on. The trick is to condition subsequent probabilities in the expression by all of the events contained in the prior probabilities.

TABLE 2.1
Number of Heads on Three Coin Tosses

Outcome	*HHH*	*HTT*	*HTH*	*HHT*	*THH*	*TTT*	*THT*	*TTH*
Random variable (number of heads)	3	1	2	2	2	0	1	1

2.3 RANDOM VARIABLES

We can associate a set of real numbers with the outcomes of random experiments by defining a random variable that transform the points of the sample space into points on the real line (that is, numbers). The function (f) that defines this transformation from the outcome space (0) to the real line is called a random variable. The value $f(0_1)$ is the value of the random variable for outcome 1.

Let us toss a fair coin three times. The outcome space is {HHH; HTT; HTH; HHT; THH; TTT; THT; TTH}. We can define a random variable as the number of heads on three tosses; the mapping of the random variable is shown in Table 2.1.

Each of these eight outcomes are mutually exclusive and have equal probabilities of 1/8. These probabilities can be specified in two ways. First, the experiment is such that we might logically assign equal probabilities to the eight events. Second, each toss is independent, with the probability of heads or tails being equal to 1/2. Therefore, the probability of each outcome is $(1/2)^3$, or 1/8. So we can assign probabilities to the number of heads by summing the probabilities of the outcomes that are mapped into a specific number of heads. For example, HHH is mapped into three so that the probability of three heads is 1/8. One head is a mapping from HTT, THT, and TTH. Since each of the mutually exclusive outcomes has a probability of 1/8, the probability of one head is P(HTT) + P(THT) + P(TTH) or 3/8. Similarly, the probability of two heads is 3/8 and the probability of no heads is 1/8.

The above definition was for a one-dimensional random variable. We can generalize the definition of a random variable to as many dimensions as we like. For example, a two-dimensional random variable transforms points in the outcome space into points in the XY plane; a three-dimensional random variable transforms points in the sample space into points in three-dimensional space. That is, each point has an x, y, and z coordinate.

We can use our sample space in the three coin-toss problem to define a three-dimensional random variable. Let our three-dimensional random variable be the number of heads on the first toss (X_1), the number of heads on the second toss (X_2), and the number of heads on the third toss (X_3). We then have a three-dimensional random variable $[X_1, X_2, X_3]$, which is a mapping of each

TABLE 2.2
Outcomes of Three Coin Tosses

	Outcome	*HHH*	*HTT*	*HTH*	*HHT*	*THH*	*TTT*	*THT*	*TTH*
Random variable	X_1	1	1	1	1	0	0	0	0
	X_2	1	0	0	1	1	0	1	0
	X_3	1	0	1	0	1	0	0	1

outcome into three values, one for each dimension of the random variable. A group of numbers or elements expressed in a row or column is called a vector. (Vectors will be discussed in the next chapter.) The mapping is shown in Table 2.2.

The probability of each of the eight outcomes associated with this three-dimensional random variable is equal to 1/8. Each of the three random variables, X_1, X_2, or X_3, can take on two values—0 or 1. That is, there can be either 0 or 1 head on each toss of the coin. The probability that X_1 takes the value of 1 is the sum of the probabilities for HHH, HTT, HTH, and HHT, which is 1/2. Likewise, the probability of X_2 and X_3 each taking the value of 1 is 1/2. The probability of the random vector ($X_1 = 1$, $X_2 = 1$, and $X_3 = 1$) or [1, 1, 1] is 1/8, since HHH, which has a probability of 1/8, maps directly into [1, 1, 1]. Likewise, the probability of the random vector [0, 1, 1] is 1/8 since THH, which also has a probability of 1/8, maps directly into [0,1,1]. It can be verified that the three random variables are independent by using the condition of independence $P[X_1, X_2, X_3] = P(X_1)P(X_2)P(X_3)$. For example, $P(1,0,1) = 1/8 = P(X_1 = 1)P(X_2 = 0)P(X_3 = 1) = (1/2)^3 = 1/8$. We can also look at other subsets of this random vector. For example, we could examine subsets $[X_1, X_2]$, $[X_1, X_3]$, and $[X_2, X_3]$. Each of these three vectors can take four forms: [1, 0], [0, 1], [1, 1], and [0, 0]. The probability of the subvector [1, 0] for $[X_1, X_2]$ is the sum of the probabilities of HTT and HTH, which is 1/4, since both HTT and HTH map into [1, 0]. Alternatively, since the two components of this subvector are independent, the probability of [1, 0] for $[X_1, X_2]$ is $p(X_1 = 1)$ $p(X_2 = 0) = (1/2)(1/2) = 1.4$.

We can also look at the conditional probabilities of various subvectors. We can examine the probability of $[X_1, X_2]$ taking certain values given that X_3 takes a specific value or the probability that X_3 takes a certain value given that the subvector $[X_1, X_2]$ takes a certain value. The conditional probability of $[X_1, X_2]$ given X_3 or $p(X_1, X_2 | X_3)$ is defined as

$$\frac{p(X_1, X_2, X_3)}{p(X_3)}$$

and the conditional probability of X_3 given $[X_1, X_2]$ or $p(X_3|X_1, X_2)$ is defined as

$$\frac{P(X_1, X_2, X_3)}{p(X_1, X_2)}$$

For example, the probability of $[X_1, X_2]$ taking the value [0,1] given that X_3 takes the value 1 is

$$\frac{P(X_1 = 0, X_2 = 1, X_3 = 1)}{p(X_3 = 1)},$$

or (1/8)/(1/2) = 1/4, and the probability that X_3 takes the value 0 given that $[X_1, X_2]$ takes the value [1,1] is

$$\frac{P(X_1 = 1, X_2 = 1, X_3 = 0)}{P(X_1 = 1, X_2 = 1)} = (1/8)/(1/4) = 1/2$$

Since the three random variables are independent, the probability distribution of X_3 does not depend on the values realized by $[X_1, X_2]$, and consequently $P(X_3) = P(X_3|X_1, X_2)$. Likewise, $P(X_1, X_2) = P(X_1, X_2|X_3)$. If random variables are independent, then their conditional and unconditional distributions are identical. The reader can verify these relationships.

The examples that we have been dealing with here involved discrete random variables. These discrete random variables take on only a finite number of values. As we have seen, discrete random variables can be either one-dimensional or multidimensional. We can also have continuous random variables that can be either one-dimensional or multidimensional. Continuous random variables take on all possible values in the real number system within a given interval. There are many continuous random variables in the behavioral and social sciences. Many of these are actually discrete random variables, but they take on so many values that for all practical purposes they can be considered and treated as continuous random variables. Some examples are intelligence, personality test scores, and attitude scale scores.

2.4 UNIVARIATE FREQUENCY DISTRIBUTIONS

Suppose we constructed a measure of self-concept and administered it to a random sample of 100 members of the population of young adults. The

TABLE 2.3
Frequency Distribution of Self-Concept Scores

	Self-Concept Scores (N = 100)									
	Low				*Average*				*High*	
	1	*2*	*3*	*4*	*5*	*6*	*7*	*8*	*9*	
Sample n_i	2	6	11	19	26	20	10	4	2	$\Sigma n_i = N = 100$
Relative frequency $p_i = \frac{n_i}{N}$	.02	.06	.11	.19	.26	.20	.10	.04	.02	$\Sigma p_i = 1$

hypothetical frequency distribution of the self-concept scores, which range from 1 (low) to 9 (high), is presented in Table 2.3.

This table indicates that the random variable self-concept (X) takes on various values X_i with various probabilities (p_i). It should be noted that we are dealing only with a relatively small sample here, and hence the relative frequencies or probabilities are estimates only of what the probabilities are in the population (that is, the population of all young adults) from which the sample came. For example, the probability of a score of 1 based on our sample is .02, whereas if we calculated it for the total population of young adults, it might be .04. The larger the sample, the more likely in a probability sense that the sample probabilities will be close to those of the population. This will be discussed later. For the present, let us ignore the distinction between a sample from a population and the population itself and concentrate on the characteristics of the frequency distribution shown in Table 2.3.

It can be seen that scores near the middle of the scale are more frequent than scores at either end of the scale. It can also be seen that the distribution is fairly symmetrical about the middle scale value of 5. This type of frequency distribution is characteristic of many psychological attributes and in many cases can be fit adequately by the normal density function, which will be discussed later in this chapter. The frequency distribution tells us that most individuals in the sample have scores in the middle range of the scale, and extremely low or high self-concept scores are much less frequent than middle-range scores.

There are two parameters that are usually used to describe a frequency distribution that is distributed like our self-concept scale. They are the mean ($\overline{X}$) and the standard deviation (s). The mean is the average value or score for the random variable. It is sometimes called a "location parameter" because it indicates where on a real line (that is, the X axis) the average or central value of the random variable is located. In a perfectly symmetrical distribution it also is the value of the random variable where an equal number of people (or other units that are measured) fall above and below that value. The median is the value of the random variable for which half of the units of observation (for example, people) fall above and below regardless of the shape of the distribution. For a perfectly symmetrical distribution, the mean and the median are identical. The median is sometimes a more appropriate measure of central tendency than the mean for nonsymmetrical frequency distributions. The formula for the mean is

$$\bar{X} = \Sigma p_i X_i$$

where p_i is the relative frequency or density of the ith value of the random variable (X_i). In our example the mean can be computed as

$$\begin{aligned}\bar{X} = \Sigma p_i X_i &= .02(1) + .06(2) + .11(3) + .19(4) + .26(5) \\ &+ .20(6) + .10(7) + .04(8) + .02(9) = 4.93\end{aligned}$$

The standard deviation (s) is a measure of the spread or dispersion of scores around its mean. Frequency distributions that have most of their scores or values of the random variable clustered closely around the mean will have a small standard deviation, and distributions with scores that are more spread out (that is, not clustered closely around the mean) will have large standard deviations. For a distribution such as self-concept, which is approximately normally distributed, about two-thirds of the people (or other units) have scores that are within one standard deviation of the mean. In other words, the probability that X falls into the interval ($\bar{X} - s$, $\bar{X} + s$) is approximately 2/3. The formula for the standard deviation is

$$s = \sqrt{\Sigma p_i (X_i - \bar{X})^2}$$

This formula shows that the standard deviation is a function of the distances of the values of the random variable from its mean (that is, $X_i - \bar{X}$) and the relative frequency of those distances (that is, p_i). We can see from this formula that if values of the random variable that are far away from the mean occur with a high relative frequency, then the standard deviation will be large. On the other hand, if values of the random variable that are close to the mean occur with a high relative frequency, then the standard deviation will be small. The relative frequency, p_i, weights the squared deviation of the random variable from its mean. The value of the standard deviation of the self-concept scale is

$$s = (\Sigma p_i(X_i - \bar{X})^2)^{1/2} = (.02(1-4.93)^2 + .06(2-4.93)^2 + .11(3-4.93)^2$$
$$+ .19(4-4.93)^2 + .26(5-4.93)^2 + .20(6-4.93)^2$$
$$+ .10(7-4.93)^2 + .04(8-4.93)^2 + .02(9-4.93)^2)^{1/2}$$
$$= 1.6628$$

The value 1.6628 is the square root of the average squared deviation from the mean. We have now summarized our frequency distribution by two parameters, the mean ($\bar{X} = 4.93$) and the standard deviation ($s = 1.6628$). These two parameters essentially summarize the characteristics of symmetrical empirical frequency distributions such as those illustrated by self-concept. The mean indicates the location of the distribution and the standard deviation its dispersion.

For nonsymmetrical distributions, statistics such as the median and interquartile range provide a better summarization than the mean and standard deviation. The median, a measure of central tendency, was discussed earlier. The interquartile range is a measure of dispersion. It is defined as the difference between the values of the random variable for which 25 percent of the sample falls below and 25 percent falls above.

2.5 BIVARIATE FREQUENCY DISTRIBUTIONS

Let us assume that we have joint measures for socioeconomic status and intelligence for a sample of 200 young adults. Furthermore, let the scale values for both intelligence and socioeconomic status run from 1 to 7. That is, the random variables intelligence and socioeconomic status take on the values 1, 2, 3, 4, 5, 6, 7 with certain probabilities. A hypothetical bivariate frequency distribution for these joint measures on the 200 sample members is presented in Table 2.4.

The manner in which the people are dispersed throughout the cells of the table indicates how the two variables, intelligence and socioeconomic status (SES), are related. Those people who have low SES scores as compared to people with high SES scores are more likely to have low intelligence (IQ) scores. Table 2.4 also exhibits the marginal frequency distribution for each variable, which can be obtained by summing across columns within rows for IQ and summing across rows within columns for SES. The $n(Y_j)$ indicates the

TABLE 2.4
Bivariate Frequency Distribution of Socioeconomic Status and Intelligence for 200 Young Adults

Y (Intelligence)	X (Socioeconomic Status) 1	2	3	4	5	6	7	$n(Y_j) = \sum_{i=1}^{7} n(X_i, Y_j)$
7					2	4	6	12
6				4	4	6	2	16
5			4	6	20	4	4	38
4		2	6	46	8	4	2	68
3	2	4	22	6	2			36
2	4	8	4	2				18
1	6	2	2	2				12
$n(X_i) = \sum_{j=1}^{7} n(X_i, Y_j)$	12	16	38	66	36	18	14	

$$N = \sum_{i=1}^{7} n(X_i) = \sum_{j=1}^{7} n(Y_j) = \sum_{i=1}^{7}\sum_{j=1}^{7} n(X_i,Y_j) = 200$$

number of individuals who score at the jth scale value of Y for IQ, $n(X_i)$ indicates the number of individuals who score at the ith scale value of X for SES, and $n(X_i, Y_j)$ indicates the number of individuals who jointly score at the ith scale value of X and the jth scale value of Y. Both subscripts i and j take on the values 1 through 7. For example, $n(X_7)$ is the number of people who scored 7 on the SES scale, $n(Y_5)$ is the number of people who scored 5 on the IQ scale, and $n(X_7, Y_5)$ is the number of people who scored 7 on SES and 5 on IQ. It follows that

$$\sum_{j=1}^{7} n(X_7, Y_j) = 0 + 0 + 0 + 0 + 2 + 4 + 6 = 12$$

is the number of people who scored 7 on IQ. The last term simply means that the number of people who scored 7 on IQ is the sum of those people who scored 7 on IQ and scored at any level on SES. Similarly, the number of people who scored 5 on SES is the sum of those people who scored 5 on SES and scored at any level on IQ. For our example, the number is

$$\sum_{i=1}^{7} n(X_i, Y_5) = 2 + 4 + 20 + 8 + 2 + 0 + 0 = 36$$

Let us now convert this frequency distribution into a relative frequency distribution or probability distribution. This can be done by dividing each n in the bivariate table by the total number of observations. For example, the probability of selecting an individual with a bivariate score of 5 on IQ and 6 on SES (that is, $[X_i = 5, Y_j = 6]$) is 4 out of 200, or .02.

2.6 MARGINAL DISTRIBUTIONS

The bivariate probability distribution shown in Table 2.5 also contains the necessary information to estimate the probability distribution for each of the two variables. For a bivariate probability distribution, the probability distribution for each variable is sometimes called a "marginal" distribution because it is obtained by summing the bivariate probabilities (densities) across all the values of the other variable for a given value of the variable of interest. For example, the probability of a score of 1 on the SES scale is the sum of the probabilities of all values of intelligence (1 through 7) in column 1 of Table 2.5. That is,

$$\sum_{i=1}^{7} p_{i1} = 0 + 0 + 0 + 0 + .01 + .02 + .03 = .06$$

where p_{i1} is the probability of having the ith value of intelligence and the first value (1) of SES. Similarly, the probability of a score of 3 on the intelligence scale is

$$\sum_{j=1}^{7} p_{3j} = .01 + .02 + .11 + .03 + .01 + .00 + .00 = .18.$$

The reader can in a similar manner construct the remaining probability elements for each of the marginal probability distributions. The probability distribution of intelligence is presented on the left of the table, and that for SES is presented at the bottom of the table.

TABLE 2.5
Bivariate Probability Distribution of Socioeconomic Status and Intelligence for 200 Young Adults

Probability Distribution of Intelligence	X (Socioeconomic Status): 1	2	3	4	5	6	7	Y (intelligence)
.06					.01	.02	.03	7
.08				.02	.02	.03	.01	6
.19			.02	.03	.10	.02	.02	5
.34		.01	.03	.23	.04	.02	.01	4
.18	.01	.02	.11	.03	.01			3
.09	.02	.04	.02	.01				2
.06	.03	.01	.01	.01				1
Probability Distribution of Socioeconomic Status	.06	.08	.19	.33	.18	.09	.07	

2.7 CONDITIONAL DISTRIBUTIONS

The concept of a conditional distribution is based upon the concept of conditional probability. Conditional probability indicates the probability of a value of one random variable occurring given that another random variable takes a specific value. If the conditional and unconditional probability distributions are identical, then the two random variables are independent; otherwise, they are dependent or one random variable is conditional upon the other. We saw that for our coin tossing experiment, the probability of heads on a given toss of the coin does not depend on the outcome of a previous toss of the coin. The two tosses are independent. On the other hand, we saw in sampling chips without replacement that the probability of drawing a certain colored chip on the second draw is dependent or conditional on what happens on the first draw. In our SES-intelligence example, we shall see that SES is conditional on intelligence and vice versa. For example, if we randomly drew a person from our hypothetical population in Table 2.5, and we knew the person's intelligence scale score was 2, then we could determine the person's probability of falling into each of the seven SES levels. This would be the conditional probability distribution of SES for an intelligence scale score of 2. The conditional probability of the ith level of SES given the jth level of intelligence is

$$p(X_i | Y_j) = \frac{p(X_i, Y_j)}{p(Y_j)}$$

where $p(X_i, Y_j)$ is the bivariate density of the ith value of SES and the jth value of intelligence and $p(Y_j)$ is the marginal density of the jth level of intelligence. Likewise, the conditional probability of the jth level of intelligence given the ith level of SES is

$$p(Y_j | X_i) = \frac{p(X_i, Y_j)}{p(X_i)}$$

With these formulas, let us construct the conditional probability distribution of intelligence given an SES score of 4. The conditional probability of an IQ score of 7 is

$$p(Y_7 | X_4) = \frac{p(X_4, Y_7)}{p(X_4)} = \frac{0}{.33} = 0$$

The conditional probability of an IQ score of 6 is

$$p(Y_6 | X_4) = \frac{p(X_4, Y_6)}{p(X_4)} = \frac{.02}{.33} = .06$$

The reader can verify that $p(Y_5 | X_4) = .09$, $p(Y_4 | X_4) = .69$, $p(Y_3 | X_4) = .09$, $p(Y_2 | X_4) = .03$, and $p(Y_1 | X_4) = .03$. These seven probabilities add up to within rounding error of one, since a conditional probability distribution has the same properties as an unconditional probability distribution. There are six

TABLE 2.6
Conditional Probability Distributions of Intelligence for Each of Seven Socioeconomic Status Levels[a]

		SES Level						
		1	2	3	4	5	6	7
	7	.00	.00	.00	.00	.06	.22	.43
	6	.00	.00	.00	.06	.11	.33	.14
	5	.00	.00	.11	.09	.56	.22	.29
Intelligence	4	.00	.13	.16	.69	.22	.22	.14
	3	.17	.25	.58	.09	.06	.00	.00
	2	.33	.50	.11	.03	.00	.00	.00
	1	.50	.13	.05	.03	.00	.00	.00

a. Conditional distributions are columns.

other conditional probability distributions of intelligence, one for each of the six remaining values of SES. The seven conditional probability distributions of intelligence given SES are presented in Table 6. As an exercise, the reader should determine the seven conditional probability distributions of SES given intelligence.

It can easily be seen from Table 2.6 that the probability of scoring at a particular intelligence level is a function of the person's SES level. For example, the probability of an IQ score of 7 given an SES score of 7 is .43, while the probability of an IQ score of 7 given an SES score of 1 is 0. We see that intelligence is dependent upon SES or that the two random variables, intelligence and SES, are not independent. If SES and intelligence were independent, then the conditional intelligence distributions would be identical since knowing the value of SES should not yield any information concerning the probability distribution of intelligence. We saw earlier that two events were independent if their joint probability of occurrence was equal to the product of their separate unconditional probabilities of occurrence. Similarly, two random variables are independent if their bivariate probability distribution is a product of their separate marginal distributions. That is, $P(X_i, Y_j) = P(X_i)P(Y_j)$ for all values of i and j. In our example, $P(X_4, Y_5)$ would equal $P(X_4)P(Y_5)$ if intelligence and SES were independent. However, $P(X_4, Y_5) = .03$ and $P(X_4)P(Y_5) = (.33)(.19) = .06$ so that $P(X_4, Y_5) \neq P(X_4)P(Y_5)$, and therefore the random variables intelligence and SES are not independent of one another.

2.8 REGRESSION AND CORRELATION

In the previous section we computed the conditional probability distributions of intelligence for each of the seven SES levels. Using these seven conditional probability distributions, let us compute the mean and standard deviation for each one. The mean of intelligence for SES level 1 is

$$\bar{X}_{(IQ|SES1)} = \sum_{i=1}^{7} p_{i1} X_i$$

where p_{i1} is the conditional probability of score i on intelligence for SES level 1 and X_i is the corresponding score for the ith level of intelligence. Using the probability distribution in the first column of Table 2.6, it can be seen that

$$\bar{X}_{(IQ|SES1)} = \sum_{i=1}^{7} p_{i1} X_i = .50(1) + .33(2) + .17(3) + .00(4) + .00(5) + .00(6) + .00(7) = 1.67$$

The standard deviation of this conditional distribution is

$$S_{(IQ|SES1)} = \sqrt{\sum_{i=1}^{7} p_{i1} \left(X_i - \bar{X}_{(IQ|SES1)}\right)^2}$$

which is

$$\left(.50(1-1.67)^2 + .33(2-1.67)^2 + .17(3-1.67)^2 + .00(4-1.67)^2 \right.$$
$$\left. .00(5-1.67)^2 + .00(6-1.67)^2 + .00(7-1.67)^2\right)^{1/2} \text{ or } .75$$

The remaining six conditional means and standard deviations for intelligence are calculated in the same manner. All seven conditional means and standard deviations as well as the unconditional or marginal mean and standard deviation are presented in Table 2.7.

It can be seen from this table that both the conditional means and conditional standard deviations for intelligence differ across the seven SES levels, and they all also differ from the unconditional mean and standard deviation. This is another way of examining the interdependence between SES and intelligence. If SES and intelligence were independent random variables, then

TABLE 2.7
Conditional Means and Standard Deviations for Intelligence Given SES

	SES Level							
Intelligence	*1*	*2*	*3*	*4*	*5*	*6*	*7*	*Unconditional*
$\overline{X}$	1.67	2.40	3.20	3.93	4.94	5.50	5.86	3.99
s	0.75	0.87	0.94	0.90	0.89	1.06	1.12	1.46

the conditional means and standard deviations would all be equal to each other. That is, they would all have the same mean and standard deviation as the total or unconditional distribution. In the present case, knowing the SES level of the individual yields information regarding the respondent's intelligence. If the person falls in SES level 1, then we know that people at that level, on the average, score at 1.67 on this particular IQ scale and that the scores are dispersed around this mean with a standard deviation of .75. On the other hand, a person at SES level 7 would be expected to have, on the average, an IQ score of 5.86, and the dispersion of IQ scores is somewhat greater at the highest SES level (1.12 versus .75). In general, as SES increases, average intelligence increases and the IQ scores become more dispersed. There is more variability in intelligence at the higher SES levels.[1]

The means for intelligence and the individual data points for each level of SES are plotted in Figure 2.3. The number beside each point indicates the number of observations that the point represents.

The lines connecting the seven means for intelligence show that the mean increase of intelligence with increases in SES is almost linear. The trend among the means shows some deviations from a straight line or linear relationship, but for our purposes we shall consider it as a linear trend.

Since it is assumed that the data can be summarized by a straight-line relationship, it would be worthwhile to find the equation of the straight line that best fits the data in some sense and effectively summarizes the relationship between intelligence and SES. A criterion of fit that is often used by statisticians in a situation like this is to find the equation of the line that minimizes the sum of the squared deviations of the intelligence scores from that line. That is, find the line that minimizes

$$\sum_{i=1}^{200} e_i^2$$

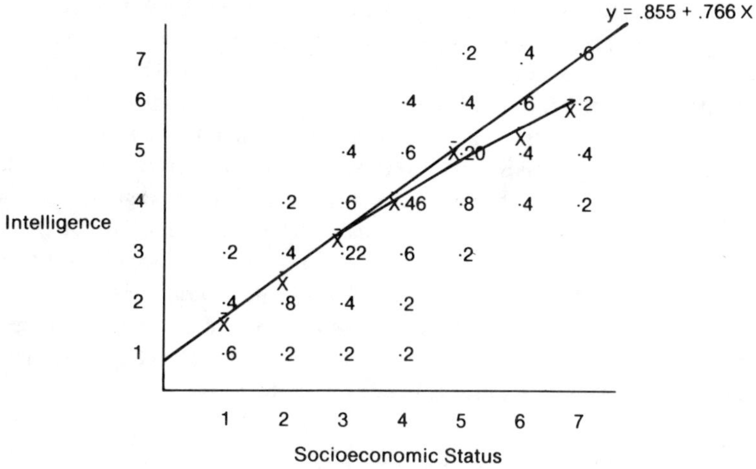

Figure 2.3 Scatter Plot of Intelligence and Socioeconomic Status

where e_i is the deviation of the ith individual's intelligence score from that line. We call the line minimizing Σe_i^2 the regression line of intelligence on SES, or we say that we are regressing intelligence on SES. Intuitively, the regression line should be close to the line connecting the means as shown in the scatter plot. In fact, the curve that would best fit the data in a least-squares sense (that is, minimum $\sum_i e_i^2$) is the curve that connects the means as shown in the scatter plot. The reason for this is that the sum of squared deviations of the observations from the mean is smaller than the sum of squared deviations from any other constant.[2]

We obviously cannot fit the seven intelligence means with a straight line and therefore cannot get the best fit in a least-squares sense, but we can come close. The problem boils down to finding the parameters a and b of the line $y_i = a + bx_i$ where y is the predicted intelligence score (that is, the dependent variable) and x is SES (that is, the independent variable) such that $\sum_i [y_i - (a + bx_i)]^2$ is minimized. Expanding, we have

$$\sum_i (y_i - a - bx_i)^2 = \sum_i (y_i^2 - 2ay_i - 2bx_iy_i + 2abx_i + b^2x_i^2 + a^2)$$

$$= \sum_i y_i^2 - 2a\sum_i y_i - 2b\sum_i x_iy_i + 2ab\sum_i x_i + b^2\sum_i x_i^2 + na^2$$

In order to find the value of a (intercept) and b (slope) that minimizes $\sum_i (y_i - a - bx_i)^2$, we need to take the partial derivative of the expression with respect to a and with respect to b and set these two partial derivative equations equal to zero. This will yield two equations in the two unknowns, a and b, that can then be solved for a and b. The partial derivative of $\sum_i (y_i - a - bx_i)^2 = \theta$ with respect to a is a function that expresses the ratio of the change in θ to the change in a as the change in a approaches zero. Likewise, the partial derivative of θ with respect to b is a function that expresses the ratio of the change in θ to the change in b as the change in b approaches zero. In order for θ to be a minimum, both partial derivatives have to be equal to zero, since this indicates the point where θ is no longer changing (that is, getting larger or smaller) as a and b change. The partial derivatives of θ with respect to a and θ with respect to b are symbolized as $\delta\theta / \delta a$ and $\delta\theta / \delta b$, respectively. For those readers who have had elementary calculus, it can easily be seen that

$$\frac{\partial \theta}{\partial a} = -2\sum_i y_i + 2na + 2b\sum_i x_i$$

$$\frac{\partial \theta}{\partial b} = -2\sum_i x_i y_i + 2a\sum_i x_i + 2b\sum_i x_i^2$$

For those readers who have not had elementary calculus, the results can be taken on faith.

Setting each partial derivative equal to zero and simplifying, we have the two simultaneous equations[3]

$$an + b\sum_i x_i = \sum_i y_i$$

$$a\sum_i x_i + b\sum_i x_i^2 = \sum_i x_i y_i$$

We can compute the constants $\sum_i x_i$, $\sum_i y_i$, $\sum_i x_i^2$, and $\sum_i x_i y_i$ from our data and, of course, n is also known. The terms $\sum x_i^2$ and $\sum x_i y_i$ are referred to as the sum of squares and the sum of cross products, respectively.

With our knowledge of elementary algebra[4] we can show that

$$b = \frac{\sum_i x_i y_i - \frac{\left(\sum_i x_i\right)\left(\sum_i y_i\right)}{n}}{\sum_i x_i^2 - \frac{\left(\sum_i x_i\right)^2}{n}}$$

$$a = \bar{y} - \left[\frac{\sum_i x_i y_i - \frac{\left(\sum_i x_i\right)\left(\sum_i y_i\right)}{n}}{\sum_i x_i^2 - \frac{\left(\sum_i x_i\right)^2}{n}}\right] \bar{x} = \bar{y} - b\bar{x}$$

The numerator of b, the slope parameter, is called the corrected (adjusted for the mean) sum of cross products or sum of cross products about the mean and is equal to $\sum_i (x_i - \bar{x})(y_i - \bar{y})$. Similarly, the denominator of b is called the corrected (adjusted for the mean) sum of squares or sum of squares about the mean and is equal to $\sum_i (x_i - \bar{x})^2$. Consequently, b can be expressed as

$$\frac{\sum_i (x_i - \bar{x})(y_i - \bar{y})}{\sum_i (x_i - \bar{x})^2}$$

but expressing b in the previous form is easier computationally since we do not need to calculate deviation scores before summing. It is a general practice to compute b first and then a, since a can be written as $\bar{y} - b\bar{x}$.

Using the data from Table 2.4, let us solve for the parameters a and b for our hypothetical data set. Cursory examination of the formulas for the two parameters indicates that the two parameters can easily be calculated, once $\sum_i x_i$, $\sum_i y_i$, $\sum_i x_i^2$, $\sum_i y_i^2$, and $\sum_i x_i y_i$ are known. In the above notation, x_i, indicates the value of the ith individual of the random variable x (that is, SES) where i ranges from 1 to 200. The value of $\sum_i x_i^2$ is $12(1)^2 + 16(2)^2 + 38(3)^2 + \ldots + 14(7)^2$, or 3708. The computation is simple since there are only seven values of the random variable x and each value is taken on by numerous individuals. To compute the value of $\sum_i x_i y_i$, for each cell we multiply the number of observations by the row and column value of the random variables and sum this triple product across all nonempty cells. Starting with column 1 and continuing column by column, we find $\sum_i x_i y_i$ equals 2(3)(1) + 4(2)(1) + 6(1)(1) + . . . + 2(4)(7), or 3558. The reader should verify that $\sum_i x_i = 808$, $\sum_i y_i = 798$, and $\sum_i y_i^2 = 3610$. Since n equals 200,

$$b = \frac{3558 - \dfrac{(808)(798)}{200}}{3708 - \dfrac{(808)^2}{200}} = .776$$

and

$$a = \frac{798}{200} - .776\left(\frac{808}{200}\right) = .855$$

Therefore, the equation of the regression line is $y_i = .855 + .776x_i$ and is shown on the scatter plot of Figure 2.3. Notice that the regression line comes pretty close to the series of lines connecting the means. For a simple function, it gives a pretty good fit to the data. Let us see if we can now find one number that summarizes how much IQ is related to SES.

First, the total sum of squares about the mean of the dependent variable, IQ, is $\sum_i (y_i - \bar{y})^2$. This sum of squares can be broken down into two component sums of squares, the predicted or regression sum of squares and the error sum of squares. Since $y_i - \bar{y} = (y_i - \hat{y}_i) + (\hat{y}_i - \bar{y})$,

$$\sum_i (y_i - \bar{y})^2 = \sum_i [(y_i - \hat{y}_i) + (\hat{y}_i - \bar{y})]^2$$
$$= \sum_i (y_i - \hat{y}_i)^2 + \sum_i (\hat{y}_i - \bar{y})^2 + 2\sum_i (y_i - \hat{y}_i)(\hat{y}_i - \bar{y})$$

the term $\sum_i (y_i - \hat{y}_i)^2$ is the sum of squares of the deviation of the observed values of y_i from the predicted values. If we let $e_i = y_i - \hat{y}_i$, then $\sum_i (y_i - \hat{y}_i)^2$ can be more simply expressed as $\sum_i e_i^2$. The predicted values are the values y_i that fall on the regression line. Since we are concerned here with deviations from the regression line or predicted values, $\sum_i e_i^2$ is called the error sum of squares.

The term $\sum_i (\hat{y}_i - \bar{y})^2$ is the sum of squares of the deviation of the predicted values from the overall mean of y. It is called the regression sum of squares. If y did not vary with x, then all of the predicted values, $\hat{y}_i$, would be equal to the overall mean $\bar{y}$. If the values of $\hat{y}_1$ differ from $\bar{y}$, then $\sum_i (\hat{y}_i - \bar{y})^2$ is positive and the independent variable x explains some of the variation in y since $\hat{y}_i = a + bx_i$.

This term is consequently sometimes called the sum of squares due to the regression model.

The term $2\sum_i (y_i - \hat{y}_i)(\hat{y}_i - \bar{y})$ involves the cross product of the error in the regression model and the deviation of the predicted value from the overall mean. It can be shown that this term is equal to zero.

Consequently,

$$\sum_i (y_i - \bar{y})^2 = \sum_i (\hat{y}_i - \bar{y})^2 + \sum_i (y_i - \hat{y}_i)^2$$

and the total sum of squares can be partitioned into a sum of squares due to regression plus a sum of squares due to error. If we form the ratio

$$\frac{\sum_i (\hat{y}_i - \bar{y})^2}{\sum_i (y_i - \bar{y})^2}$$

then we have an index of the amount of variation in y explained by the independent variable in the regression model. This ratio is sometimes referred to as r^2.

Similarly,

$$\frac{\sum_i (y_i - \hat{y}_i)^2}{\sum_i (y_i - \bar{y})^2}$$

is an index of the amount of variation in y that cannot be explained by the regression model.

Since $\hat{y}_i = a + bx_i$ and $\bar{y} = a + b\bar{x}$, the proportion of variance due to regression can also be expressed as

$$\frac{\sum_i [b(x_i - \bar{x})]^2}{\sum_i (y_i - \bar{y})^2} \quad \text{or} \quad \frac{b^2 \sum_i (x_i - \bar{x})^2}{\sum_i (y_i - \bar{y})^2} = r^2$$

where $b^2 \sum_{i=1} (x_i - x)^2$ is the regression sum of squares.

If we take the square root of r^2, we than have

$$r = \frac{b\sqrt{\sum_i (x_i - \bar{x})^2}}{\sqrt{\sum_i (y_i - \bar{y})^2}}$$

This r is called the correlation coefficient between x and y and is simply the square root of the proportion of the total variation that is explained by the regression model.

We can also express the correlation in terms of the x and y variables since

$$b = \frac{\sum_i (x_i - \bar{x})(y_i - \bar{y})}{\sum_i (x_i - \bar{x})^2}$$

and consequently,

$$r = \frac{\sum_i (x_i - \bar{x})(y_i - \bar{y})}{\sqrt{\sum_i (x_i - \bar{x})^2}\sqrt{\sum_i (y_i - \bar{y})^2}}$$

From our regression data, calculating the total sum of squares for the dependent variable (SS_T), the regression sum of squares (SS_R), and the error sum of squares (SS_E), we have

$$SS_T = \sum_{i=1}^{n} (y_i - \bar{y})^2 = \Sigma y_i^2 - \frac{(\Sigma y_i)^2}{n} = 3610 - \frac{(798)^2}{200} = 425.98$$

$$SS_R = b^2 \sum_{i=1}^{n} (x_i - \bar{x})^2 = b^2 \left[\Sigma x_i^2 - \frac{(\Sigma x_i)^2}{n}\right]$$

$$= (.753)^2 \left[3708 - \frac{(808)^2}{200}\right] = 251.57$$

and

$$SS_e = SS_T - SS_R = 425.98 - 251.57 = 174.41$$

The proportion of total variance explained by x is

$$\frac{SS_R}{SS_T} = \frac{251.57}{425.98} = .591$$

The correlation between x and y ($r_{x,y}$) is

$$\sqrt{\frac{SS_R}{SS_T}} = \sqrt{.591} = .768$$

We can also use the formula

$$r_{x,y} = \frac{\sum_{i=1}^{n} (x_i - \bar{x})(y_i - \bar{y})}{\sqrt{\sum_{i=1}^{n} (x_i - \bar{x})^2} \sqrt{\sum_{i=1}^{n} (y_i - \bar{y})^2}}$$

$$= \frac{334.08}{\sqrt{443.68}\sqrt{425.98}} = .768$$

since

$$\sum_{i=1}^{n} (x_i - \bar{x})(y_i - \bar{y}) = \sum_i x_i y_i - \frac{(\sum_i x_i)(\sum_i y_i)}{n}$$

$$= 3558 - \frac{(800)(798)}{200} = 334.08$$

The correlation, r, is sometimes expressed another way. We can divide the numerator and denominator of our last expression for r by n without changing the value of r. This gives

$$r = \frac{\sum_i \frac{(x_i - \bar{x})(y_i - \bar{y})}{n}}{\frac{1}{n}\sqrt{\sum_i (x_i - \bar{x})^2}\sqrt{\sum_i (y_i - \bar{y})^2}} = \frac{\sum_i \frac{(x_i - \bar{x})(y_i - y)}{n}}{\sqrt{\frac{\sum_i (x_i - \bar{x})^2}{n}}\sqrt{\frac{\sum_i (y_i - \bar{y})^2}{n}}}$$

The numerator of this expression for r is called the covariance of the random variables x and y. It is the average of the sum of the cross products of deviation (from the mean) scores. The denominator is the product of thc two corresponding standard deviations, a concept introduced earlier in this chapter. This formula is sometimes written as

$$r = \frac{s_{xy}}{s_x s_y}$$

where s_{xy} is the covariance of x and y and s_x and s_y are the corresponding standard deviations.

To better understand the meaning of r, we can express it in yet another way. From the former two expressions

$$r = \frac{1}{n} \sum_i \frac{(x_i - \bar{x})}{s_x} \frac{(y_i - \bar{y})}{s_y} = \frac{\sum_i z_{x_i} z_{y_i}}{n}$$

where

$$z_{x_i} = \frac{x_i - \bar{x}}{s_x} \quad \text{and} \quad z_{y_i} = \frac{y_i - \bar{y}}{s_y}$$

are called the standardized or z scores of x and y, respectively. As an exercise, the reader can show that a z score has a mean of 0 and a standard deviation of 1. If the z scores for x and y corresponding to an individual tend to be similar, then the correlation is positive and the two variables are said to be positively related to each other. On the other hand, if the z scores corresponding to an individual tend to be similar in magnitude but opposite in sign, then r is negative and the two variables are said to be negatively related. A correlation varies between –1 and 1. An r of 1 indicates a perfect positive relationship and an r of –1 indicates a perfect negative relationship. An r of 0 indicates a lack of relationship. For example, when r equals 1, the z_x and z_y are identical for each individual or unit although the values across individuals or units will, of course, vary. (If they do not, then the correlation is not defined.) Therefore

$$\sum_i z_{x_i} z_{y_i} = \sum_i z_{x_i}^2 = n$$

since

$$\frac{\sum_i z_{x_i}^2}{n} = 1$$

and therefore r = n/n = 1. The correlation for our example was .768, which indicates a high positive relationship.

Up to this point we have been discussing descriptive statistics and have not differentiated between a sample and a population, nor have we discussed the concept of statistical inference. We will now review some important concepts in these areas.

2.9 NORMAL DISTRIBUTION

Inferential statistics is concerned with drawing a random sample of observations from a population and making inferences about certain characteristics (or parameters) of the population from information provided by the sample.

For our previous example of self-concept, the 100 observations might have been a random sample from an extremely large or infinite population of, say, six-year-old children. The researcher would probably be more interested in estimating the mean self-concept of all six-year-old children (the population of six-year-old children) than he or she would be in just describing the particular sample of children who happened to be selected. In the regression analysis example, a researcher would probably be more interested in how the

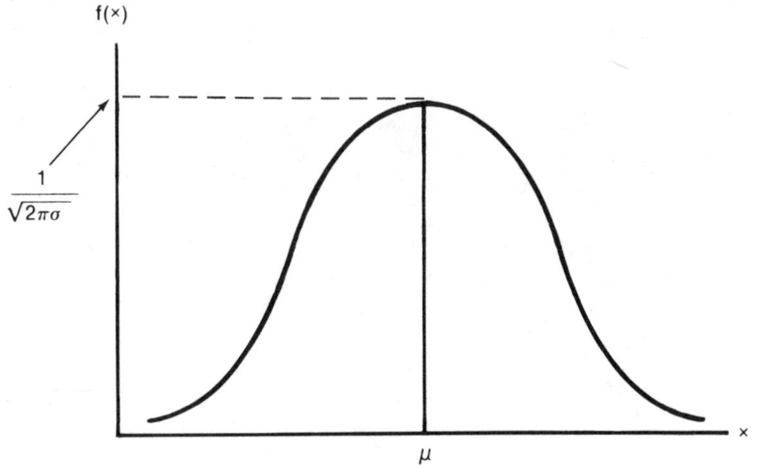

Figure 2.4 A Normal Density Function

regression parameter estimates a and b derived from the sample would correspond with the respective values if all cases in the population from which the sample was drawn were included.

For the purposes of developing a model of statistical inference, it is assumed for most of the statistical models in this book that the random variable in the population from which the sample observations are drawn is normally distributed. A normally distributed variable has a density function given by

$$f(x) = \frac{1}{\sqrt{2\pi\sigma}} e^{-\frac{1}{2}\left(\frac{x-\mu}{\sigma}\right)^2}$$

where σ is the standard deviation of the variable x in the population, μ is the mean of all of the values of x in the population, π is the constant 3.14, and e is the constant 2.718. For a given value of the variable x, we can substitute it in the above formula and obtain a specific value of f(x) that is the density of that particular value of x. The more relatively frequent a value of x is in the population, the greater its density. A normal density function is presented in Figure 2.4.

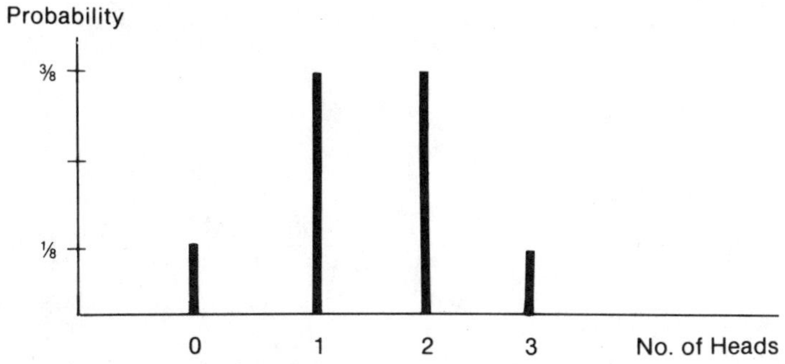

Figure 2.5 Probability Distribution of Number of Heads in Three Tosses of a Coin

From Figure 2.4, it can be seen that the variable x is distributed symmetrically about its mean in a bell-shaped manner. The density of x is greatest at the population mean where its value is

$$\frac{1}{\sqrt{2\pi\sigma}}$$

which can be verified by substituting μ for x in the formula for the density function. As the value of x moves further away from the mean in either direction, the density or relative frequency becomes smaller. The figure is just a plotting of all possible values that the random variable x can realize and the corresponding f(x) for the normal density function. Note that f(x) is only a function of x in the formula since all the other values in the function are either given constants (that is, π and e) or are assumed to be known constants (that is, μ and σ) for the population in question. The constants μ and σ are known as the parameters of the density function since, once they are specified, the density of a particular value of x can be specified.

The density function for a continuous variable is, in many respects, analogous to the probability function of a discrete variable. We previously discussed a discrete probability distribution—the number of heads occurring in three tosses of a coin. This probability distribution is shown in Figure 2.5.

Like the normal density function, this probability distribution can also be summarized by a formula. The applicable probability distribution is a special case of the binomial distribution. The binomial distribution describes the probability distribution of the number of outcomes of interest (such as heads) occurring in n trials (such as the number of coin tosses) if the outcome of interest for each trial is independent and occurs with a constant probability, p (for example, .50 for heads). Then, according to the binomial distribution, the probability of x favorable outcomes (that is, outcomes of interest) is

$$p(x) = \frac{n!}{x!(n-x)!} p^x(1-p)^{n-x}$$

where n is the number of trials, x is the number of favorable outcomes, and p is the probability of the favorable outcome occurring in a single trial. Ther term n! is called n factorial and is defined as n(n – 1) (n – 2) . . . (1); for example, 4! = 4.3.2.1 = 24.

In our example, the number of trials was 3 and the probability of a favorable outcome (heads) was .5. Therefore, the specific binomial distribution applicable to our example is

$$p(x) = \frac{3!}{x!(3-x)!} \left(\frac{1}{2}\right)^x \left(\frac{1}{2}\right)^{3-x}$$

where x is the number of heads in three coin tosses. The probability of 0 heads is

$$p(0) = \frac{3!}{0!3!} \left(\frac{1}{2}\right)^0 \left(\frac{1}{2}\right)^3 = \frac{1}{8}$$

where 0! is defined as 1. The probability of 1 head occurring is

$$p(1) = \frac{3!}{1!2!} \left(\frac{1}{2}\right)^1 \left(\frac{1}{2}\right)^2 = \frac{3}{8}$$

The parameters of the binomial are n and p. For our example, n was 3 and p was 1/2. Like the normal density function, the probabilities of various values of the random variable, number of heads, is determined once n and p are specified.

The probability that x takes the values 0, 1, or 2 can be expressed as

$$\sum_{x=0}^{2} p(x) = \sum_{x=0}^{2} \frac{3!}{x!(3-x)!} \left(\frac{1}{2}\right)^x \left(\frac{1}{2}\right)^{3-x} = \frac{1}{8} + \frac{3}{8} + \frac{3}{8} = \frac{7}{8}$$

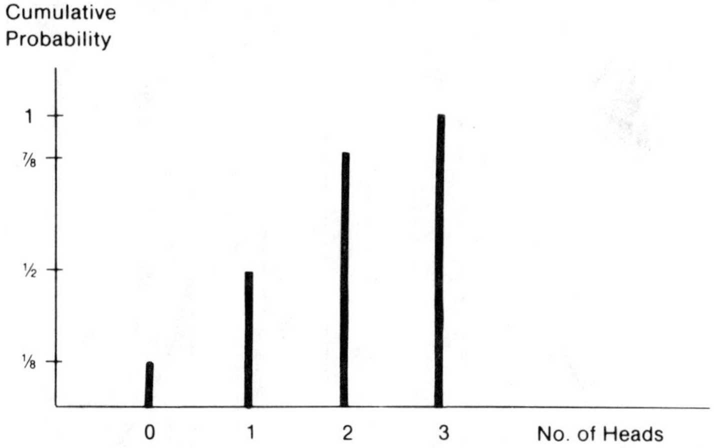

Figure 2.6 Cumulative Probability Distribution of Number of Heads in Three Tosses of a Coin

We simply sum the probabilities corresponding to the values of interest for the random variable. Sometimes, a cumulative probability distribution is used to summarize the information in a probability distribution. The cumulative probability distribution gives the probability of a particular value of the random variable or any value smaller than it. The cumulative probability distribution for our example is presented in Figure 2.6.

The probability of 0 heads is 1/8; the probability of 0 or 1 head is 1/2; the probability of 2 or fewer heads is 7/8; and the probability of 3 or fewer heads, the certain event, is 1.

In the case of continuous variables such as represented by the normal density function, we have an infinite number of values for the density function and they simply cannot be summed like the probabilities of discrete variables. There is, however, an analogous operation, called integration in calculus, that is signified by $\int$ and that can be loosely interpreted as a summation operator. The integral (summation) operation on the density function is denoted as

$$\int_a^b f(x)\,dx = \frac{1}{\sqrt{2\pi\sigma}} \int_a^b e^{-\frac{1}{2}\left(\frac{x-\mu}{\sigma}\right)^2} dx$$

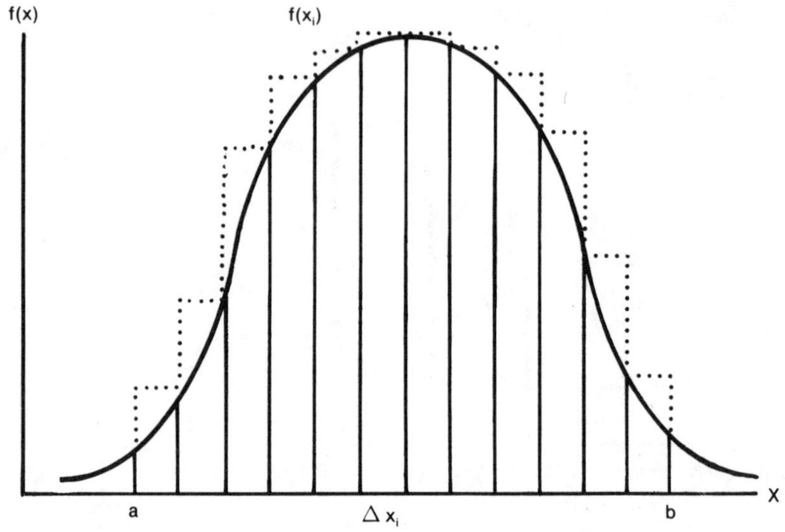

Figure 2.7 Approximation of the Area Under a Curve

where a and b are the lower and upper limits of integration, respectively. This is the definition of the area under the density function (that is, normal curve) between any two different points a and b on the x axis.

The dx can be interpreted as an infinitesimal change in x. The complete equation can be interpreted as multiplying the density by a small change in x and summing up the infinite number of products thus generated from the value x = a to x = b. This is diagrammed in Figure 2.7.

We can approximate the area under the normal curve from a to b by forming a number of rectangles as shown in Figure 2.7 and summing up their areas. That is, the area under the curve from a to b can be approximated as

$$\sum_i f(x_i)\Delta x_i$$

As the Δx_i become smaller, the approximation becomes closer to the true value of the area. In the limit, as Δx_i approaches zero, the approximation approaches the true area. This is expressed as the integral of the density function. The $\int$ resembles a summation sign and the dx can be interpreted as an infinitesimal change in x.

The area under the normal curve between any two different points a and b on the axis is defined as the probability that x takes a value between a and b. That is

$$\text{Probability } (a \leqslant x \leqslant b) = \int_a^b f(x)dx$$

where f(x) is the density function. This definition applies to any density function. It is important to note that while a specific value of x has a density, f(x), associated with it, the density is not a probability since there is no area under the curve associated with it.

It can be shown that the value of the integral from $-\infty$ to ∞ of the normal density function is one. This is true of any density function. That is,

$$\frac{1}{\sqrt{2\pi\sigma}} \int_{-\infty}^{\infty} e^{-\frac{1}{2}\left(\frac{x-\mu}{\sigma}\right)^2} dx = 1$$

This definition of a density function is analogous to the requirement that the sum of the probabilities of the values of a discrete variable value sum to one.

There are other analogies between discrete probability distributions and continuous density functions. In particular, the probability of a particular value of x exceeding x_c can be determined by integrating the density function from x_c to ∞, which, for the normal density, is

$$\frac{1}{\sqrt{2\pi\sigma}} \int_{x_c}^{\infty} e^{-\frac{1}{2}\left(\frac{x-\mu}{\sigma}\right)^2} dx$$

Similarly, the probability of x taking a value less than x_c can be determined by integrating from $-\infty$ to x_c, which, for the normal density, is

$$\frac{1}{\sqrt{2\pi\sigma}} \int_{-\infty}^{x_c} e^{-\frac{1}{2}\left(\frac{x-\mu}{\sigma}\right)^2} dx$$

A cumulative distribution function can also be defined for any density function. It is analogous to the cumulative probability distribution function for discrete variables discussed earlier. The cumulative distribution function gives the probability of the random variable, x, taking a value equal or less than a given value of x. It is defined in general as

$$F(x) = \int_{-\infty}^{x} f(x)dx$$

where f(x) is an arbitrary density function; for the normal density, it is

$$F(x) = \frac{1}{\sqrt{2\pi\sigma}} \int_{-\infty}^{x} e^{-\frac{1}{2}\left(\frac{x-\mu}{\sigma}\right)^2} dx$$

F(x) is called a distribution function since it indicates how much of the density is distributed at or below x or the probability of a value falling at or below x. The above integral can be shown to be equal to

$$F(z) = \frac{1}{2\pi} \int_{-\infty}^{z} e^{-\frac{1}{2}z^2} dz$$

where z is the standardized value of x (that is, $(x - \mu)/\sigma$). From the above integral expression, it can be seen that the density of z is

$$\frac{1}{2\pi} e^{-\frac{1}{2}z^2}$$

since $\sigma = 1$ and $\mu = 0$. To find the value of the distribution function for x, convert it to a standardized variable and enter its value in a table for a standard normal distribution function. This will yield the probability of a variable taking a value at or below the specified value of x.

The cumulative distribution function F(x) is illustrated in Figure 2.8. $F(x_a)$ is the probability that x is equal to or less than x_a.

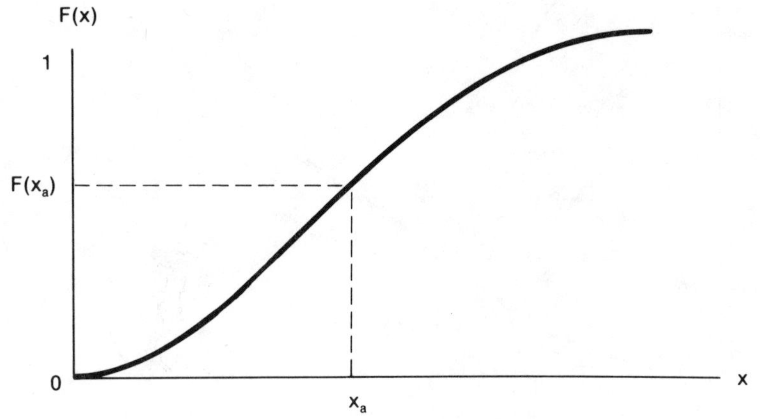

Figure 2.8 Cumulative Distribution Function of x

Since the function indicates the amount of density falling at or below a particular value of x, its value can only range from 0 to 1. As x becomes large, most of the density is to the left of x. When x is transformed to

$$z = \left(\frac{x - \mu}{\sigma} \right)$$

the distribution function for which tables are available is illustrated in Figure 2.9.

We can see from this figure that half of the distribution of z is contained at or below the mean, which is zero in the case of standardized variables. Another property of normally distributed variables is that approximately 68 percent of the distribution falls between one standard deviation below the mean and one standard deviation above the mean. Approximately 95 percent of the distribution falls between two standard deviations below the mean and two standard deviations above the mean. Since standardized variables are centered about 0 and have a standard deviation of one, the probability of z falling between –1 and 1 is .68 and the probability of z falling between –2 and 2 is .95.

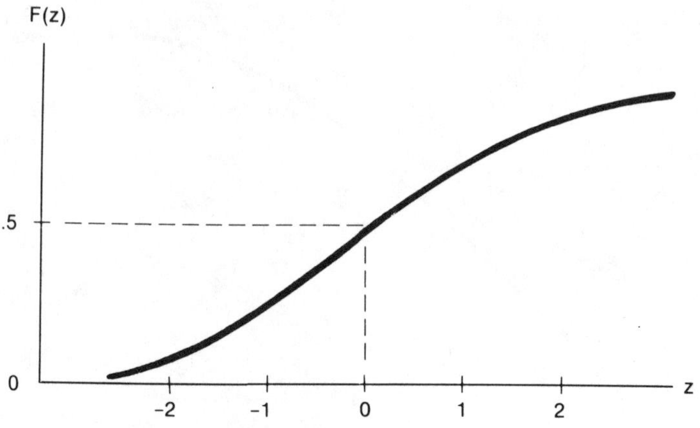

Figure 2.9 Cumulative Distribution Function of z

2.10 SAMPLING DISTRIBUTION OF THE MEAN

Let us return to our self-concept example. If we knew the population mean and standard deviation for self-concept, and if we assumed that self-concept was distributed normally, then we could estimate the probability of a randomly selected child's score lying in any specified interval of the self-concept scale. For example, 95 times out of 100 a randomly selected child's score will lie within two standard deviations of the mean ($\mu \pm 2\sigma_x$). Approximately 2 1/2 times out of a 100 a randomly selected child's score will lie two standard deviations above the mean, and so on. This is the sampling distribution of a single observation from a normal distribution with known mean and standard deviation.

In the self-concept example, we are more interested in the sampling distribution of the mean from a normal population. That is, what does the density function of means rather than individual observations look like and how can the information provided by the sample be used to infer something about the mean of the population.

Let us now turn to the sampling distribution (or density function) of the sample mean for a normal distribution. If the variance of a single observation from a normally distributed random variable is σ^2, then the variance of a mean from a randomly selected sample from that population is normally distributed with variance σ^2/n, where n is the size of the sample. Although the variance of a linear combination of random variables, of which the sample mean is a specific case, is treated in more detail in *Introduction to Multivariate Analysis*, a proof that the sample mean

$$\bar{x} = \frac{\sum_{i=1}^{n} x_i}{n}$$

is distributed normally with variance σ^2/n will be sketched here.

The variance of a linear combination of independent variables, $ax_1 + bx_2 + cx_3$, is given by $a^2\sigma_{x_1}^2 + b^2\sigma_{x_2}^2 + c^2\sigma_{x_3}^2$. This can be generalized to any arbitrary number of variables. Independence, as we have seen, means that the probability of selecting any particular value of one independent variable is not influenced by the value selected for another independent variable comprising the linear combination. We can tailor this general theorem to the case of the sample mean,

$$\bar{x} = \sum_{i=1}^{n} \frac{x_i}{n}$$

which can be expressed as a linear combination of independent variables,

$$\bar{x} = \frac{1}{n} x_1 + \frac{1}{n} x_2 \ldots + \frac{1}{n} x_3$$

The coefficient for each variable is $1/n$ and the variance of each x_i is σ^2 since each observation is drawn from the same population. Consequently, the variance of

$$\bar{x} = \sum_{i=1}^{n} \frac{x_i}{n} = \frac{1}{n} x_1 + \frac{1}{n} x_2 \ldots + \frac{1}{n} x_3$$

is

$$\frac{1\sigma^2}{n^2} + \frac{1\sigma^2}{n^2} \ldots + \frac{1\sigma^2}{n^2} = \frac{n\sigma^2}{n^2} = \frac{\sigma^2}{n}$$

The standard deviation of the sampling distribution of the mean is therefore $\sigma/\sqrt{n}$. Another theorem states that a linear composite of normally distributed

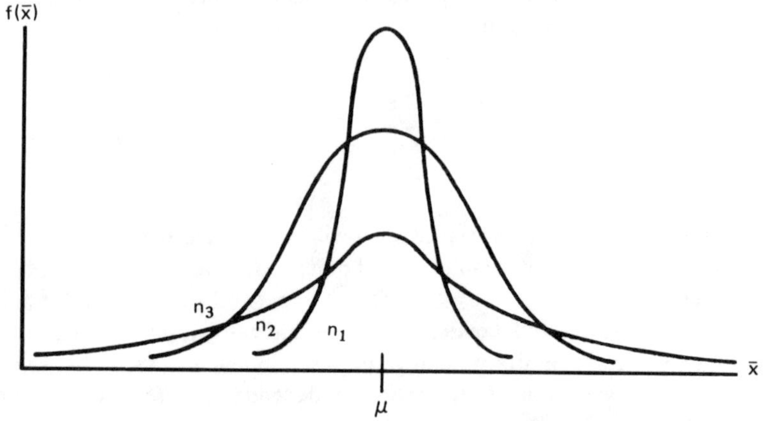

Figure 2.10 Sampling Distribution (Density Function) of the Mean from a Normally Distributed Variable with Mean, μ, and Standard Deviation, σ, as n Increases ($n_1 > n_2 > n_3$)

variables is itself normally distributed, so that $\bar{x}$ is normally distributed with a standard deviation of $\sigma/\sqrt{n}$ and mean μ.

The variance term for the distribution of the sample mean indicates that as the sample size increases, the variance of the sample mean about the population mean decreases. This is illustrated in Figure 2.10.

We can see that the sample means become closely clustered about the population mean as n gets large. The sampling distribution of the mean indicates what the hypothetical distribution of an infinite number of sample means for a given sample size would look like. In practice we usually only have a sample mean based on a single sample, but the known properties of its hypothetical distribution allow us to make certain statements concerning the likelihood of our single estimate being close to the population mean.

The sample mean, $\bar{x}$, is a good estimator of the population mean for three primary reasons. First, if we select an infinite number of means from the sampling distribution and averaged them, their average would be equal to the population mean itself. The sample mean is said to be an unbiased estimator of μ. Second, as the sample size increases, the probability of the sample mean lying in a small interval about the population mean increases, as illustrated in Figure 2.10. This is known as the consistency of the estimator. Another way of expressing this is to say that the standard error of the estimator

$$\frac{\sigma}{\sqrt{n}}$$

becomes smaller as the sample size increases. The third characteristic of a "good" estimator such as the sample mean is that its standard error is smaller than any other linear unbiased estimator of the same population parameter. This is termed "efficiency."

The proof that the mean is unbiased is sketched as follows. The expected value of x, denoted as E(x), is defined as the average of an infinite number of independent selections of x from the population, but this is equivalent to the population mean of the continuous variable x defined as

$$E(x) = \int_{-\infty}^{+\infty} xf(x)dx = \frac{1}{\sqrt{2\pi\sigma}} \int_{-\infty}^{+\infty} x \cdot e^{\frac{1}{2}\left(\frac{x-\mu}{\sigma}\right)^2} dx = \mu$$

which is the analogue to determining the population mean of a discrete variable. We take the value of x, multiply it by its probability, and sum these products to find the mean. For example, the expected number of heads in three tosses of a coin is

$$E(H) = \sum_{i=0}^{3} p_i H_i = \frac{1}{8}(0) + \frac{3}{8}(1) + \frac{3}{8}(2) + \frac{1}{8}(3) = \frac{12}{8} = 1.5$$

Since $E(x) = \mu$,

$$E(\bar{x}) = E\left(\frac{x_1}{n} + \frac{x_2}{n} \ldots + \frac{x_n}{n}\right) = E\left(\frac{x_1}{n}\right) + E\left(\frac{x_2}{n}\right) \ldots + E\left(\frac{x_n}{n}\right)$$

$$= \frac{\mu}{n} + \frac{\mu}{n} \ldots + \frac{\mu}{n} = \frac{n\mu}{n} = \mu$$

Notice that the expectation operator operates like a summation sign, Σ. That is,

$$\sum_{i=1}^{n} (ax_i + by_i) = a \sum_{i=1}^{n} x_i + b \sum_{i=1}^{n} y_i$$

In summary, the sample mean, $\bar{x}$, based upon n independent observations from a normally distributed population with mean μ and standard deviation σ is normally distributed with mean μ and standard deviation $\sigma/\sqrt{n} = \sigma_{\bar{x}}$.

2.11 CONFIDENCE INTERVAL FOR SAMPLE MEAN

The standard error of the mean or the standard deviation of the sampling distribution of the mean indicates how close the sample mean is likely to be to the population mean. Approximately 95 out of 100 estimates will fall in the interval ($\mu - 2\sigma_{\bar{x}}$, $\mu + 2\sigma_{\bar{x}}$). An estimate of μ such as $\bar{x}$ is known as a point estimate. However, the point estimate has an error attached to it that is reflected by $\sigma_{\bar{x}}$. This information can be used to develop an interval estimate of μ that indicates how likely it is, in a probability sense, that a given interval will contain the population mean. It is conventional to use a 95 (or 99) percent confidence interval, which means that 95 out of 100 times a confidence interval based upon a sample will contain the population mean. As the probability of a confidence interval covering μ gets larger, the corresponding interval gets larger. Let us develop this concept further.

Since $\bar{x}$ is normally distributed with mean μ and standard deviation $\sigma/\sqrt{n}$, $\bar{x}$ can be standardized as

$$\frac{\bar{x} - \mu}{\sigma/\sqrt{n}} \quad \text{or} \quad \frac{\sqrt{n}(\bar{x} - \mu)}{\sigma}$$

This standardized variable is normally distributed with mean 0 and standard deviation 1 denoted as N(0,1). Consequently, 95 percent of the standardized sample means drawn independently will lie between −1.96 and +1.96. This can be stated as

$$-1.96 \leqslant \frac{\sqrt{n}(\bar{x} - \mu)}{\sigma} \leqslant +1.96$$

and will be true 95 times out of 100. The above statement is equivalent to

$$\bar{x} - \frac{1.96\sigma}{\sqrt{n}} \leqslant \mu \leqslant \bar{x} + \frac{1.96\sigma}{\sqrt{n}}$$

which is also true 95 times out of 100.[6] Notice that $\bar{x}$ is a random variable, and hence the location of the confidence interval is itself random. However, 95 times out of 100, the random confidence interval will contain the population mean.

We can use any probability level that we wish for constructing a confidence interval by referring to a table for the cumulative normal distribution function to select a z, such that $-z$ and z form a confidence interval with the required probability level, and substituting that value for 1.96 in the above expression. For example, a 99 percent confidence interval is given by

$$\bar{x} - \frac{2.58\sigma}{\sqrt{n}} \leqslant \mu \leqslant \bar{x} + \frac{2.58\sigma}{\sqrt{n}}$$

We can see that a 99 percent confidence interval is wider than a 95 percent confidence interval. If we want to be almost certain that a particular confidence interval covers the mean, then that interval needs to be relatively large. If our standard error is small, however, even a high confidence level can be satisfied by a small confidence interval. The general expression for a confidence interval for a sample mean when σ is known is

$$\bar{x} - z_{\frac{\alpha}{2}} \frac{\sigma}{\sqrt{n}} \leqslant \mu \leqslant \bar{x} + z_{\frac{\alpha}{2}} \frac{\sigma}{\sqrt{n}}$$

where α is one minus the probability attached to the confidence interval and $z_{\alpha/2}$ is the value of z corresponding to 1/2 of this probability, since the probability must be divided equally between the tails.

To take an example, let us assume that our mean self-concept of 4.93 based upon a sample of 100 observations was generated from a normal population with σ^2 equal to 4. The mean (4.93) is a point estimate of the population mean, and its 95 percent confidence interval is

$$4.93 - 1.96 \frac{\sqrt{4}}{\sqrt{100}} \leqslant \mu \leqslant 4.93 + 1.96 \frac{\sqrt{4}}{\sqrt{100}}$$

or

$$4.54 \leqslant \mu \leqslant 5.32$$

This means that this interval has a probability of .95 of containing μ. *It does not mean that μ falls into that interval with probability .95. The end points of the interval are the random variables; μ is a constant.*

In most inference problems, σ^2 is not known. However, an unbiased estimate of σ^2 can be obtained from the sample and used to approximate a standard error of the mean and to construct a confidence interval. Like any estimator, we would like our estimator of σ^2, denoted as $\hat{\sigma}^2$, to be unbiased, consistent, and efficient. Intuitively, it would seem that a reasonable estimator of σ^2 would be

$$\hat{\sigma}^2 = \frac{\sum_{i=1}^{n} (x_i - \bar{x})^2}{n}$$

since this is analogous to how we would calculate a population variance if all of the values were known.

As it turns out, this is a biased estimator of the population variance except in the case where n approaches ∞. On the average, this estimator is $n/n - 1$ times as large as the population variance. That is, the expectation of this estimator ($E(\sigma^2)$) is $[(n - 1)/n]\sigma^2$ so that this estimate is on the average smaller than the true value of σ^2. This is because the deviations are taken from the sample mean rather than the unknown population mean and the deviations tend to be smaller from their own sample mean than from some other constant such as the population mean, μ. We can easily correct for this bias by multiplying our estimator by $n/n - 1$, giving the unbiased estimator of σ^2 as

$$\hat{\sigma}^2 = \frac{\sum_{i=1}^{n} (x_i - \bar{x})^2}{n - 1}$$

The estimated standard error of the mean is given by

$$\frac{\hat{\sigma}}{\sqrt{n}} = \sqrt{\frac{\sum_{i=1}^{n} (x_i - \bar{x})^2}{n(n - 1)}}$$

It should be noted that this is an estimate of $\sigma/\sqrt{n}$, which has an associated standard error. This added uncertainty increases the length of the confidence interval, as we shall see below.

When both μ and σ^2 are unknown, which is the case in most practical applications, then the random variable

$$\frac{\bar{x} - \mu}{\hat{\sigma}/\sqrt{n}}$$

has what is known as a t distribution with n – 1 degrees of freedom. Like the z distribution, tables for the t distribution exist, so that the probabililty of a t value falling above or below a given value can be determined when the table is entered with the appropriate degrees of freedom. Since the distribution of the statistic t is known, we can again construct a confidence interval for μ of any desired confidence level. We can develop a confidence interval with confidence level 1 – α by noting that

$$t = \frac{\bar{x} - \mu}{\hat{\sigma}/\sqrt{n}}$$

lies in the interval

$$-t_{n-1,\frac{\alpha}{2}} \leqslant \frac{\bar{x} - \mu}{\hat{\sigma}/\sqrt{n}} \leqslant t_{n-1,\frac{\alpha}{2}}$$

with probability 1 – α. The subscripts of t indicate that the t value is determined from a t distribution with n – 1 degrees of freedom and its value is such that it is equal to or exceeded with probability $\alpha/2$. The reader can demonstrate that this expression is equivalent to

$$\bar{x} - t_{n-1,\frac{\alpha}{2}} \frac{\hat{\sigma}}{\sqrt{n}} \leqslant \mu \leqslant \bar{x} + t_{n-1,\frac{\alpha}{2}} \frac{\hat{\sigma}}{\sqrt{n}}$$

which is the confidence interval for μ with confidence level 1 – α when σ is unknown and has to be estimated.

Let us again use the self-concept data to establish a 95 percent confidence interval using the t distribution. Before doing so, however, we have to note that our estimate of the standard deviation was biased since we divided by n rather than n – 1. This can be compensated for by dividing the sample standard deviation by $\sqrt{n-1}$ rather than $\sqrt{n}$. Given our sample standard deviation of 1.6628, the estimated standard error of the mean becomes

$$\frac{1.6628}{\sqrt{99}} = .167$$

For a confidence level of .95, α equals .05, $\alpha/2$ equals .025, and t is distributed with 99 of freedom. Using the self-concept mean of 4.93, and substituting into the t-value confidence interval expression, we find

$$4.93 - 1.99(.167) \leqslant \mu \leqslant 4.93 + 1.99(.167) = 4.60 \leqslant \mu \leqslant 5.26$$

as the confidence interval with a confidence level of .95.

If the actual, rather than the estimated, standard error of the mean was .167, then the confidence interval based on z scores would be slightly smaller since the multiplier of the actual standard error would be 1.96 rather than 1.99. As the sample size increases without limit, t becomes distributed as z and the two methods of constructing confidence intervals become equivalent.

2.12 HYPOTHESIS TESTING INVOLVING MEANS

Sampling distribution theory also allows us to test certain hypotheses concerning the parameters of a normal distribution. We shall be concerned in this section with hypotheses regarding the mean of a normal distribution. Suppose we are interested in testing the hypothesis that $\mu = \mu_o$ or that the population mean takes on a hypothesized value μ_o. The hypothesis $\mu = \mu_o$ is called the null hypothesis. The alternative hypothesis is that $\mu \neq \mu_o$ or that μ takes on some other value in the parameter space Ω. The parameter space Ω of μ is the admissible values that μ can assume. In the case of the mean, it is most likely all real numbers between $-\infty$ and ∞.

Suppose the null hypothesis is that $\mu = \mu_o$ and also that the population variance σ^2 is known. The sample data can then be used to test this hypothesis. For a given sample size n_o from a normal population with mean μ_o and variance σ_o^2, we know that the sampling distribution of the mean will have expectation μ_o (that is, the mean of the sample means will be μ_o) and that the sample means will be distributed normally with a standard error or standard deviation of $\sigma_o/\sqrt{n_o}$. If the null hypothesis is true, then approximately 95 percent of the sample means from a sample of size n_o will fall within two standard errors of the mean, while 5 percent of the sample means will lie further than two standard deviations from μ_o. The sampling distribution is shown in Figure 2.11.

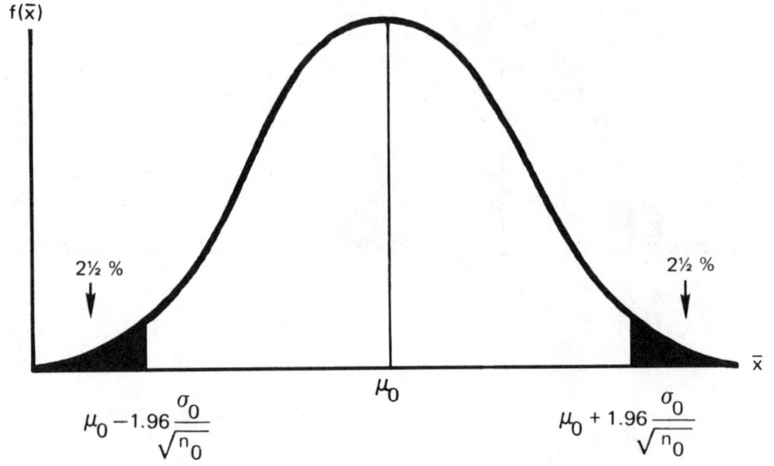

Figure 2.11 Sampling Distribution of the Sample Mean Under the Null Hypothesis That $\mu = \mu_o$

Since it is unlikely to obtain sample means in either tail under the null hypothesis that $\mu = \mu_o$, we would reject the null hypothesis if our sample mean $\bar{x}$ fell in the shaded area of either tail. The shaded areas,

$$\bar{x} \leqslant \mu_o - 1.96 \frac{\sigma_o}{\sqrt{n_o}} \quad \text{and} \quad \bar{x} \geqslant \mu_o + 1.96 \frac{\sigma_o}{\sqrt{n_o}}$$

are called the critical regions for the test statistic. If the sample mean that is a random variable falls into the a priori determined critical region, we reject the null hypothesis; otherwise, we accept the null hypothesis.

By accepting the null hypothesis, it does not mean that we have proved that $\mu = \mu_o$; it simply means that we do not have enough to evidence to reject it. It may have been clearer to some readers if the term "failed to reject" had been used instead of "accept."

However, if the null hypothesis is true, we will be wrong 5 percent of the time. This is called the α level or signficance level of the test. It is the probability of rejecting the null hypothesis when it is in fact true. Rejecting a hypothesis when it is true is known as a Type I error.

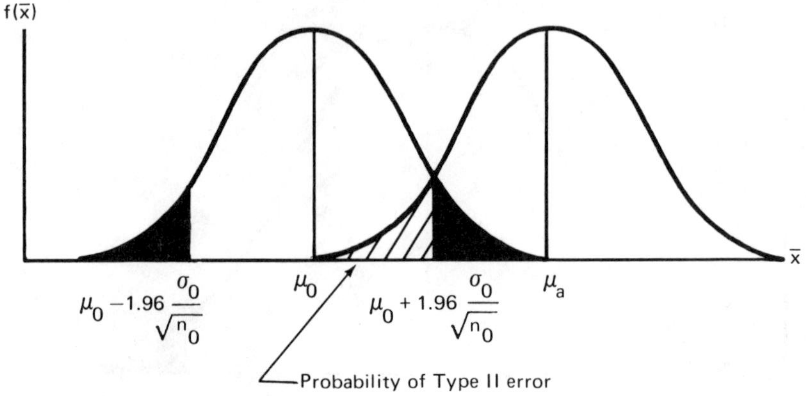

Figure 2.12 Type II Error

There is also another type of error that we need to be concerned about in hypothesis testing. This is known as a Type II error, which is accepting the null hypothesis when it is false. When the sample mean is in actuality generated from some other population with a different population mean, then there is a probability that a sample mean generated from this alternate population will fall within the acceptance region (unshaded region in Figure 2.11) and the null hypothesis that $\mu = \mu_o$ will be erroneously accepted. The situation is illustrated in Figure 2.12.

Referring to Figure 2.12, it can be seen that if the population mean is really μ_a, then the sampling distribution from this population will be distributed around μ_a with variance $\sigma_a/\sqrt{n}$. Consequently, we would expect that a sample mean generated from this alternate population would fall into the acceptance region with a given probability. This probability is represented by the lightly shaded area and is called the probability of a Type II error. In this case, the probability of a Type II error is the probability that a sample mean drawn from the alternate population is less than

$$\mu_o + 1.96 \frac{\sigma_o}{\sqrt{n_o}}$$

The α level or probability of a Type I error can be set at any level desired by the researcher. Most frequently α is set at .05 or .01. Ideally, we would like to minimize both Type I and Type II errors. However, we can see from Figure 2.12 that, as the probability of a Type I error is decreased, the probability of a Type II error is increased since the critical region is moved further to the right, which will decrease the darkly shaded area (probability of Type I error) but increase the lightly shaded area (probability of Type II error). All that can be done is to fix the α level or probability of a Type I error and then define a critical region that yields the smallest Type II error given the Type I error level. The probability of a Type II error will really depend upon the true value of μ. If μ_a is far away from μ_o, then the probability of a Type II error will be small, since there is little chance for a sample mean generated from this population to fall within the acceptance region. As μ_a moves closer to μ_o, the probability of a Type II error increases. The probability of rejecting the null hypothesis when it is false is one minus the probability of a Type II error, which is called the power of the test. As we have shown, the power of a test depends upon the true value of μ. As the true value of μ moves further away from μ_o specified by the null hypothesis, the power of the test increases.

Let us test the hypothesis that $\mu_o = 10$, based upon a sample mean of 12 from a sample of 100 observations. Assume that the variance is known to be 100. Using an α of .01, the critical region is defined as

$$\bar{x} < \mu_o - 2.58 \frac{\sigma_o}{\sqrt{n}} \quad \text{and} \quad \bar{x} > \mu_o + 2.58 \frac{\sigma_o}{\sqrt{n}}$$

Substituting the available information, we find the critical region

$$\bar{x} < 10 - 2.58 \frac{(10)}{(10)} = 7.42 \quad \text{and} \quad \bar{x} > 10 + 2.58 \frac{(10)}{(10)} = 12.58$$

The sample mean of 12 does not fall within the critical region and hence the null hypothesis is accepted.

The above discussion has concerned what is known as a two-tailed test. If we can specify our alternative hypothesis in more detail, a one-tailed test, which would be more powerful than a two-tailed test, can sometimes be utilized. For example, if the null hypothesis was $\mu = \mu_o$ and the alternative hypothesis was $\mu > \mu_o$, then we would want all our critical region to be in the right tail of the sampling distribution under the null hypothesis since this test would be more powerful than a two-tailed test, which splits the probability of a Type I area equally between the two tails. The increased power is demonstrated in Figure 2.13.

From this figure, it can be seen that the probability of a Type II error is decreased or the power increased for alternative values of μ greater than μ_o since sample means generated from this population are less likely to fall into the acceptance region based upon a one-tailed test then they are for a two-tailed test.

One problem with this approach to hypothesis testing is that in practical

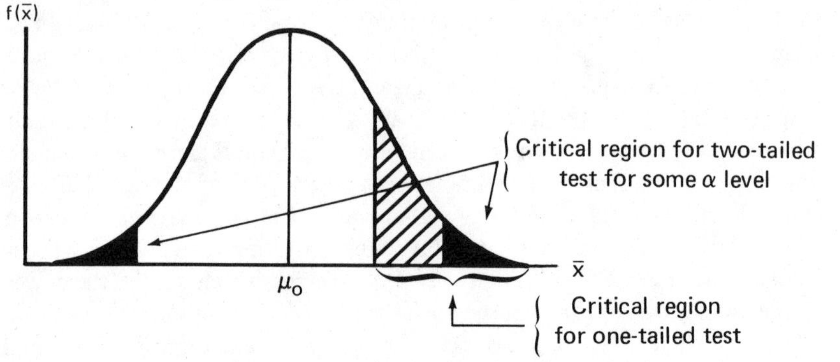

Figure 2.13 Critical Region for One-Tailed Test of $\mu = \mu_o$ versus $\mu > \mu_o$

situations, the variance, σ^2, of the population from which the sample was drawn is usually unknown, and hence needs to be estimated from the sample itself. This is similar to the problem encountered in making interval estimates. We have seen that an unbiased estimate of σ^2 is

$$\hat{\sigma}^2 = \frac{\sum_{i=1}^{n} (x_i - x)^2}{n - 1}$$

and that an unbiased estimate of the standard deviation of the sampling distribution of means is

$$\frac{\hat{\sigma}}{\sqrt{n}} \cdot$$

It is also true that when $\mu = \mu_o$,

$$\frac{\bar{x} - \mu_o}{\hat{\sigma}/\sqrt{n}}$$

is distributed as t with n – 1 degrees of freedom. Considering the alternative hypothesis that $\mu \neq \mu_o$ and thereby using a two-tailed test with a given α level, the critical region would be

$$\bar{x} \leqslant \mu_o - t_{\frac{\alpha}{2}, n-1} \frac{\hat{\sigma}}{\sqrt{n}} \quad \text{and} \quad \bar{x} \geqslant \mu_o + t_{\frac{\alpha}{2}, n-1} \frac{\hat{\sigma}}{\sqrt{n}}$$

Returning to the self-concept example, let us test the hypothesis that $\mu = 5$ with α set to .05 against the alternative hypothesis that $\mu \neq 5$. Substituting into the above formula, we find the critical region to be

$$\bar{x} \leqslant 5 - 1.99(.167) = 4.67 \quad \text{and} \quad \bar{x} \geqslant 5 + 1.99(.167) = 5.33$$

since

$$t_{\frac{\alpha}{2}, n-1} = t_{.025,99} = 1.99 \quad \text{and} \quad \frac{\hat{\sigma}}{\sqrt{n}} = .167$$

Since the sample mean is 4.93, it does not fall within the critical region and, consequently, the null hypothesis, $\mu = 5$, is accepted at the .05 level.

The hypothesis-testing approach is closely related to the confidence-interval approach. If the hypothesized value of μ, μ_o, falls within the 95 percent confidence interval, then the sample mean will also fall within the acceptance region defined by the critical values of the test statistic. As the sample increases in size, the t distribution approaches the z distribution. This is because the estimate of σ^2 based upon a large n will contain little sampling error, and, for all practical purposes, $\hat{\sigma}$ can be substituted for σ and probability statements can be made using the z distribution. For values of n greater than, say, 200, z can be used in lieu of t. For small n's (for example, less than 50), confidence intervals based upon t will be considerably wider than the corresponding interval based upon z. In a hypothesis-testing framework, this means that the critical regions based upon t will be further from the hypothesized μ than the corresponding critical regions based upon the z distribution. Intuitively, this follows, since z involves the distribution of one random variable ($\bar{x}$) while t involves the distribution of a statistic that contains two random variables, $\bar{x}$ and $\hat{\sigma}$. More variability would be expected from a statistic involving two random variables compared to a statistic such as z, which involves only one random variable.

The t-test procedure can be extended to test the hypothesis that the means from two independent samples came from the same population. The null hypothesis is that $\mu_1 = \mu_2$ and the alternative hypothesis is that $\mu_1 \neq \mu_2$. One assumption that needs to be made is that the variance of each of the two populations is the same, although unknown.

Although linear composites from normal distributions will be treated in greater detail in a later chapter, I will show that the difference of means, $\bar{x}_1 - \bar{x}_2$, from two independent samples with sample sizes of n_1 and n_2, respectively, has an estimated standard error (or estimated standard deviation of the sampling distribution of mean differences) of

$$\hat{\sigma}\sqrt{\frac{1}{n_1} + \frac{1}{n_2}}$$

where $\hat{\sigma}^2$ is a pooled estimate of the common variance with $n_1 + n_2 - 2$ degrees of freedom (one degree of freedom is lost for each of the two means that have to be estimated). The estimated variance of a linear composite of n independently distributed random variables is

$$\sum_i^n a_i^2 \hat{\sigma}_i^2$$

The estimated variance of each mean can be expressed as

$$\sum_i^n \left(\frac{1}{n}\right)^2 \hat{\sigma}_i^2 = \left(\frac{1}{n}\right)^2 \sum_i^n \hat{\sigma}_i^2 = \frac{n}{n^2}\hat{\sigma}^2 = \frac{\hat{\sigma}^2}{n}$$

since each observation is drawn from a population with common variance, σ^2. It follows that the estimated variance of

$$\bar{x}_1 - \bar{x}_2 \text{ equals } \sum_{i=1}^{n_1}\left(\frac{1}{n_1}\right)^2 \hat{\sigma}^2 + \sum_{i=1}^{n_2}\left(\frac{-1}{n_2}\right)^2 \hat{\sigma}^2 = \frac{\hat{\sigma}^2}{n_1} + \frac{\hat{\sigma}^2}{n_2}$$

or estimated standard deviation of

$$\sqrt{\frac{\hat{\sigma}^2}{n_1} + \frac{\hat{\sigma}^2}{n_2}} = \sqrt{\hat{\sigma}^2\left(\frac{1}{n_1} + \frac{1}{n_2}\right)} = \hat{\sigma}\sqrt{\frac{1}{n_1} + \frac{1}{n_2}}$$

if the null hypothesis is $\mu_1 = \mu_2 = 0$, then $\mu_1 - \mu_2 = 0$, and

$$\frac{(\bar{x}_1 - \bar{x}_2) - (\mu_1 - \mu_2)}{\hat{\sigma}\sqrt{\frac{1}{n_1} + \frac{1}{n_2}}} = \frac{\bar{x}_1 - \bar{x}_2}{\hat{\sigma}\sqrt{\frac{1}{n_1} + \frac{1}{n_2}}}$$

is distributed as t with $n_1 + n_2 - 2$ degrees of freedom.

Suppose that from a sample of 50 black children (sample 1) we found a mean of 4.8 on our self-concept scale and that from a sample of 50 white children (sample 2) the mean was 4.7. Let us further assume that the variances of self-concept scores for black children and white children were 2.1 and 2.2, respectively. Let us test the null hypothesis that the mean self-concept scores for black and white children are equal with α set at .01. The pooled estimate of variance is

$$\frac{\sum_{i=1}^{n_1} (x_{1i} - \bar{x}_1)^2 + \sum_{i=1}^{n_2} (x_{2i} - \bar{x}_2)^2}{n_1 + n_2 - 2}$$

where n_1 and n_2 are the sample sizes for blacks and whites, respectively, and $\bar{x}_1$ and $\bar{x}_2$ are the corresponding sample means for blacks and whites, respectively. The 2 subtracted from the total sample size in the denominator is a consequence of losing one degree of freedom for each of the two means that were estimated.

Since

$$\hat{\sigma}_1^2 = \frac{\sum_{i=1}^{n_1} (x_{1i} - \bar{x}_1)^2}{n_1 - 1} \quad \text{and} \quad \hat{\sigma}_2 = \frac{\sum_{i=1}^{n_2} (x_{2i} - \bar{x}_2)^2}{n_2 - 1}$$

then

$$\sum_{i=1}^{n_1} (x_{1i} - \bar{x}_1)^2 = (n_1 - 1)\hat{\sigma}_1^2 \quad \text{and} \quad \sum_{i=1}^{n_2} (x_{2i} - \bar{x}_2)^2 = (n_2 - 1)\hat{\sigma}_2^2$$

and the pooled estimate of variance $\hat{\sigma}^2$ can be expressed in terms of the individual sample variances as

$$\frac{(n_1 - 1)\hat{\sigma}_1^2 + (n_2 - 1)\hat{\sigma}_2^2}{n_1 + n_2 - 2}$$

For our example, we have

$$\hat{\sigma} = \sqrt{\frac{(n_1 - 1)\hat{\sigma}_1^2 + (n_2 - 1)\hat{\sigma}_2^2}{n_1 + n_2 - 2}} = \sqrt{\frac{49(2.1) + 49(2.2)}{98}} = 1.467$$

Substituting into the above formula for t, we find

$$t = \frac{4.8 - 4.7}{1.467\sqrt{\frac{1}{50} + \frac{1}{50}}} = \frac{.1}{.293} = .341$$

For a two-tailed t-test with $\alpha/2 = .005$ and degrees of freedom equal to 98, we need a t of 2.63 to reject the null hypothesis that $\mu_1 = \mu_2$; consequently, we must accept the null hypothesis that $\mu_1 = \mu_2$.

2.13 TESTING HYPOTHESES CONCERNING β

In our previous example of regressing intelligence on socioeconomic status, we calculated for the sample of 100 observations a regression slope based upon least squares. This regression slope is certainly descriptive of how the mean of intelligence varies with socioeconomic level of our sample. In most cases like this, however, once again the interest is on inferring from the sample estimate, b, what the value of the slope parameter would be if the entire population of children were available for calculating b. Let us call the population slope parameter β, and its sample estimate $\hat{\beta}$. Like the estimator for the mean, we want an estimator of β that is unbiased (that is, $E(\hat{\beta}) = \beta$), and has minimal variance in the class of unbiased, linear estimators. In many instances for bivariate regression, interest lies in testing the hypothesis $\beta = 0$ against the alternative hypothesis $\beta \neq 0$. This is equivalent to the hypothesis that there is no relationship between the two variables.

Let us now examine an inference model for β, the population slope parameter in a bivariate regression framework. The model is $y_i = \alpha + \beta x_i + \epsilon_i$. First, as with all statistical or mathematical models, a number of assumptions have to be made. One assumption is that the x values of the independent variables are fixed in repeated sampling and the y values for a given value of x are random and independent observations. Another assumption is that the errors associated with the model have expectation zero and are uncorrelated with equal variances. That is, the ϵ_i associated with each x_i has a mean of zero and a common variance σ_ϵ^2. And since the observations are independently selected from the population, they have a zero covariance or correlation. Putting it another way, if for a given value x_i we drew an infinite number of y_i's, then the mean of ϵ_i would be zero ($E(\epsilon_i) = 0$) and the variance of ϵ_i would be σ_ϵ^2.

The estimate $\hat{\beta}$ of β is actually a linear combination of the sample values of y_i, the dependent variable and is therefore called a linear estimator. That is, $\hat{\beta} = \sum_i c_i y_i$. We know from previous discussions that the variance of a linear composite $\sum_i c_i y_i$ of independent observations is $\sum_i c_i^2 \sigma_i^2$. All we have to do is to determine the c_i's of the linear composite. Previously, we showed that the least-squares estimate of β was

$$\hat{\beta} = \frac{\sum_{i=1}^{n} (x_1 - \bar{x})(y_i - \bar{y})}{\sum_{i=1}^{n} (x_i - \bar{x})^2}$$

This can be expressed as

$$\hat{\beta} = \frac{\sum_{i=1}^{n} (x_i - \bar{x})y_i - \sum_{i=1}^{n} (x_i - \bar{x})\bar{y}}{\sum_{i=1}^{n} (x_i - \bar{x})^2}$$

Since

$$\sum_{i=1}^{n} (x_i - \bar{x}) = 0,$$

the last term in the numerator disappears and we have

$$\hat{\beta} = \frac{\sum_{i=1}^{n} (x_i - \bar{x})y_i}{\sum_{i=1}^{n} (x_i - \bar{x})^2}$$

This is clearly a linear combination of the y_i, since

$$c_i = \frac{(x_i - \bar{x})}{\sum_{i=1}^{n} (x_i - \bar{x})^2}$$

is assumed constant across samples, since the x_i's are assumed to be fixed values. Therefore,

$$c_i^2 = \frac{(x_i - \bar{x})^2}{\left(\sum_{i=1}^{n} (x_i - \bar{x})^2 \right)^2}$$

and the variance of $\hat{\beta}$ is then

$$\frac{\sum_{i=1}^{n} (x_i - \bar{x})^2 \, \sigma_{y_i}^2}{\left(\Sigma (x_i - \bar{x})^2 \right)^2}$$

Our regression model states that the population mean or expectation of y_i is $\alpha + \beta x_i$, so that the variance of y_i is

$$\sigma_{y_i}^2 = E[y_i - (\alpha + \beta x_i)]^2$$

but $[y_i - (\alpha + \beta x_i)]$ is the error, ϵ_i, associated with the ith observation and therefore $\sigma_{y_i}^2 = E(\epsilon_i)^2$. The error variance for the ith observation is $E[\epsilon_i - E(\epsilon_i)]^2$ and, since $E(\epsilon_i) = 0$ by assumption, $\sigma_{\epsilon i}^2 = E(\epsilon_i)^2$ and consequently $\sigma_{y_i}^2 = \sigma_{\epsilon i}^2$. Remember that x_i remains constant across samples so that $\alpha + \beta x_i$ is a fixed value, the mean of the ith observation, y_i, on the dependent variable, but that y_i is a random variable that varies around this fixed mean across samples.

Since the regression model assumes that the error variance for each observation is identical, $\sigma_{\epsilon_i}^2 = \sigma_\epsilon^2$ and the variance of β, $\sigma_{\hat{\beta}}^2$ can be written

$$\sigma_{\hat{\beta}}^2 = \frac{\sigma_\epsilon^2 \sum_{i=1}^{n} (x_i - \bar{x})^2}{\left(\sum_{i=1}^{n} (x_i - x)^2 \right)^2} = \frac{\sigma_\epsilon^2}{\sum_{i=1}^{n} (x_i - \bar{x})^2}$$

The standard error of $\hat{\beta}$ (that is, the standard deviation of the sampling distribution of $\hat{\beta}$) is

$$\sigma_{\hat{\beta}} = \frac{\sigma_\epsilon}{\sqrt{\sum_{i=1}^{n} (x_i - \bar{x})^2}}$$

Since y_i is normally distributed about its mean, $\alpha + \beta x_i$, and $\hat{\beta}$ is a linear composite of these normally distributed observations, $\hat{\beta}$ itself is normally distributed with the standard error given above. Similar to the previous inference models, we can now proceed to test various hypotheses about β. Of most interest would be to test the null hypotheses $\beta = 0$ against the alternative hypothesis that $\beta \neq 0$. We want to determine if our estimate of β could have come from a population regression where β was, in fact, zero. Once again, we can rely upon the z distribution to test the hypothesis that $\beta = 0$. If β did come from a population with $\beta = 0$, and since β is normally distributed with standard deviation,

$$\frac{\sigma_\epsilon}{\sqrt{\sum_{i=1}^{n} (x_i - \bar{x})^2}}$$

then

$$\frac{\hat{\beta} - 0}{\sigma_\epsilon \Big/ \sqrt{\sum_{i=1}^{n} (x_i - \bar{x})^2}}$$

is distributed as z. If we use a two-tailed test with a given α level, then we would reject the hypothesis if z fell into the critical region. Once again, we run into the problem that σ_ϵ^2 is unknown and must be estimated from the data. The procedure for estimating σ_ϵ^2 is to take the deviation of each observation from the *sample* regression line, sum these squared deviations, and divide by the appropriate degrees of freedom. It can be shown that an unbiased estimator ($\hat{\sigma}_\epsilon^2$) of σ_ϵ^2 is

$$\frac{\sum_{i=1}^{n} e_i^2}{n-2} = \frac{\sum_{i=1}^{n} \left[y_i - (\hat{\alpha} + \hat{\beta} x_i)^2\right]}{n-2}$$

The numerator is the error sum of squares and the denominator is the degrees of freedom. Although our sample size is n, two degrees of freedom are lost because two parameters (α and β) have to be estimated, and these two parameter estimates determine the orientation of the sample regression line from which the error sum of squares is computed. If we divide by n, our estimate will be on the average too small (biased), since we are using the sample itself both to determine the regression line and the sum of the squared deviations from the regression line. This is conceptually similar to the loss of a degree of freedom in estimating the variance of a random variable. It can be shown that

$$\frac{\hat{\beta} - 0}{\hat{\sigma}_\epsilon \Big/ \sqrt{\sum_{i=1}^{n} (x_i - \bar{x})^2}}$$

is distributed as t with n – 2 degrees of freedom.

Let us test the null hypothesis that $\beta = 0$ in our example involving the regression of intelligence on socioeconomic level.

Using our sample data and substituting into the formula for t, we find

$$t = \frac{.753 - 0}{\dfrac{.939}{21.063}} = 16.89$$

since

$$\hat{\sigma}_\epsilon = \sqrt{\frac{SS_e}{n-2}} = \sqrt{\frac{174.41}{198}} = .939$$

and

$$\sqrt{\sum_{i=1}^{n} (x_i - \bar{x})^2} = \sqrt{443.68} = 21.063$$

With 198 degrees of freedom, t approaches z, and we find by referring to a z table that a value of z this large under the null hypothesis is so rare that it is not even tabled. A value of z of 4.417 is significant at the .00001 level. Clearly, t falls into the critical region irrespective of the α level that is considered.

Consequently, the null hypothesis is rejected at an extremely high significance level.

2.14 PROBLEMS

(1) From the sample data in Appendix A, what are the following estimated probabilities?

(a) being in a four-year college
(b) being in a four-year college and being white
(c) being black given that respondent is in the lowest SES level
(d) having the highest high school grades given that the respondent is white and of the highest SES level

(2) Calculate the mean and standard deviation of the Scaled Vocabulary Score (variable 1).

(3) Find the bivariate distribution of college status (variable 9) and SES (variable 10). From the bivariate distribution, find the marginal distribution of each variable. What is the conditional distribution of college status for level 3 of SES?

(4) Find the mean and standard deviation of the conditional distribution of Scaled Vocabulary Scores (variable 1) for each of the three levels of SES (variable 10). Plot the means against the three SES levels.

(5) Find the correlation between the Scaled Vocabulary Scores (variable 1) and SES (variable 10). Regress the Scaled Vocabulary Scores on SES and find the intercept and slope parameters. Considering the plot of means from 4, do you think the regression analysis does a good job in summarizing the relationship between the two variables?

(6) From the mean and standard deviation calculated in problem 2, find the z score associated with a scaled vocabulary score of 65. Refer to a z table and find the probability of a vocabulary score exceeding a value of 65.

(7) From the results of problem 2, estimate the variance of the mean for Scaled Vocabulary Scores.

(8) Find the 95 percent confidence interval for the mean Scaled Vocabulary Scores.

(9) Using the 5 percent level of significance and a two-tailed test, test the hypothesis that the means of the Scaled Vocabulary Scores are equal for levels 1 and 3 of SES (variable 10). (Use the results of problem 4, above.)

(10) Test the hypothesis that the slope parameter found in problem 5 is zero. Do the results of this test and the one for problem 9 support one another?

NOTES

1. Many of the linear models that we will be discussing assume that the conditional standard deviations are constant. This assumption, which is discussed in more detail later, is known as homoscedasticity. When this assumption is violated, as appears to be the case in our example, then the model should be modified to accommodate this condition, which is known as heteroscedasticity.

2. Simple algebra will suffice to prove this statement. The sum of squared deviations from the mean, $\sum_i (x_i - \bar{x})^2$, equals

$$\sum_i (x_i^2 - 2\bar{x}x_i + \bar{x}^2) = \sum_i x_i^2 - 2\bar{x}\sum_i x_i + \sum_i \bar{x}^2 = \sum_i x_i^2 - 2n\bar{x}^2 + n\bar{x}^2$$

$$= \sum_i x_i^2 - n\bar{x}^2$$

since $\sum_i \bar{x} = n\bar{x}$ and $\sum_i \bar{x}^2 = n\bar{x}^2$ (that is, a constant summed i times is the constant multiplied by the number of times, i, that it is summed). The next step is to compute the sum of squared deviations from any arbitrary constant b not equal to the mean, $\bar{x}$. Then, we can express b as $a + \bar{x}$ where a is any number not equal to zero. Finding the sum of squares of the x_i from b, we have

$$\sum_i (x_i - b)^2 = \sum (x_i^2 - 2x_i b + b^2) = \sum_i x_i^2 - 2bn\bar{x} + nb^2$$

Substituting $a + \bar{x}$ for b, we have

$$\sum x_i^2 - 2(a + \bar{x})n\bar{x} + n(a + \bar{x})^2 = \sum x_i^2 - 2an\bar{x} - 2n\bar{x}^2 + na^2 + 2na\bar{x} + n\bar{x}^2$$

$$= \sum x_i^2 - n\bar{x}^2 + na^2$$

Since a is not zero, the term na^2 is positive and $\sum x_i^2 - n\bar{x}^2$ is less than $\sum x_i^2 - n\bar{x}^2 + na^2$ for any value of a different from zero or, equivalently, any constant differing from the mean, $\bar{x}$.

3. There is another way to derive the two linear simultaneous equations, sometimes called the normal equations, needed for solving a and b without the use of calculus. The observation on the dependent variable for the ith person can be written as

$$y_i = a + bx_i + e_i$$

where e_i is the error in the prediction from the straight line $a + bx_i$. Least-squares estimates of a and b produce e_i's that have the following two properties. They sum to zero over individuals (that is, $\sum_i e_i = 0$) and the sum of the cross products of x_i and e_i over individuals is zero (that is, $\sum x_i e_i = 0$). With these two properties, we can derive the two normal equations by: (1) summing the equations over individuals and (2) multiplying the equation by x_i and summing across indviduals. Doing this, we have

$$\sum_i y_i = \sum_i (a + bx_i + e_i) = \sum_i a + \sum_i bx_i + \sum_i e_i = na + b\sum_i x_i$$

and

$$\sum_i x_i y_i = \sum_i x_i (a + bx_i + e_i) = \sum_i x_i a + \sum_i x_i x_i + \sum_i x_i e_i = a\sum_i x_i + \sum_i x_i^2$$

These equations are identical to those previously derived.

4. From the knowledge of matrix algebra to be gained in the following chapter, we will see that these two equations can be expressed in matrix form, giving

$$\begin{bmatrix} n & \sum_i x_i \\ \sum_i x_i & \sum_i x_i^2 \end{bmatrix} \begin{bmatrix} a \\ b \end{bmatrix} = \begin{bmatrix} \sum_i y_i \\ \sum_i x_i y_i \end{bmatrix}.$$

and that the solution is

$$\begin{bmatrix} a \\ b \end{bmatrix} = \begin{bmatrix} n & \sum_i x_i \\ \sum_i x_i & \sum_i x_i^2 \end{bmatrix}^{-1} \begin{bmatrix} \sum_i y_i \\ \sum_i x_i y_i \end{bmatrix}$$

where $\begin{bmatrix} n & \sum_i x_i \\ \sum_i x_i & \sum_i x_i^2 \end{bmatrix}^{-1}$ is called the inverse of $\begin{bmatrix} n & \sum_i x_i \\ \sum_i x_i & \sum_i x_i^2 \end{bmatrix}$

5. Since $\hat{y}_i = a + bx_i$ and $a = \bar{y} - b\bar{x}$, as previously presented,

$$y_i - \hat{y}_i = y_i - (a + bx_i) = y_i - (\bar{y} - b\bar{x} + bx_i) = (y_i - \bar{y}) - b(x_i - \bar{x})$$

Since $\bar{y}$ equals $a + b\bar{x}$, and $\hat{y}_i = a + bx_i$, $\hat{y}_i - \bar{y}$ can be expressed as

$$[(a + bx_i) - (a + b\bar{x})] = b(x_i - \bar{x})$$

Substituting $(y_i - \bar{y}) - b(x_i - \bar{x})$ for $(y_i - \hat{y}_i)$, and $b(x_i - \bar{x})$ for $(\hat{y}_i - \bar{y})$, we have

$$2\sum_i (y_i - \hat{y}_i)(\hat{y}_i - \bar{y}) = 2\sum_i [(y_i - \bar{y}) - b(x_i - \bar{x})]\ [b(x_i - \bar{x})]$$

$$= 2b\sum_i (y_i - \bar{y})(x_i - \bar{x}) - 2b^2\sum_i (x_i - \bar{x})^2.$$

Since

$$b = \frac{\sum_i (x_i - \bar{x})(y_i - \bar{y})}{\sum_i (x_i - \bar{x})^2},$$

substituting $b\sum_i (x_i - \bar{x})^2$ for $\sum_i (y_i - \bar{y})(x_i - \bar{x})$ in the above, we find

$$2b^2 \sum_i (x_i - \bar{x})^2 - 2b^2 \sum_i (x_i - \bar{x})^2 = 0$$

and the cross product term vanishes.

6. The two statements are identical because the statement

$$-1.96 \leqslant \frac{\sqrt{n}(\bar{x} - \mu)}{\sigma} \leqslant 1.96$$

is equivalent to

$$-\frac{1.96\sigma}{\sqrt{n}} \leqslant (\bar{x} - \mu) \leqslant \frac{1.96\sigma}{\sqrt{n}}$$

which, in turn, is equivalent to

$$-\bar{x} - \frac{1.96\sigma}{\sqrt{n}} \leqslant -\mu \leqslant -\bar{x} + \frac{1.96\sigma}{\sqrt{n}}$$

Multiplying all terms by –1 reverses the direction of the inequalities, resulting in

$$\bar{x} - \frac{1.96\sigma}{\sqrt{n}} \leqslant \mu \leqslant \bar{x} + \frac{1.96\sigma}{\sqrt{n}}$$

3 Matrix Algebra

3.1 INTRODUCTION

The statistical techniques discussed in this book are much easier to understand and apply when treated within the context of matrix algebra. This chapter covers the basic concepts of matrix algebra that are used to elucidate the statistical models in the remainder of the book.

Section 3.2 defines vectors and matrices, which are basically, as the reader will see, ordered arrays of numbers or elements. Section 3.3 further describes the characteristics of vectors. As with real numbers, certain operations on vectors are permissible while others are not. They are described in section 3.4. A vector can be represented geometrically as a point in space. This suggests that a vector can be characterized by such properties as length and distance from other vectors. All of these concepts are discussed in section 3.5. A set of vectors can also be characterized in terms of whether or not the vectors are independent of one another (section 3.6) or whether or not they form a basis from which other vectors can be expressed (section 3.7). Vectors are useful in describing and interpreting statistical models, as illustrated in section 3.8.

We then turn to a further study of matrices. This discussion parallels the discussion of vectors. Characteristics of matrices are covered in section 3.9, while matrix operations are covered in section 3.10. Additional aspects of matrices, the trace of a matrix and the partitioning of a matrix, are discussed in sections 3.11 and 3.12, respectively. A set of linear equations in several unknowns can be expressed conveniently in matrix form. This allows for the use of the matrix inverse (section 3.13) to solve readily for the unknowns. Simultaneous equations and their solution using the matrix inverse are discussed in section 3.14. Quadratic forms that play a role in testing the statistical significance of regression parameters are discussed in section 3.15. The final section, section 3.16, defines the latent roots and vectors of a matrix. All of the topics discussed in this chapter play important roles in the chapters that lie ahead. Some topics will be developed further as the need arises.

3.2 VECTORS AND MATRICES

For our purposes, a vector can be considered an ordered array of real numbers. (A vector can be an ordered array of any type of elements—for example, complex numbers—but we shall be concerned only with real numbers.) If the numbers are arrayed in a column, then we have a column vector. A column vector with m elements can be written as

$$\mathbf{x} = \begin{bmatrix} x_1 \\ x_2 \\ \cdot \\ \cdot \\ \cdot \\ x_m \end{bmatrix}$$

where x_1 is the first real number in the array and x_m is the mth real number in the array. Vectors are usually represented by lowercase boldface type. We shall see later that a vector is a special type of matrix that has m rows and only one column, where matrices in general have m rows and n columns. When n = 1, we have the special case of a vector. As an example, a vector might represent the reading scores of a class of third graders. If there were six children in the class, with scores of 45, 50, 52, 58, 37, and 63, respectively, then we could represent these scores as the vector below:

$$\mathbf{x} = \begin{bmatrix} x_1 \\ x_2 \\ x_3 \\ x_4 \\ x_5 \\ x_6 \end{bmatrix} = \begin{bmatrix} 45 \\ 50 \\ 52 \\ 58 \\ 39 \\ 63 \end{bmatrix}$$

We could also present these six scores as a row vector rather than as a column vector and denote the row vector as

$$\mathbf{x}' = [x_1, x_2, x_3, x_4, x_5, x_6] = [45, 50, 52, 58, 39, 63]$$

We call the row vector **x′** the "transpose" of the column vector **x**. Transpose is the operation of interchanging the columns and rows of a matrix, which in the case of a vector means changing the single column into a row.

A matrix is an m × n rectangular array of numbers. That is, it is a set of real numbers presented in an array that has m rows and n columns. It is written as

$$\underset{(m\times n)}{\mathbf{A}} = \begin{bmatrix} a_{11} & a_{12} & \cdots & a_{1n} \\ a_{21} & \cdot & \cdots & a_{2n} \\ \cdot & \cdot & \cdots & \cdot \\ \cdot & \cdot & \cdots & \cdot \\ a_{m1} & a_{m2} & \cdots & a_{mn} \end{bmatrix}$$

where the (m × n) under the **A** indicates the dimension of the matrix (that is, the number of rows and columns). Matrices are usually represented by uppercase boldface type. Where the dimension of the matrix can be inferred from its context, it will not be so labeled.

The transpose of the matrix **A** is defined as

$$\underset{(n\times m)}{\mathbf{A}'} = \begin{bmatrix} a_{11} & a_{21} & \cdots & a_{m1} \\ a_{12} & \cdot & \cdots & a_{m2} \\ \cdot & \cdot & \cdots & \cdot \\ \cdot & \cdot & \cdots & \cdot \\ a_{1n} & a_{2n} & \cdots & a_{mn} \end{bmatrix}$$

where the rows of **A** now become the columns of **A′**, the second subscript indicates the row number and the first subscript indicates the column number, whereas for **A** the first subscript indicates the row number and the second subscript indicates the column number.

A typical element of **A** can be indicated as a_{ij}, where i represents the row and j represents the column in which the element a_{ij} is located. For example, the element a_{34} is the element located at the intersection of the third row and fourth column (that is, the number that is in both the third row and the fourth column). A typical element of **A′** can be indicated as a_{ji}, which means that the a_{ij} th element of **A** is now the a_{ji} th element of **A′**. For example, a_{34} of **A** becomes a_{43} of **A′**. That is, the element in the third row and fourth column of **A** becomes the element in the fourth row and third column of **A′**.

Suppose that in addition to the reading scores for the six children we also had scores for arithmetic and vocabulary. Then each of the six children would have three scores, and we could present all of this information in a 6×3 matrix in which each of the six rows represents a child and each of the three columns represents a test score. These data presented in matrix form would be

$$\mathbf{X} = [x_{ij}] = \begin{bmatrix} x_{11} & x_{12} & x_{13} \\ x_{21} & x_{22} & x_{23} \\ x_{31} & x_{32} & x_{33} \\ x_{41} & x_{42} & x_{43} \\ x_{51} & x_{52} & x_{53} \\ x_{61} & x_{62} & x_{63} \end{bmatrix}$$

where x_{ij} represents a typical element in the ith row and j^{th} column of matrix **X**.

If column subscript 1 represented reading, column subscript 2 represented arithmetic, and column subscript 3 represented vocabulary, then the element x_{42} of x would represent the fourth child's (i = 4) arithmetic score (j = 2).

Suppose that the vector of arithmetic score was

$$\begin{bmatrix} 47 \\ 55 \\ 50 \\ 60 \\ 44 \\ 65 \end{bmatrix}$$

and the vector of vocabulary score was

$$\begin{bmatrix} 50 \\ 60 \\ 48 \\ 56 \\ 40 \\ 62 \end{bmatrix}$$

then the 6×3 matrix of scores would be

$$X = \begin{bmatrix} x_{11} & x_{12} & x_{13} \\ x_{21} & x_{22} & x_{23} \\ x_{31} & x_{32} & x_{33} \\ x_{41} & x_{42} & x_{43} \\ x_{51} & x_{52} & x_{53} \\ x_{61} & x_{62} & x_{63} \end{bmatrix} = \begin{bmatrix} 45 & 47 & 50 \\ 50 & 55 & 60 \\ 52 & 50 & 48 \\ 58 & 60 & 56 \\ 39 & 44 & 40 \\ 64 & 65 & 62 \end{bmatrix}$$

The score of the fourth child on the second test, or x_{42}, is 60. The transpose of **X** is

$$X' = \begin{bmatrix} x_{11} & x_{21} & x_{31} & x_{41} & x_{51} & x_{61} \\ x_{12} & x_{22} & x_{32} & x_{42} & x_{52} & x_{62} \\ x_{13} & x_{23} & x_{33} & x_{43} & x_{53} & x_{63} \end{bmatrix} = \begin{bmatrix} 45 & 50 & 52 & 58 & 39 & 64 \\ 47 & 55 & 50 & 60 & 44 & 65 \\ 50 & 60 & 48 & 56 & 40 & 62 \end{bmatrix}$$

It can be seen that the fourth child's second test score of 60 (x_{42} of **X**) is now located in the 2nd row and 4th column of **X′**. That is, the element x_{42} of **X** becomes the element x_{24} of **X′**.

3.3 CHARACTERISTICS OF VECTORS

Two vectors **x** and **y** are called equal if each element or component of **x** equals the corresponding element of **y**. That is, **x** = **y** if and only if the ith element of **x** equals the ith element of **y** for each i where i goes from 1 to m, m being the number of elements. The two vectors **x** and **y** below are equal

$$x = \begin{bmatrix} 3 \\ 4 \\ 5 \\ 3 \\ 2 \end{bmatrix} \qquad y = \begin{bmatrix} 3 \\ 4 \\ 5 \\ 3 \\ 2 \end{bmatrix}$$

since their corresponding elements are equal. The two vectors **x** and **y** below are not equal

$$x = \begin{bmatrix} 3 \\ 4 \\ 5 \\ 3 \\ 2 \end{bmatrix} \qquad y = \begin{bmatrix} 3 \\ 4 \\ 6 \\ 3 \\ 2 \end{bmatrix}$$

since the third element of **x**, which is 5, does not equal the third element of **y**, which is 6, although the remaining four corresponding elements of **x** and **y** are equal.

3.4 VECTOR OPERATIONS

Unlike the real numbers, only two basic operations can be performed with vectors. For single numbers, which we shall call scalars, there are a number of permissible operations, such as addition, multiplication, and division, while for vectors there are only two basic operations, vector addition and multiplication of a vector by a scalar. Any algebraic operations on real numbers result in another real number. For example, $(2 + 2) \times 2 = 8$, so that performing permissible operations on the real numbers produces another real number. Similarly, the two permissible vector operations produce another vector, as we shall see below. The operation of vector addition is defined as

$$x + y = \begin{bmatrix} x_1 \\ x_2 \\ \cdot \\ \cdot \\ \cdot \\ x_m \end{bmatrix} + \begin{bmatrix} y_1 \\ y_2 \\ \cdot \\ \cdot \\ \cdot \\ y_m \end{bmatrix} = \begin{bmatrix} x_1 + y_1 \\ x_2 + y_2 \\ \cdot \\ \cdot \\ \cdot \\ x_m + y_m \end{bmatrix} = z$$

Adding the vectors **x** and **y** results in a vector **z** where the ith component of **z** (z_i) is the sum of the corresponding i^{th} components for **x** and **y** (that is, x_i and y_i). It is obvious from this definition that both of the vectors that are to be added must contain the same number of elements. If we call the reading scores of the six children $\mathbf{x}_1$ and the arithmetic scores of the six children $\mathbf{x}_2$, then we can obtain a vector $\mathbf{y}$ of reading plus arithmetic scores by adding the vectors $\mathbf{x}_1$ and $\mathbf{x}_2$ as below.

$$x_1 + x_2 = \begin{bmatrix} 45 \\ 50 \\ 52 \\ 58 \\ 39 \\ 64 \end{bmatrix} + \begin{bmatrix} 47 \\ 55 \\ 50 \\ 60 \\ 44 \\ 65 \end{bmatrix} = \begin{bmatrix} 92 \\ 105 \\ 102 \\ 118 \\ 83 \\ 129 \end{bmatrix} = y$$

The first element of $\mathbf{y}$ is obtained by adding the first element of $\mathbf{x}_1$ to the first element of $\mathbf{x}_2$. Similarly, the fourth element of $\mathbf{y}$ is obtained by adding the fourth element of $\mathbf{x}_1$ to the fourth element of $\mathbf{x}_2$. Adding the vector $\mathbf{x}_1$ to $\mathbf{x}_2$ produces another vector $\mathbf{y}$. We could, in turn, add another vector $\mathbf{x}_3$ to $\mathbf{y}$ to produce another vector $\mathbf{z} = \mathbf{y} + \mathbf{x}_3 = \mathbf{x}_1 + \mathbf{x}_2 + \mathbf{x}_3$. For example, we could obtain the total of all three scores ($\mathbf{z}$) for the six children by adding the vector of vocabulary scores ($\mathbf{x}_3$) to the vector $\mathbf{y} = \mathbf{x}_1 + \mathbf{x}_2$ calculated above. By doing this, we have

$$z = x_1 + x_2 + x_3 = y + x_3 = \begin{bmatrix} 92 \\ 105 \\ 102 \\ 118 \\ 83 \\ 129 \end{bmatrix} + \begin{bmatrix} 50 \\ 60 \\ 48 \\ 56 \\ 40 \\ 62 \end{bmatrix} = \begin{bmatrix} 142 \\ 165 \\ 150 \\ 174 \\ 123 \\ 191 \end{bmatrix}$$

The vector $\mathbf{z}$ contains the total of all three test scores for the six children. As in scalar algebra, where $3 + 2 = 2 + 3$ (the commutative property), the addition of vectors is defined so that $\mathbf{x} + \mathbf{y} = \mathbf{y} + \mathbf{x}$. If

$$x = \begin{bmatrix} 1 \\ 2 \\ 3 \end{bmatrix} \text{ and } y = \begin{bmatrix} 3 \\ 2 \\ 1 \end{bmatrix}$$

$$\text{then } \mathbf{x} + \mathbf{y} = \begin{bmatrix} 1 \\ 2 \\ 3 \end{bmatrix} + \begin{bmatrix} 3 \\ 2 \\ 1 \end{bmatrix} = \begin{bmatrix} 4 \\ 4 \\ 4 \end{bmatrix} = \begin{bmatrix} 3 \\ 2 \\ 1 \end{bmatrix} + \begin{bmatrix} 1 \\ 2 \\ 3 \end{bmatrix} = \mathbf{y} + \mathbf{x}$$

The operation of multiplying a vector **x** by a scalar a (remembering that a scalar is a single real number) is defined as

$$a\mathbf{x} = a \begin{bmatrix} x_1 \\ x_2 \\ \cdot \\ \cdot \\ \cdot \\ x_m \end{bmatrix} = \begin{bmatrix} ax_1 \\ ax_2 \\ \cdot \\ \cdot \\ \cdot \\ ax_m \end{bmatrix}$$

It can easily be seen that to multiply a vector **x** by a scalar a we simply multiply each element of **x** by the scalar a to get the new vector a**x**. If a = 2 and

$$\mathbf{x} = \begin{bmatrix} 3 \\ 2 \\ 1 \\ 4 \end{bmatrix} \quad \text{then } a\mathbf{x} = 2 \begin{bmatrix} 3 \\ 2 \\ 1 \\ 4 \end{bmatrix} = \begin{bmatrix} 6 \\ 4 \\ 2 \\ 8 \end{bmatrix}$$

As in vector addition, multiplying a vector by a scalar also produces a vector of the same dimension as the vector that was multiplied by the scalar.

As with scalar algebra, where we can combine the operations of + and × to produce another number (for example, [2 + 2] × 3 = 12), we can combine the operations of scalar multiplication and vector addition to produce another vector of the same dimension as the original vectors on which we operated.

That is, a**x** + b**y** exists for all scalars a and b and all vectors **x** and **y** of the same dimension. Furthermore, since a**x** + b**y** results in a vector **z**, we could, in turn, form c**z** + d**r** to produce another vector **s**. For example, we might want to form a linear combination of the three test scores by applying differential weights to each of the test scores. In terms of vector operations, our new weighted total scores would become $\mathbf{y} = a\mathbf{x}_1 + b\mathbf{x}_2 + c\mathbf{x}_3$, where a, b, and c are scalars (weights for our example) and $\mathbf{x}_1$, $\mathbf{x}_2$, and $\mathbf{x}_3$ are vectors representing the reading, arithmetic, and vocabulary scores, respectively. If we wanted to give twice as much weight to the reading score relative to the other two scores, then we would have

$$\mathbf{y} = \begin{bmatrix} y_1 \\ y_2 \\ y_3 \\ y_4 \\ y_5 \\ y_6 \end{bmatrix} = 2\begin{bmatrix} 45 \\ 50 \\ 52 \\ 58 \\ 39 \\ 64 \end{bmatrix} + 1\begin{bmatrix} 47 \\ 55 \\ 50 \\ 60 \\ 44 \\ 65 \end{bmatrix} + 1\begin{bmatrix} 50 \\ 60 \\ 48 \\ 56 \\ 40 \\ 62 \end{bmatrix} = \begin{bmatrix} 90 \\ 100 \\ 104 \\ 116 \\ 78 \\ 128 \end{bmatrix} + \begin{bmatrix} 47 \\ 55 \\ 50 \\ 60 \\ 44 \\ 65 \end{bmatrix} + \begin{bmatrix} 50 \\ 60 \\ 48 \\ 56 \\ 40 \\ 62 \end{bmatrix} = \begin{bmatrix} 187 \\ 215 \\ 202 \\ 232 \\ 162 \\ 255 \end{bmatrix}$$

where **y** is the vector of weighted scores for the six children.

Like scalar algebra, the rules of vector operations have the distributive property, which is defined as $a(\mathbf{x} + \mathbf{y}) = a\mathbf{x} + a\mathbf{y}$. If we wanted to find the vector of average scores for the six children, then

$$\mathbf{y} = \frac{1}{3}(\mathbf{x}_1 + \mathbf{x}_2 + \mathbf{x}_3) = \frac{1}{3}\mathbf{x}_1 + \frac{1}{3}\mathbf{x}_2 + \frac{1}{3}\mathbf{x}_3,$$

where **y** is the vector of average scores. For our example,

$$\mathbf{y} = \frac{1}{3}\left[\begin{bmatrix} 45 \\ 50 \\ 52 \\ 58 \\ 39 \\ 64 \end{bmatrix} + \begin{bmatrix} 47 \\ 55 \\ 50 \\ 60 \\ 44 \\ 65 \end{bmatrix} + \begin{bmatrix} 50 \\ 60 \\ 48 \\ 56 \\ 40 \\ 62 \end{bmatrix}\right] = \frac{1}{3}\begin{bmatrix} 45 \\ 50 \\ 52 \\ 58 \\ 39 \\ 64 \end{bmatrix} + \frac{1}{3}\begin{bmatrix} 47 \\ 55 \\ 50 \\ 60 \\ 44 \\ 65 \end{bmatrix} + \frac{1}{3}\begin{bmatrix} 50 \\ 60 \\ 48 \\ 56 \\ 40 \\ 62 \end{bmatrix} = \begin{bmatrix} 47\frac{1}{3} \\ 55 \\ 50 \\ 58 \\ 41 \\ 63\frac{2}{3} \end{bmatrix}$$

If we want to subtract one vector **y** from another vector **x** we can do this by using the two vector operations. That is, set the scalar a equal to –1 and form the linear combination $\mathbf{x} + (-1)\mathbf{y} = \mathbf{x} - \mathbf{y}$. For example, if

$$\mathbf{x} = \begin{bmatrix} 1 \\ 2 \end{bmatrix} \text{ and } \mathbf{y} = \begin{bmatrix} 2 \\ 3 \end{bmatrix},$$

then $$\mathbf{x} - \mathbf{y} = \begin{bmatrix} 1 \\ 2 \end{bmatrix} + (-1)\begin{bmatrix} 2 \\ 3 \end{bmatrix} = \begin{bmatrix} 1 \\ 2 \end{bmatrix} + \begin{bmatrix} -2 \\ -3 \end{bmatrix} = \begin{bmatrix} -1 \\ -1 \end{bmatrix}$$

We simply take the differences in corresponding elements.

Two vectors of the same dimension can be multiplied to produce a scalar or single number. Remember, the previous operations produced vectors, not scalars. In order to multiply two vectors, **x** and **y**, we take the transpose of either vector and postmultiply it by the remaining vector. The multiplication operation is symbolized by **x′y** and is defined as

$$\mathbf{x}'\mathbf{y} = [x_1, x_2, x_3 \ldots, x_n] \begin{bmatrix} y_1 \\ y_2 \\ y_3 \\ \cdot \\ \cdot \\ \cdot \\ y_n \end{bmatrix} = \sum_{i=1}^{n} x_i y_i$$

For example, if $\mathbf{x} = \begin{bmatrix} 2 \\ 1 \\ 4 \end{bmatrix}$ and $\mathbf{y} = \begin{bmatrix} 3 \\ 2 \\ 5 \end{bmatrix}$,

then $$\mathbf{x}'\mathbf{y} = [2,1,4] \begin{bmatrix} 3 \\ 2 \\ 5 \end{bmatrix} = 2(3) + 1(2) + 4(5) = 28.$$

Note that **x′y** = **y′x** and **x′y** is not defined if **x** and **y** have a different number of elements. The vector product **x′y** is referred to as the "inner product." The multiplication of two vectors is a special case of matrix multiplication in which each matrix has only one row or column. Matrix multiplication is discussed later in this chapter.

3.5 GEOMETRICAL REPRESENTATION OF VECTORS AND RELATED CHARACTERISTICS

Vectors can be represented as points in Euclidean space. That is, a vector with two elements,

$$\mathbf{x} = \begin{bmatrix} x_1 \\ x_2 \end{bmatrix}$$

can be represented as a point in the real plane; a vector with three elements,

$$\mathbf{x} = \begin{bmatrix} x_1 \\ x_2 \\ x_3 \end{bmatrix}$$

can be represented as a point in three-dimensional Euclidean space; and a vector of higher dimension, such as

$$\mathbf{x} = \begin{bmatrix} x_1 \\ x_2 \\ x_3 \\ x_4 \\ x_5 \end{bmatrix}$$

can be represented as a point in five-dimensional Euclidean space. However, we can only visualize and, consequently, diagram vectors up to three-dimensional Euclidean space, although the analogy holds for Euclidean space of arbitrary dimension. The vectors for the three children can be represented in six-dimensional Euclidean space, although, as we shall see later, they form a three-dimensional subspace within the six-dimensional Euclidean space.

The vectors

$$\mathbf{x}_1 = \begin{bmatrix} 2 \\ 1 \end{bmatrix}, \mathbf{x}_2 = \begin{bmatrix} 3 \\ 3 \end{bmatrix}, \text{ and } \mathbf{x}_3 = \begin{bmatrix} 1 \\ -2 \end{bmatrix}$$

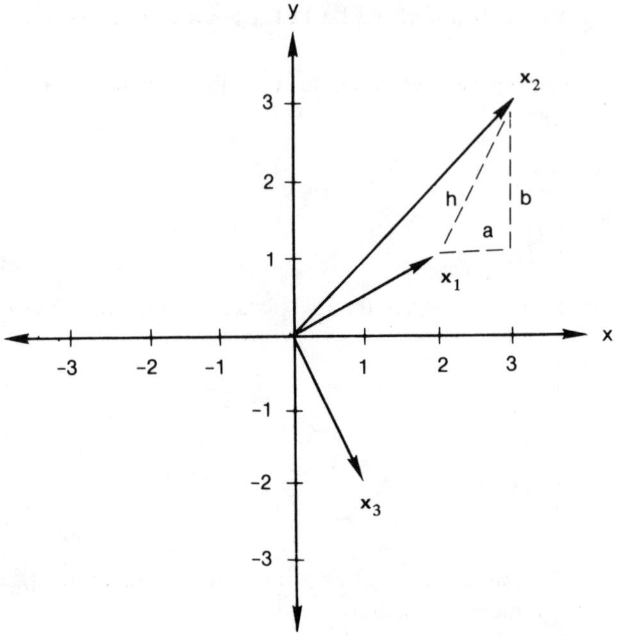

Figure 3.1 Vectors in the Plane

are represented as points in the two-dimensional Euclidean space (the real plane) in Figure 3.1, where the first component of the vector represents the x coordinate and the second component represents the y coordinate. Arrows are sometimes used, as they are in Figure 3.1, to represent vectors. The length of a vector, sometimes referred to as its norm, is defined as the positive square root of the sum of the squared elements of the vector, or

$$(\mathbf{x}'\mathbf{x})^{\frac{1}{2}} = \left[[x_1, x_2, \ldots x_m] \begin{bmatrix} x_1 \\ x_2 \\ \cdot \\ \cdot \\ \cdot \\ x_m \end{bmatrix} \right]^{\frac{1}{2}} = (x_1^2 + x_2^2 \ldots x_m^2)^{\frac{1}{2}} = \left(\sum_{i=1}^{m} x_i^2 \right)^{\frac{1}{2}}$$

The length of vector $\mathbf{x}_2$ equals the positive square root of

$$[x_1, x_2] \begin{bmatrix} x_1 \\ x_2 \end{bmatrix} = [3, 3] \begin{bmatrix} 3 \\ 3 \end{bmatrix} = (3)(3) + (3)(3) = 18$$

which is roughly 4.3. If we draw a perpendicular line from the end of the vector $\mathbf{x}_2$ to the x axis, we have formed a right triangle, and we know from high school geometry that the hypotenuse of a right triangle is equal to $\sqrt{a^2 + b^2}$, where a and b are the lengths of the remaining two sides of the right triangle. In this instance, a is the coordinate of x (that is, 3) and b is the coordinate of y (3). Put another way, a is the projection of the vector $\mathbf{x}$ on the x axis and b is the projection of the vector $\mathbf{x}$ on the y axis. As an exercise, the reader can compute the lengths of $\mathbf{x}_1$ and $\mathbf{x}_3$. Each vector in Euclidean space may be characterized by its length.

When the inner product $\mathbf{x'y}$ equals zero, then we say that the two vectors are orthogonal to one another. This means that the two vectors are perpendicular to one another or, equivalently, that the cosine of the angle between them equals zero. The vectors $\mathbf{x}_1$ and $\mathbf{x}_3$ are orthogonal (see Figure 3.1), since

$$\mathbf{x}_1' \mathbf{x}_3 = [2,1] \begin{bmatrix} 1 \\ -2 \end{bmatrix} = 2(1) + 1(-2) = 0$$

The reader should determine if any other pair of vectors in figure 3.1 is orthogonal.

The relationship between two vectors may also be characterized by their distance from each other. The distance between any two vectors $\mathbf{x}$ and $\mathbf{y}$ is defined as the positive square root of

$$[\mathbf{x} - \mathbf{y}]' \, [\mathbf{x} - \mathbf{y}] = [(x_1 - y_1), (x_2 - y_2) \ldots, (x_m - y_m)] \begin{bmatrix} x_1 - y_1 \\ x_2 - y_2 \\ \cdot \\ \cdot \\ \cdot \\ x_m - y_m \end{bmatrix}$$

$$= (x_1 - y_1)^2 + (x_2 - y_2)^2 + \ldots + (x_m - y_m)^2$$

$$= \sum_{i=1}^{m} (x_i - y_i)^2$$

The distance between $\mathbf{x}_1$ and $\mathbf{x}_2$ is the positive square root of

$$[x_1 - x_2]' [x_1 - x_2] = [(2-3), (1-3)] \begin{bmatrix} 2-3 \\ 1-3 \end{bmatrix} = [-1, -2] \begin{bmatrix} -1 \\ -2 \end{bmatrix} = 5$$

The distance is $\sqrt{5}$ or approximately 2.3. The reader should calculate the distances between the remaining two pairs of vectors. Cursory examination of Figure 3.1 reveals that the distance between the vectors $\mathbf{x}_1$ and $\mathbf{x}_2$ is less than the distance between vectors $\mathbf{x}_2$ and $\mathbf{x}_3$. Using elementary geometry, we can support this definition of distance by noting that the line between the two points is the hypotenuse (h) of a right triangle shown by the dotted lines. Since $h = \sqrt{a^2 + b^2}$, the length of a = 3 – 2, and the length of b = 3 – 1, we have $h = \sqrt{1^2 + 2^2} = \sqrt{5}$. The length of a is simply the absolute difference between the first component of $\mathbf{x}_1$ and the first component of $\mathbf{x}_2$ (that is, the difference in x coordinates). Similarly, the length of b is the absolute difference between the second (last) component of $\mathbf{x}_1$ and the second (last) component of $\mathbf{x}_2$ (that is, the difference in y coordinates).

Note that these last few operations with vectors do not produce another vector, but produce a single number or index, which we refer to as a scalar.

3.6 LINEAR INDEPENDENCE OF VECTORS

A set of vectors can also be characterized by another property, called "independence." A set of vectors is independent if no one vector in the set can be written as a linear combination of the others in the set. More formally, a set of vectors $\mathbf{x}_1, \mathbf{x}_2, \mathbf{x}_3, \ldots, \mathbf{x}_n$ is independent if there are no scalars $c_1, c_2, c_3, \ldots, c_n$ different from zero such that

$$c_1x_1 + c_2x_2 + c_3x_3 \ldots + c_nx_n = \mathbf{0}, \text{ where } \mathbf{0} \text{ is the zero vector } \begin{bmatrix} 0 \\ 0 \\ \cdot \\ \cdot \\ \cdot \\ 0 \end{bmatrix}$$

with the number of elements, of course, equal to the number of elements in the remaining vectors $\mathbf{x}_1, \mathbf{x}_2, \mathbf{x}_3, \ldots, \mathbf{x}_n$. If there is a linear combination $c_1\mathbf{x}_1 + c_2\mathbf{x}_2 + c_3\mathbf{x}_3 \ldots + c_n\mathbf{x}_n = \mathbf{0}$ where not all of the c_i (that is, $c_i, c_2, c_3, \ldots, c_n$) are zero, then we say that the set of vectors is linearly dependent. The vectors

$$\begin{bmatrix} 1 \\ 2 \end{bmatrix} \text{ and } \begin{bmatrix} 2 \\ 1 \end{bmatrix}$$

are independent since there is no c_1 and c_2 different from zero such that

$$c_1 \begin{bmatrix} 1 \\ 2 \end{bmatrix} + c_2 \begin{bmatrix} 2 \\ 1 \end{bmatrix} = \begin{bmatrix} 0 \\ 0 \end{bmatrix}$$

The set of vectors

$$\mathbf{x}_1 = \begin{bmatrix} 3 \\ 2 \end{bmatrix}, \mathbf{x}_2 = \begin{bmatrix} 1 \\ 0 \end{bmatrix}, \text{ and } \mathbf{x}_3 = \begin{bmatrix} 1 \\ 2 \end{bmatrix}$$

is not linearly independent since a set of c's can be found not all zero such that $c_1\mathbf{x}_1 + c_2\mathbf{x}_2 + c_3\mathbf{x}_3 = \mathbf{0}$. One set of c's is $c_1 = -1$, $c_2 = 2$, and $c_3 = 1$, since

$$-1 \begin{bmatrix} 3 \\ 2 \end{bmatrix} + 2 \begin{bmatrix} 1 \\ 0 \end{bmatrix} + 1 \begin{bmatrix} 1 \\ 2 \end{bmatrix} = \begin{bmatrix} 0 \\ 0 \end{bmatrix}$$

We can rewrite this expression as

$$\begin{bmatrix} 3 \\ 2 \end{bmatrix} = 2 \begin{bmatrix} 1 \\ 0 \end{bmatrix} + 1 \begin{bmatrix} 1 \\ 2 \end{bmatrix}$$

so that the vector $\mathbf{x}_1$ can be expressed as a linear combination of the vectors $\mathbf{x}_2$ and $\mathbf{x}_3$, that is, $\mathbf{x}_1 = 2\mathbf{x}_2 + 1\mathbf{x}_3$. Conversely, we could express $\mathbf{x}_2$ as a linear combination of $\mathbf{x}_1$ and $\mathbf{x}_3$(that is, $\mathbf{x}_2 = \frac{1}{2}\,\mathbf{x}_1 - \frac{1}{2}\,\mathbf{x}_3$) or $\mathbf{x}_3$ as a linear combination of $\mathbf{x}_1$ and $\mathbf{x}_2$ ($\mathbf{x}_3 = \mathbf{x}_1 - 2\mathbf{x}_2$).

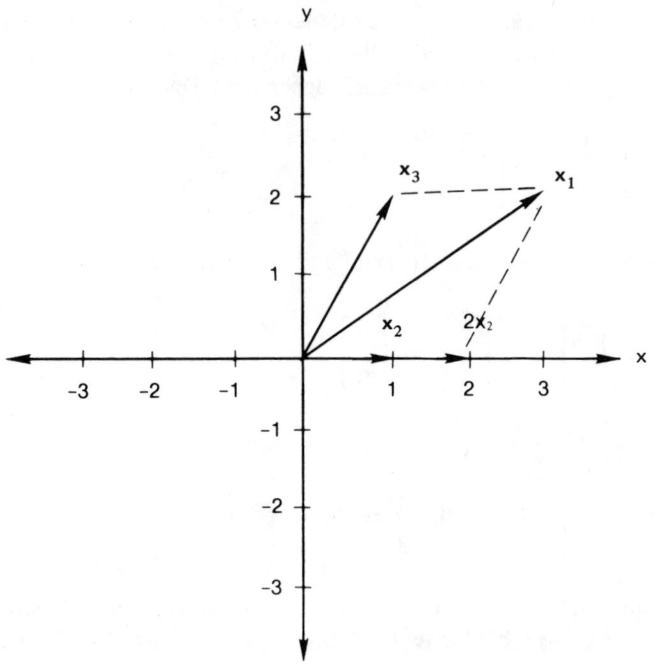

Figure 3.2 Linear Dependence of Vectors in the Plane

In order to contribute to an intuitive understanding of what is meant by the linear independence and dependence of vectors with two components, Figure 3.2 portrays the set of vectors

$$\mathbf{x}_1 = \begin{bmatrix} 3 \\ 2 \end{bmatrix}, \mathbf{x}_2 = \begin{bmatrix} 1 \\ 0 \end{bmatrix}, \text{ and } \mathbf{x}_3 = \begin{bmatrix} 1 \\ 2 \end{bmatrix}$$

as directed lines in the plane.

It can be seen geometrically from this figure that if we add $2\mathbf{x}_2$ and $\mathbf{x}_3$, we obtain the vector $\mathbf{x}_1$. Multiplying $\mathbf{x}_2$ by the scalar doubles the size of each coordinate of $\mathbf{x}_2$ and hence doubles the length of the vector $\mathbf{x}_2$. Geometrically, vectors are added according to the parallelogram rule, whereby the endpoint of the vector sum is at the intersection of the two imaginary sides (the dotted lines in Figure 3.2) needed to form a parallelogram from the two vectors to be added. Another interpretation is that $\mathbf{x}_1$ must have a projection on $\mathbf{x}_2$ that is twice the length of the vector $\mathbf{x}_2$ and at the same time must project on $\mathbf{x}_3$ only once its length. (Projection lines on a particular vector are paralled to the remaining vector. In the case of orthogonal vectors the projections are perpendicular.) As an exercise the reader can demonstrate geometrically that $\mathbf{x}_2 = \frac{1}{2}\mathbf{x}_1 - \frac{1}{2}\mathbf{x}_3$ and $\mathbf{x}_3 = \mathbf{x}_1 - 2\mathbf{x}_3$. Furthermore, any two component vectors can be written as a linear combination of $\mathbf{x}_2$ and $\mathbf{x}_3$. In other words, there exist scalars a and b such that any other vector in the plane can be expressed as a linear combination of $\mathbf{x}_2$ and $\mathbf{x}_3$.

3.7 BASIS OF A VECTOR SPACE

A vector space is a set of vectors (for example, points in a plane) for which the vector operations defined above are permissible. That is, if $\mathbf{x}_1$ and $\mathbf{x}_2$ are members of the vector space, then so is $a\mathbf{x}_i + b\mathbf{x}_2$. When any other vector in the space under consideration (such as a plane) can be written as a linear combination of a set of independent vectors, we call this set of vectors a "basis" for the vector space. As we shall see, there are many possible choices for a basis. The basis of a vector space can also be defined as the minimum number of independent vectors needed to span the space. "Spanning the space" means that all other vectors in the vector space can be expressed as a linear combination of these basis vectors. Accordingly, $\mathbf{x}_3$ and $\mathbf{x}_1$ form a basis for E^2 (the plane); each of the pairs of vectors $(\mathbf{x}_1, \mathbf{x}_2)$ and $(\mathbf{x}_2, \mathbf{x}_3)$ also forms a basis for E^2.

In E^2 (the plane or two-dimensional Euclidean space), the basis consists of two vectors, each vector consisting of two elements or components. This is true because three or more vectors with two components must be linearly dependent (see Figure 3.2) and one vector spans a subspace of E^2, the real line (E^1). The number of vectors in a basis must be equal to the dimension of the vector space. Figure 3.3 illustrates that one vector in E^2 cannot be a basis for E^2 because it does not span E^2, but is a basis for a one-dimensional subspace of E^2.

We can see from Figure 3.3 that any linear combination of $\mathbf{x}$ (that is, $a\mathbf{x}$, with a being any scalar) results in a vector colinear with $\mathbf{x}$, which means that the vector $a\mathbf{x}$ is a vector in the same direction as $\mathbf{x}$. Two vectors have the same direction if their angles with the x axis are equal. The set of vectors $a\mathbf{x}$ for all a's simply forms a line (E^1) in E^2.

Although any two independent vectors in E^2 form a basis for E^2, as we have seen above, it is sometimes convenient to have the basis vectors orthogonal by being colinear with the x and y axes and of unit length. The reader should verify that the three possible sets of basis vectors formed from $\mathbf{x}_1$, $\mathbf{x}_2$, and $\mathbf{x}_3$ in Figure 3.2 do not satisfy either of these two conditions.

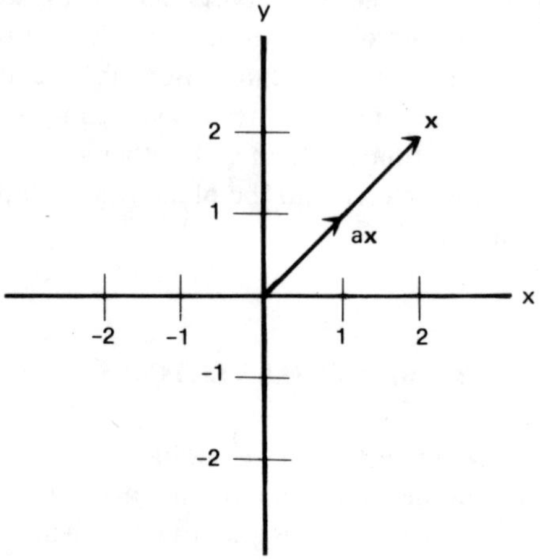

Figure 3.3 A Vector in E^2

Two unique vectors in E^2 satisfy these two conditions. The two unique vectors are

$$\mathbf{e}_1 = \begin{bmatrix} 1 \\ 0 \end{bmatrix} \text{ and } \mathbf{e}_2 = \begin{bmatrix} 0 \\ 1 \end{bmatrix}$$

and are geometrically portrayed in Figure 3.4.

The reader can verify that $\mathbf{e}_1$ and $\mathbf{e}_2$ are orthogonal and of unit length. Any vector in E_2 can be expressed as a linear combination of $\mathbf{e}_1$ and $\mathbf{e}_2$. For example, the vector

$$\mathbf{x} = \begin{bmatrix} 2 \\ 1 \end{bmatrix} \text{ can be expressed as}$$

$$2\mathbf{e}_1 + 1\mathbf{e}_2 = 2\begin{bmatrix} 1 \\ 0 \end{bmatrix} + 1\begin{bmatrix} 0 \\ 1 \end{bmatrix} = \begin{bmatrix} 2 \\ 1 \end{bmatrix} = \mathbf{x}$$

The vector $\mathbf{x}$ expressed as a linear combination of $\mathbf{e}_1$ and $\mathbf{e}_2$ is shown in Figure 3.4.

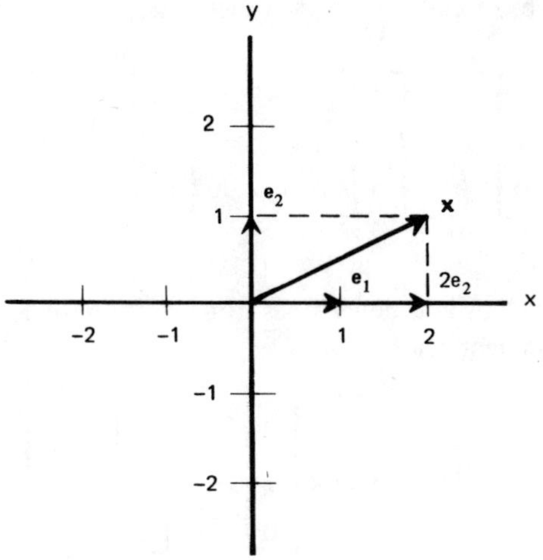

Figure 3.4 The Basis e_1 and e_2

Let us now turn to three-dimensional Euclidean space (E^3), where a vector is represented as a point with x, y, and z coordinates in three-dimensional space. For example, the vector

$$\mathbf{x} = \begin{bmatrix} 2 \\ 1 \\ 2 \end{bmatrix}$$

is a vector in three-dimensional Euclidean space. A basis for E^3 is any set of three independent vectors. The set of vectors

$$\mathbf{x}_1 = \begin{bmatrix} 2 \\ 1 \\ 0 \end{bmatrix}, \mathbf{x}_2 = \begin{bmatrix} 1 \\ 2 \\ 1 \end{bmatrix}, \text{ and } \mathbf{x}_3 = \begin{bmatrix} 1 \\ 1 \\ 2 \end{bmatrix}$$

forms a basis for E^3 since there are no scalars a, b, and c different from zero such that $a\mathbf{x}_1 + b\mathbf{x}_2 + c\mathbf{x}_3 = \mathbf{0}$. On the other hand, the set of vectors

$$\mathbf{x}_1 = \begin{bmatrix} 2 \\ 1 \\ 0 \end{bmatrix}, \mathbf{x}_2 = \begin{bmatrix} 1 \\ 1 \\ 2 \end{bmatrix}, \text{ and } \mathbf{x}_3 = \begin{bmatrix} 3 \\ 1 \\ -2 \end{bmatrix}$$

is linearly dependent and hence does not form a basis for E^3. These three vectors are dependent since

$$2\mathbf{x}_1 - 1\mathbf{x}_2 - 1\mathbf{x}_3 = \mathbf{0}, \text{ or } 2\begin{bmatrix} 2 \\ 1 \\ 0 \end{bmatrix} - 1\begin{bmatrix} 1 \\ 1 \\ 2 \end{bmatrix} - 1\begin{bmatrix} 3 \\ 1 \\ -2 \end{bmatrix} = \begin{bmatrix} 0 \\ 0 \\ 0 \end{bmatrix}$$

That is, there is a set of scalars a, b, and c not equal to zero such that $a\mathbf{x}_1 + b\mathbf{x}_2 + c\mathbf{x}_3 = \mathbf{0}$. In the present example, $a = 2$, $b = -1$, and $c = -1$. Equivalently, each of the vectors can be written as a linear combination of the remaining two vectors. For example, $\mathbf{x}_3 = 2\mathbf{x}_1 - \mathbf{x}_2$.

The vectors

$$\mathbf{x}_1 = \begin{bmatrix} 1 \\ 2 \\ 3 \end{bmatrix} \text{ and } \mathbf{x}_2 = \begin{bmatrix} 2 \\ 1 \\ 2 \end{bmatrix}$$

are independent of each other and are in E^3. They do not, however, form a basis for E^3. Taking all possible linear combinations of these two vectors with all possible scalars a and b would produce a two-dimensional subspace (E^2) of the three-dimensional space (E^3). That is, these two vectors would span a plane or, equivalently, be the basis of a plane (E^2) embedded in E^3. This is analogous to the situation discussed earlier, where one vector in E^2 cannot be a basis for E^2, but is the basis for a one-dimensional subspace of E^2, a line in E^1. Analogous to the situation for E^2, it is sometimes convenient to use the unique

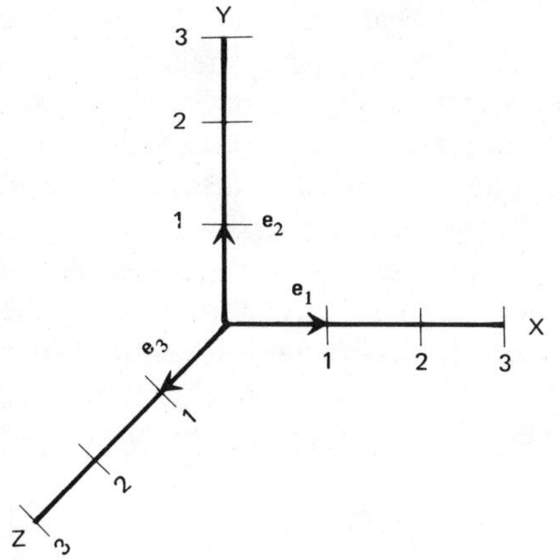

Figure 3.5 The Basis e_1, e_2, and e_3 for E^3

set of basis vectors that are orthogonal by being colinear with the x, y, and z coordinate axes and are of unit length. These vectors are denoted as

$$e_1 = \begin{bmatrix} 1 \\ 0 \\ 0 \end{bmatrix}, e_2 = \begin{bmatrix} 0 \\ 1 \\ 0 \end{bmatrix}, \text{ and } e_3 = \begin{bmatrix} 0 \\ 0 \\ 1 \end{bmatrix}$$

and are geometrically portrayed in Figure 3.5.

A vector is colinear with another vector if the two have the same direction; the two vectors do not have to have the same length. The vector $\mathbf{e}_1$ is colinear with the x axis and has zero projections on the y and z axis; $\mathbf{e}_2$ is colinear with the y axis and has zero projections on x and z; and $\mathbf{e}_3$ is colinear with the z axis and has zero projections on x and y. The set of vectors $\mathbf{e}_1$, $\mathbf{e}_2$, and $\mathbf{e}_3$ forms an orthogonal basis for E^3. Every vector in E^3 can be expressed as $a\mathbf{e}_1 + b\mathbf{e}_2 + c\mathbf{e}_3$ where a, b, and c are scalars and $\mathbf{e}_1$, $\mathbf{e}_2$, and $\mathbf{e}_3$ are the basis vectors

$$\begin{bmatrix} 1 \\ 0 \\ 0 \end{bmatrix}, \begin{bmatrix} 0 \\ 1 \\ 0 \end{bmatrix}, \text{ and } \begin{bmatrix} 0 \\ 0 \\ 1 \end{bmatrix}, \text{ respectively.}$$

It can also be seen from Figure 3.5 that $\mathbf{e}_1$ and $\mathbf{e}_2$ do not span E^3 but do span or form a basis for E^2, a subspace embedded in E^3. Any vector in the x, y plane can be expressed as a linear combination of $\mathbf{e}_1$ and $\mathbf{e}_2$. Likewise, the two independent vectors $\mathbf{e}_1$ and $\mathbf{e}_3$ span another two-dimensional subspace (E^2) of E^3, the x, z plane. The reader can verify that any four three-dimensional vectors in E^3 are necessarily linearly dependent.

The results for three-dimensional Euclidean space are easily generalized to higher-dimensional Euclidean spaces (for example, E^4, E^{100}, and so on), even though we cannot visualize such a higher-dimensional space. Let us now return to our earlier example of six children with three scores each. These data were represented as three six-component vectors, with each vector representing the scores of six children on a particular test. The three vectors were for reading, arithmetic, and vocabulary scores for the six children and were

$$\begin{bmatrix} 45 \\ 50 \\ 52 \\ 58 \\ 39 \\ 63 \end{bmatrix}, \begin{bmatrix} 47 \\ 55 \\ 50 \\ 60 \\ 44 \\ 65 \end{bmatrix}, \begin{bmatrix} 50 \\ 60 \\ 48 \\ 56 \\ 40 \\ 62 \end{bmatrix}, \text{ respectively.}$$

These three vectors can be represented as points in six-dimensional Euclidean space (E^6). These are an independent set of vectors and form a three-dimensional subspace embedded in E^6. Generalizing from E^2 and E^3, we need six independent vectors to form a basis for E^6. Again, generalizing from E^2 and E^3, an orthogonal basis for E^6 would be

$$\mathbf{e}_1 = \begin{bmatrix} 1 \\ 0 \\ 0 \\ 0 \\ 0 \\ 0 \end{bmatrix}, \mathbf{e}_2 = \begin{bmatrix} 0 \\ 1 \\ 0 \\ 0 \\ 0 \\ 0 \end{bmatrix}, \mathbf{e}_3 = \begin{bmatrix} 0 \\ 0 \\ 1 \\ 0 \\ 0 \\ 0 \end{bmatrix}, \mathbf{e}_4 = \begin{bmatrix} 0 \\ 0 \\ 0 \\ 1 \\ 0 \\ 0 \end{bmatrix}, \mathbf{e}_5 = \begin{bmatrix} 0 \\ 0 \\ 0 \\ 0 \\ 1 \\ 0 \end{bmatrix}, \text{ and } \mathbf{e}_6 = \begin{bmatrix} 0 \\ 0 \\ 0 \\ 0 \\ 0 \\ 1 \end{bmatrix}$$

Each of these vectors are also of unit length as well as orthogonal. For example, $\sqrt{\mathbf{e}_1'\mathbf{e}_1} = 1$, $\mathbf{e}_1'\mathbf{e}_2 = 0$, and so on.

3.8 VECTOR REPRESENTATION OF STATISTICAL MODELS

Many of the statistical models (such as regression) can be described using vector space terminology. For example, we might like to be able to represent the vector of scores $\mathbf{y}$ on a dependent variable as a linear combination of a number of vectors, each representing an independent variable. If we could predict the scores of $\mathbf{y}$ from the scores of the independent vectors $\mathbf{x}_1$ and $\mathbf{x}_2$, then $\mathbf{y}$ could be represented as a linear combination of the two vectors $\mathbf{x}_1$ and $\mathbf{x}_2$ (that is, $\mathbf{y} = a\mathbf{x}_1 + b\mathbf{x}_2$). In this case of perfect prediction, the vector of dependent variable scores, $\mathbf{y}$, would lie in the subspace spanned by the independent variable vectors $\mathbf{x}_1$ and $\mathbf{x}_2$. For example, if the five individual scores for a dependent variable were

$$y = \begin{bmatrix} 2 \\ 1 \\ 3 \\ 5 \\ 2 \end{bmatrix}$$

and the score vectors for independent variables $\mathbf{x}_1$ and $\mathbf{x}_2$ were

$$x_1 = \begin{bmatrix} 0 \\ -1 \\ 1 \\ 1 \\ 0 \end{bmatrix} \text{ and } x_2 = \begin{bmatrix} 1 \\ 1 \\ 1 \\ 2 \\ 1 \end{bmatrix}$$

$$\text{then } y = 1x_1 + 2x_2 = 1 \begin{bmatrix} 0 \\ -1 \\ 1 \\ 1 \\ 0 \end{bmatrix} + 2 \begin{bmatrix} 1 \\ 1 \\ 1 \\ 2 \\ 1 \end{bmatrix} = \begin{bmatrix} 2 \\ 1 \\ 3 \\ 5 \\ 2 \end{bmatrix}$$

and the dependent vector $\mathbf{y}$ is a linear combination of the independent vectors $\mathbf{x}_1$ and $\mathbf{x}_2$. The subspace spanned by $\mathbf{x}_1$ and $\mathbf{x}_2$ is a two-dimensional subspace of E^5. The vector $\mathbf{y}$, since it can be expressed as a linear combination of $\mathbf{x}_1$ and $\mathbf{x}_2$, must lie in the subspace spanned by $\mathbf{x}_1$ and $\mathbf{x}_2$.

In practice, we never find that a dependent variable vector **y** can be expressed exactly as a linear combination of independent vectors $\mathbf{x}_1, \mathbf{x}_2, \ldots, \mathbf{x}_n$. What is possible, however, is to find a vector $\hat{\mathbf{y}}$ that lies in the subspace spanned by $\mathbf{x}_1, \mathbf{x}_2, \ldots, \mathbf{x}_n$ (that is, $\hat{\mathbf{y}} = a\mathbf{x}_1 + b\mathbf{x}_2 \ldots, z\mathbf{x}_n$) and is also the closest vector to **y** of any vector lying in that subspace. We define closeness in terms of the distance of $\hat{\mathbf{y}}$ from **y**, that is $(\hat{\mathbf{y}} - \mathbf{y})'(\hat{\mathbf{y}} - \mathbf{y})$. In other words, $\hat{\mathbf{y}}$ is such that it lies in the subspace spanned by $\mathbf{x}_1, \mathbf{x}_2, \ldots, \mathbf{x}_n$ and $(\hat{\mathbf{y}} - \mathbf{y})'(\hat{\mathbf{y}} - \mathbf{y})$ is a minimum. We shall see in the next chapter that scalars a, b, . . . , z can be found that produce a **y** which lies in the subspace spanned by $\mathbf{x}_1, \mathbf{x}_2, \ldots, \mathbf{x}_n$ and is the closest to **y** (that is, minimum value of $[\hat{\mathbf{y}} - \mathbf{y}]'[\hat{\mathbf{y}} - \mathbf{y}]$). For example, if

$$\mathbf{y} = \begin{bmatrix} 5 \\ 4 \\ 1 \\ 2 \\ 8 \\ 6 \\ 7 \\ 5 \end{bmatrix}$$

is a dependent variable vector of scores, and

$$\mathbf{x}_1 = \begin{bmatrix} 2 \\ 1 \\ 0 \\ 2 \\ 6 \\ 3 \\ 5 \\ 2 \end{bmatrix} \quad \text{and } \mathbf{x}_2 = \begin{bmatrix} 2 \\ 3 \\ 1 \\ 0 \\ 2 \\ 3 \\ 2 \\ 3 \end{bmatrix}$$

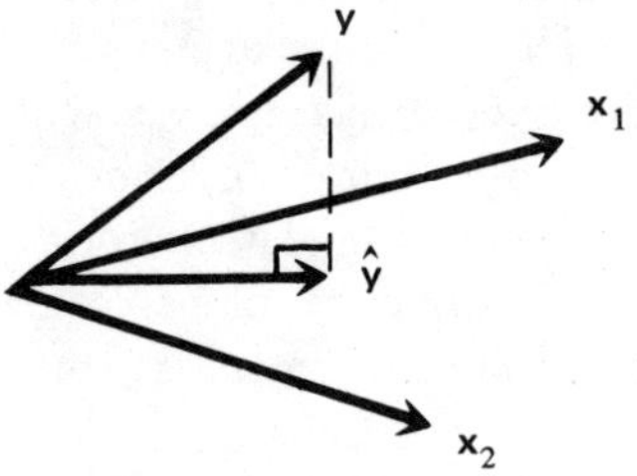

Figure 3.6 Prediction of y from $\mathbf{x}_1$ and $\mathbf{x}$

are independent variable vectors, then **y** cannot be expressed as $a\mathbf{x}_1 + b\mathbf{x}_2$ and hence does not lie in the two-dimensional subspace spanned by $\mathbf{x}_1$ and **x**. That is, **y** is not perfectly predicted from $\mathbf{x}_1$ and $\mathbf{x}_2$. However,

$$\hat{\mathbf{y}} = \begin{bmatrix} 4 \\ 4 \\ 1 \\ 2 \\ 8 \\ 6 \\ 7 \\ 5 \end{bmatrix}$$

does lie in the subspace spanned by $\mathbf{x}_1$ and $\mathbf{x}_2$ because

$$\hat{\mathbf{y}} = 1\mathbf{x}_1 + 1\mathbf{x}_2 = \begin{bmatrix} 2 \\ 1 \\ 0 \\ 2 \\ 6 \\ 3 \\ 5 \\ 2 \end{bmatrix} + \begin{bmatrix} 2 \\ 3 \\ 1 \\ 0 \\ 2 \\ 3 \\ 2 \\ 3 \end{bmatrix} = \begin{bmatrix} 4 \\ 4 \\ 1 \\ 2 \\ 8 \\ 6 \\ 7 \\ 5 \end{bmatrix}$$

and $\hat{\mathbf{y}}$ is close to $\mathbf{y}$ since the distance between $\hat{\mathbf{y}}$ and $\mathbf{y}$, $(\hat{\mathbf{y}}-\mathbf{y})'(\hat{\mathbf{y}}-\mathbf{y})$, equals 1, as the reader can verify. The predicted vector $\hat{\mathbf{y}}$ differs from the observed vector $\mathbf{y}$ only in the first element and hence is close to and would be a good predictor of $\mathbf{y}$. The case of one dependent variable vector, $\mathbf{y}$, and two independent variable vectors, $\mathbf{x}_1$ and $\mathbf{x}_2$, is illustrated in Figure 3.6. From this figure we can see that $\hat{\mathbf{y}}$ lies in the plane spanned by $\mathbf{x}_1$ and $\mathbf{x}_2$ and is as close as possible to $\mathbf{y}$ since $\hat{\mathbf{y}}$ is a perpendicular projection of $\mathbf{y}$ onto the plane spanned by $\mathbf{x}_1$ and $\mathbf{x}_2$. (The shortest distance between a point and a plane is in the direction perpendicular to the plane.)

Another model discussed in *Introduction to Multivariate Analysis* is factor analysis. The aim of factor analysis is to be able to express the scores on an observed variable such as a test score in terms of more latent fundamental or basic variables. Our aim here is to be able to express the vector of observed scores $\mathbf{y}$ as a linear combination of vectors of latent variables $\mathbf{x}_1, \mathbf{x}_2, \ldots, \mathbf{x}_n$, that is, $\mathbf{y} = a\mathbf{x}_1 + b\mathbf{x}_2 \ldots + c\mathbf{x}_n$.

3.9 CHARACTERISTICS OF MATRICES

For our purposes, we can define a matrix as an m by n array of numbers where m is the number of rows in the array and n is the number of columns in the array. An example of a 4×3 matrix is

$$\begin{bmatrix} 4 & 5 & 0 \\ 3 & 6 & 1 \\ 1 & 8 & 2 \\ 2 & 3 & 4 \end{bmatrix}$$

This matrix has 4 rows and 3 columns and is a 4×3 array of 12 numbers or elements. An element of a matrix can be denoted as a_{ij}, which means the element is contained in the ith row and j^{th} column of the matrix. The element a_{32} of the above matrix is 8. It is the element in the third row and second column. Sometimes a matrix is denoted by $[a_{ij}]$ where the a_{ij} in the brackets represents the typical element. Matrices will always be identified by placing brackets around the array of numbers. Sometimes matrices are denoted by uppercase boldface letters. The first part of this chapter dealt with a special kind of matrix, a vector. A vector is an $n \times 1$ vector. That is, it is composed of n rows and only one column.

One of the most common matrices that is utilized in the behavioral and social science areas is the correlation matrix, which we will denote by $\mathbf{R}$ or $[r_{ij}]$.

The element r_{ij} is the correlation of the ith row variable with the jth column variable. An example of a correlation matrix is

	1	2	3	4
1	1.00	.50	.30	.60
2	.50	1.00	.40	.50
3	.30	.40	1.00	.40
4	.60	.50	.40	1.00

For a correlation matrix, the row variables are the same as the column variables. The element r_{21} is the correlation of the variable represented by the second row with the variable represented by the first column, which is .50 in the above correlation matrix. The element r_{33} is the correlation of the third row variable with the third column variable, which is 1, because the third row variable is the same as the third column variable and the correlation of a variable with itself is, of course, 1. The correlation matrix has a number of different properties. First, it is square in that the number of rows, n, equals the number of columns, m, that is, $m = n$. In the above example $m = 4$ and $n = 4$, or $m = n = 4$. Second, it is symmetric, meaning that the $r_{ij}{}^{th}$ element is equal to the $r_{ji}{}^{th}$ element. If $r_{ij} = r_{23}$, then $r_{ji} = r_{32}$ and $r_{23} = r_{32}$. In the above correlation matrix, $r_{23} = .40$ and $r_{32} = .40$, and so $r_{23} = r_{32} = .40$. A matrix is defined as being symmetric if $\mathbf{A} = \mathbf{A}'$ where $\mathbf{A}'$ is called the transpose of **A**. The transpose of **A**, as mentioned earlier, is constructed from **A** by forming a matrix where the rows of **A** become the columns of a new matrix, **A′**, or vice versa by forming a matrix where the columns of **A** become the rows of a new matrix, **A′**. For example, the transpose of **R** above, or **R′**, is found by making the first row of **R** the first column of **R′**; making the second row of **R** the second column of **R′**; and so on. The first row of **R** is [1.0, .50, .30, .60] and this becomes the first column of **R′**. The second row of **R** is [.50, 1.00, .40, .50] and this becomes the second column of **R′**, and so on for the remaining two rows of **R**. The reader should verify that $\mathbf{R} = \mathbf{R}'$ and so **R** is a symmetric matrix. Another useful square symmetric matrix is the identity matrix, which is commonly expressed as **I**. **I** is an $n \times n$ matrix that has all elements in the principal diagonal equal to 1 and all off-diagonal elements equal to zero. The principal diagonal is defined as those elements where the row subscript equals the column subscript or those elements r_{ij} where i equals j. A 5 × 5 identity matrix is

$$\mathbf{I} = \begin{bmatrix} 1 & 0 & 0 & 0 & 0 \\ 0 & 1 & 0 & 0 & 0 \\ 0 & 0 & 1 & 0 & 0 \\ 0 & 0 & 0 & 1 & 0 \\ 0 & 0 & 0 & 0 & 1 \end{bmatrix}$$

The principal diagonal is the string of 1's from the upper left to the lower right of the matrix. They are the elements $r_{11} = 1$, $r_{22} = 1$, $r_{33} = 1$, $r_{44} = 1$, and $r_{55} = 1$. The off-diagonal elements are those elements r_{ij} where the subscript i does not equal j. The element $r_{12} = 0$ is an off-diagonal element because the row subscript 1 does not equal the column subscript 2. In fact, all of the 0 elements in **I** are off-diagonal elements since the row subscript does not equal the column subscript for any of the 0 elements in **I**. The reader can easily verify that **I** = **I′**. **I** can be of any size; for convenience we used a 5 × 5 identity matrix. An example of an identity matrix would be a correlation matrix representing a set of variables that are uncorrelated with one another. We shall see later in this chapter that **I** plays the same role in matrix multiplication that 1 plays in scalar multiplication. That is, if we multiply a matrix **A** by **I**, we get **AI** = **IA** = **A**, analogous to the scalar result a1 = a.

3.10 MATRIX OPERATIONS

We will now turn to a discussion of the various permissible operations that can be performed on matrices. First, we can multiply a matrix **A** by a scalar c to obtain a matrix c**A**. The elements of c**A** are $[ca_{ij}]$. The matrix c**A** is obtained from the matrix **A** by multiplying each of the elements of **A** by the scalar c. For example, let c = 3 and

$$\mathbf{A} = \begin{bmatrix} 3 & 1 & 0 \\ 3 & 2 & 1 \\ 5 & 2 & 3 \end{bmatrix}, \text{ then } c\mathbf{A} = 3 \begin{bmatrix} 3 & 1 & 0 \\ 3 & 2 & 1 \\ 5 & 2 & 3 \end{bmatrix} = \begin{bmatrix} 9 & 3 & 0 \\ 9 & 6 & 3 \\ 15 & 6 & 9 \end{bmatrix}$$

The scalar multiplication of a matrix is defined so that c**A** = **A**c.

Two matrices **A** and **B** are equal if and only if each of the corresponding elements of **A** and **B** are equal. That is, $a_{ij} = b_{ij}$ for i = 1, . . . , n and j = 1, . . . , m.

If

$$\mathbf{A} = \begin{bmatrix} 3 & 4 & 3 \\ 2 & 1 & 2 \\ 1 & 7 & 1 \\ 5 & 0 & 5 \end{bmatrix} \quad \text{and } \mathbf{B} = \begin{bmatrix} 3 & 4 & 3 \\ 2 & 1 & 2 \\ 1 & 7 & 1 \\ 5 & 0 & 7 \end{bmatrix}$$

then $\mathbf{A} \neq \mathbf{B}$ since element a_{43} of **A**, which is 5, does not equal b_{43} of **B**, which is 7. If both of these elements were equal, then **A** would equal **B**. Notice that the order of the two matrices must be the same when referring to equality. That is, each matrix must have the same number of rows and the same number of columns.

If two matrices **A** and **B** are of the same order, then the addition of **A** and **B** is defined by adding the corresponding elements of the two matrices to produce a new matrix **C**. More specifically, **A** + **B** = **C** where the elements of **C** are $c_{ij} = a_{ij} + b_{ij}$. This equality can also be expressed as $[a_{ij}] + [b_{ij}] = [a_{ij} + b_{ij}]$. If we added the matrices **A** and **B** above, we would have

$$\mathbf{A} + \mathbf{B} = \begin{bmatrix} 3 & 4 & 3 \\ 2 & 1 & 2 \\ 1 & 7 & 1 \\ 5 & 0 & 5 \end{bmatrix} + \begin{bmatrix} 3 & 4 & 3 \\ 2 & 1 & 2 \\ 1 & 7 & 1 \\ 5 & 0 & 7 \end{bmatrix} = \begin{bmatrix} 6 & 8 & 6 \\ 4 & 2 & 4 \\ 2 & 14 & 2 \\ 10 & 0 & 12 \end{bmatrix} = \mathbf{C}$$

The operations of scalar multiplication and matrix addition can be combined such that

$$a\,\mathbf{A} + b\,\mathbf{B} + c\,\mathbf{C} + \ldots + z\,\mathbf{Z} = \theta$$

where θ is a new matrix formed by using jointly the operations of matrix addition and multiplication of a matrix by a scalar. For example,

$$-1\mathbf{A} + 3\mathbf{B} = -1 \begin{bmatrix} 3 & 4 & 3 \\ 2 & 1 & 2 \\ 1 & 7 & 1 \\ 5 & 0 & 5 \end{bmatrix} + 3 \begin{bmatrix} 3 & 4 & 3 \\ 2 & 1 & 2 \\ 1 & 7 & 1 \\ 5 & 0 & 7 \end{bmatrix}$$

$$= \begin{bmatrix} -3 & -4 & -3 \\ -2 & -1 & -2 \\ -1 & -7 & -1 \\ -5 & 0 & -5 \end{bmatrix} + \begin{bmatrix} 9 & 12 & 9 \\ 6 & 2 & 6 \\ 3 & 21 & 3 \\ 15 & 0 & 21 \end{bmatrix} = \begin{bmatrix} 6 & 8 & 6 \\ 4 & 2 & 4 \\ 2 & 14 & 2 \\ 10 & 0 & 16 \end{bmatrix}$$

The reader should verify the following results concerning the properties of multiplication of a matrix by a scalar and matrix addition:

(1) $\mathbf{A} + \mathbf{B} = \mathbf{B} + \mathbf{A}$

(2) $\mathbf{A} + \mathbf{B} + \mathbf{C} = (\mathbf{A} + \mathbf{B}) + \mathbf{C} = \mathbf{A} + (\mathbf{B} + \mathbf{C})$

(3) $a(\mathbf{A} + \mathbf{B}) = a\mathbf{A} + a\mathbf{B}$

(4) $(a + b)\mathbf{A} = a\mathbf{A} + b\mathbf{A}$

(5) $a(b\mathbf{A}) = ab\mathbf{A}$

Rules 1 and 2 are familiar for the real numbers, where we can add (matrices, in this case) in any order we please. Rules 3, 4, and 5 are generalizations of rules for the real numbers where $3(2 + 2) = 3(2) + 3(2)$, $(3 + 2)2 = 3(2) + 2(2)$, and $2(3 \cdot 4) = 2 \cdot 3 \cdot 4$.

We can subtract matrix **A** from **B** by changing the sign of every element of **A** by multiplying **A** by the scalar -1 and adding the result to **A** to obtain

$$\mathbf{B} + (-1)\mathbf{A} = \mathbf{B} - \mathbf{A}$$

which, for our example matrices **A** and **B**, gives

$$\begin{bmatrix} 3 & 4 & 3 \\ 2 & 1 & 2 \\ 1 & 7 & 1 \\ 5 & 0 & 7 \end{bmatrix} + (-1) \begin{bmatrix} 3 & 4 & 3 \\ 2 & 1 & 2 \\ 1 & 7 & 1 \\ 5 & 0 & 5 \end{bmatrix} = \begin{bmatrix} 3 & 4 & 3 \\ 2 & 1 & 2 \\ 1 & 7 & 1 \\ 5 & 0 & 7 \end{bmatrix} + \begin{bmatrix} -3 & -4 & -3 \\ -2 & -1 & -2 \\ -1 & -7 & -1 \\ -5 & 0 & -5 \end{bmatrix}$$

$$= \begin{bmatrix} 0 & 0 & 0 \\ 0 & 0 & 0 \\ 0 & 0 & 0 \\ 0 & 0 & 2 \end{bmatrix}$$

A matrix in which the elements are all zero is called a zero matrix, and when it is added to any matrix **A**, it results in

$$\mathbf{A} + \mathbf{O} = \mathbf{A}$$

The zero matrix must, of course, have the same number of rows and columns as **A** in order for **A** + **0** to be defined. The zero matrix behaves as an identity matrix for addition just like 0 is an identity element for the addition of real numbers where $x + 0 = x$.

Two matrices **A** and **B** may be multiplied to produce the product **AB** = **C** under certain conditions. In order to find the matrix product **AB**, **A** must have the same number of columns as **B** has rows. If this condition is violated, then the matrix product **AB** is not defined. However, the matrix product **BA** might be defined if **B** has the same number of columns as **A** has rows. Consequently, when we refer to matrix multiplication, we must specify the order in which the matrices are multiplied. In the case of **AB**, we say that **B** is premultiplied by **A** or, equivalently, **A** is postmultiplied by **B**. Most generally, $\mathbf{AB} \neq \mathbf{BA}$. Matrices whose rows and columns are such that a matrix product is defined are said to be "conformable" for multiplication. For two conformable matrices **A** and **B**, the product **AB** produces a matrix **C** whose c_{ij}^{th} element is formed by multiplying row i of **A** with the jth column of **B**. That is

$$[c_{ij}] = [a_{i1}\, a_{i2} \ldots a_{in}] \begin{bmatrix} b_{1j} \\ b_{2j} \\ \cdot \\ \cdot \\ \cdot \\ b_{nj} \end{bmatrix}$$

We can see from this definition that the element c_{ij} is the inner product of the ith row of **A** with the jth column of **B**, which can also be expressed as

$$\sum_{k=1}^{n} a_{ik} b_{kj}$$

where n is the number of columns of **A** and the number of rows of **B**.

If

$$\mathbf{A} = \begin{bmatrix} a_{11} & a_{12} \\ a_{21} & a_{22} \\ a_{31} & a_{32} \end{bmatrix} \text{ and } \mathbf{B} = \begin{bmatrix} b_{11} & b_{12} & b_{13} \\ b_{21} & b_{22} & b_{23} \end{bmatrix},$$

then c_{21} of **C** would be $[a_{21}\ a_{22}] \begin{bmatrix} b_{11} \\ b_{21} \end{bmatrix} = a_{21} b_{11} + a_{22} b_{21}$ or equivalently,

$$\sum_{k=1}^{2} a_{2k} b_{k1}$$

The element c_{33} of **C** would be the inner product of row 3 of **A** with column 3 or **B** or

$$\sum_{k=1}^{2} a_{3k} b_{k3} = a_{31} b_{13} + a_{32} b_{23}$$

All of the elements of the complete matrix product **C** are formed by taking each row of **A** and multiplying it by each column of **B**. There are nine possible inner products that form the nine elements of the 3 × 3 matrix **C**. The reader should verify that **AB** equals

$$\mathbf{C} = \begin{bmatrix} c_{11} = & c_{12} = & c_{13} = \\ (a_{11}b_{11} + a_{12}b_{21}) & (a_{11}b_{12} + a_{12}b_{22}) & (a_{11}b_{13} + a_{12}b_{23}) \\ & & \\ c_{21} = & c_{22} = & c_{23} = \\ (a_{21}b_{11} + a_{22}b_{21}) & (a_{21}b_{12} + a_{22}b_{22}) & (a_{21}b_{13} + a_{22}b_{23}) \\ & & \\ c_{31} = & c_{32} = & c_{33} = \\ (a_{31}b_{11} + a_{32}b_{21}) & (a_{31}b_{12} + b_{32}b_{22}) & (a_{31}b_{13} + a_{32}b_{23}) \end{bmatrix}$$

The matrix **C** is a 3 × 3 matrix. Matrix **A** has three rows and matrix **B** has three columns, so that **C** has the same number of rows as **A** and the same number of columns as **B**. The order of matrix **C** = **AB** is equal to the number of rows of **A** and the number of columns of **B** or

$$\underset{(n \times k)}{\mathbf{A}} \; \underset{(k \times m)}{\mathbf{B}} = \underset{(n \times m)}{\mathbf{C}}$$

If

$$\underset{(4\times 2)}{\mathbf{A}} = \begin{bmatrix} 4 & 2 \\ 3 & 1 \\ 5 & 0 \\ 2 & 3 \end{bmatrix} \quad \text{and} \quad \underset{(2\times 2)}{\mathbf{B}} = \begin{bmatrix} 2 & 1 \\ 1 & 2 \end{bmatrix},$$

then

$$\mathbf{AB} = \underset{(4\times 2)}{\begin{bmatrix} 4 & 2 \\ 3 & 1 \\ 5 & 0 \\ 2 & 3 \end{bmatrix}} \underset{(2\times 2)}{\begin{bmatrix} 2 & 1 \\ 1 & 2 \end{bmatrix}} = \begin{bmatrix} 4(2) + 2(1) & 4(1) + 2(2) \\ 3(2) + 1(1) & 3(1) + 1(2) \\ 5(2) + 0(1) & 5(1) + 0(2) \\ 2(2) + 3(1) & 2(1) + 3(2) \end{bmatrix} = \underset{(4\times 2)}{\begin{bmatrix} 10 & 8 \\ 7 & 5 \\ 10 & 5 \\ 7 & 8 \end{bmatrix}}$$

Note that $\mathbf{BA} = \begin{bmatrix} 2 & 1 \\ 1 & 2 \end{bmatrix} \begin{bmatrix} 4 & 2 \\ 3 & 1 \\ 5 & 0 \\ 2 & 3 \end{bmatrix}$ is not defined since the number of columns of **B** (2) does not equal the number of rows of **A** (4).

If

$$\underset{(4\times 2)}{\mathbf{A}} = \begin{bmatrix} 1 & 2 \\ 2 & 1 \\ 0 & 3 \\ 4 & 1 \end{bmatrix} \quad \text{and} \quad \underset{(2\times 4)}{\mathbf{B}} = \begin{bmatrix} 3 & 1 & 4 & 2 \\ 0 & 1 & 0 & 2 \end{bmatrix},$$

then

$$\mathbf{AB} = \begin{bmatrix} 1 & 2 \\ 2 & 1 \\ 0 & 3 \\ 4 & 1 \end{bmatrix} \begin{bmatrix} 3 & 1 & 4 & 2 \\ 0 & 1 & 0 & 2 \end{bmatrix}$$

$$= \begin{bmatrix} 1(3)+2(0) & 1(1)+2(1) & 1(4)+2(0) & 1(2)+2(2) \\ 2(3)+1(0) & 2(1)+1(1) & 2(4)+1(0) & 2(2)+1(2) \\ 0(3)+3(0) & 0(1)+3(1) & 0(4)+3(0) & 0(2)+3(2) \\ 4(3)+1(0) & 4(1)+1(1) & 4(4)+1(0) & 4(2)+1(2) \end{bmatrix}$$

$$= \begin{bmatrix} 3 & 3 & 4 & 6 \\ 6 & 3 & 8 & 6 \\ 0 & 3 & 0 & 6 \\ 12 & 5 & 16 & 10 \end{bmatrix}$$

However, the reader should verify that

$$\mathbf{BA} = \begin{bmatrix} 3 & 1 & 4 & 2 \\ 0 & 1 & 0 & 2 \end{bmatrix} \begin{bmatrix} 1 & 2 \\ 2 & 1 \\ 0 & 3 \\ 4 & 1 \end{bmatrix} = \begin{bmatrix} 13 & 21 \\ 10 & 3 \end{bmatrix}$$

so that **AB** clearly does not equal **BA**. **AB** and **BA** are not of the same order. **AB** is 4×4 and **BA** is 2×2. Although in scalar algebra multiplication is commutative in that $xy = yx$, this is not generally so for matrix algebra, where **AB** does not in general equal **BA**. Consequently, we must be careful to define the order in which matrices are multiplied.

If $xy = 0$ in scalar algebra, then either x or y must be equal to zero. In matrix algebra $\mathbf{AB} = \mathbf{0}$ does not imply that either **A** or **B** are zero matrices. For example, given

$$\mathbf{A} = \begin{bmatrix} 3 & 1 & 0 \\ 2 & 0 & 0 \\ 5 & 2 & 0 \end{bmatrix} \text{ and } \mathbf{B} = \begin{bmatrix} 0 & 0 & 0 \\ 0 & 0 & 0 \\ 3 & 2 & 4 \end{bmatrix}, \text{ then}$$

$$\mathbf{AB} = \begin{bmatrix} 3 & 1 & 0 \\ 2 & 0 & 0 \\ 5 & 2 & 0 \end{bmatrix} \begin{bmatrix} 0 & 0 & 0 \\ 0 & 0 & 0 \\ 3 & 2 & 4 \end{bmatrix} = \begin{bmatrix} 0 & 0 & 0 \\ 0 & 0 & 0 \\ 0 & 0 & 0 \end{bmatrix} = \mathbf{0}$$

Furthermore, if $yx = yz$ in scalar algebra, then $x = z$. This does not hold for matrix algebra where $\mathbf{AB} = \mathbf{AC}$ does not imply that $\mathbf{B} = \mathbf{C}$. For example, given

$$\mathbf{A} = \begin{bmatrix} 1 & 3 & 0 \\ 2 & 2 & 0 \\ 1 & -2 & 0 \end{bmatrix}, \mathbf{B} = \begin{bmatrix} 1 & 2 & 1 \\ -1 & -2 & 0 \\ 1 & 0 & -1 \end{bmatrix}, \text{ and } \mathbf{C} = \begin{bmatrix} 1 & 2 & 1 \\ -1 & -2 & 0 \\ 1 & 2 & 3 \end{bmatrix}$$

then the reader should verify that

$$\mathbf{AB} = \begin{bmatrix} -2 & -4 & 1 \\ 0 & 0 & 2 \\ 3 & 6 & 1 \end{bmatrix} \text{ and } \mathbf{AC} = \begin{bmatrix} -2 & -4 & 1 \\ 0 & 0 & 2 \\ 3 & 6 & 1 \end{bmatrix}$$

We have shown that $\mathbf{AB} = \mathbf{AC}$, but that $\mathbf{B} \neq \mathbf{C}$. The above discussion has indicated that some of the rules that apply to scalar algebra do not apply to matrix algebra.[1] However, the important rules of multiplication being associative (that is, $[xy]z = x[yz]$ in scalar algebra) and of multiplication being distributive with respect to multiplication (that is, x[y + z] = xy + xz) do apply.

The associative rule for matrix multiplication states that (**AB**)**C** = **A**(**BC**). If

$$\mathbf{A} = \begin{bmatrix} 1 & 0 & -1 \\ 2 & 1 & 0 \\ -1 & -2 & 1 \end{bmatrix}, \mathbf{B} = \begin{bmatrix} 0 & 0 & 1 \\ 1 & 0 & -2 \\ 2 & 1 & 1 \end{bmatrix}, \text{ and } \mathbf{C} = \begin{bmatrix} 0 & -1 & 1 \\ 0 & 2 & 0 \\ 1 & 1 & 1 \end{bmatrix},$$

$$\text{then } (\mathbf{AB})\mathbf{C} = \begin{bmatrix} -2 & -1 & 0 \\ 1 & 0 & 0 \\ 0 & 1 & 4 \end{bmatrix} \begin{bmatrix} 0 & -1 & 1 \\ 0 & 2 & 0 \\ 1 & 1 & 1 \end{bmatrix} = \begin{bmatrix} 0 & 0 & -2 \\ 0 & -1 & 1 \\ 4 & 6 & 4 \end{bmatrix}$$

$$\text{and } \mathbf{A}(\mathbf{BC}) = \begin{bmatrix} 1 & -0 & -1 \\ 2 & 1 & 0 \\ -1 & -2 & 1 \end{bmatrix} \begin{bmatrix} 1 & 1 & 1 \\ -2 & -3 & -1 \\ 1 & 1 & 3 \end{bmatrix} = \begin{bmatrix} 0 & 0 & -2 \\ 0 & -1 & 1 \\ 4 & 6 & 4 \end{bmatrix}$$

$$\text{Thus, we see that } (\mathbf{AB})\mathbf{C} = \mathbf{A}(\mathbf{BC}) = \begin{bmatrix} 0 & 0 & -2 \\ 1 & -1 & 1 \\ 4 & 6 & 4 \end{bmatrix}$$

Using the same matrices **A**, **B**, and **C**, we shall show that the distributive property **A**(**B** + **C**) = **AB** + **AC** holds.

$$\mathbf{A}(\mathbf{B} + \mathbf{C}) = \begin{bmatrix} 1 & 0 & -1 \\ 2 & 1 & 0 \\ -1 & -2 & 1 \end{bmatrix} \begin{bmatrix} 0 & -1 & 2 \\ 1 & 2 & 2 \\ 3 & 2 & 2 \end{bmatrix} = \begin{bmatrix} -3 & -3 & 0 \\ 1 & 0 & 2 \\ 1 & -1 & 4 \end{bmatrix}$$

and

$$\mathbf{AB} + \mathbf{AC} = \begin{bmatrix} 1 & 0 & -1 \\ 2 & 1 & 0 \\ -1 & -2 & 1 \end{bmatrix} \begin{bmatrix} 0 & 0 & 1 \\ 1 & 0 & -2 \\ 2 & 1 & 1 \end{bmatrix} + \begin{bmatrix} 1 & 0 & -1 \\ 2 & 1 & 0 \\ -1 & -2 & 1 \end{bmatrix} \begin{bmatrix} 0 & -1 & 1 \\ 0 & 2 & 0 \\ 1 & 1 & 1 \end{bmatrix}$$

$$= \begin{bmatrix} -2 & -1 & 0 \\ 1 & 0 & 0 \\ 0 & 1 & 4 \end{bmatrix} + \begin{bmatrix} -1 & -2 & 0 \\ 0 & 0 & 2 \\ 1 & -2 & 0 \end{bmatrix} = \begin{bmatrix} -3 & -3 & 0 \\ 1 & 0 & 2 \\ 1 & -1 & 4 \end{bmatrix}$$

so that $\mathbf{A}(\mathbf{B} + \mathbf{C}) = \mathbf{AB} + \mathbf{AC} = \begin{bmatrix} -3 & -3 & 0 \\ 1 & 0 & 2 \\ 1 & -1 & 4 \end{bmatrix}$

There are some further properties of the matrix transpose operation that will prove useful. The reader can verify using matrices **A** and **B** above that

(a) $(\mathbf{A}')' = \mathbf{A}$

(b) $(\mathbf{A} + \mathbf{B})' = \mathbf{A}' + \mathbf{B}'$

(c) $(a\mathbf{A})' = a\mathbf{A}'$

(d) $(\mathbf{AB})' = \mathbf{B}'\mathbf{A}'$

3.11 TRACE OF A MATRIX

The sum of the diagonal elements of a square matrix is called the trace of the matrix. If **A** is square, then tr(**A**) is equal to

$$\sum_{i=1}^{n} a_{ii}$$

Using the matrices **A**, **B**, and **C** above, we find that

$$\mathrm{tr}(\mathbf{A}) = \mathrm{tr} \begin{bmatrix} 1 & 0 & -1 \\ 2 & 1 & 0 \\ -1 & -2 & 1 \end{bmatrix} = \sum_{i=1}^{3} a_{ii} = a_{11} + a_{22} + a_{33} = 1 + 1 + 1 = 3$$

and the reader can verify that tr**B** and tr**C** are 1 and 3, respectively. The reader can also verify using our **A**, **B**, and **C** matrices the following rules concerning the trace operation: tr(**A** + **B**) = tr(**A**) + tr(**B**); tr(c**A**) = ctr(**A**); and tr(**AB**) = tr(**BA**) if both products are defined.

3.12 PARTITIONED MATRICES

Given a matrix **A**, it may be partitioned into a number of submatrices. For example, if

$$\mathbf{A} = \begin{bmatrix} 1 & 0 & -1 \\ 2 & 1 & 0 \\ -1 & -2 & 1 \end{bmatrix}$$

then we could form the following partition of **A**:

$$\mathbf{A} = [\mathbf{A}_1, \mathbf{A}_2] \text{ where } \mathbf{A}_1 = \begin{bmatrix} 1 & 0 \\ 2 & 1 \\ -1 & -2 \end{bmatrix} \text{ and } \mathbf{A}_2 = \begin{bmatrix} -1 \\ 0 \\ 1 \end{bmatrix}.$$

We can denote this partition of **A** as

$$\left[\begin{array}{cc|c} 1 & 0 & -1 \\ 2 & 1 & 0 \\ -1 & -2 & 1 \end{array}\right]$$

The dotted line indicates that we have partitioned **A** into the two submatrices $\mathbf{A}_1$ and $\mathbf{A}_2$.

We could also partition **A** into

$$\begin{bmatrix} \mathbf{A}_{11} & \mathbf{A}_{12} \\ \mathbf{A}_{21} & \mathbf{A}_{22} \end{bmatrix} \text{ where } \mathbf{A}_{11} = \begin{bmatrix} 1 & 0 \\ 2 & 1 \end{bmatrix},$$

$\mathbf{A}_{12} = \begin{bmatrix} -1 \\ 0 \end{bmatrix}$, $\mathbf{A}_{21} = [-1\ -2]$, and $\mathbf{A}_{22} = [1]$ so that the partitioned matrix would be

$$\left[\begin{array}{cc|c} 1 & 0 & -1 \\ 2 & 1 & 0 \\ \hline -1 & -2 & 1 \end{array}\right]$$

Whenever a matrix is partitioned, the dotted lines must go completely through the matrix. For example, we could not have the following partition of **A**

$$\left[\begin{array}{cc|c} 1 & 0 & -1 \\ 2 & 1 & 0 \\ \hline -1 & -2 & 1 \end{array}\right]$$

because the horizontal dotted line does not go all the way through **A**. The reader is invited to find other ways to partition **A**.

If **A** and **B** are matrices of the same order and are identically partitioned, then the two partitioned matrices, **A** and **B**, may be added according to the following rule:

$$\begin{bmatrix} \mathbf{A}_{11} & \mathbf{A}_{12} \\ \mathbf{A}_{21} & \mathbf{A}_{22} \end{bmatrix} + \begin{bmatrix} \mathbf{B}_{11} & \mathbf{B}_{12} \\ \mathbf{B}_{21} & \mathbf{B}_{22} \end{bmatrix} = \begin{bmatrix} (\mathbf{A}_{11} + \mathbf{B}_{11}) & (\mathbf{A}_{12} + \mathbf{B}_{12}) \\ (\mathbf{A}_{21} + \mathbf{B}_{21}) & (\mathbf{A}_{22} + \mathbf{B}_{22}) \end{bmatrix}$$

For example, if

$$\begin{bmatrix} \mathbf{A}_{11} & \mathbf{A}_{12} \\ \mathbf{A}_{21} & \mathbf{A}_{22} \end{bmatrix} = \left[\begin{array}{cc|c} 1 & 0 & -1 \\ 2 & 1 & 0 \\ \hline -1 & -2 & 1 \end{array}\right], \text{ and } \begin{bmatrix} \mathbf{B}_{11} & \mathbf{B}_{12} \\ \mathbf{B}_{21} & \mathbf{B}_{22} \end{bmatrix} = \left[\begin{array}{cc|c} 0 & 0 & 1 \\ 1 & 0 & -2 \\ \hline 2 & 1 & 1 \end{array}\right]$$

then

$$\left[\begin{array}{cc|c} 1 & 0 & -1 \\ 2 & 1 & 0 \\ \hline -1 & -2 & 1 \end{array}\right] + \left[\begin{array}{cc|c} 0 & 0 & 1 \\ 1 & 0 & -2 \\ \hline 2 & 1 & 1 \end{array}\right] = \left[\begin{array}{cc|c} 1 & 0 & 0 \\ 3 & 1 & -2 \\ \hline 1 & -1 & 2 \end{array}\right]$$

$$= \begin{bmatrix} (\mathbf{A}_{11} + \mathbf{B}_{11}) & (\mathbf{A}_{12} + \mathbf{B}_{12}) \\ (\mathbf{A}_{21} + \mathbf{B}_{21}) & (\mathbf{A}_{22} + \mathbf{B}_{22}) \end{bmatrix}$$

Note that if **B** were partitioned as

$$\left[\begin{array}{cc|c} 0 & 0 & 1 \\ \hline 1 & 0 & -2 \\ 2 & 1 & 1 \end{array}\right] = \begin{bmatrix} \mathbf{B}_{11} & \mathbf{B}_{12} \\ \mathbf{B}_{21} & \mathbf{B}_{22} \end{bmatrix},$$

then

$$\left[\begin{array}{cc|c} 1 & 0 & -1 \\ 2 & 1 & 0 \\ \hline -1 & -2 & 1 \end{array}\right] + \left[\begin{array}{cc|c} 0 & 0 & 1 \\ \hline 1 & 0 & -2 \\ 2 & 1 & 1 \end{array}\right]$$

is not defined since

$$\mathbf{A}_{11} = \begin{bmatrix} 1 & 0 \\ 2 & 1 \end{bmatrix} \text{ and } \mathbf{B}_{11} = [0 \ \ 0]$$

are not conformable for addition. We have seen that for two partitioned matrices to be added they must be identically partitioned. We now turn to the multiplication of partitioned matrices.

In order to form the matrix product of two partitioned matrices, the two matrices must be partitioned such that

$$\begin{bmatrix} \mathbf{A}_{11} & \mathbf{A}_{12} \\ \mathbf{A}_{21} & \mathbf{A}_{22} \end{bmatrix} \begin{bmatrix} \mathbf{B}_{11} & \mathbf{B}_{12} \\ \mathbf{B}_{21} & \mathbf{B}_{22} \end{bmatrix} = \begin{bmatrix} (\mathbf{A}_{11}\mathbf{B}_{11} + \mathbf{A}_{12}\mathbf{B}_{21}) & (\mathbf{A}_{11}\mathbf{B}_{12} + \mathbf{A}_{12}\mathbf{B}_{22}) \\ (\mathbf{A}_{21}\mathbf{B}_{11} + \mathbf{A}_{22}\mathbf{B}_{21}) & (\mathbf{A}_{21}\mathbf{B}_{12} + \mathbf{A}_{22}\mathbf{B}_{22}) \end{bmatrix}$$

That is, the matrices must be partitioned in such a way that certain multiplications of submatrices are defined. For example, if

$$A = \begin{bmatrix} A_{11} & A_{12} \\ A_{21} & A_{22} \end{bmatrix} = \left[\begin{array}{cc|cc} 1 & 0 & -1 & 1 \\ 2 & 1 & 0 & 2 \\ \hline -1 & -2 & 1 & 1 \\ 0 & 1 & 0 & 2 \end{array}\right] \text{ and}$$

$$\begin{bmatrix} B_{11} & B_{12} \\ B_{21} & B_{22} \end{bmatrix} = \left[\begin{array}{cc|cc} 0 & 0 & 1 & 1 \\ 1 & 0 & -2 & 1 \\ \hline 2 & 1 & 1 & 0 \\ 2 & 1 & 0 & 1 \end{array}\right] \text{, then}$$

$$AB = \begin{bmatrix} A_{11} & A_{12} \\ A_{21} & A_{22} \end{bmatrix} \begin{bmatrix} B_{11} & B_{12} \\ B_{21} & B_{22} \end{bmatrix} = \begin{bmatrix} (A_{11}B_{11} + A_{12}B_{21}) & (A_{11}B_{12} + A_{12}B_{22}) \\ (A_{21}B_{11} + A_{22}B_{21}) & (A_{21}B_{22} + A_{22}B_{22}) \end{bmatrix}$$

$$\begin{bmatrix} \begin{bmatrix} 1 & 0 \\ 2 & 1 \end{bmatrix}\begin{bmatrix} 0 & 0 \\ 1 & 0 \end{bmatrix} + \begin{bmatrix} -1 & 1 \\ 0 & 2 \end{bmatrix}\begin{bmatrix} 2 & 1 \\ 2 & 1 \end{bmatrix} & \begin{bmatrix} 1 & 0 \\ 2 & 1 \end{bmatrix}\begin{bmatrix} 1 & 1 \\ -2 & 1 \end{bmatrix} + \begin{bmatrix} -1 & 1 \\ 0 & 2 \end{bmatrix}\begin{bmatrix} 1 & 1 \\ -2 & 1 \end{bmatrix} \\ \begin{bmatrix} -1 & -2 \\ 0 & 1 \end{bmatrix}\begin{bmatrix} 0 & 0 \\ 1 & 0 \end{bmatrix} + \begin{bmatrix} 1 & 1 \\ 0 & 2 \end{bmatrix}\begin{bmatrix} 2 & 1 \\ 2 & 1 \end{bmatrix} & \begin{bmatrix} 1 & -2 \\ 0 & 1 \end{bmatrix}\begin{bmatrix} 1 & 1 \\ -2 & 1 \end{bmatrix} + \begin{bmatrix} 1 & 1 \\ 0 & 2 \end{bmatrix}\begin{bmatrix} 1 & 0 \\ 0 & 1 \end{bmatrix} \end{bmatrix}$$

$$= \begin{bmatrix} 0 & 0 & -2 & 1 \\ 5 & 2 & -4 & 5 \\ 2 & 2 & 6 & 0 \\ 5 & 2 & -2 & 3 \end{bmatrix}$$

The multiplication of partitioned matrices is analogous to regular matrix multiplication where the elements of the matrix are scalars instead of matrices.

That is, the elements are now matrices that are conformable for multiplication, but the rules for forming the matrix product are the same as if the matrices were scalars.

3.13 MATRIX INVERSION

In scalar algebra, for every real number a, other than 0, there is a unique number a^{-1} such that $aa^{-1} = a^{-1}a = 1$. For certain types of matrices there is an analogous concept. If a matrix is square and its rank (that is, number of independent row vectors or, equivalently, column vectors) is equal to the number of its rows or, equivalently, its columns, then for any matrix **A** that meets these specifications, there is a matrix $\mathbf{A}^{-1}$ such that $\mathbf{AA}^{-1} = \mathbf{A}^{-1}\mathbf{A} = \mathbf{I}$. The matrix $\mathbf{A}^{-1}$ is called the inverse of **A**, and **I** is the identity matrix of appropriate dimensions. Furthermore, similar to the scalar situation, $\mathbf{A}^{-1}$ is unique. It should be emphasized that for a unique inverse to exist, the matrix **A** must be full rank. This means that the column or, equivalently, the row vectors must be a linearly independent set. Putting it another way, no row (column) vector of the matrix **A** can be expressed as a linear combination of the remaining row (column) vectors. The row (column) vectors form the basis of an n dimensional space where n is the number of rows (columns).

An equivalent condition for the inverse of **A** to exist is that its determinant does not vanish. The determinant of **A** denoted as $|\mathbf{A}|$ is a scalar that is a function of the elements of **A**. The value of $|\mathbf{A}|$ is obtained by summing all the products consisting of all possible products with one element from each row and column and giving each product to be summed a negative sign if the inversions of the column subscript are odd. An inversion is when a higher-column subscript precedes a lower-column subscript. This is a formal definition of $|\mathbf{A}|$. For example, the determinant of the matrix

$$A = \begin{bmatrix} a_{11} & a_{12} \\ a_{21} & a_{22} \end{bmatrix}$$

is $a_{11}a_{22} - a_{12}a_{21}$. The row subscripts are always kept in correct order, but the column subscripts will be out of order for some products. The first product has the correct order of column subscripts and, hence, no inversions, which is equivalent to an even number of inversions. Therefore, it has a positive sign. The second product has a negative sign because the two column subscripts are inverted. Specific formulas for calculating the value of the determinants of small matrices will be given when the need arises. The inverse of a diagonal matrix is easy to compute. Let

$$\mathbf{A} = \begin{bmatrix} a_1 & 0 & 0 \\ 0 & a_2 & 0 \\ 0 & 0 & a_3 \end{bmatrix}, \text{ then } \mathbf{A}^{-1} = \begin{bmatrix} \frac{1}{a_1} & 0 & 0 \\ 0 & \frac{1}{a_2} & 0 \\ 0 & 0 & \frac{1}{a_3} \end{bmatrix}, \text{ since}$$

$$\mathbf{AA}^{-1} = \begin{bmatrix} a_1 & 0 & 0 \\ 0 & a_2 & 0 \\ 0 & 0 & a_3 \end{bmatrix} \begin{bmatrix} \frac{1}{a_1} & 0 & 0 \\ 0 & \frac{1}{a_2} & 0 \\ 0 & 0 & \frac{1}{a_3} \end{bmatrix} = \begin{bmatrix} 1 & 0 & 0 \\ 0 & 1 & 0 \\ 0 & 0 & 1 \end{bmatrix} = \mathbf{A}^{-1}\mathbf{A}$$

For diagonal matrices, the rule is simply to substitute the reciprocals of the diagonal elements to generate the inverse. Other nondiagonal matrices are not so easy to invert. In fact, it is not feasible to invert large matrices by manual computation. Consequently, matrix inversion routines have been extensively programmed on electronic computers. We shall subsequently need to compute matrix inverses and methods will later be shown for inverting small matrices.

There are other types of inverses besides the unique inverse for a full rank square matrix. We know that an inverse satisfying $\mathbf{AA}^{-1} = \mathbf{A}^{-1}\mathbf{A} = \mathbf{I}$ cannot be generated for a rectangular matrix since $\mathbf{AB} \neq \mathbf{BA}$ so that an inverse as defined above does not exist. There are, however, "left" and "right" inverses of rectangular matrices. That is, if **A** is rectangular, then under certain conditions an inverse of **A** exists such that $\mathbf{A}_1^{-1}\mathbf{A} = \mathbf{I}$, or $\mathbf{AA}_2^{-1} = \mathbf{I}$, but that $\mathbf{A}_1^{-1}$ does not equal $\mathbf{A}_2^{-1}$ where $\mathbf{A}_1^{-1}$ is a left inverse and $\mathbf{A}_2^{-1}$ is a right inverse. This discussion will not be concerned specifically with left and right inverses, but with what is called a "generalized" inverse.

A generalized inverse is a matrix **G** such that $\mathbf{AGA} = \mathbf{A}$. The matrix **A** can be rectangular or square. If **A** is square, then it need not be nonsingular for a generalized inverse to exist. The generalized inverse will be used in some instances to solve for the parameters of linear statistical models. In most cases, it will be found for square matrices that are singular. A square singular matrix has row (or, equivalently, column) vectors that are not linearly independent. In this instance, the determinant of **A** is zero and a unique inverse does not exist. When the matrix **A** is square and nonsingular (full rank), a unique inverse $\mathbf{A}^{-1}$ is defined, and this is the only generalized inverse of the matrix since in this case $\mathbf{AA^{-1}A = A}$. In the case of a square singular matrix, we shall see that there are an infinite number of inverses **G** such that **AGA** = **A**. However, we shall also see that we need only solve for any one of them in order to solve the linear equations of interest. A method of solving for generalized inverses will be described when the methodology is needed for solving for estimates of statistical parameters in subsequent chapters.

3.14 SIMULTANEOUS LINEAR EQUATIONS

An example of a set of three simultaneous equations in three unknowns is

$$2x_1 + 3x_2 + x_3 = 8$$

$$x_1 + 2x_2 + 3x_3 = 4$$

$$3x_1 + x_2 + 4x_3 = 2$$

This set of three simultaneous equations can be expressed as $\mathbf{Ax} = \mathbf{b}$ where

$$\mathbf{A} = \begin{bmatrix} 2 & 3 & 1 \\ 1 & 2 & 3 \\ 3 & 1 & 4 \end{bmatrix}, \mathbf{x} = \begin{bmatrix} x_1 \\ x_2 \\ x_3 \end{bmatrix}, \text{ and } \mathbf{b} = \begin{bmatrix} 8 \\ 4 \\ 2 \end{bmatrix}$$

The reader can verify that

$$\begin{bmatrix} 2 & 3 & 1 \\ 1 & 2 & 3 \\ 3 & 1 & 4 \end{bmatrix} \begin{bmatrix} x_1 \\ x_2 \\ x_3 \end{bmatrix} = \begin{bmatrix} 8 \\ 4 \\ 2 \end{bmatrix}$$

is equivalent to the set of simultaneous equations given above. Matrix notation results in a more compact way of expressing a set of simultaneous equations than expressing each equation in scalar form. If **A** and **b** are known, as they are in the example above, then the unknowns x_1, x_2, x_3, or, in matrix terminology, the vector $\mathbf{x} = [x_1, x_2, x_3]$, may be solved for by first finding $\mathbf{A}^{-1}$ if **A** is nonsingular or any **G** of **A** if **A** is singular. Then, premultiplying **b** by $\mathbf{A}^{-1}$ or any **G** of **A**, if **A** is singular, will yield the solution vector, **x**. In the above example **A** is nonsingular so that a solution for the vector **x** is $\mathbf{A}^{-1}\mathbf{b}$. This was obtained by premultiplying both sides of $\mathbf{Ax} = \mathbf{b}$ by $\mathbf{A}^{-1}$ which gives $\mathbf{A}^{-1}\mathbf{Ax} = \mathbf{A}^{-1}\mathbf{b}$ or $\mathbf{x} = \mathbf{A}^{-1}\mathbf{b}$ since $\mathbf{A}^{-1}\mathbf{A} = \mathbf{I}$ and $\mathbf{Ix} = \mathbf{x}$. The reader may verify that

$$A^{-1} = \begin{bmatrix} .25 & -.55 & .35 \\ .25 & .25 & -.25 \\ -.25 & .35 & .05 \end{bmatrix}$$

so that $\mathbf{x} = \mathbf{A}^{-1}\mathbf{b} = \begin{bmatrix} 1.2 \\ 2.0 \\ -.4 \end{bmatrix}$

We could, of course, have solved for **x** by the algebraic procedure that we encountered in high school algebra, but this becomes a cumbersome procedure for large sets of simultaneous equations. $\mathbf{A}^{-1}$ is also the unique generalized inverse for the nonsingular matrix. If **A** is singular, then $\mathbf{x} = \mathbf{Gb}$ for any of an infinite number of **G** matrices that satisfy $\mathbf{AGA} = \mathbf{A}$. To show that $\mathbf{x} = \mathbf{Gb}$ is a solution of $\mathbf{Ax} = \mathbf{b}$, premultiply the solution by **A**. This gives $\mathbf{Ax} = \mathbf{AGb}$. But since $\mathbf{b} = \mathbf{Ax}$, $\mathbf{AGb} = \mathbf{AGAx} = \mathbf{Ax} = \mathbf{b}$, and so $\mathbf{Ax} = \mathbf{b}$. Thus the solution satisfies the equation.

In the set of three simultaneous linear equations below,

$$2x_1 + 3x_2 + x_3 = 8$$

$$x_1 + 2x_2 + 3x_3 = 4$$

$$4x_1 + 7x_2 + 7x_3 = 6$$

the matrix $= \begin{bmatrix} 2 & 3 & 1 \\ 1 & 2 & 3 \\ 4 & 7 & 7 \end{bmatrix}$ is singular since the third row vector is a linear combination of the first two rows. That is,

$$\begin{bmatrix} 4 \\ 7 \\ 7 \end{bmatrix} = 2 \begin{bmatrix} 1 \\ 2 \\ 3 \end{bmatrix} + 1 \begin{bmatrix} 2 \\ 3 \\ 1 \end{bmatrix}$$

In this situation we can find any **G** such that **AGA** = **A** and then find **x** as **Gb**. This, of course, means that **x** = **Gb** is not a unique solution. Since **G** can take on an infinite number of values, so can **x**.

In this case we have only two linearly independent equations in three unknowns. The third equation is redundant. Let us examine the first two linearly independent equations

$$2x_1 + 3x_2 + x_3 = 8$$

$$x_1 + 2x_2 + 3x_3 = 4$$

These two equations are equivalent to

$$2x_1 + 3x_2 = 8 - x_3$$

$$x_1 + 2x_2 = 4 - 3x_3$$

and can be expressed in matrix form as

$$\begin{bmatrix} 2 & 3 \\ 1 & 2 \end{bmatrix} \begin{bmatrix} x_1 \\ x_2 \end{bmatrix} = \begin{bmatrix} 8 - x_3 \\ 4 - 3x_3 \end{bmatrix}$$

The matrix $\begin{bmatrix} 2 & 3 \\ 1 & 2 \end{bmatrix}$ is nonsingular so that its inverse exists, and so

$$\begin{bmatrix} x_1 \\ x_2 \end{bmatrix} = \begin{bmatrix} 2 & 3 \\ 1 & 2 \end{bmatrix}^{-1} \begin{bmatrix} 8 - x_3 \\ 4 - 3x_3 \end{bmatrix}$$

We can see from the general form of the solution that both x_1 and x_2 depend upon the value of x_3. The infinite number of solutions for

$$\mathbf{x} = \begin{bmatrix} x_1 \\ x_2 \\ x_3 \end{bmatrix}$$

comes about because x_3 can be assigned any value arbitrarily and the values of x_1 and x_2 will be accordingly affected. If we set $x_3 = 0$, then x_1 and x_2 will be uniquely determined since

$$\begin{bmatrix} x_1 \\ x_2 \end{bmatrix} = \begin{bmatrix} 2 & 3 \\ 1 & 2 \end{bmatrix}^{-1} \begin{bmatrix} 8 \\ 4 \end{bmatrix}$$

and we therefore have one solution for **x**. There is a **G** matrix associated with this particular solution (that is, when $x_3 = 0$), and it is

$$\mathbf{G} = \begin{bmatrix} \begin{bmatrix} 2 & 3 \\ 1 & 2 \end{bmatrix}^{-1} & \begin{matrix} 0 \\ 0 \end{matrix} \\ \begin{matrix} 0 & 0 \end{matrix} & 0 \end{bmatrix}$$

It can be shown that

$$\mathbf{AGA} = \begin{bmatrix} 2 & 3 & 1 \\ 1 & 2 & 3 \\ 4 & 7 & 7 \end{bmatrix} \begin{bmatrix} \begin{bmatrix} 2 & 3 \\ 1 & 2 \end{bmatrix}^{-1} & \begin{matrix} 0 \\ 0 \end{matrix} \\ \begin{matrix} 0 & 0 \end{matrix} & 0 \end{bmatrix} \begin{bmatrix} 2 & 3 & 1 \\ 1 & 2 & 3 \\ 4 & 7 & 7 \end{bmatrix} = \begin{bmatrix} 2 & 3 & 1 \\ 1 & 2 & 3 \\ 4 & 7 & 7 \end{bmatrix} = \mathbf{A}$$

Another way of looking at the problem of solving two independent linear equations in three unknowns is that one additional equation must be specified for a unique solution to exist. If we specified the third equation as $x_3 = 0$, then a unique solution (a specific **G**) exists. We shall see later that other constraints or restrictions on the unknowns such as $x_1 + x_2 + x_3 = 0$ can be used. In general, if the number of unknowns is n, and the number of linearly independent equations is k, then a unique value must be specified for any arbitrary n – k unknowns. For example, if n = 5, and k = 2, then x_1, x_2 and x_3 can be set to zero and a unique solution will exist for x_4 and x_5.

In summary, two types of sets of linear equations will be encountered in our subsequent discussions of statistical models. One type of set has as many independent linear equations as unknowns, and a unique solution for the unknowns exists. The other type of set has fewer independent linear equations than unknowns and an infinite number of solutions. Solving for any one of the infinite number of generalized inverses **G** will yield a solution **x** = **Gb**, where **b** is the vector of constants on the right-hand side of the linear equations.

There are other types of linear equation sets, which we shall discuss briefly for the sake of completeness even though they are rarely encountered in statistical modeling. There is the case of inconsistent equations for which no solution exists. For example, the two equations

$$3x_1 + 3x_2 = 2$$

$$x_1 + x_2 = 6$$

are inconsistent because the first equation implies that $x_1 = 2/3 - x_2$ while the second equation implies that $x_1 = 6 - x_2$. Clearly one equation is inconsistent with the other. They are actually two parallel lines that do not intersect and therefore do not have a solution. The remaining case involves the situation in which there are more equations than unknowns. In this situation, we find a full set of linearly independent equations and solve for **x**. If the number of linearly independent equations is smaller than the number of unknowns, then we can solve for **x** through a generalized inverse. If the number of linearly independent equations is equal to the number of unknowns, then a unique solution for **x** can be found.

3.15 QUADRATIC FORMS

A function such as $y = ax_1^2 + bx_2^2 + cx_1x_2$ is called a "quadratic form" in two variables. It can be expressed in matrix notation as **x′Ax** where

$$\mathbf{x} = \begin{bmatrix} x_1 \\ x_2 \end{bmatrix}, \text{ and } \mathbf{A} = \begin{bmatrix} a & \frac{c}{2} \\ \frac{c}{2} & b \end{bmatrix}$$

A quadratic form can be generalized to three or more variables. We will encounter quadratic forms later, in our discussion of testing statistical hypotheses for various linear models. If the matrix **A** is such that **x′Ax** is greater than zero for any **x** not equal to **0**, then **A** is called positive definite. If the matrix **A** is such that **x′Ax** is equal to or greater than zero for any **x**, then **A** is called positive semidefinite.

3.16 LATENT ROOTS AND VECTORS

In some multivariate analysis models, such as principal components analysis, discussed in *Introduction to Multivariate Analysis*, we will encounter such matrix expressions as $\mathbf{Ax} = \lambda\mathbf{x}$ where $\mathbf{A}$ is a square matrix of order n, $\mathbf{x}$ is an $n \times 1$ vector, and λ is a scalar. This matrix expression can also be written as $(\mathbf{A}-\mathbf{I}\lambda)\mathbf{x} = \mathbf{0}$. The expression $\mathbf{Ax} = \lambda\mathbf{x}$ means that there is a linear transformation of the vector $\mathbf{x}$ by the transformation matrix $\mathbf{A}$ such that this transformation is equivalent to "stretching" the vector $\mathbf{x}$ by multiplying it by the scalar λ. That is, the transformation of $\mathbf{x}$ by $\mathbf{A}$ only alters the length of the vector $\mathbf{x}$ but does not change its orientation (that is, direction cosines in regard to its basis) in n space. Expressions such as this result from trying to maximize some function of random variables. If $\mathbf{A}$ is a known $n \times n$ matrix, then one or more λ and associated vectors $\mathbf{x}$ can be found that satisfy this equation. A way of finding the solutions that make up pairs of λ and $\mathbf{x}$ is presented in *Introduction to Multivariate Analysis* as the need arises.

3.17 PROBLEMS

(1) From the sample data in the Appendix,[2] compute the inner product of variable 7 with variable 8 (that is, consider each column as a vector). Develop a simple counting rule that generates this inner product directly.

(2) Let vectors $\mathbf{x}_1$, $\mathbf{x}_2$, $\mathbf{x}_3$, and $\mathbf{x}_4$ be the first 5 values of variables 1, 2, 3, and 4, respectively. Find the vector $2\mathbf{x}_1 + \mathbf{x}_2 + 3\mathbf{x}_3 + 4\mathbf{x}_4$. Do the vectors $\mathbf{x}_1$, $\mathbf{x}_2$, $\mathbf{x}_3$, $\mathbf{x}_4$, and $2\mathbf{x}_1 + \mathbf{x}_2 + 3\mathbf{x}_3 + 4\mathbf{x}_4$ constitute a linearly independent set?

(3) What is the length of $\mathbf{x}_1$? What is the distance between $\mathbf{x}_2$ and $\mathbf{x}_4$? What is the inner product of $\mathbf{x}_2$ and $\mathbf{x}_3$? Are vectors $\mathbf{x}_2$ and $\mathbf{x}_3$ orthogonal? (Use vectors from problem 2.)

(4) What do you think is the dimension of the space spanned by $\mathbf{x}_1$, $\mathbf{x}_2$; $\mathbf{x}_3$, and $\mathbf{x}_4$? What did you assume in arriving at your answer? (Use vectors from problem 2.)

(5) Let the matrix $\mathbf{X} = [\mathbf{x}_1, \mathbf{x}_2, \mathbf{x}_3, \mathbf{x}_4]$. What is the dimension of $\mathbf{X}$? Find $\mathbf{X}'$ and $\mathbf{X}'\mathbf{X}$. Is $\mathbf{XX}'$ defined? Find $10\mathbf{X}$. (Use vectors from problem 2.)

(6) Let $\mathbf{x}_5$ and $\mathbf{x}_6$ be the first 5 values of variables of 5 and 6, respectively, and then let $\mathbf{X}_1 = [\mathbf{x}_1, \mathbf{x}_2, \mathbf{x}_3]$ and $\mathbf{X}_2 = [\mathbf{x}_4, \mathbf{x}_5, \mathbf{x}_6]$. Find $2\mathbf{X}_1 - 3\mathbf{X}_2$. Find $\mathbf{X}_1'\mathbf{X}_2$ and $\mathbf{X}_1\mathbf{X}_2'$. What are the dimensions of each product? What are the traces of $\mathbf{X}_1'\mathbf{X}_2$ and $\mathbf{X}_1\mathbf{X}_2'$? (Use vectors from problem 2.)

(7) Partition $\mathbf{X}_1$ and $\mathbf{X}_2$ from problem 6 such that their sum is defined in terms of the partitions. Partition $\mathbf{X}_1'$ and $\mathbf{X}_2$ such that their product is defined in terms of the partitions.

(8) Using $\mathbf{X}_1'\mathbf{X}_2$ from problem 6 as a coefficient matrix of a set of simultaneous linear equations, do you think a solution exists for

$$\begin{bmatrix} X_1'X_2 \end{bmatrix} \begin{bmatrix} x_1 \\ x_2 \\ x_3 \end{bmatrix} = \begin{bmatrix} 5 \\ 3 \\ 4 \end{bmatrix} ?$$

Is the solution unique? Why?

Do you think a solution exists for

$$X_1 \begin{bmatrix} x_1 \\ x_2 \\ x_3 \end{bmatrix} = \begin{bmatrix} 5 \\ 4 \\ 3 \\ 2 \\ 1 \end{bmatrix} ?$$

Is the solution unique? Why?

Do you think a solution exists for

$$X_1' \begin{bmatrix} x_1 \\ x_2 \\ x_3 \\ x_4 \\ x_5 \end{bmatrix} = \begin{bmatrix} 5 \\ 3 \\ 4 \end{bmatrix} ?$$

Is the solution unique? Why?

(9) Using $\mathbf{X}_1\mathbf{X}_2'$ from problem 6 as the constant matrix of a quadratic form, calculate the value of the quadratic form $\mathbf{x}_1' \mathbf{X}_1 \mathbf{X}_2' \mathbf{x}_1$.

(10) Is

$$\begin{bmatrix} 2 \\ 1 \\ 3 \end{bmatrix}$$

a latent vector and 3 its associated latent root of the matrix $\mathbf{X}_1'\mathbf{X}_2$ from problem 6?

(11) Verify that the inverse of

$$\mathbf{A} = \begin{bmatrix} 2 & -2 & -1 \\ 1 & 1 & -2 \\ 1 & 0 & -1 \end{bmatrix} \text{ is } \begin{bmatrix} -1 & -2 & 5 \\ -1 & -1 & 3 \\ -1 & -2 & 4 \end{bmatrix}$$

(12) Using the **A** from problem 11, solve the following for **x**:

$$\mathbf{Ax} = \begin{bmatrix} 3 \\ 5 \\ 2 \end{bmatrix}$$

(13) If

$$\begin{bmatrix} 1 \\ 2 \\ -2 \end{bmatrix}$$

is a latent vector of

$$\begin{bmatrix} 3 & -6 & -4 \\ -6 & 4 & 2 \\ -4 & 2 & -1 \end{bmatrix}$$

find its associated latent root.

NOTES

1. There are certain matrix operations that have analogies to operations with real numbers under certain conditions. For example, if the matrices **A**, **B**, and **C** are each square, nonsingular, and conformable for matrix multiplication, then **AB** = **AC** implies

that **B** = **C**. (A matrix is nonsingular if it has a determinant not equal to 0. A determinant is only defined for square matrices. It is a scalar or number that is a specific function of the elements in the matrix and is discussed in more detail later in this and subsequent chapters.) Another example is that if **A** is a square and nonsingular matrix, then a matrix $\mathbf{A}^{-1}$, called the inverse of **A**, exists that has the property that $\mathbf{A}\mathbf{A}^{-1} = \mathbf{A}^{-1}\mathbf{A} = \mathbf{I}$. (The inverse matrix is discussed later in this chapter and in subsequent chapters throughout the book.) This is analogous to the operation of taking the reciprocal of a real number, since for any number other than 0, $a^{-1}a = aa^{-1} = 1$; for example, $5(1/5) = 1$. Finally, for any square matrix **A**, singular or nonsingular, $\mathbf{A}^n$ is defined as **A A A** . . . **A** so that the analogue of exponentiation holds under certain conditions.

2. For these problems, use the data found in the Appendix.

4 Multiple Regression Analysis

4.1 INTRODUCTION

This section introduces multiple regression, the extension of our earlier-discussed regression model with a single continuous independent variable to one that has two or more continuous independent variables.

Section 4.2 discusses the basic assumptions of the multiple regression model. These assumptions, along with the formulation of the multiple regression model presented in this section, enable us, in section 4.3, to use the principle of least squares to generate the matrix expression (that is, the normal equations) to be solved for the regression parameter estimates. The procedure for solving the normal equations is illustrated in section 4.4 on a small hypothetical data set. Instead of working with the original measures on the variables, one could subtract the mean from each variable and estimate the regression coefficients using these deviation scores. There are some advantages to working with deviation scores, and the procedure is illustrated in section 4.5. Similarly, all of the variables can be standardized to have means of zero and standard deviations of one. This is often done when the measurement units of the original variables are arbitrary and meaningless.

Section 4.6 illustrates the estimation of standardized regression coefficients. The properties of the regression parameter estimates (such as expectation and variance) are discussed in section 4.7. The estimation of the error variance for the multiple regression model is discussed in section 4.8. In section 4.9, the reader will see that the total sum of squares can be partitioned into two components: a sum of squares due to regression and a sum of squares due to error. These two sums of squares can be used to develop an index to summarize the overall relationship between the set of independent variables and the dependent variable. This index is known as the "multiple correlation coefficient." It is a generalization of the simple correlation coefficient, and is discussed in section 4.10. With all of this background, the statistical testing of various hypotheses concerning the regression parameters is discussed in section 4.11.

Section 4.12 briefly considers some generalizations of the basic multiple regression model brought about by the relaxation of certain assumptions. Section 4.13 discusses nonlinear models for cases in which the relationship between the dependent variable and the independent variables is not linear. Section 4.14 describes some popular computer software packages available for conducting multiple regression analyses. The last section presents an interesting application of multiple regression analysis.

We previously discussed a regression model for describing the relationship between one independent and one dependent variable. The model was

$$y_i = \alpha + \beta x_i + \epsilon_i$$

and the problem was to estimate the parameters α, β, and the common variance of the ϵ_i (σ_ϵ^2) given certain assumptions. The regression equation describes a line in a plane, such as that shown in Figure 4.1.

The expected value of y (population mean) for a given value of $x(x_i)$ is $\alpha + \beta x_i$, and a single observed value of y_i for a given x_i has a deviation of ϵ_i (that is, error) from its expected value. This simple model can be extended to include an arbitrary number of independent variables. It can also be extended to include an arbitrary number of dependent variables, an extension termed "multivariate regression analysis." However, the present discussion will be limited to one dependent variable and an arbitrary number of continuous independent variables. For simplicity, we will start with a discussion of two independent variables and then generalize to k independent variables.

If we postulate a linear relationship between the dependent variable y and the two independent variables x_1 and x_2, then the expected value or population mean of y associated with the ith observation can be expressed as

$$E(y_i) + \beta_o + \beta_1 x_{1i} + \beta_2 x_{2i}$$

If we consider the value of a single observation, y_i (rather than its expectation), when x_1 is fixed at x_{1i} and x_2 is fixed at x_{2i}, then we have to add an error component, ϵ_i, since a particular observation can deviate from the expected value or mean of all observations on y_i at x_{1i} and x_{2i}. So the model for y_i becomes

$$y_i = \beta_o + \beta_1 x_{1i} + \beta_2 x_{2i} + \epsilon_i$$

For the case of two independent variables, the former equation for the expected value of y describes a plane in the three-dimensional Euclidean space with x_1, x_2, and y as the coordinate axes. The geometrical representation of the

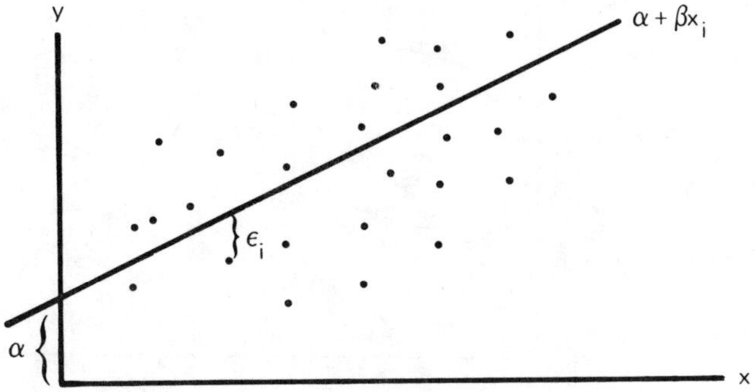

Figure 4.1 Simple Regression Line for Bivariate Regression

regression equation is presented in Figure 4.2. The intercept of the plane on the y axis is β_o, and β_1 and β_2 measure the slopes of the plane in the direction of the x_1 and x_2 axes, respectively. We shall see later that these slopes measure the influence of the independent variables, x_1 and x_2, respectively, on the dependent variable, y.

Let us assume that we have a sample of n observations on y for n selected joint values of x_1 and x_2; then the sample of observations can be expressed as

$$y_1 = \beta_o + \beta_1 x_{11} + \beta_2 x_{21} + \epsilon_1$$

$$y_2 = \beta_o + \beta_1 x_{12} + \beta_2 x_{22} + \epsilon_2$$

$$\cdots\cdots\cdots$$

$$\cdots\cdots\cdots$$

$$\cdots\cdots\cdots$$

$$y_n = \beta_o + \beta_1 x_{1n} + \beta_2 x_{2n} + \epsilon_n$$

or

$$y_i = \beta_o + \beta_1 x_{1i} + \beta_2 x_{2i} + \epsilon_i, \quad \text{where } i = 1, 2, \ldots, n.$$

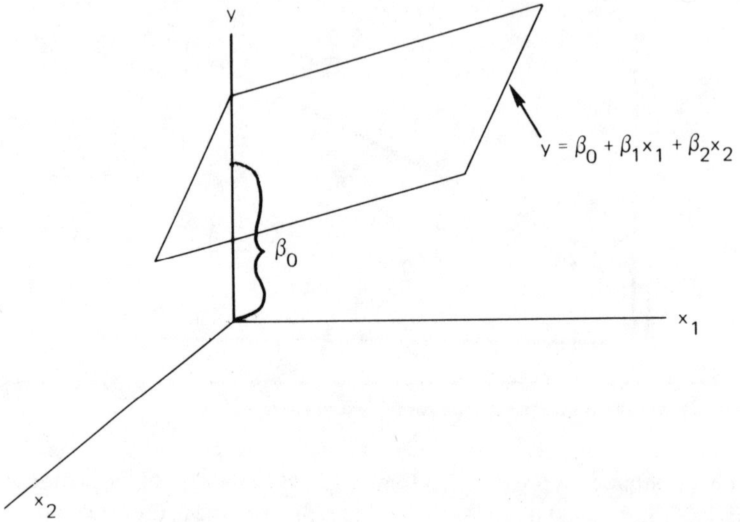

Figure 4.2 Multiple Regression Plane

Let us use our knowledge of matrix algebra developed in the previous chapter and express the n sample equations in matrix form. Let

$$\mathbf{y} = \begin{bmatrix} y_1 \\ y_2 \\ \cdot \\ \cdot \\ \cdot \\ y_n \end{bmatrix}$$

be a column vector of the n values of the dependent variable y; let

$$\mathbf{X} = \begin{bmatrix} 1 & x_{11} & x_{21} \\ 1 & x_{12} & x_{22} \\ \cdot & \cdot & \cdot \\ \cdot & \cdot & \cdot \\ \cdot & \cdot & \cdot \\ 1 & x_{1n} & x_{2n} \end{bmatrix}$$

be an n $\times$ 3 matrix with a column of n 1's in the first column, the n values of x_{1i} in the second column, and the n values of x_{2i} in the third column. Then let the parameters (regression coefficients) β_o, β_1, and β_2 be represented by the 3 $\times$ 1 column vector

$$\beta = \begin{bmatrix} \beta_o \\ \beta_1 \\ \beta_2 \end{bmatrix}$$

and finally let the n errors (ϵ_i) be represented by an n $\times$ 1 column vector

$$\epsilon = \begin{bmatrix} \epsilon_1 \\ \epsilon_2 \\ \cdot \\ \cdot \\ \cdot \\ \epsilon_n \end{bmatrix}$$

Using the matrix and vectors defined in this manner, the reader can verify that the n equations can be represented in matrix algebra as

$$\begin{bmatrix} y_1 \\ y_2 \\ \cdot \\ \cdot \\ \cdot \\ y_n \end{bmatrix} = \begin{bmatrix} 1 & x_{11} & x_{21} \\ 1 & x_{12} & x_{22} \\ \cdot & \cdot & \cdot \\ \cdot & \cdot & \cdot \\ \cdot & \cdot & \cdot \\ 1 & x_{1n} & x_{2n} \end{bmatrix} \begin{bmatrix} \beta_o \\ \beta_1 \\ \beta_2 \end{bmatrix} + \begin{bmatrix} \epsilon_1 \\ \epsilon_2 \\ \cdot \\ \cdot \\ \cdot \\ \epsilon_n \end{bmatrix}$$

It can be seen that the leading column of ones in the **X** matrix is needed to represent the constant β_o, the intercept, which is present in all n equations.

The above can be expressed more compactly as

$$y = \mathbf{X}\beta + \epsilon$$

It can be seen that the dependent variable **y** can be decomposed into a deterministic component $\mathbf{X}\boldsymbol{\beta}$ and a random or stochastic component $\boldsymbol{\epsilon}$.

4.2 BASIC ASSUMPTIONS OF MULTIPLE REGRESSION

The objective of regression analysis is to estimate the parameters β_o, β_1, β_2, and the variance of ϵ_i on the basis of the sample data. In order to do this, we have to make certain assumptions about the model. One assumption is that the values of x_{1i} and x_{2i} are fixed in repeated sampling and that the only random component in the model is ϵ_i. That is, the matrix **X** is fixed but the vector ϵ is random, which will yield different values in repeated sampling. It can be shown that this assumption can be relaxed to provide for X's that are randomly selected (called stochastic regressors) for each sample replication and the classical model based upon the assumption of fixed regressors will still apply. That is, the parameters are estimated in exactly the same way, and hypothesis testing of these parameters proceeds identically. We choose to explicate estimation and hypothesis testing using the fixed model because it is conceptually simpler and, at this stage of development, more instructive than the random model.

Another assumption is that each ϵ_i is normally distributed with mean zero, common variance σ^2, and the ϵ_i's are uncorrelated. The first part of the assumption can be expressed as

$$\begin{bmatrix} E(\epsilon_1) \\ E(\epsilon_2) \\ \cdot \\ \cdot \\ \cdot \\ E(\epsilon_n) \end{bmatrix} = E \begin{bmatrix} \epsilon_1 \\ \epsilon_2 \\ \cdot \\ \cdot \\ \cdot \\ \epsilon_n \end{bmatrix} = E(\epsilon) = \mathbf{0}$$

since the E before the vector means to take the expectation of every element in the vector. The expectation of a random variable is its average over an infinite number of observations or its average in the population.[1]

Another way to look at the assumption, $E(\epsilon_i) = 0$, is that, if $\beta_o + \beta_1 x_{1i} + \beta_2 x_{2i}$ is the population mean, $\mu_i = E(y_i)$, then the deviations, ϵ_i, around this mean must sum to zero since $E(\epsilon_i) = E(y_i - \mu_i) = E(y_i) - E(\mu_i) = \mu_i - \mu_i = 0$.

The remaining assumptions concerning ϵ_i can be expressed as

$$\begin{bmatrix} E(\epsilon_1^2) & E(\epsilon_1\epsilon_2) & \cdots & E(\epsilon_1\epsilon_n) \\ E(\epsilon_2\epsilon_1) & E(\epsilon_2^2) & \cdots & E(\epsilon_2\epsilon_n) \\ \cdot & \cdot & & \cdot \\ \cdot & \cdot & & \cdot \\ \cdot & \cdot & & \cdot \\ E(\epsilon_n\epsilon_1) & E(\epsilon_n\epsilon_2) & \cdots & E(\epsilon_n^2) \end{bmatrix}$$

$$= E \begin{bmatrix} \epsilon_1 \\ \epsilon_2 \\ \cdot \\ \cdot \\ \cdot \\ \epsilon_n \end{bmatrix} [\epsilon_1 \epsilon_2 \; . \; . \; . \; \epsilon_n]$$

$$= E(\epsilon\epsilon') = \sigma^2 \mathbf{I}_{nxn}$$

since by assumption of independence the off-diagonal elements of the matrix (that is, covariances) must be zero and each diagonal element reflects the common variance, σ^2. Normally, the covariance between ϵ_i and ϵ_j would be expressed as $E[\epsilon_i - E(\epsilon_i)][\epsilon_j - E(\epsilon_j)]$, but since $E(\epsilon_i) = E(\epsilon_j) = 0$, the covariance expression simplifies to $E(\epsilon_i\epsilon_j)$. $E(\epsilon_i\epsilon_j)$ is the average of the infinite number of random cross-products $\epsilon_i\epsilon_j$ that would be generated by an infinite number of replications of the regression model. It is the numerator in the formula for the correlation coefficient, and if it is zero, then the correlation must be zero.[2]

The final assumption is that the rank of the matrix **X** must be equal to the number of parameters being estimated (three in the case of two independent variables) and the number of parameters to be estimated must be less than the number of sample observations. Since the number of regression parameters equals the number of columns of **X**, the rank condition will be satisfied if the column vectors form a linearly independent set. The first part of this assumption is important since the matrix **X′X**, which is k by k (3 by 3 in the case of two independent variables), must be inverted in order to estimate the parameters. Note that k is equal to the number of columns of **X** or, equivalently, the number of regression parameters. If **X** is less than rank k, then **X′X** is less than k in rank (a theorem of matrix algebra states that the rank of the product of two matrices is equal to or less than the matrix with the lowest rank), and hence singular, and cannot be inverted. We will see further on that the second part of the assumption is important for hypothesis testing because if this assumption is not fulfilled the error variance cannot be estimated.

For estimation purposes, we do not need to specify the density function of ϵ_i, but for hypothesis testing we must assume that ϵ_i is normally distributed so that the distribution of the estimators themselves will be normal and the machinery of normal distribution theory can be applied.

4.3 LEAST-SQUARES ESTIMATION OF THE REGRESSION PARAMETERS

Given the assumed model, $\mathbf{y} = \mathbf{X}\boldsymbol{\beta} + \boldsymbol{\epsilon}$, the object is to estimate $\boldsymbol{\beta}$ and the common variance of the ϵ_i, σ_ϵ^2, from the known fixed matrix $\mathbf{X}$ and the associated vector of random observations, $\mathbf{y}$. The vector $\mathbf{y}$ is random because it is a sum of the random vector $\boldsymbol{\epsilon}$ and the fixed vector $\mathbf{X}\boldsymbol{\beta}$.

The principle of least squares, which was discussed in Chapter 3, leads to estimators with desirable properties under the above assumptions. We want to find an estimate of $\boldsymbol{\beta}$ denoted as $\hat{\boldsymbol{\beta}}$ that will minimize the error sum of squares, Σe_i^2. From our knowledge of matrix algebra, Σe_i^2 can be written as $\mathbf{e}'\mathbf{e}$ where $\mathbf{e}' = [e_1, e_2 \ldots, e_n]$. Note that the residuals e_i that are minimized are not the actual ϵ_i's, but estimates of the ϵ_i's based upon the $\hat{\boldsymbol{\beta}}$ that minimizes $\mathbf{e}'\mathbf{e}$. The population model is

$$\mathbf{y} = \mathbf{X}\boldsymbol{\beta} + \boldsymbol{\epsilon}$$

whereas the model based upon least-squares estimation is

$$\mathbf{y} = \mathbf{X}\hat{\boldsymbol{\beta}} + \mathbf{e}$$

where $\hat{\boldsymbol{\beta}}$ is the least-squares estimator of $\boldsymbol{\beta}$ and $\mathbf{e}$ is the vector of estimated residuals from the least-squares regression plane.

Since $\hat{\boldsymbol{\beta}}$ has probability zero[3] of being exactly equal to $\boldsymbol{\beta}$, the vector of empirically determined residuals $\mathbf{e}$ will differ from the actual population vector $\boldsymbol{\epsilon}$.

By subtracting $\mathbf{X}\hat{\boldsymbol{\beta}}$ from both sides of the above equation, $\mathbf{e}$ can be expressed as

$$\mathbf{e} = \mathbf{y} - \mathbf{X}\hat{\boldsymbol{\beta}}$$

and consequently,

$$\mathbf{e}'\mathbf{e} = (\mathbf{y} - \mathbf{X}\hat{\boldsymbol{\beta}})'(\mathbf{y} - \mathbf{X}\hat{\boldsymbol{\beta}})$$

Since $\mathbf{X}$ and $\mathbf{y}$ are known, they are considered as constants, and the vector $\hat{\boldsymbol{\beta}}$ is considered as a variable. We want to find a particular value of the variable vector $\hat{\boldsymbol{\beta}}$ such that $\mathbf{e}'\mathbf{e}$ is the smallest possible value that can be found. In order to minimize $\mathbf{e}'\mathbf{e}$, we must resort to the tool of partial differentiation. The reader who has not had calculus can try to develop an intuitive feeling for the minimization process as described below.

With $\hat{\beta}$ considered in this framework as the independent variable, we must find a value of $\hat{\beta}$ such that

$$\frac{\partial e'e}{\partial \hat{\beta}} = 0$$

This means that at the minimum value any minute change in the elements of the vector $\hat{\beta}$ will lead to no change in the value of **e′e**. The situation for a regression vector

$$\hat{\beta} = \begin{bmatrix} \hat{\beta}_o \\ \hat{\beta}_1 \end{bmatrix}$$

containing two elements (for example, intercept and slope for bivariate regression) is presented geometrically in Figure 4.3.

At the point where **e′e** is a minimum, we can draw a tangent plane that is parallel to the plane formed by $\hat{\beta}_o$ and $\hat{\beta}_1$ indicating that at the point β_1^*, β_o^* the change in **e′e** with respect to both $\hat{\beta}_o$ and $\hat{\beta}_1$ is zero. The slopes of the plane in the directions of both $\hat{\beta}_o$ and $\hat{\beta}_1$ are zero.

Since the minimization of **e′e** requires

$$\frac{\partial e'e}{\partial \hat{\beta}} = 0 = -2X'y + 2X'X\hat{\beta}$$

$\hat{\beta}$ must satisfy the matrix equation $\mathbf{X'X}\hat{\beta} = \mathbf{X'y}$.[4]

This matrix expression, the end result of the least-squares principle, is known as the set of normal equations. The $\hat{\beta}$ that satisfies these equations minimizes **e′e**. Since **X′** is 3 × n for multiple regression with two independent variables, this means that there are three normal equations, one for each parameter to be estimated in the model. A well-known theorem states that, in order to obtain a unique solution for $\hat{\beta}$, we must have at least as many linearly independent equations as there are parameters. Let us now examine these equations in more details. Substituting the appropriate elements into the matrix expression for the normal equations, we find for our two-independent-variable multiple regression problem that the normal equations are

$$\begin{bmatrix} 1 & 1 & \cdots & 1 \\ x_{11} & x_{12} & \cdots & x_{1n} \\ x_{21} & x_{22} & \cdots & x_{2n} \end{bmatrix} \begin{bmatrix} 1 & x_{11} & x_{21} \\ 1 & x_{12} & x_{22} \\ \vdots & \vdots & \vdots \\ 1 & x_{1n} & x_{2n} \end{bmatrix} \begin{bmatrix} \hat{\beta}_o \\ \hat{\beta}_1 \\ \hat{\beta}_2 \end{bmatrix}$$

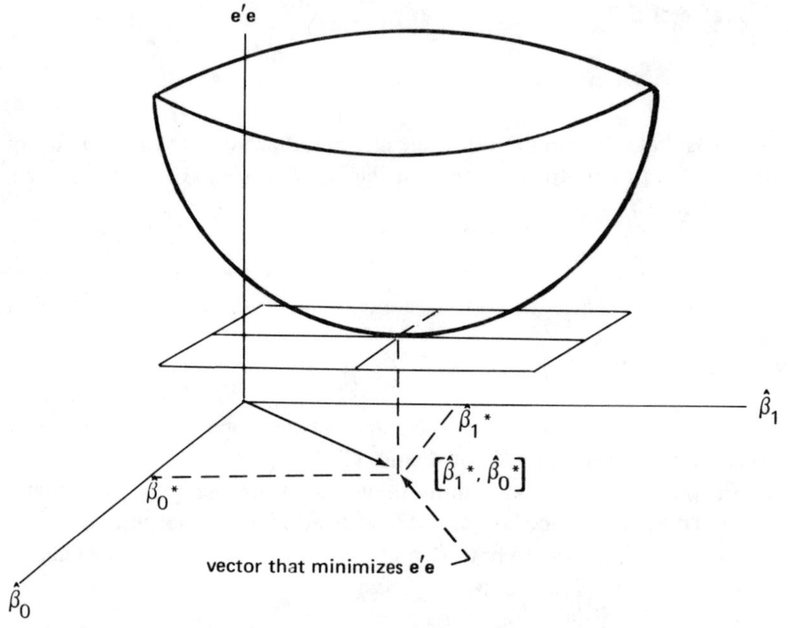

Figure 4.3 Minimization of e′e with Respect to β_0 and β_1

$$= \begin{bmatrix} 1 & 1 & \cdots & 1 \\ x_{11} & x_{12} & \cdots & x_{1n} \\ x_{21} & x_{22} & \cdots & x_{2n} \end{bmatrix} \begin{bmatrix} y_1 \\ y_2 \\ \vdots \\ y_n \end{bmatrix}$$

or

$$\begin{bmatrix} n & \sum_{i=1}^{n} x_{1i} & \sum_{i=1}^{n} x_{2i} \\ \sum_{i=1}^{n} x_{1i} & \sum_{i=1}^{n} x_{1i}^2 & \sum_{i=1}^{n} x_{1i}x_{2i} \\ \sum_{i=1}^{n} x_{2i} & \sum_{i=1}^{n} x_{2i}x_{1i} & \sum_{i=1}^{n} x_{2i}^2 \end{bmatrix} \begin{bmatrix} \hat{\beta}_o \\ \hat{\beta}_1 \\ \hat{\beta}_2 \end{bmatrix} = \begin{bmatrix} \sum_{i=1}^{n} y_i \\ \sum_{i=1}^{n} x_{1i}y_i \\ \sum_{i=1}^{n} x_{2i}y_i \end{bmatrix}$$

The matrix on the left (**X′X**) contains the sample size in the upper left-hand corner. It is also symmetric and bordered by the sum of each of the two independent variables. The sum of squares of the two independent variables is given as the last two elements of the principal diagonal and the remaining off-diagonal element is the sum of cross products of the independent variables x_1 and x_2. The vector on the right side of the equation, **X′y**, contains the sum of the y_i, the sum of cross products between x_1 and y, and the sum of cross products between x_2 and y, respectively.

Multiplying out the left side of the above equation, we have three simultaneous equations in the three unknowns.

$$\hat{\beta}_o n + \hat{\beta}_1 \sum_{i=1}^{n} x_{1i} + \hat{\beta}_2 \sum_{i=1}^{n} x_{2i} = \sum_{i=1}^{n} y_i$$

$$\hat{\beta}_o \sum_{i=1}^{n} x_{1i} + \hat{\beta}_1 \sum_{i=1}^{n} x_{1i}^2 + \hat{\beta}_2 \sum_{i=1}^{n} x_{1i}x_{2i} = \sum_{i=1}^{n} x_{1i}y_i$$

$$\hat{\beta}_o \sum_{i=1}^{n} x_{2i} + \hat{\beta}_1 \sum_{i=1}^{n} x_{2i}x_{1i} + \hat{\beta}_2 \sum_{i=1}^{n} x_{2i}^2 = \sum_{i=1}^{n} x_{2i}y_i$$

where $\hat{\beta}_o$, $\hat{\beta}_1$, and $\hat{\beta}_2$ are the three unknowns and the remaining terms are constants provided by the sample data. The next step is to solve these three simultaneous equations for β_o, β_1, and β_2 or, equivalently, the vector $\boldsymbol{\beta}$. In order to find a way of doing this, it is best to return to the matrix form of the normal equations,

$$\mathbf{X'X}\hat{\boldsymbol{\beta}} = \mathbf{X'y}$$

Since **X′X** is a square $k \times k$ matrix (in this case a 3×3 matrix) that is assumed to be nonsingular and hence invertible, we can premultiply both sides of the normal equations by $(\mathbf{X'X})^{-1}$ to obtain

$$(X'X)^{-1}(X'X)\hat{\beta} = (X'X)^{-1}X'y$$

or

$$\hat{\beta} = (X'X)^{-1}X'y \quad \text{since} \quad (X'X)^{-1}(X'X) = I.$$

4.4 SOLVING THE NORMAL EQUATIONS FOR $\hat{\beta}$

We can now see why it is important for **X** and consequently **X′X** to be equal in rank to the number of parameters in the model. In order to find $\hat{\boldsymbol{\beta}}$, all we need to do is form **X′X**, compute its inverse, and postmultiply the inverse by **X′y**. This procedure is generalizable to any number of independent variables, but

TABLE 4.1
Hypothetical Scores on V, Q, and GPA for 15 College Students

Student Identification Number	*V* x_1	*Q* x_2	*GPA* y
1	1	2	2
2	2	5	1
3	2	3	2
4	2	2	2
5	3	4	1
6	3	5	3
7	4	6	2
8	5	5	3
9	5	6	4
10	5	7	3
11	6	8	4
12	7	6	2
13	8	4	4
14	8	9	3
15	9	8	4

the two independent variable case will now be illustrated using some hypothetical data concerning the prediction of college grade-point average (GPA) from the quantitative (Q) and verbal (V) sections of an aptitude test. The data are presented in Table 4.1.

From this table we can easily construct the matrix **X**. It is a column vector of 15 one's adjoined to the first two data columns of the table. Therefore,

$$\mathbf{X} = \begin{bmatrix} 1 & 1 & 2 \\ 1 & 2 & 5 \\ 1 & 2 & 3 \\ 1 & 2 & 2 \\ 1 & 3 & 4 \\ 1 & 3 & 5 \\ 1 & 4 & 6 \\ 1 & 5 & 5 \\ 1 & 5 & 6 \\ 1 & 5 & 7 \\ 1 & 6 & 8 \\ 1 & 7 & 6 \\ 1 & 8 & 4 \\ 1 & 8 & 9 \\ 1 & 9 & 8 \end{bmatrix}$$

The matrix $\mathbf{X'X}$ is

$$\begin{bmatrix} 1 & 1 & 1 & 1 & 1 & 1 & 1 & 1 & 1 & 1 & 1 & 1 & 1 & 1 & 1 \\ 1 & 2 & 2 & 2 & 3 & 3 & 4 & 5 & 5 & 5 & 6 & 7 & 8 & 8 & 9 \\ 2 & 5 & 3 & 2 & 4 & 5 & 6 & 5 & 6 & 7 & 8 & 6 & 4 & 9 & 8 \end{bmatrix} \begin{bmatrix} 1 & 1 & 2 \\ 1 & 2 & 5 \\ 1 & 2 & 3 \\ 1 & 2 & 2 \\ 1 & 3 & 4 \\ 1 & 3 & 5 \\ 1 & 4 & 6 \\ 1 & 5 & 5 \\ 1 & 5 & 6 \\ 1 & 5 & 7 \\ 1 & 6 & 8 \\ 1 & 7 & 6 \\ 1 & 8 & 4 \\ 1 & 8 & 9 \\ 1 & 9 & 8 \end{bmatrix} = \begin{bmatrix} 15 & 70 & 80 \\ 70 & 415 & 429 \\ 80 & 429 & 490 \end{bmatrix}$$

The sample size is 15, $\sum_{i=1}^{n} x_{1i} = 70$, $\sum_{i=1}^{n} x_{2i} = 80$, $\sum_{i=1}^{n} x_{1i}^2 = 415$,

$\sum_{i=1}^{n} x_{2i}^2 = 490$, and $\sum_{i=1}^{n} x_{1i}x_{2i} = 429$.

The next step is to invert this matrix. We could do so using the method of cofactors to be illustrated in a subsequent chapter, but let us use another method so that we can become more adept at matrix operations. We can perform certain row operations on a matrix. In particular, we can divide each element in a row by a scalar, or we can add (subtract) a particular row that has been multiplied by a scalar constant to another row. Row operations on a matrix can be done by premultiplying the matrix by another matrix, E. For example, if we want to divide each element in the first row of $\mathbf{X'X}$ by 15, we could premultiply $\mathbf{X'X}$ by

$$\mathbf{E}_1 = \begin{bmatrix} \frac{1}{15} & 0 & 0 \\ 0 & 1 & 0 \\ 0 & 0 & 1 \end{bmatrix}$$

for

$$\mathbf{E}_1\,[\mathbf{X'X}] = \begin{bmatrix} \frac{1}{15} & 0 & 0 \\ 0 & 1 & 0 \\ 0 & 0 & 1 \end{bmatrix} \begin{bmatrix} 15 & 70 & 80 \\ 70 & 415 & 429 \\ 80 & 429 & 490 \end{bmatrix} = \begin{bmatrix} 1 & \frac{70}{15} & \frac{80}{15} \\ 70 & 415 & 429 \\ 80 & 429 & 490 \end{bmatrix}$$

Likewise, we could subtract two times row one from row three by premultiplying **X′X** by

$$\mathbf{E}_2 = \begin{bmatrix} 1 & 0 & 0 \\ 0 & 1 & 0 \\ -2 & 0 & 1 \end{bmatrix}$$

for

$$\mathbf{E}_2(\mathbf{X'X}) = \begin{bmatrix} 1 & 0 & 0 \\ 0 & 1 & 0 \\ -2 & 0 & 1 \end{bmatrix} \begin{bmatrix} 15 & 70 & 80 \\ 70 & 415 & 429 \\ 80 & 429 & 490 \end{bmatrix}$$

$$= \begin{bmatrix} 15 & 70 & 80 \\ 70 & 415 & 429 \\ 80-2(15) & 429-2(70) & 490-2(80) \end{bmatrix} = \begin{bmatrix} 15 & 70 & 80 \\ 70 & 415 & 429 \\ 50 & 289 & 330 \end{bmatrix}$$

Now, if we can premultiply **X′X** by a sequence of matrices, $\mathbf{E}_i$, such that

$$\mathbf{E}_n \ldots \mathbf{E}_2\mathbf{E}_1\,[\mathbf{X'X}] = \mathbf{I},$$

then $[\mathbf{E}_n \ldots \mathbf{E}_2\mathbf{E}_1]$ must be the inverse of **X′X**.

Since

$$[\mathbf{E}_n \ldots \mathbf{E}_2\mathbf{E}_1]\,\mathbf{I} = [\mathbf{E}_n \ldots \mathbf{E}_2\mathbf{E}_1]$$

performing the same elementary row operations on **I** that we did on **X′X** to reduce it to **I** will yield $[\mathbf{X'X}]^{-1}$. The sequence of **E** matrices simply represents performing a series of elementary row operations (either multiplying a particular row by a scalar constant or adding [subtracting] the multiple of a particular row to another row) on **X′X**. We do not have to construct the **E** matrices to reduce **X′X** to **I**. We can simply perform these admissible operations step by step and come out with the same result. This procedure is called the abbreviated Gauss-Doolittle technique. We begin by adjoining the 3 × 3 identity matrix to the **X′X** matrix as

$$[\mathbf{X'X}\ \mathbf{I}] = \begin{bmatrix} 15 & 70 & 80 & 1 & 0 & 0 \\ 70 & 415 & 429 & 0 & 1 & 0 \\ 80 & 429 & 490 & 0 & 0 & 1 \end{bmatrix}$$

We then proceed with a sequence of row operations that will reduce **X′X** to **I**, and by applying these same operations to the **I** matrix on the right determine $[\mathbf{X'X}]^{-1}$. The procedure is illustrated below step by step. The first thing that we want to do is convert the 15 in the upper-left corner to 1. We can do this by dividing each of the six elements in row one by 15. Doing this to all the elements in the row means that we are doing the same thing to both **X′X** and **I**. This step results in a new matrix,

$$\begin{bmatrix} 1 & 4.666 & 5.333 & .0666 & 0 & 0 \\ 70 & 415 & 429 & 0 & 1 & 0 \\ 80 & 429 & 490 & 0 & 0 & 1 \end{bmatrix}$$

We can now reduce the second element in column one to zero by subtracting 70 times row one from row two, giving

$$\begin{bmatrix} 1 & 4.666 & 5.333 & .0666 & 0 & 0 \\ 0 & 88.333 & 55.666 & -4.666 & 1 & 0 \\ 80 & 429 & 490 & 0 & 0 & 1 \end{bmatrix}$$

The third element in column one can be reduced to zero by subtracting 80 times row one from row three, giving

$$\begin{bmatrix} 1 & 4.666 & 5.333 & .0666 & 0 & 0 \\ 0 & 88.333 & 55.666 & -4.666 & 1 & 0 \\ 0 & 55.666 & 63.333 & -5.333 & 0 & 1 \end{bmatrix}$$

We can see that we already turned column one into the first column of an identity matrix. Let us do the same thing to column two. The first thing we do when switching from one column to the next is transform the diagonal value into a one. This can be done by dividing all of the elements in row two by 88.333, giving

$$\begin{bmatrix} 1 & 4.666666 & 5.333333 & .066666 & 0 & 0 \\ 0 & 1 & .630189 & -.052830 & .011321 & 0 \\ 0 & 55.666666 & 63.333333 & -5.333333 & 0 & 1 \end{bmatrix}$$

As we go along, we want to retain as many significant figures as possible since there can be considerable round-off error. Since the elements of $\mathbf{X'X}$ are fairly large, the elements of $[\mathbf{X'X}]^{-1}$ will be in general pretty small since row one of $\mathbf{X'X}$ multiplied by column one of $[\mathbf{X'X}]^{-1}$ must be equal to one.

The next step is to reduce the 4.666666 to zero. This can be done by subtracting 4.666666 times row two from row one, which gives

$$\begin{bmatrix} 1 & 0 & 2.392451 & .313207 & .052831 & 0 \\ 0 & 1 & .630189 & .052830 & .011321 & 0 \\ 0 & 55.666666 & 63.333333 & 5.333333 & 0 & 1 \end{bmatrix}$$

As an exercise, the reader can verify that the end result of this procedure is

$$\begin{bmatrix} 1 & 0 & 0 & .515800 & .000521 & .084668 \\ 0 & 1 & 0 & .000521 & .024749 & .021753 \\ 0 & 0 & 1 & .084668 & .021753 & .034909 \end{bmatrix}$$

where $\mathbf{X'X}$ has been reduced to $\mathbf{I}$ and the original $\mathbf{I}$ matrix on the right transformed to $[\mathbf{X'X}]^{-1}$.

It can be verified that the matrix on the right is the correct inverse since

$$\begin{bmatrix} .515800 & .000521 & -.084668 \\ .000521 & .024749 & -.021753 \\ -.084668 & -.021753 & .034909 \end{bmatrix} \begin{bmatrix} 15 & 70 & 80 \\ 70 & 415 & 429 \\ 80 & 429 & 490 \end{bmatrix} = \begin{bmatrix} 1 & 0 & 0 \\ 0 & 1 & 0 \\ 0 & 0 & 1 \end{bmatrix}$$

Since

$$
X'y = \begin{bmatrix} 1 & 1 & 1 & 1 & 1 & 1 & 1 & 1 & 1 & 1 & 1 & 1 & 1 & 1 & 1 \\ 1 & 2 & 2 & 2 & 3 & 3 & 4 & 5 & 5 & 5 & 6 & 7 & 8 & 8 & 9 \\ 2 & 5 & 3 & 2 & 4 & 5 & 6 & 5 & 6 & 7 & 8 & 6 & 4 & 9 & 8 \end{bmatrix} \begin{bmatrix} 2 \\ 1 \\ 2 \\ 2 \\ 1 \\ 3 \\ 2 \\ 3 \\ 4 \\ 3 \\ 4 \\ 2 \\ 4 \\ 3 \\ 4 \end{bmatrix} = \begin{bmatrix} 40 \\ 212 \\ 229 \end{bmatrix}
$$

then

$$
\hat{\beta} = \begin{bmatrix} \hat{\beta}_0 \\ \hat{\beta}_1 \\ \hat{\beta}_2 \end{bmatrix} = [X'X]^{-1}X'y = \begin{bmatrix} .515800 & .000521 & -.084668 \\ .000521 & .024749 & -.021753 \\ -.084668 & -.021753 & .034909 \end{bmatrix} \begin{bmatrix} 40 \\ 212 \\ 229 \end{bmatrix}
$$

$$
= \begin{bmatrix} 1.353480 \\ .286191 \\ -.004195 \end{bmatrix}
$$

Our estimated regression equation is then

$$
\hat{y} = 1.353480 + .286191x_1 - .004195x_2
$$

The constant 1.353480 is the point at which the estimated regression plane intercepts the y axis. It reflects the height of the regression plane. The estimated regression coefficient $\hat{\beta}_1$, (.286191) indicates the slope of the regression plane in the direction of x_1 and $\hat{\beta}_2$ indicates the slope of the regression plane in the direction of x_2. For every unit change in x_1, y changes .286191 units; and for every unit change in x_2, y changes – .004195 units. It seems that x_1 (verbal ability) is the more important variable.[5] This equation can also be used to predict the value of y given a particular set of values for x_1 and x_2. More will be said later concerning the interpretation and testing of hypotheses concerning $\hat{\boldsymbol{\beta}}$.

This method of estimation is completely general and can be used for any number of continuous independent variables and, as we shall see later, can even be modified to accommodate categorical independent variables by the use of indicator variables. Before turning to other aspects of the multiple regression model, let us return to the problem of estimating $\hat{\boldsymbol{\beta}}$.

If **X** is a random matrix generated from a stochastic process (that is, a random sample of values rather than a fixed set of numbers) and is independently distributed from $\boldsymbol{\epsilon}$, then the least-squares estimates of $\boldsymbol{\beta}$ under these conditions have basically the same properties as under the fixed model. This is an important result, because it means that we can make inferences from an **X** matrix generated from a probability sample as well as from a fixed matrix **X**.[6] In the social sciences, we frequently cannot control **X** and must rely upon a probability sample for our inferences. It is comforting that this result holds true.

Let us return to our estimated regression equation

$$\mathbf{y} = \mathbf{X}\hat{\boldsymbol{\beta}} + \mathbf{e}$$

where $\hat{\boldsymbol{\beta}}$ is the least-squares estimate of $\boldsymbol{\beta}$ and **e** is the vector of sample residuals, and premultiply both sides by $\mathbf{X}'$. This yields

$$\mathbf{X}'\mathbf{y} = \mathbf{X}'\mathbf{X}\hat{\boldsymbol{\beta}} + \mathbf{X}'\mathbf{e}.$$

If we assume in the case of stochastic regressor variables that the same properties for the sample data hold as for the population data, $\mathbf{X}'\mathbf{e}$ becomes zero and we have the normal equation $\mathbf{X}'\mathbf{y} = \mathbf{X}'\mathbf{X}\hat{\boldsymbol{\beta}}$. A characteristic of least squares is that $\mathbf{X}'\mathbf{e}$ is zero; hence least squares intuitively seems to be a reasonable estimator.

4.5 MULTIPLE REGRESSION WITH DEVIATION SCORES

We can also estimate $\hat{\boldsymbol{\beta}}$ by using deviation scores, that is, $(x_{1i} - \bar{x}_1)$, $(x_{2i} - \bar{x}_2)$, and $(y_i - \bar{y})$, instead of the raw scores from the original **X** matrix. As we shall see, there are two advantages in using deviation scores. First, the new $\mathbf{X}'\mathbf{X}$ matrix formed from the deviation scores has a rank of one less than the raw score $\mathbf{X}'\mathbf{X}$ matrix and is hence simpler to invert. Second, frequently a covariance matrix of all the variables including the dependent variable is available and we can work directly with this covariance matrix to solve directly for β_1

and β_2 and indirectly for $\hat{\beta}_0$. This is especially important in secondary data analysis where the **X′X** matrix based upon raw scores is not readily available, but the covariance matrix and the vector of means is available. Let us now examine how the vector $\boldsymbol{\beta}$ is obtained through the use of deviation scores.

We know that $\bar{y} = \hat{\beta}_0 + \hat{\beta}_1\bar{x}_1 + \hat{\beta}_2\bar{x}_2$ since

$$\bar{y} = \frac{\Sigma y_i}{n} = \sum_{i=1}^{n} \frac{\hat{\beta}_0 + \hat{\beta}_1 x_{1i} + \hat{\beta}_2 x_{2i} + e_i}{n}$$

$$= \frac{n\hat{\beta}_0}{n} + \frac{\hat{\beta}_1 \Sigma x_{1i}}{n} + \frac{\hat{\beta}_2 \Sigma x_{2i}}{n} + \frac{\Sigma e_i}{n} = \hat{\beta}_0 + \hat{\beta}_1\bar{x}_1 + \hat{\beta}_2\bar{x}_2$$

(Note that $\frac{\Sigma e_i}{n} = 0$ is a property of a least-squares solution.)

If we subtract $\bar{y}$ from both sides of our original estimated regression equation, we have

$$y_i - \bar{y} = \hat{\beta}_0 + \hat{\beta}_1 x_{1i} + \hat{\beta}_2 x_{2i} + e_i - (\hat{\beta}_0 + \hat{\beta}_1\bar{x}_1 + \hat{\beta}_2\bar{x}_2)$$

Simplifying, we have

$$y_1 - \bar{y} = \hat{\beta}_1(x_{1i} - \bar{x}_1) + \hat{\beta}_2(x_{2i} - \bar{x}_2) + e_i$$

The reader can verify that the normal equations for this model are

$$\mathbf{X}_d'\mathbf{X}_d\hat{\beta}_* = \mathbf{X}_d'\mathbf{y}_d$$

where the subscript d indicates that deviation scores are being used and the asterisk attached to $\hat{\beta}$ indicates that $[\hat{\beta}_1, \hat{\beta}_2]'$ is being estimated rather than $\hat{\beta} = [\hat{\beta}_0, \hat{\beta}_1, \hat{\beta}_2]'$. The matrix $\mathbf{X}_d$ and the vector $\mathbf{y}_d$ take the form given below.

$$\mathbf{X}_d = \begin{bmatrix} x_{11} - \bar{x}_1 & x_{21} - \bar{x}_2 \\ x_{12} - \bar{x}_1 & x_{22} - \bar{x}_2 \\ \vdots & \vdots \\ x_{1n} - \bar{x}_1 & x_{2n} - \bar{x}_2 \end{bmatrix}$$

and

$$\mathbf{y} = \begin{bmatrix} y_1 - \bar{y} \\ y_2 - \bar{y} \\ \cdot \\ \cdot \\ \cdot \\ y_n - \bar{y} \end{bmatrix}$$

We can form deviation scores from the scores in Table 4.1 by subtracting the appropriate mean from the elements in each of the three columns. Subtracting $\bar{x}_1 = 4.666$ from each element of the first column, $\bar{x}_2 = 5.333$ from each element of the second column, and $\bar{y} = 2.666$ from each element of the third column, we arrive at the deviation score matrix, $\mathbf{X}_d$, as shown in Table 4.2.

The first two columns of Table 4.2 constitute the $\mathbf{X}_d$ matrix of deviation scores and the last column is the $\mathbf{y}_d$ vector of deviation scores for the dependent variable.

The reader can verify that

$$\mathbf{X}_d'\mathbf{X}_d = \begin{bmatrix} -3.666 & -2.666 & . & . & . & 4.333 \\ -3.333 & -.333 & . & . & . & 2.666 \end{bmatrix} \begin{bmatrix} -3.666 & -3.333 \\ -2.666 & -.333 \\ \cdot & \cdot \\ \cdot & \cdot \\ \cdot & \cdot \\ 4.333 & 2.666 \end{bmatrix}$$

$$= \begin{bmatrix} 89.333 & 55.666 \\ 55.666 & 63.333 \end{bmatrix}$$

There is an easier way to compute $\mathbf{X}_d'\mathbf{X}_d$ than to subtract the appropriate mean for each individual observation first as was done in Table 4.2. Note that the two columns of the deviation score matrix can be expressed as

$$\mathbf{X}_d = [\mathbf{x}_1 - \bar{x}_1\mathbf{1}, \mathbf{x}_2 - \bar{x}_2\mathbf{1}] = \left[\begin{bmatrix} 1 \\ 2 \\ \cdot \\ \cdot \\ \cdot \\ 9 \end{bmatrix} - 4.666 \begin{bmatrix} 1 \\ 1 \\ \cdot \\ \cdot \\ \cdot \\ 1 \end{bmatrix}, \begin{bmatrix} 2 \\ 5 \\ \cdot \\ \cdot \\ \cdot \\ 8 \end{bmatrix} - 5.333 \begin{bmatrix} 1 \\ 1 \\ \cdot \\ \cdot \\ \cdot \\ 1 \end{bmatrix} \right]$$

TABLE 4.2
Hypothetical Deviation Scores
on V, Q, and GPA for 15 College Students

Student Identification Number	*V* $x_1 - \bar{x}_1$	*Q* $x_2 - \bar{x}_2$	*GPA* $y - \bar{y}$
1	–3.666	–3.333	– .666
2	–2.666	– .333	–1.666
3	–2.666	–2.333	– .666
4	–2.666	–3.333	– .666
5	–1.666	–1.333	–1.666
6	–1.666	– .333	.333
7	– .666	.666	– .666
8	.333	– .333	.333
9	.333	.666	1.333
10	.333	1.666	.333
11	1.333	2.666	1.333
12	2.333	.666	– .666
13	3.333	–1.333	1.333
14	3.333	3.666	.333
15	4.333	2.666	1.333

where $\mathbf{x}_1$ is the column vector of raw scores for variable one, $\bar{x}_1$ is the mean of variable one (a scalar), and **1** is a column vector of 1's with n (number of sample observations, which is 15 in this example) rows. Then

$$\mathbf{X}_d'\mathbf{X}_d = \begin{bmatrix} \mathbf{x}_1' - \bar{x}_1\mathbf{1}' \\ \mathbf{x}_2' - \bar{x}_2\mathbf{1}' \end{bmatrix} [\mathbf{x}_1 - \bar{x}_1\mathbf{1} \quad \mathbf{x}_2 - \bar{x}_2\mathbf{1}]$$

$$= \begin{bmatrix} \mathbf{x}_1'\mathbf{x}_1 - n\bar{x}_1^2 & \mathbf{x}_1'\mathbf{x}_2 - n\bar{x}_1\bar{x}_2 \\ \mathbf{x}_2'\mathbf{x}_1 - n\bar{x}_2\bar{x}_1 & \mathbf{x}_2'\mathbf{x}_2 - n\bar{x}_2^2 \end{bmatrix} = \mathbf{X}'\mathbf{X} - n\bar{\mathbf{x}}\bar{\mathbf{x}}'$$

where $\mathbf{X}'\mathbf{X}$ is the raw score sum of squares and cross products (SSCP) and $\bar{\mathbf{x}}'$ is the row vector of the two means, $[\bar{x}_1, \bar{x}_2]$.

The SSCP matrix gets its name from the fact that the diagonal elements are the sum of squares for each of the independent variables and the off-diagonal elements are the cross products between all pairs of variables. Note that in this case **X** does not contain a leading column of ones. The column of ones is not needed because there is no constant or intercept term in the deviation score model. Also note that the $\mathbf{X}'\mathbf{X}$ matrix can be recovered from $\mathbf{X}_d'\mathbf{X}_d$ if we also know n and $\bar{x}$. Using this matrix formula, we do not have to form a deviation score matrix, but can simply correct the SSCP matrix by subtracting out the corrections for the means. These corrections are represented by the matrix

$n\bar{\mathbf{x}}\bar{\mathbf{x}}'$. We can look upon the elements of the SSCP matrix as based upon deviation scores from zero. We need deviation scores from the mean so the SSCP matrix must be corrected or adjusted accordingly. The reader can verify the above expression for $\mathbf{X}_d'\mathbf{X}_d$ using the hypothetical data set.

Next,

$$\mathbf{X}_d'\mathbf{y}_d = \begin{bmatrix} -3.666 & -.2666 & \cdots & 4.333 \\ -3.333 & -.333 & \cdots & 2.666 \end{bmatrix} \begin{bmatrix} -.666 \\ -1.666 \\ \cdot \\ \cdot \\ \cdot \\ 1.333 \end{bmatrix} = \begin{bmatrix} 25.333 \\ 15.666 \end{bmatrix}$$

This matrix can also be expressed as $\mathbf{X}_d'\mathbf{y}_d = \mathbf{X}'\mathbf{y} - n\bar{y}\bar{\mathbf{x}}$, so that the raw-score cross products matrix, $\mathbf{X}'\mathbf{y}$, can likewise be corrected for the means to yield the deviation score cross products matrix, $\mathbf{X}_d'\mathbf{y}_d$.

$$\text{Since } \hat{\beta}_* = \begin{bmatrix} \hat{\beta}_1 \\ \beta_2 \end{bmatrix} = [\mathbf{X}_d'\mathbf{X}_d]^{-1}\mathbf{X}_d'\mathbf{y}_d$$

we need to find the inverse of the 2×2 matrix $\mathbf{X}_d'\mathbf{X}_d$ and postmultiply it by the vector $\mathbf{X}_d'\mathbf{y}_d$. We could use the Gauss-Doolittle method to find that

$$[\mathbf{X}_d'\mathbf{X}_d]^{-1} = \begin{bmatrix} .024749 & -.021753 \\ -.021753 & .034909 \end{bmatrix}$$

and that, consequently,

$$\hat{\beta}_* = \begin{bmatrix} \hat{\beta}_1 \\ \hat{\beta}_2 \end{bmatrix} = \begin{bmatrix} .024749 & -.021753 \\ -.021753 & .034909 \end{bmatrix} \begin{bmatrix} 25.333 \\ 15.666 \end{bmatrix} = \begin{bmatrix} .286191 \\ -.004195 \end{bmatrix}$$

Then $\hat{\beta}_o$ can be found by substituting the means and regression coefficients into

$$\hat{\beta}_o = \bar{y}_1 - \hat{\beta}_1\bar{x}_1 - \hat{\beta}_2\bar{x}_2$$

which gives

$$\hat{\beta}_o = 2.666666 - .286196\,(4.666666) - [(-.004195)\,(5.333333)]$$

$$= 1.353480$$

Frequently, the value of the intercept parameter, $\hat{\beta}_0$, is of little interest to researchers since it is an arbitrary function of the scaling of the variables in the model. Consequently, the regression analysis with deviation scores directly yields estimates of the regression parameters of interest (that is, $\hat{\beta}_1$ and $\hat{\beta}_2$).

The matrix $\mathbf{X}_d'\mathbf{X}_d$ contains the sum of squares and cross products of deviation scores. That is,

$$\mathbf{X}_d'\mathbf{X}_d = \begin{bmatrix} \sum_{i=1}^{n} (x_{1i} - \bar{x}_1)^2 & \sum_{i=1}^{n} (x_{1i} - \bar{x}_1)(x_{2i} - \bar{x}_2) \\ \sum_{i=1}^{n} (x_{2i} - \bar{x}_2)(x_{1i} - \bar{x}_1) & \sum_{i=1}^{n} (x_{2i} - \bar{x}_2)^2 \end{bmatrix}$$

Consequently, an unbiased estimate of the covariance matrix for the independent variables is

$$\frac{1}{n-1}[\mathbf{X}_d'\mathbf{X}_d]$$

Likewise, $\mathbf{X}_d'\mathbf{y}_d$ contains the sum of cross-products of deviation scores for each independent variable with the dependent variable. That is,

$$\mathbf{X}_d'\mathbf{y}_d = \begin{bmatrix} \sum_{i=1}^{n} (x_{1i} - \bar{x}_1)(y_i - \bar{y}) \\ \sum_{i=1}^{n} (x_{2i} - \bar{x}_2)(y_i - \bar{y}) \end{bmatrix}$$

and an unbiased estimate of this vector of covariances is

$$\frac{1}{n-1}[\mathbf{X}_d'\mathbf{y}_d]$$

As mentioned earlier, data are frequently available in the form of a covariance matrix. We can use the covariances to find $\hat{\beta}_*$, since

$$\left[\frac{1}{n-1}\mathbf{X}_d'\mathbf{X}_d\right]^{-1}\left[\frac{1}{n-1}\mathbf{X}_d'\mathbf{y}_d\right] = \left[(n-1)[\mathbf{X}_d'\mathbf{X}_d]^{-1}\right]\left[\frac{1}{n-1}\mathbf{X}_d'\mathbf{y}_d\right]$$

$$= [\mathbf{X}_d'\mathbf{X}_d]^{-1}\mathbf{X}_d'\mathbf{y}_d = \hat{\beta}_*$$

Summarizing, if $\mathbf{C}_x$ is the covariance matrix of the independent variables and $\mathbf{c}_{x,y}$ is the vector containing the covariance of each independent variable with y, then $\beta_* = \mathbf{C}_x^{-1}\mathbf{c}_{x,y}$.

4.6 MULTIPLE REGRESSION WITH STANDARDIZED SCORES

Frequently, the types of independent and dependent variables encountered in behavioral and social science research are measured in such a way that the measurement units are arbitrary and hence noncomparable across variables. In our example, Q is measured on one scale, V on another, and GPA on yet another. A larger score on one variable as contrasted to another does not imply that the larger score possesses more of its own attribute than the amount of the attribute reflected by the other score. Similarly, a change of one unit on one variable may not be comparable to a change of one unit on another variable. For example, a change in one unit in Q has less significance than a change of one unit of GPA since Q is measured on a nine-point scale and GPA is measured on a four-point scale. The measurement unit for the three variables is arbitrary; hence, if raw scores are used in the regression analysis, it is difficult to interpret and compare the regression parameters since they reflect the change in an arbitrary scaled score of y for a unit change in the arbitrary scale of one of the independent variables.

A solution to this problem of the arbitrary scaling of social and psychological variables is to use variables that are standardized to have a common mean of zero and a common standard deviation of one. Standardized variables are measured in standard deviation units, and from the characteristics of a normal or "quasi"-normal distribution, we know the meaning of a standardized score. For example, we know that for a normal distribution, 50 percent of the values of the variable fall below the standardized score of zero, roughly 84 percent fall below a standardized score of one, and roughly 98 percent fall below a standardized score of two.

A standardized score is defined as

$$z_i = \frac{x_i - \bar{x}}{s_x}$$

where s_x is the sample standard deviation $\left(\frac{\sum_{i=1}^{n}(x_i - \bar{x})^2}{n}\right)^{\frac{1}{2}}$

Our deviation score matrix, $\mathbf{X}_d$, can be converted to a standardized score matrix $\mathbf{Z}$ by dividing each element in a deviation score column by the appropriate standard deviation. The vector $\mathbf{y}_d$ can similarly be converted to a standardized score vector $\mathbf{y}_z$ by dividing each element by s_y.

If we transformed our variables to standardized scores, and conducted a regression analysis using standardized scores, then the solution vector for $\hat{\boldsymbol{\beta}}_z$ would be $\hat{\boldsymbol{\beta}}_z = (\mathbf{Z}'\mathbf{Z})^{-1}\mathbf{Z}'\mathbf{y}_z$ since the regression model would now be expressed as $\mathbf{y}_z = \mathbf{Z}\boldsymbol{\beta} + \mathbf{e}$, the normal equation of which is $\mathbf{Z}'\mathbf{y}_z = \mathbf{Z}'\mathbf{Z}\hat{\boldsymbol{\beta}}$. The matrix $\mathbf{Z}$ is the matrix of standardized scores for the independent variables, that is

$$\mathbf{Z} = \begin{bmatrix} \dfrac{x_{11} - \bar{x}_1}{s_{x_1}} & \dfrac{x_{21} - \bar{x}_2}{s_{x_2}} \\ \dfrac{x_{12} - \bar{x}_1}{s_{x_1}} & \dfrac{x_{22} - \bar{x}_2}{s_{x_2}} \\ \vdots & \vdots \\ \dfrac{x_{1n} - \bar{x}_1}{s_{x_1}} & \dfrac{x_{2n} - \bar{x}_2}{s_{x_2}} \end{bmatrix}$$

and $\mathbf{y}_z$ is the vector of standardized scores on the dependent variable. That is,

$$y_z = \begin{bmatrix} \dfrac{y_1 - \bar{y}}{s_y} \\ \dfrac{y_2 - \bar{y}}{s_y} \\ \vdots \\ \dfrac{y_n - \bar{y}}{s_y} \end{bmatrix}$$

Let

$$\mathbf{D}_s^{-1} = \begin{bmatrix} 1/s_{x_1} & 0 \\ 0 & 1/s_{x_2} \end{bmatrix}, \text{ then } \mathbf{Z} = \mathbf{X}_d \mathbf{D}_s^{-1}$$

We can now calculate $\mathbf{Z}'\mathbf{Z}$:

$$\mathbf{Z}'\mathbf{Z} = \left[\mathbf{X}_d \mathbf{D}_s^{-1}\right]' \mathbf{X}_d \mathbf{D}_s^{-1} = \mathbf{D}_s^{-1} \mathbf{X}_d' \mathbf{X}_d \mathbf{D}_s^{-1}$$

since the transpose of a diagonal (that is, $\mathbf{D}_s^{-1}$) or symmetrical matrix is equal to the original matrix itself, and the transpose of a product of two matrices is equal to their transposes multiplied in reverse order.

Similarly,

$$\mathbf{Z}'\mathbf{y}_z = \left[\mathbf{X}_d \mathbf{D}_s^{-1}\right]' \left[\mathbf{y}_d (s_y^{-1})\right] = \left[\mathbf{D}_s^{-1} \mathbf{X}_d' \mathbf{y}_d\right] s_y^{-1}$$

where s_y^{-1} is a scalar equal to the inverse of the standard deviation of y.

We will show how the standardized regression coefficients can be obtained directly from the unstandardized regression coefficients. Substituting from above, we find

$$\begin{aligned}
\hat{\beta}_z &= (\mathbf{Z}'\mathbf{Z})^{-1} \mathbf{Z}'\mathbf{y}_z \\
&= \frac{1}{s_y} [\mathbf{D}_s^{-1} (\mathbf{X}_d' \mathbf{X}_d) \mathbf{D}_s^{-1}]^{-1} [\mathbf{D}_s^{-1} \mathbf{X}_d' \mathbf{y}_d] \\
&= \frac{1}{s_y} \mathbf{D}_s (\mathbf{X}_d' \mathbf{X}_d)^{-1} \mathbf{D}_s \mathbf{D}_s^{-1} \mathbf{X}_d' \mathbf{y}_d \\
&= \frac{1}{s_y} \mathbf{D}_s (\mathbf{X}_d' \mathbf{X}_d)^{-1} \mathbf{X}_d' \mathbf{y}_d = \frac{1}{s_y} \mathbf{D}_s \hat{\beta}_*
\end{aligned}$$

where $\hat{\beta}_*$ is the vector of unstandardized regression coefficients. In the above matrix manipulations, we used the following matrix properties: $[\mathbf{A\ B\ C}]' = \mathbf{C}'\ \mathbf{B}'\ \mathbf{A}'$; and $[\mathbf{A\ B\ C}]^{-1} = \mathbf{C}^{-1}\ \mathbf{B}^{-1}\ \mathbf{A}^{-1}$ if **A**, **B**, and **C** are nonsingular matrices.

Let us now solve for $\hat{\boldsymbol{\beta}}_z$. First, we must compute the standard deviations for x_1, x_2, and y:

$$s_{x_1} = \sqrt{\frac{\sum_{i=1}^{15} (x_{1i} - \bar{x}_1)^2}{15}} = 2.4404$$

$$s_{x_2} = \sqrt{\frac{\sum_{i=1}^{15} (x_{2i} - \bar{x}_2)^2}{15}} = 2.0548$$

$$s_y = \sqrt{\frac{\sum_{i=1}^{15} (y_i - \bar{y})^2}{15}} = 1.0110$$

Then,

$$\hat{\boldsymbol{\beta}}_z = \frac{1}{s_y} \mathbf{D}_s \hat{\boldsymbol{\beta}}_* = \frac{1}{1.0110} \begin{bmatrix} 2.4404 & 0 \\ 0 & 2.0548 \end{bmatrix} \begin{bmatrix} .286191 \\ -.004195 \end{bmatrix}$$

$$= \begin{bmatrix} .6907 \\ -.0087 \end{bmatrix}$$

We can also transform $\boldsymbol{\beta}_z$ to $\boldsymbol{\beta}_*$ by the inverse transformation. That is, we can multiply both sides of $\hat{\boldsymbol{\beta}}_z = \left(\frac{1}{s_y} \mathbf{D}_s\right)^{-1}$.

This gives

$$\left(\frac{1}{s_y} \mathbf{D}_s\right)^{-1} \hat{\boldsymbol{\beta}}_z = \hat{\boldsymbol{\beta}}_* \text{ or } \hat{\boldsymbol{\beta}}_* = s_y \mathbf{D}_s^{-1} \boldsymbol{\beta}_z.$$

For example,

$$\hat{\boldsymbol{\beta}}_* = 1.0110 \begin{bmatrix} \frac{1.0000}{2.4404} & 0 \\ 0 & \frac{1.0000}{2.0548} \end{bmatrix} \begin{bmatrix} .6907 \\ -.0087 \end{bmatrix} = \begin{bmatrix} .2862 \\ -.0042 \end{bmatrix}$$

The above discussion shows us that an unstandardized regression coefficient can be transformed into a standardized one by multiplying the unstandardized coefficient by s_x/s_y, where s_x is the standard deviation of the independent variable associated with the regression coefficient. Conversely, a standardized regression coefficient can be transformed into an unstandardized coefficient by the inverse of s_x/s_y or s_y/s_x.

The regression equation for standardized variables is

$$y_z = .6907z_1 - .0086z_2$$

These standardized regression weights tell us that a change in one standard deviation unit of x_1 results in a change of .69 standard deviation units in the dependent variable, and that changes in x_2 produce virtually no changes in the dependent variable.

The matrix **Z′Z** can be converted into a correlation matrix by multiplying all of the elements in **Z′Z** by the scalar 1/n or, in the present case, 1/15. Thus

$$\frac{1}{n}[\mathbf{Z'Z}] = \mathbf{R}_x = \begin{bmatrix} 1.00 & .74 \\ .74 & 1.00 \end{bmatrix}$$

This matrix is useful in that it indicates the degree of relationship among the independent variables. The size of an element of a covariance matrix is a function of the measurement scale of the particular variables it involves and reflects little about the degree of relationship, except that the sign of the covariance will indicate the direction of the correlation (that is, positive or negative). The raw score **X′X** matrix tells us absolutely nothing about the relationships among the independent variables. The matrix **R** indicates that the two variables are highly related in that they correlate .74.

Likewise, the $\mathbf{Z'y}_z$ matrix can be converted to a correlation matrix by multiplying the elements of this vector by 1/15;

$$\frac{1}{15}(\mathbf{Z'y}_z) = \begin{bmatrix} .68 \\ .50 \end{bmatrix} = \mathbf{r}_{x,y}$$

Many times the correlation matrix among the independent and dependent variables is available. The standardized regression weights can be computed from the intercorrelation matrix for the independent variables and the vector of correlations between the independent variables and the dependent variables, since

$$\mathbf{R}_x^{-1}\mathbf{r}_{x,y} = \left[\frac{1}{n}\mathbf{Z'Z}\right]^{-1}\left[\frac{1}{n}\mathbf{Z'y}_z\right] = [\mathbf{Z'Z}]^{-1}\mathbf{Z'y}_z = \hat{\beta}_z$$

We have discussed three ways in which to estimate multiple regression weights. First, we can operate on raw-score cross-product matrices and obtain the raw-score regression weights. Second, we can operate on deviation-score cross-product (or covariance) matrices and obtain deviation-score regression weights. (The only difference between the first and second regression model is that the first model contains an intercept parameter—the remaining regression parameters are identical.) Third, we can operate on standardized-score cross-product (or correlation) matrices to obtain standardized regression coefficients. We have also shown how the different types of regression coefficients can be transformed from one to the other.

Most of the discussion concerned the multiple regression model with two independent variables, but the above results are generalizable to any number of independent variables provided that the rank of **X** is equal to the number of parameters to be estimated. Let us now turn to some of the properties of our least-squares estimate of the regression vector $\boldsymbol{\beta}$.

4.7 PROPERTIES OF $\hat{\boldsymbol{\beta}}$

In order to make inferences about the population vector of parameters $\boldsymbol{\beta}$, we need to determine the characteristics of the sampling distribution of $\hat{\boldsymbol{\beta}}$. That is, we need to determine its mean, variance, and the form of the density function (for example, normal). The mean of the sampling distribution of $\hat{\boldsymbol{\beta}}$ is the expectation of $\hat{\boldsymbol{\beta}}$, that is, $E(\hat{\boldsymbol{\beta}})$. Remember, the expectation of a random variable is its average over an infinite number of random drawings or replications. It is also sometimes helpful to consider expectation as the average population value. Before finding

$$E(\hat{\beta}) = E\begin{bmatrix} \hat{\beta}_o \\ \hat{\beta}_1 \\ \cdot \\ \cdot \\ \cdot \\ \beta_p \end{bmatrix}$$

where $\hat{\boldsymbol{\beta}}$ is our previously discussed least-squares estimator, we first have to convert our estimator $\hat{\boldsymbol{\beta}}$ into a function of both $\boldsymbol{\beta}$ and $\boldsymbol{\epsilon}$, where $\boldsymbol{\beta}$ is the regression coefficient vector for the population and $\boldsymbol{\epsilon}$ is the random vector of residuals from the population model. That is, we convert the estimator into a function of the parameters we are interested in estimating and a random component reflecting sampling variation. Thus

$$\hat{\beta} = [X'X]^{-1}X'y = [X'X]^{-1}X'[X\beta + \epsilon] = \beta + [X'X]^{-1}X'\epsilon$$

since

$$[X'X]^{-1}X'X = I$$

Taking expectations, we find

$$E(\hat{\beta}) = E[\beta + [X'X]^{-1}X'\epsilon] = \beta + [X'X]^{-1}X'E(\epsilon)$$

since the expectation of a constant (that is, $\boldsymbol{\beta}$) is that constant and the expectation of a fixed matrix postmultiplied by a random vector is the fixed matrix postmultiplied by the expectation of the random vector. That is, $E(\mathbf{Ax}) = \mathbf{A}E(\mathbf{x})$, where $\mathbf{A}$ is fixed and $\mathbf{x}$ is a random vector. In this instance, $\mathbf{A} = [\mathbf{X'X}]^{-1}\mathbf{X'}$.[7] The last step is to use the assumption that $E(\epsilon) = \mathbf{0}$, and we find that

$$E(\hat{\boldsymbol{\beta}}) = \boldsymbol{\beta}, \text{ since } [\mathbf{X'X}]^{-1}\mathbf{X'}E(\epsilon) = \mathbf{0}$$

We can see that our least-squares estimator $\hat{\boldsymbol{\beta}}$ is an unbiased estimator of $\boldsymbol{\beta}$ regardless of the sample size use to estimate $\boldsymbol{\beta}$. It should be pointed out that the unbiasedness of $\hat{\boldsymbol{\beta}}$ was demonstrated by using the assumption that the design matrix $\mathbf{X}$ is a fixed set of numbers and the only random variables are $\boldsymbol{\epsilon}$ or $\mathbf{y}$ since $\mathbf{y}$ is a constant (that is, $\mathbf{X}\boldsymbol{\beta}$) plus the random vector $\boldsymbol{\epsilon}$. It can be shown that $\hat{\boldsymbol{\beta}} = (\mathbf{X'X})^{-1}\mathbf{X'y}$ is a best linear unbiased estimator (BLUE). A BLUE estimator is the estimator with the smallest variance of any estimator in the class of linear unbiased estimators. If $\mathbf{X}$ is also assumed to be stochastic (that is, to vary randomly from one replication to another), then if $\mathbf{X}$ is assumed to be statistically independent of $\boldsymbol{\epsilon}$ it can be shown that $\hat{\boldsymbol{\beta}}$ is a consistent estimator or $\boldsymbol{\beta}$, meaning that as the sample size increases, the probability of $\hat{\boldsymbol{\beta}}$ falling close to $\boldsymbol{\beta}$ increases.

Let us now examine the covariance matrix of $\hat{\boldsymbol{\beta}}$. The covariance matrix of $\hat{\boldsymbol{\beta}}$ can be expressed as

$$E[\hat{\beta} - E(\hat{\beta})]\ [\hat{\beta} - E(\hat{\beta})]'$$

which is

$$E[\hat{\beta} - \beta]\ [\hat{\beta} - \beta]'$$

since we have just proved that $E(\hat{\boldsymbol{\beta}}) = \boldsymbol{\beta}$. The elements of this matrix are simply the variances and covariances of the regression parameters since

$$E[\hat{\beta} - \beta]\,[\hat{\beta} - \beta]' = E\begin{bmatrix} \hat{\beta}_o - \beta_o \\ \hat{\beta}_1 - \beta_1 \\ \cdot \\ \cdot \\ \cdot \\ \hat{\beta}_n - \beta_n \end{bmatrix} [\hat{\beta}_o - \beta_o, \hat{\beta}_1 - \beta_1, \ldots, \hat{\beta}_n - \beta_n]$$

$$= E\begin{bmatrix} (\hat{\beta}_o - \beta_o)^2 & (\hat{\beta}_o - \beta_o)(\hat{\beta}_1 - \beta_1) & \cdots & (\hat{\beta}_o - \beta_1)(\hat{\beta}_n - \beta_n) \\ (\hat{\beta}_1 - \beta_1)(\hat{\beta}_o - \beta_o) & (\hat{\beta}_1 - \beta_1)^2 & \cdots & (\hat{\beta}_1 - \beta_1)(\hat{\beta}_n - \beta_n) \\ \vdots & \vdots & & \vdots \\ (\hat{\beta}_n - \beta_n)(\hat{\beta}_o - \beta_o) & (\hat{\beta}_n - \beta_n)(\hat{\beta}_1 - \beta_1) & \cdots & (\hat{\beta}_n - \beta_n)^2 \end{bmatrix}$$

$$= \begin{bmatrix} E(\hat{\beta}_o - \beta_o)^2 & E(\hat{\beta}_o - \beta_o)(\hat{\beta}_1 - \beta_1) & \cdots & E(\hat{\beta}_o - \beta_o)(\hat{\beta}_n - \beta_n) \\ E(\hat{\beta}_1 - \beta_1)(\hat{\beta}_o - \beta_o) & E(\hat{\beta}_1 - \beta_1)^2 & \cdots & E(\hat{\beta}_1 - \beta_1)(\hat{\beta}_n - \beta_n) \\ \vdots & \vdots & & \vdots \\ E(\hat{\beta}_n - \beta_n)(\hat{\beta}_o - \beta_o) & E(\hat{\beta}_n - \beta_n)(\hat{\beta}_1 - \beta_1) & \cdots & E(\hat{\beta}_n - \beta_n)^2 \end{bmatrix}$$

The diagonal values of this matrix are the variances for each of the regression parameters. The off-diagonal elements are the covariances between the parameter estimates. More attention is usually focused on the diagonal elements of this matrix since they reflect the variability of each of the elements of the regression parameter vector. The covariance elements come into play when we need to estimate the variance of a linear composite or contrast of the elements of $\boldsymbol{\beta}$ since the covariances of the components enter into the formula for the variance of a linear composite of random variables.

To find the covariance matrix of $\hat{\boldsymbol{\beta}}$, we must reexpress

$$E(\hat{\beta} - \beta)(\hat{\beta} - \beta)' = \text{cov}(\beta)$$

to a more basic form that contains the random vector ϵ, which reflects sampling variation, and functions of the design matrix **X**. These are the two basic components that will determine $\text{cov}(\hat{\boldsymbol{\beta}})$. Let us proceed to find the $\text{cov}(\hat{\boldsymbol{\beta}})$. First, we need to express $\hat{\boldsymbol{\beta}} - \boldsymbol{\beta}$ in terms of **X** and ϵ. Since

$$\hat{\beta} = \beta + [X'X]^{-1}X'\epsilon$$

as shown earlier in the derivation of $E(\beta)$, then

$$[\beta - \beta] = [X'X]^{-1} X'\epsilon$$

and, substituting, we find

$$\text{cov}(\hat{\beta}) = E[\hat{\beta} - \beta]\ [\hat{\beta} - \beta]' = E\left[[X'X]^{-1} X'\epsilon\epsilon' X [X'X]^{-1}\right]$$

since

$$[\hat{\beta} - \beta]' = [[X'X]^{-1} X'\epsilon]' = \epsilon' X [X'X]^{-1}$$

Because matrix expressions involving **X** are fixed and only ϵ is random,

$$E\left[[X'X]^{-1} X'\epsilon\epsilon' X [X'X]^{-1}\right] = [X'X]^{-1} X' E(\epsilon\epsilon') X [X'X]^{-1}$$

The matrix $E(\epsilon\epsilon')$ is the covariance matrix of the residual errors, that is,

$$E(\epsilon\epsilon') = \begin{bmatrix} E(\epsilon_1)^2 & E(\epsilon_1\epsilon_2) & \cdots & E(\epsilon_1\epsilon_n) \\ E(\epsilon_2\epsilon_1) & E(\epsilon_2)^2 & \cdots & E(\epsilon_2\epsilon_n) \\ \vdots & \vdots & & \vdots \\ E(\epsilon_n\epsilon_1) & E(\epsilon_n\epsilon_2) & \cdots & E(\epsilon_n)^2 \end{bmatrix}$$

and since by assumption the errors have constant variances and are uncorrelated,

$$E(\epsilon\epsilon') = \sigma^2 \mathbf{I}$$

where σ^2 is the common residual variance and **I** is an identity matrix of order n. Therefore,

$$\begin{aligned} [X'X]^{-1} X' E(\epsilon\epsilon') X [X'X]^{-1} &= [X'X]^{-1} X' [\sigma^2 I]\, X [X'X]^{-1} \\ &= \sigma^2 [X'X]^{-1} X' I X [X'X]^{-1} \\ &= \sigma^2 [X'X]^{-1} \end{aligned}$$

since $X'IX = X'X$ and $[X'X]^{-1}[X'X] = \mathbf{I}$

Thus

$$\text{cov}(\hat{\beta}) = E(\hat{\beta} - \beta)(\hat{\beta} - \beta)' = \sigma^2 [X'X]^{-1}$$

and we can see that the standard error of a regression coefficient is a function of the common residual variation, σ^2, and the elements of the matrix $[\mathbf{X'X}]^{-1}$.

Other things being equal, a larger residual variance results in larger standard errors for the regression parameters. The characteristics of $[\mathbf{X'X}]^{-1}$ are also important. If the diagonal elements are large, then the standard errors will be large. It can be shown that, if the rows of $\mathbf{X}'$ are highly correlated (or one or more rows are essentially a linear combination of the remaining rows), then the diagonal elements of $[\mathbf{X'X}]^{-1}$ will be large. This is called the problem of multicolinearity because it signifies that the vectors of regressor variables are moving in the same direction since they are highly correlated; hence not enough unique variation exists for some of the independent variables so that their regression parameters can be estimated accurately. If some rows of $\mathbf{X}'$ can "almost" be expressed as linear combinations of other rows, then $\mathbf{X'X}$ will be close to being singular and the value of the determinant will be small. (Remember, a singular matrix is a square matrix, such as $\mathbf{X'X}$, the rank of which is less than its order. The determinant of a singular matrix is zero.) Since the cofactor expansion method of solving for the inverse, as we shall see, results in the denominator of each element of the inverse being the determinant of the matrix, small values of $|\mathbf{X'X}|$ result in large values for the elements of $[\mathbf{X'X}]^{-1}$. In the extreme case where any one row of $\mathbf{X}'$ can be expressed exactly as a linear combination of the other rows of $\mathbf{X}'$, then $|\mathbf{X'X}|$ is zero, $[\mathbf{X'X}]^{-1}$ does not exist, and there is no unique solution for $\hat{\boldsymbol{\beta}}$.

A geometrical interpretation of multicolinearity can begin by examining Figure 4.4, where a deviation score model with two independent variables is represented.

The regression model can be expressed in terms of vectors as

$$y = \hat{\beta}_1 x_1 + \hat{\beta}_2 x_2 + e$$

since

$$\mathbf{X}\hat{\beta} = \begin{bmatrix} x_{11} & x_{21} \\ x_{12} & x_{22} \\ \cdot & \cdot \\ \cdot & \cdot \\ \cdot & \cdot \\ x_{1n} & x_{2n} \end{bmatrix} \begin{bmatrix} \hat{\beta}_1 \\ \hat{\beta}_2 \end{bmatrix} = \begin{bmatrix} \hat{\beta}_1 x_{11} + \hat{\beta}_2 x_{21} \\ \hat{\beta}_1 x_{12} + \hat{\beta}_2 x_{22} \\ \cdot \quad\quad \cdot \\ \cdot \quad\quad \cdot \\ \cdot \quad\quad \cdot \\ \hat{\beta}_1 x_{1n} + \hat{\beta}_2 x_{2n} \end{bmatrix} = \hat{\beta}_1 \mathbf{x}_1 + \hat{\beta}_2 \mathbf{x}_2$$

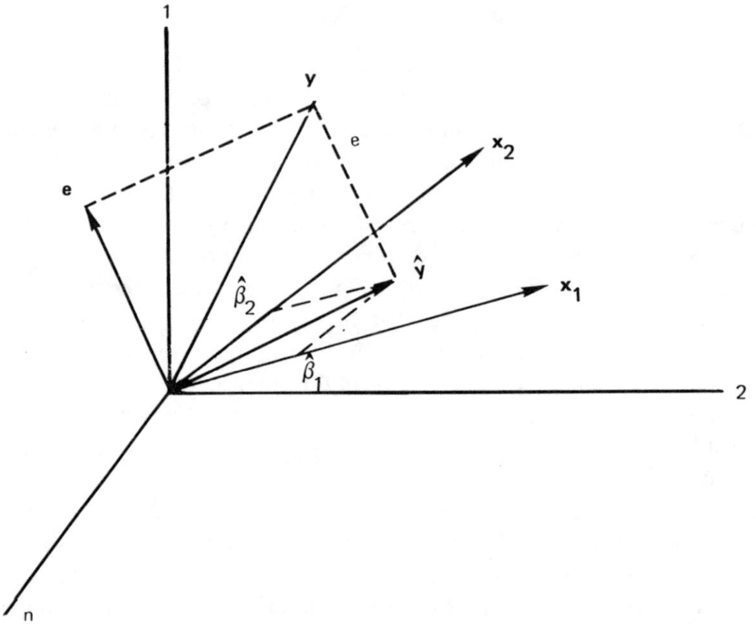

Figure 4.4 Geometrical Model of Multiple Regression

Geometrically, least squares finds the vector $\hat{\boldsymbol{\beta}}$ that will minimize the length of vector **e** given the data vectors $\mathbf{x}_1$, $\mathbf{x}_2$, and **y**. The length of the vector **e** is $[\mathbf{e}'\mathbf{e}]^{1/2}$ or, in scalar algebra, $\sqrt{\Sigma e_i^2}$. The vectors $\mathbf{x}_1$, $\mathbf{x}_2$, and **y** are n-dimensional vectors in n (that is, number of sample observations) space where, of course, in Figure 4.4 only three of the n coordinate vectors can be portrayed. For the vector of n observations on the dependent variable represented by **y**, **e** is the shortest length vector from **y** perpendicular to the plane in which $\mathbf{x}_1$ and $\mathbf{x}_2$ lie. (The residual vector **e** is perpendicular to this plane because least squares results in a residual vector that is orthogonal or uncorrelated with each of the independent variables and hence is orthogonal to the plane in which they lie.) Since $\hat{\mathbf{y}} = \hat{\beta}_1\mathbf{x}_1 + \hat{\beta}_2\mathbf{x}_2$, $\hat{\mathbf{y}}$ must be a vector in the plane defined by $\mathbf{x}_1$ and $\mathbf{x}_2$. That is, the vector $\hat{\mathbf{y}}$ is a linear combination of the vectors $\mathbf{x}_1$ and $\mathbf{x}_2$, and $\hat{\beta}_1$ and $\hat{\beta}_2$ are the coordinates of the projection of $\hat{\mathbf{y}}$ on $\mathbf{x}_1$ and $\mathbf{x}_2$, respectively. Also, $\hat{\mathbf{y}}$ is the perpendicular projection of **y** on the plane defined by $\mathbf{x}_1$ and $\mathbf{x}_2$. The projection is perpendicular since it must minimize the distance between **y** and the plane defined by $\mathbf{x}_1$ and $\mathbf{x}_2$. This minimal distance is the length (or norm) of the vector **e** (that is, $[\mathbf{e}'\mathbf{e}]^{1/2}$). Our main interest lies in the projections $\hat{\beta}_1$ and $\hat{\beta}_2$ and how these projections are affected by multicolinearity.

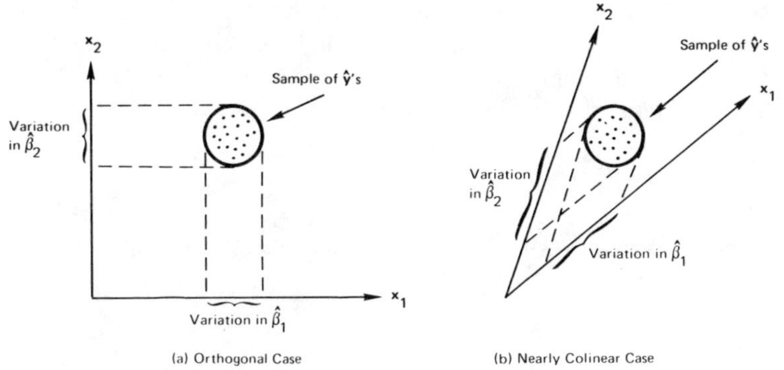

Figure 4.5 Geometrical Illustration of Sampling Variability of the Vector β for Orthogonal and Nearly Colinear Independent Variables

Upon repeated sampling of the vector **y**, the **y**'s will concentrate in a spherical pattern in n space since each element of the vector is an independent observation. The perpendicular projection of this spherical pattern on the plane defined by $\mathbf{x}_1$ and $\mathbf{x}_2$ will be a circle. This circular projection reflects the variation in $\hat{\mathbf{y}}$ and can be projected onto the vectors $\mathbf{x}_1$ and $\mathbf{x}_2$ to represent the sampling variation in $\hat{\beta}_1$ and $\hat{\beta}_2$, respectively. Figure 4.5 shows the range of the projections ($\hat{\beta}_1$ and $\hat{\beta}_2$) in the case in which the two vectors $\mathbf{x}_1$ and $\mathbf{x}_2$ are orthogonal and in the case in which they are nearly colinear or where one vector is nearly a scalar multiple of another.

It can easily be seen by comparing a and b of Figure 4.5 that the same amount of sampling dispersion of $\hat{\mathbf{y}}$ results in considerably more variation in the parameters $\hat{\beta}_1$ and $\hat{\beta}_2$ in the nearly colinear case.

The matrix $E[(\hat{\beta} - \beta)(\hat{\beta} - \beta)]'$, like $E[\beta]$, was derived under the assumption that **X** is a matrix of fixed numbers. If **X** is a stochastic matrix, then under certain assumptions it can be shown that $\sigma^2[\mathbf{X}'\mathbf{X}]^{-1}$ is a consistent estimator of $\text{cov}[\hat{\beta}]$ in that as the sample size increases each element of the matrix converges to the proper value of the variance (or covariance) for the estimator.

4.8 ESTIMATION OF σ^2 AND $\sigma^2(\mathbf{X}'\mathbf{X})^{-1}$

In the most practical situations, σ^2 is unknown and has to be estimated from sample data. It can be shown that s^2 is an unbiased estimator of σ^2 where

$$s^2 = \frac{e'e}{n-k}$$

e is the sample vector of least square residuals, n is the sample size, and k is the number of estimated regression parameters in the model.[8] For two independent variables, k equals 3 since $\hat{\beta}_o$, $\hat{\beta}_1$ and $\hat{\beta}_2$ must be estimated. Since $(\mathbf{X'X})^{-1}$ is fixed in repeated samples, an unbiased estimator of $\sigma^2(\mathbf{X'X})^{-1}$ is $s^2(\mathbf{X'X})^{-1}$.

The calculation of **e'e** is simple, since

$$\begin{aligned} e'e &= (y - X\hat{\beta})'(y - X\hat{\beta}) \\ &= (y' - \hat{\beta}'X')(y - X\hat{\beta}) = y'y - y'X\hat{\beta} - \hat{\beta}'X'y + \hat{\beta}'X'X\hat{\beta} \\ &= y'y - 2\hat{\beta}'X'y + \hat{\beta}'X'X\hat{\beta} \end{aligned}$$

since both $\mathbf{y'X}\hat{\beta}$ and $\hat{\beta}'\mathbf{X'y}$ are scalars or matrices with a single element, $\hat{\beta}'\mathbf{X'y}$ is the transpose of $\mathbf{y'X}\hat{\beta}$, and hence the single elements of each matrix must be equal to each other.

Furthermore,

$$\hat{\beta}'X'X\hat{\beta} = \hat{\beta}'X'X[X'X]^{-1}X'y = \hat{\beta}X'y$$

since $[\mathbf{X'X}]^{-1}\mathbf{X'y}$ can be substituted for $\hat{\beta}$ and $[\mathbf{X'X}][\mathbf{X'X}]^{-1} = \mathbf{1}$.

Substituting $\hat{\beta}'\mathbf{X'y}$ for $\hat{\beta}'\mathbf{X'X}\hat{\beta}$ in the last expression above for **e'e**, we find

$$e'e = y'y - \hat{\beta}'X'y$$

Using this last expression, let us calculate s^2, and finally the estimated covariance matrix of $\hat{\beta}$ from our hypothetical example. Substituting into the above formula, we find

$$e'e = [2\ 1\ \ldots\ 4]\begin{bmatrix} 2 \\ 1 \\ \cdot \\ \cdot \\ \cdot \\ 4 \end{bmatrix} = [1.35348\ \ .28619\ \ -.00419]\begin{bmatrix} 40 \\ 212 \\ 229 \end{bmatrix} = 8.15$$

Since $n - k = 12$,

$$s^2 = \frac{e'e}{n-k} = \frac{8.15}{12} = .6792,$$

and the estimated covariance matrix of $\hat{\beta}$ is

$$s^2[X'X]^{-1} = .6792 \begin{bmatrix} .515800 & .000521 & -.084668 \\ .000521 & .024749 & -.021753 \\ -.084668 & -.021753 & .034909 \end{bmatrix}$$

$$= \begin{matrix} \\ \hat{\beta}_o \\ \hat{\beta}_1 \\ \hat{\beta}_2 \end{matrix} \begin{matrix} \hat{\beta}_o \quad\quad\quad \hat{\beta}_1 \quad\quad\quad \hat{\beta}_2 \\ \begin{bmatrix} .350331 & .000354 & -.057507 \\ .000354 & .016810 & -.014775 \\ -.057507 & -.014775 & .023710 \end{bmatrix} \end{matrix}$$

The diagonal elements of this matrix are the estimated sampling variances of $\hat{\beta}_o$, $\hat{\beta}_1$, and $\hat{\beta}_2$, respectively. The off-diagonals are the covariances between the various parameter estimates. For example, the covariance between $\hat{\beta}_o$ and $\hat{\beta}_1$ is virtually zero, and the covariance between $\hat{\beta}_0$ and $\hat{\beta}_2$ is –.057507. The main interest lies in the sampling variances of β_1 and β_2, as they will be used to test statistical hypotheses concerning β_1 and β_2. The parameter β_o is of little interest since it simply reflects the level of the regression plane, but tells us nothing about relationships. Before turning to hypothesis testing and other problems of inference, let us examine how a multiple regression model partitions the total sum of squares.

4.9 PARTITIONING THE TOTAL SUM OF SQUARES IN THE MULTIPLE REGRESSION MODEL

We saw that the error sum of squares could be expressed as

$$\mathbf{e'e} = \mathbf{y'y} - \hat{\boldsymbol{\beta}}'\mathbf{X'y}$$

It follows then that the total sum of squares can be expressed as

$$\mathbf{y'y} = \hat{\boldsymbol{\beta}}'\mathbf{X'y} + \mathbf{e'e}$$

where $\hat{\boldsymbol{\beta}}'\mathbf{X'y}$ is the sum of squares due to regression. As an exercise, the reader can directly demonstrate this partition of the total sum of squares by using the fact that $\mathbf{y} = \mathbf{X}\hat{\boldsymbol{\beta}} + \mathbf{e}$ and substituting this into $\mathbf{y'y}$. This formulation is in terms of raw scores; thus the model is explaining the sum of squares of y about the origin. We are more interested in explaining the sum of squares of y about the mean of $\bar{y}$ or, equivalently, the variance of y. The explained variation in y is a function of $\hat{\beta}_1$ and $\hat{\beta}_2$ rather than $\hat{\beta}_0$ since $\hat{\beta}_0$ is the y intercept of the regression plane and does not reflect the slopes of the regression plane as do $\hat{\beta}_1$ and $\hat{\beta}_2$. We can convert the above equation, which partitions the sum of squares about zero into the partition of the sums of squares of y about the mean of y, by subtracting from both sides of the equation a correction factor for the mean of the dependent variable. This correction factor is $n\bar{y}^2$. Subtracting $n\bar{y}^2$ from both sides of $\mathbf{y'y} = \hat{\boldsymbol{\beta}}'\mathbf{X'y} + \mathbf{e'e}$, we have $\mathbf{y'y} - n\bar{y}^2 = (\hat{\boldsymbol{\beta}}'\mathbf{X'y} - n\bar{y}^2) + \mathbf{e'e}$ where now the sum of squares of y about the mean, $\mathbf{y'y} - n\bar{y}^2$, can be partitioned into a sum of squares about the mean due to regression $(\hat{\boldsymbol{\beta}}'\mathbf{X'y} - n\bar{y}^2)$ and a sum of squares due to error $(\mathbf{e'e})$. Notice that $\mathbf{e'e}$ is the same in both models; only the regression sum of squares is adjusted. Thus, if we use the raw score intercept model, then we must correct both $\mathbf{y'y}$ and $\hat{\boldsymbol{\beta}}'\mathbf{X'y}$ if we want the partition to reflect the sum of squares about the mean.

If we had used deviation scores in our regression model, then our model would be directly explaining the variation of y about the mean and no correction would be needed since

$$y_d'y_d = \hat{\beta}_*'X_d'y_d + e'e$$

and this is equivalent to $\mathbf{y'y} - n\bar{y}^2 = (\hat{\boldsymbol{\beta}}'\mathbf{X'y} - n\bar{y}^2) + \mathbf{e'e}$.

4.10 MULTIPLE CORRELATION

The relationship between a set of independent variables and a dependent variable can be summarized by a multiple correlation coefficient in the same way the relationship between one independent and one dependent variable can be summarized by a correlation coefficient. In both instances the correlation is the square root of the proportion of variation in y explained by the independent variable(s). The amount of variation explained by regression is $\hat{\boldsymbol{\beta}}_*'\mathbf{X}_d\mathbf{y}_d$ so that the proportion of the total variation explained by the regression model is

$$\frac{\hat{\beta}_*'X_d'y_d}{y_d'y_d} = R^2$$

and the multiple correlation (R) is

$$\sqrt{\frac{\hat{\beta}_*'X_d'y_d}{y_d'y_d}} \quad \text{or} \quad \sqrt{\frac{\hat{\beta}'X'y - n\bar{y}^2}{y'y - n\bar{y}^2}}.$$

The multiple correlation can also be interpreted as the correlation between y and

$$\hat{y} = \hat{\beta}_0 + \hat{\beta}_1 x_1 + \hat{\beta}_2 x_2$$

just as the correlation between y and x in the bivariate case is equal to the correlation between y and

$$\hat{y} = \hat{\beta}_0 + \hat{\beta}_1 x$$

since $\hat{y}$ is a linear transformation of x and the correlation between two variables is not altered by a linear transformation of either or both variables.

We can also show that the proper R^2 results from using the regression sum of squares and total sum of squares resulting from a multiple regression analysis with standardized variables. Using standardized variables, the sum of squares can be partitioned as

$$\mathbf{y}_z'\mathbf{y}_z = \hat{\boldsymbol{\beta}}_z \mathbf{Z}'\mathbf{y}_z + \mathbf{e}_z'\mathbf{e}_z$$

The subscript z has been added to **e** to remind the reader that $\mathbf{e}_z'\mathbf{e}_z$ will be different than the $\mathbf{e}'\mathbf{e}$ of the previous two regression models. This is because all of the variables have been rescaled to have variances of unity and this will affect the magnitudes of the residuals. However, we can show that

$$R^2 = \frac{\boldsymbol{\beta}_z'\mathbf{Z}'\mathbf{y}_z}{\mathbf{y}_z'\mathbf{y}_z}$$

by substituting some identities discussed earlier. Since

$$\mathbf{y}_z'\mathbf{y}_z = \sum_{i=1}^{n} \frac{(y_i - \bar{y})^2}{s_y^2} = \frac{ns_y^2}{s_y^2} = n$$

R^2 can be reexpressed as $\dfrac{\hat{\boldsymbol{\beta}}_z'\mathbf{Z}'\mathbf{y}_z}{n}$

We showed that

$$\hat{\boldsymbol{\beta}}_z' = \frac{1}{s_y} \hat{\boldsymbol{\beta}}_*' \mathbf{D}_s$$

where s_y is the sample standard deviation of y, $\hat{\boldsymbol{\beta}}_*' = [\hat{\beta}_1, \hat{\beta}_2]$

and

$$D_s = \begin{bmatrix} s_{x_1} & o \\ o & s_{x_2} \end{bmatrix}$$

is a diagonal matrix containing the sample standard deviations of x_1 and x_2, respectively. We also showed that

$$Z'y_z = \frac{1}{s_y} D_s^{-1} X_d' y_d$$

where $\mathbf{X}'_d$ is the k $\times$ n matrix of deviation scores for the k independent variables and $\mathbf{y}_d$ is the column vector of deviation scores for the dependent variable.

Substituting these two equalities into the R^2 based upon standardized variables, we find that

$$R^2 = \frac{\hat{\beta}_z' Z' y_z}{n} = \left[\frac{1}{s_y} \hat{\beta}_*' D_s\right]\left[\frac{1}{s_y} D_s^{-1} X_d' y_d\right] \cdot \frac{1}{n}$$

$$= \frac{1}{ns_y^2} \hat{\beta}_*' X_d' y_d = \frac{\hat{\beta}_*' X_d' y_d}{y_d' y_d}$$

since the three scalars multiply to yield

$$\frac{1}{ns_y^2}; \frac{1}{ns_y^2} = \frac{1}{y_d' y_d}; \text{ and } \mathbf{D}_s \mathbf{D}_s^{-1} = \mathbf{I}$$

Let us now compute R^2 from the sums of squares resulting from the deviation score regression analysis of our GPA multiple regression problem. We have

$$R^2 = \frac{\hat{\beta}_*' X_d' y_d}{y_d' y_d} = \frac{[.286191, -.004195] \begin{bmatrix} 25.3333 \\ 15.6666 \end{bmatrix}}{15.3333} = .4686$$

and the multiple correlation, $R = \sqrt{.4686} = .68$.

As an exercise the reader can calculate R from the data associated with the standardized multiple regression model. Let us now turn to statistical inference procedures involving multiple regression.

4.11 HYPOTHESIS TESTING OF $\hat{\beta}$

If the variance (σ^2) of the disturbance is known, then any null hypothesis regarding the value of any element of the vector $\boldsymbol{\beta}$ can be tested by appealing to the z distribution since $\hat{\beta}_i$ is normally distributed[9] with variance $\sigma^2 a^{ii}$ where a^{ii} is the ith diagonal element of $[\mathbf{X'X}]^{-1}$, corresponding to the parameter of interest, β_i. However, σ^2 is usually not known, but can be estimated as

$$\frac{e'e}{n - k}$$

and it can be shown that

$$\frac{\hat{\beta}_i - \beta_i}{\sqrt{a^{ii}} \sqrt{\dfrac{e'e}{n - k}}} = \frac{\hat{\beta}_i - \beta_i}{\hat{\sigma} \sqrt{a^{ii}}}$$

is distributed as t with n – k degrees of freedom.

The appropriate number of degrees of freedom is the number available for estimating the variance, which, in the regression framework, is the number of observations (n) minus the number of regression parameters estimated (k). We saw earlier the same rationale used for testing hypotheses concerning a single population mean or the differences between two population means. The formal proof that

$$\frac{\hat{\beta}_i - \beta_i}{\hat{\sigma} \sqrt{a^{ii}}}$$

is distributed as t with n – k degrees of freedom hinges on showing that

$$\frac{e'e}{\sigma^2}$$

can be transformed into the sum of squares of n – k independent normal variates, that is

$$\frac{\sum_{i=1}^{n} e_i^2}{\sigma^2} = \sum_{i=1}^{n-k} z_i^2$$

where z_i is a standardized normal variable. This sum of squares is distributed as χ^2 with n – k degrees of freedom. Since t is a random variable that is defined as the ratio of a standardized normal variable (z) to the square root of an independently distributed χ^2 variable divided by its degrees of freedom,

$$t = \frac{\dfrac{\hat{\beta}_i - \beta_i}{\sigma\sqrt{a^{ii}}}}{\sqrt{\dfrac{e'e}{\sigma^2} \cdot \dfrac{1}{n-k}}} = \frac{\hat{\beta}_i - \beta_i}{\sqrt{a^{ii}}\sqrt{\dfrac{e'e}{n-k}}} = \frac{\hat{\beta}_i - \beta_i}{\hat{\sigma}\sqrt{a^{ii}}}$$

For our hypothetical example, let us test the hypothesis that $\beta_1 = 0$. Referring to our covariance matrix of $\hat{\beta}$ we saw that the diagonal element corresponding to $\hat{\beta}_1$ is .016810 and hence $\sigma\sqrt{a^{ii}}$ or the estimated standard error of $\hat{\beta}_1$ is $\sqrt{.016810} = .1297$. Therefore,

$$t = \frac{\hat{\beta}_1 - \beta_1}{.1297} = \frac{.2862 - 0}{.1297} = 2.21$$

which, with n – k or 12 degrees of freedom is significant at the .05 level. This indicates that a t value more extreme than 2.21 is unlikely to occur under the null hypothesis that $\beta_1 = 0$ and therefore the null hypothesis that $\beta_1 = 0$ is rejected at the .05 level. The reader can verify that the t value associated with the null hypothesis that $\beta_2 = 0$ is not significant at the .05 level and hence the null hypothesis that $\beta_2 = 0$ is accepted at the .05 level. Confidence intervals for both β_1 and β_2 can be constructed easily for any given confidence level. For example, the 95 percent confidence interval for β_1 is

$$\beta_1 \pm t_{(.025,12)}\sqrt{a^{ii}}\hat{\sigma} = .2862 \pm (2.179)(.1297)$$

or

$$.004 \leqslant \beta_1 \geqslant .567$$

and we see that zero is not covered by the confidence interval. The reader can verify that the 95 percent confidence interval for β_2 covers zero as would be expected.

Many times the researcher is interested in a joint test of several or all of the β_i's. In the present example, we might want to test the joint hypothesis that

$$\beta_* = \begin{bmatrix} \beta_1 \\ \beta_2 \end{bmatrix} = 0$$

or that the independent variables as a set do not explain any variation in the dependent variable.

The statistical test of the hypothesis that $\boldsymbol{\beta}_* = \boldsymbol{\beta}_H$ is based upon the F distribution, which is the ratio of two independent chi-square variates, each divided by their appropriate degrees of freedom. That is,

$$F = \frac{\dfrac{\chi_1^2}{df_1}}{\dfrac{\chi_2^2}{df_2}}$$

The distribution of the random variable F is a function of the degrees of freedom in the numerator and the degrees of freedom in the denominator. Since χ^2 is the sum of k-squared standardized normal variables, we must show that the numerator of F under the null hypothesis $\boldsymbol{\beta}_* = \boldsymbol{\beta}_H$ can be expressed as the sum of df_1-squared standardized variables. Likewise, the denominator must be shown to be independently distributed under the null hypothesis $\boldsymbol{\beta}_* = \boldsymbol{\beta}_H$ as the sum of df_2-squared standardized normal variables.

It can be shown that

$$\frac{\dfrac{(\hat{\boldsymbol{\beta}}_* - \boldsymbol{\beta}_H)' \mathbf{X}_d' \mathbf{X}_d (\hat{\boldsymbol{\beta}}_* - \boldsymbol{\beta}_H)}{k\sigma^2}}{\dfrac{e'e}{(n - k - 1)\,\sigma^2}}$$

is distributed as F with k, and n – k – 1 degrees of freedom under the null hypothesis that $\boldsymbol{\beta}_* = \boldsymbol{\beta}_H$.

As mentioned earlier, frequently the interest lies in the hypothesis that $\boldsymbol{\beta}_* = \mathbf{0}$ or that there is no relationship between the independent variables and the dependent variable. For this instance, the above F ratio simplifies as follows:

$$\frac{(n - k - 1)\,\hat{\boldsymbol{\beta}}_*' \mathbf{X}_d' \mathbf{X}_d \hat{\boldsymbol{\beta}}_*}{ke'e} = \frac{(n - k - 1)\,\hat{\boldsymbol{\beta}}_*' \mathbf{X}_d' \mathbf{y}_d}{ke'e} = \frac{\dfrac{\hat{\boldsymbol{\beta}}_*' \mathbf{X}_d' \mathbf{y}_d}{k}}{\dfrac{e'e}{n - k - 1}} =$$

This last expression indicates that the numerator of the F ratio is the sum of squares about the mean due to regression divided by its degrees of freedom while the denominator is the error sum of squares divided by its degrees of freedom.

The test of the hypothesis that $\boldsymbol{\beta}_* = \mathbf{0}$ can be summarized in an analysis of variance table in which the sources of variation and associated information

TABLE 4.3
Analysis of Variance Table for Testing $\begin{bmatrix}\beta_1\\ \beta_2\end{bmatrix} = \mathbf{0}$

Source of Variation	*Sum of Squares*	*Degrees of Freedom*	*Mean Square*	*F*
Regression	$\hat{\boldsymbol\beta}_*'\mathbf{X}_d'\mathbf{y}_d$	k	$\frac{\boldsymbol\beta_*'\mathbf{X}_d'\mathbf{y}_d}{k}$	$\frac{(n-k-1)\,\boldsymbol\beta_*'\mathbf{X}_d'\mathbf{y}_d}{k(\mathbf{e}'\mathbf{e})}$
Residual	$\mathbf{e}'\mathbf{e} = \mathbf{y}_d'\mathbf{y}_d - \hat{\boldsymbol\beta}_*'\mathbf{X}_d'\mathbf{y}_d$	n−k−1	$\frac{\mathbf{e}'\mathbf{e}}{n-k-1}$	with k and n−k−1 degrees of freedom
Total	$\mathbf{y}_d'\mathbf{y}_d$	n−1		

necessary for testing significance are presented. Table 4.3 is an analysis of variance table for testing the hypothesis that $\boldsymbol\beta_* = \mathbf{0}$. It can be generalized to any number of regression parameters.

Let us fill in Table 4.3 from the results of our deviation score regression analysis on our hypothetical data set. The results are presented in Table 4.4. The reader can verify the tabled entries by substituting into the appropriate matrix expressions. The F statistic of 5.29 can be referred to a table of the upper percentage points of the F distribution with 2 degrees of freedom for the numerator and 12 degrees of freedom for the denominator. The value of F needed to fall into the upper 5 percent of the F distribution is 3.89 and so the null hypothesis that

$$\boldsymbol\beta_* = \begin{bmatrix}\beta_1\\ \beta_2\end{bmatrix} = 0$$

can be rejected at the .05 level. A value of F this extreme would occur infrequently under the null hypothesis. It should be pointed out that this test only considers the upper tail of the F distribution since only large values of F indicate a departure from the null hypothesis.

The test of the null hypothesis $\hat{\boldsymbol\beta}_* = \mathbf{0}$ can also be formulated in terms of R^2 (the percentage of variance of the dependent variable that is accounted for jointly by the independent variables). First, we note that

$$R^2 = \frac{\hat{\boldsymbol\beta}_*'\mathbf{X}_d'\mathbf{y}_d}{\mathbf{y}_d'\mathbf{y}_d} \quad \text{and therefore} \quad \hat{\boldsymbol\beta}_*'\mathbf{X}_d'\mathbf{y}_d = \mathbf{y}_d'\mathbf{y}_d R^2;$$

$$\text{and } 1 - R^2 = \frac{\mathbf{e}'\mathbf{e}}{\mathbf{y}_d'\mathbf{y}_d} \quad \text{and therefore} \quad \mathbf{e}'\mathbf{e} = \mathbf{y}_d'\mathbf{y}_d\,(1 - R^2).$$

Substituting the above into

$$F = \frac{(n - k - 1)\,\hat{\beta}_*' X_d' y_d}{k\,(e'e)}\text{, we find that}$$

$$F = \frac{(n - k - 1)\,(y_d' y_d)\,R^2}{k\,(y_d' y_d)\,(1 - R^2)} = \frac{(n - k - 1)\,R^2}{k\,(1 - R^2)}$$

This formula is convenient in situations where only the multiple correlation is available. Previously we individually tested each regression coefficient and found that β_1 was significant while β_2 was not. The proper procedure is to test first the overall hypothesis $\boldsymbol{\beta}_* = \mathbf{0}$ and, if it is rejected at a specified significance level, then conduct tests on sets of regression coefficients. In order to be operating at the correct level of significance, the tests should be hypothesized a priori. If one searches a posteriori for significant regression parameters, then he or she is capitalizing on chance since some estimated regression parameters will be statistically significant even if the corresponding population regression parameter is zero. In the present case, individual regression coefficients would be tested, since there are only two in the model.

The general procedure for conducting statistical tests on sets of regression coefficients involves the following steps:

(1) Calculate the regression sum of squares for the full model containing all independent variables (Q_1).
(2) Calculate the regression sum of squares for the model excluding the variables that are to be tested for significance (Q_2).
(3) Take the difference, $Q_1 - Q_2$, and divide it by the difference in degrees of freedom for regression between the two models. This results in $(Q_1 - Q_2)/(k_1 - k_2)$, where k_1 is the degrees of freedom for the full model and k_2 is the degrees of freedom for the reduced model. (Q_1 is at least as large as Q_2 since the additional variables included in the model associated with Q_1 cannot reduce the amount of explained variation, but rather, in most instances, increase it.) The numerator of the F ratio is $(Q_1 - Q_2)/(k_1 - k_2)$.
(4) The denominator of the F ratio is the error sum of squares associated with the full model ($\mathbf{e'e}$) divided by its appropriate degrees of freedom $(n - k_1 - 1)$. The F ratio becomes

$$\frac{\dfrac{Q_1 - Q_2}{k_1 - k_2}}{\dfrac{e'e}{n - k_1 - 1}} \quad \text{or} \quad \frac{(n - k_1 - 1)\,(Q_1 - Q_2)}{(k_1 - k_2)\,e'e}$$

which is distributed with $k_1 - k_2$ and $n - k_1 - 1$ degrees of freedom.

As an example, let us test the hypothesis that $\beta_2 = 0$. We have $Q_1 = \hat{\beta}_* \mathbf{X}_d' \mathbf{y}_d = 7.1845$, as calculated earlier. The sum of squares, Q_2, is obtained by regressing y on variable x_1 since the set of variables (in this case 1) to be excluded under the null hypothesis is variable 2. Using deviation scores, we find that $Q_2 = \hat{\beta}_1 \mathbf{x}_{d1}' \mathbf{y}_d$ where $\hat{\beta}_1$ is a scalar equal to the regression coefficient of x_1 and $\mathbf{x}_{d1}'$ is the vector of deviation scores for variable 1. Since $\mathbf{x}_{d1}'\mathbf{x}_{d1}$ is a scalar, its inverse is

$$\frac{1}{\mathbf{x}_{d1}'\mathbf{x}_{d1}} \quad \text{and} \quad \hat{\beta}_1 = \frac{\mathbf{x}_{d1}'\mathbf{y}_d}{\mathbf{x}_{d1}'\mathbf{x}_{d1}}$$

or, in scalar algebra,

$$\frac{\sum_{i=1}^{n} (x_{1i} - \bar{x}_1)(y_i - \bar{y})}{\sum_{i=1}^{n} (x_{1i} - \bar{x})^2}$$

Therefore

$$Q_2 = \frac{(\mathbf{x}_{d1}'\mathbf{y}_d)^2}{\mathbf{x}_{d1}'\mathbf{x}_{d1}} \quad \text{or} \quad \frac{\left[\sum_{i=1}^{n} (x_{1i} - \bar{x}_1)(y_i - \bar{y})\right]^2}{\sum_{i=1}^{n} (x_{1i} - \bar{x})^2}$$

Previous calculations showed that $\mathbf{x}_{d1}'\mathbf{y}_d = 25.3333$ and $\mathbf{x}_{d1}'\mathbf{x}_{d1} = 89.3333$, so that

$$Q_2 = \frac{(25.3333)^2}{89.3333} = 7.1841$$

TABLE 4.4
Analysis of Variance of GPA Data

Source of Variation	*Sum of Squares*	*Degrees of Freedom*	*Mean Square*	*F*
Regression	7.1845	2	3.5923	5.29
Residual	8.1488	12	.6791	
Total	15.3333	14		

and

$$F = \frac{(15 - 2 - 1)(7.1845 - 7.1841)}{(2 - 1)(8.1488)} = .000589$$

which we know to be insignificant without referring to an F table. It turns out that this test is equivalent to the t test for $\beta_2 = 0$ discussed earlier since $t^2 = F$ when the numerator of F has only one degree of freedom.

This testing procedure involving a subset of regression coefficients, like the overall test, can be expressed in terms of R^2. The reader should verify that

$$\frac{(n - k_1 - 1)(R_1^2 - R_2^2)}{(k_1 - k_2)(1 - R_1^2)}$$

is equivalent to

$$\frac{(n - k_1 - 1)(Q_1 - Q_2)}{(k_1 - k_2)\,e'e}$$

and is thus distributed as F with $k_1 - k_2$ and $n - k_1 - 1$ degrees of freedom under the null hypothesis. R_1^2 is the proportion of variation that the full model explains and R_2^2 is the proportion of variation that the reduced model (variables for which the associated β_i's are hypothesized to be zero are deleted). It should be emphasized that this test if fully generalizable to any subset of coefficients of a larger model.

The hypothesis testing procedure can be conducted in raw score or deviation score form. The above discussion assumed that deviation scores were used. If raw scores are used, then both Q_1 and Q_2 are based upon intercept parameters being included in each model and are therefore regression sums of squares about the origin. But if we take the difference between the raw score Q_1 and Q_2 and divide by the difference in the number of parameters in the two models, then the numerator of the F test is the same as that derived on the basis of deviation scores.

We have centered our discussion on the two independent variable multiple regression model because of computational and conceptual conveniences, but the methods discussed in this chapter are completely generalizable to any number of continuous independent variables. The ease of this generalization is enhanced by the tools of matrix algebra.

4.12 GENERALIZATIONS OF THE CLASSICAL REGRESSION MODEL

The classsical regression model has been discussed thoroughly throughout this chapter. The model of course has to fulfill a number of assumptions and some of these assumptions might not be plausible in some practical research settings. One assumption is that the design matrix **X** is fixed. In many applied research situations the assumption that **X** is stochastic seems more realistic (for example, sample survey data where the independent as well as the dependent variables are sampled). As was discussed, most of the results from classical regression conveniently apply to the case of stochastic regressors.

Another assumption of the classical model is that sometimes violated is $E(\mathbf{ee}') = \sigma^2\mathbf{I}$. This assumption, as we saw, means that the residual or error variance for each row of **X** is constant and that the errors are independent. In some situations, the error variance may be different for the various rows of **X**. For example, achievement scores as a dependent variable may become more variable as the socioeconomic status of the child increases and hence

$$E(\mathbf{ee}') \neq \sigma^2\mathbf{I},$$

but rather

$$E(\mathbf{ee}') = \begin{bmatrix} \sigma_1^2 & & & \bigcirc \\ & \sigma_2^2 & & \\ & & \ddots & \\ \bigcirc & & & \sigma_n^2 \end{bmatrix} = \begin{bmatrix} k_1\sigma^2 & & & \bigcirc \\ & k_2\sigma^2 & & \\ & & \ddots & \\ \bigcirc & & & k_n\sigma^2 \end{bmatrix} = \sigma^2 \begin{bmatrix} k_1 & & & \bigcirc \\ & k_2 & & \\ & & \ddots & \\ \bigcirc & & & k_n \end{bmatrix} = \sigma^2\Omega$$

where σ^2 is a scale factor and Ω is a diagonal matrix. The large O's indicate that the errors are uncorrelated. This situation, known as "heteroscedasticity," is illustrated in Figure 4.6.

Another situation in which the basic assumption is sometimes violated is one in which the data are generated from a time series. Although the error variance at each time on the dependent variable may be constant, the errors between times are correlated because of a carryover effect from one time period to another. A common assumption concerning ϵ_t in these types of time-series models is that $\epsilon_t = \rho\epsilon_{t-1} + \mu_t$. That is, the error in the regression model associated with the tth time period (or t^{th} row of **X**) is a linear function of the error in the previous time period plus a concurrent error or perturbation. This is called an "autoregressive model of order 1," sometimes referred to as AR(1). The errors are subscripted t rather than i to connote an ordering in

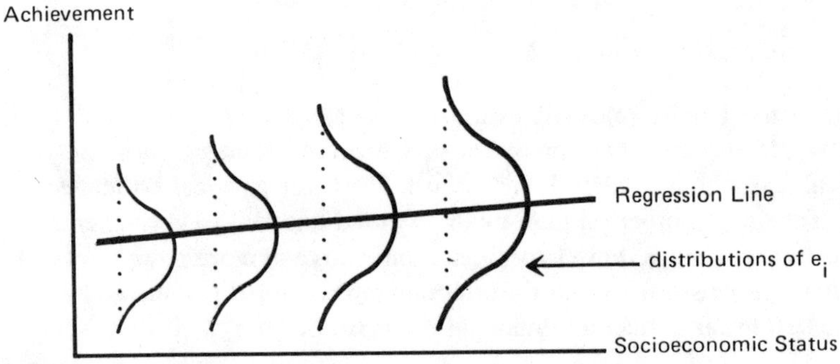

Figure 4.6 Heteroscedasticity in the Regression of Achievement on Child's Socioeconomic Status

time. Under these error assumptions, the error covariance matrix can be shown to take the form

$$\sigma^2 \begin{bmatrix} 1 & \rho & \rho^2 \ldots\ldots & \rho^{n-1} \\ \rho & 1 & \rho \ldots\ldots & \rho^{n-2} \\ \rho^2 & \rho & \cdot & \cdot \\ \cdot & \cdot & \cdot & \cdot \\ \cdot & \cdot & \cdot & \cdot \\ \cdot & \cdot & \cdot & \cdot \\ \rho^{n-1} & \rho^{n-2} & \rho^{n-3} \ldots & 1 \end{bmatrix} \text{ or } \sigma^2\Omega$$

Note that the error covariance matrix generated under the assumption of an AR(1) process has the property that the covariances among the errors become smaller as the time interval becomes longer.

Both of these error structures violate the classical assumptions, but fortunately the classical least-squares estimator $\boldsymbol{\beta} = [\mathbf{X'X}]^{-1} \mathbf{X'y}$ is still a linear unbiased estimate of $\hat{\boldsymbol{\beta}}$. Many regressions have no doubt been run with violations such as these; it is fortunate that the parameter estimates flowing from these analyses were still unbiased. The unbiasedness can be shown easily since

$$\hat{\beta} = [X'X]^{-1}X'y = [X'X]^{-1}X'[X\beta + \epsilon] = \beta + [X'X]^{-1}X'\epsilon$$

and

$$E(\hat{\beta}) = E(\beta + [X'X]^{-1}X'\epsilon) = \beta + [X'X]^{-1}X'E(\epsilon) = \beta$$

since **X** is fixed and E (ϵ) is still assumed to be **0**.

However, there are two major negative aspects associated with applying classical least squares when E ($\epsilon\epsilon'$) $\neq \sigma^2$**I**. First, the classical estimates are inefficient since another estimator can be found that will yield smaller standard errors and hence shorter confidence intervals and more power. Second, the use of the classical estimator of the standard errors of $\hat{\boldsymbol{\beta}}$ is biased.

The best linear unbiased estimate of $\boldsymbol{\beta}$ when E ($\epsilon\epsilon$) = $\sigma^2\boldsymbol{\Omega}$ is

$$\hat{\beta} = (X'\Omega^{-1}X)^{-1}X'\Omega^{-1}y$$

and its covariance matrix is

$$E[(\hat{\beta} - \beta)(\hat{\beta} - \beta)'] = \sigma^2(X'\Omega^{-1}X)^{-1}$$

The problem with this estimator is that $\boldsymbol{\Omega}$ is in most cases unknown and must itself be estimated from the sample data. In cases where an underlying model for the elements of $\boldsymbol{\Omega}$ can be postulated, then $\boldsymbol{\Omega}$ can be estimated from the data. For example, when the errors are autocorrelated, then ρ can be estimated by obtaining the classical least-squares sample residuals and correlating e_t and e_{t+1}. The estimate of $\boldsymbol{\beta}$ then becomes

$$\hat{\beta} = (X'\hat{\Omega}^{-1}X)^{-1}X'\hat{\Omega}^{-1}y$$

This approach is known as weighted least squares since $\boldsymbol{\Omega}^{-1}$ acts as a weighting matrix. For example, in the case of heteroscedastic disturbances, observations with large errors attached to them get smaller weights and hence have a smaller impact on $\hat{\boldsymbol{\beta}}$.

Another generalization of the classical model to be covered in some detail in later chapters is the use of categorical independent variables (sex, ethnicity, occupation, and the like). In this instance 0, 1 indicator or dummy variables are used to indicate whether or not an observation on the dependent variable is a member of a particular classificatory grouping. For example, if achievement is regressed upon sex, then a regression model could take the form

$$y_i = \beta_1 x_{1i} + \beta_2 x_{2i} + \epsilon_i$$

where x_{1i} equals 1 if the ith person is male, and 0 if female, and x_{2i} equals 1 if t e i^{th} person is female and 0 if male.

4.13 NONLINEAR MODELS

The models that have been discussed so far are linear. For the case of one independent variable, the equation $\hat{y} = b_0 + b_1x$ describes a line in the x, y plane. For the case of two independent variables, $\hat{y} = b_0 + b_1x_1 + b_2x_2$ describes a plane in the space defined by the x_1, x_2, and y coordinate axes. For the general case of p independent variables, $\hat{y} = b_0 + b_1x_1 + b_2x_2 + \ldots + b_px_p$ describes a hyperplane in the space defined by the $x_1, x_2, \ldots, x_p$, y coordinate axes. Of course, we can not visualize a hyperplane because it is a subspace of a space of greater than three dimensions, but its properties are analogous to those of a plane.

In many instances, these linear models are adequate. In other instances, a linear model might not fit the data very well. For example, a plot of the data might look like that shown in Figure 4.7. Certainly, as can be seen clearly in the figure, a straight line equation, $\hat{y} = b_0 + b_1x$, will not fit this data very well. We would need an equation with x^2 term to portray the nonlinear relationship between x and y. The model $\hat{y} = b_0 + b_1x + b_2x^2$ would yield better fit to the data than $\hat{y} = b_0 + b_1x$, as can be seen in Figure 4.7. We can use the technique of multiple regression to address this problem. We simply square x and treat it as a second independent variable in a multiple regression model and estimate the parameters b_0, b_1, and b_2 of the model by ordinary least squares. The coefficient b_2 associated with x^2 can be tested like any other regression coefficient. Sometimes we can tell how well a model fits the data by looking at the residuals. If we fitted $\hat{y} = b_0 + b_1x$ to the data in Figure 4.7, a plot of the residuals against x would look like the pattern portrayed in Figure 4.8.

It is apparent from Figure 4.8 that the residuals are not randomly distributed across x with about a mean of zero although the variance seems to be constant. The pattern of the residuals suggests that a nonlinear relationship exists between x and y and that an x^2 term needs to be added to the model. Therefore, let us examine the residuals from $\hat{y} = b_0 + b_1x + b_2x^2$ shown in Figure 4.9.

These residuals seem to be randomly distributed across the values of x. There are no irregularities whatsoever in the plot. The relationship between x and y could be even more complex where a higher-order polynomial such as $\hat{y} = b_0 = b_1x + b_2x^2 + b_3x^3$ might be necessary to fit the data adequately.

The same problem can occur with more than one independent variable. By examining various residual plots such as each independent variable plotted against e and the predicted value y, $\hat{y}$, plotted against e, we may find that a linear model such as $\hat{y} = b_0 + b_1x + b_2x, \ldots + b_px_p$ does not adequately fit the data. The scatter of points in the space defined by $x_1, x_i, \ldots, x_p$, y may form a complex curvilinear pattern rather than a simple linear pattern. For example, with two independent variables, we may find that a model such as $\hat{y} = b_0 + b_1x_1 + b_2x_2 + b_3x_1x_2 + b_4x_1^2 + b_5x_2^2$ might be needed to fit the swarm of points in the

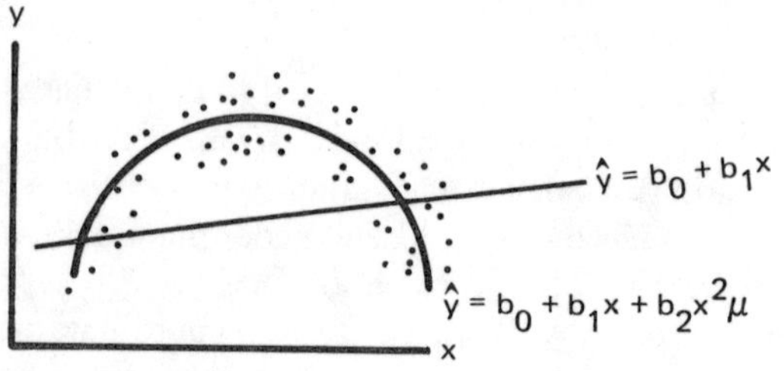

Figure 4.7 Fitting a Nonlinear Relationship

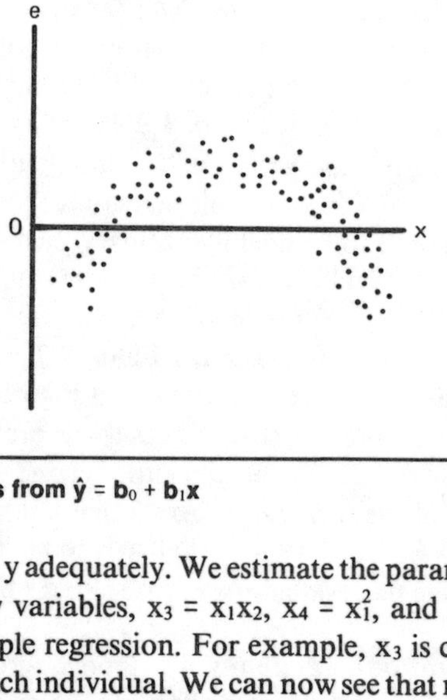

Figure 4.8 Residuals from $\hat{y} = b_0 + b_1x$

space of x_1, x_2, and y adequately. We estimate the parameters of this model by creating three new variables, $x_3 = x_1x_2$, $x_4 = x_1^2$, and $x_5 = x_2^2$, and using the technique of multiple regression. For example, x_3 is created by forming the product x_1x_2 for each individual. We can now see that multiple regression can be used to model many forms of complex relationships between the independent variable(s) and the dependent variable.

4.14 MULTIPLE REGRESSION ON A COMPUTER

We have been demonstrating the calculation of multiple regression on small data sets of a few variables and a limited number of observations. In real life, a multiple regression could involve 15 or 20 variables and hundreds or even thousands of observations. It would be impossible to analyze data sets of this magnitude by hand. We must, of necessity, turn to the computer.

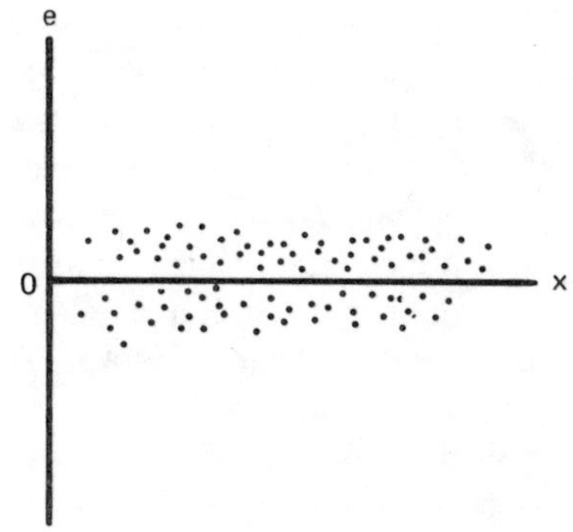

Figure 4.9 Residuals from $y = b_0 + b_1x + b_2x^2$

There are three computer software packages that are commonly used for multiple regression: SAS (Freud & Littell, 1980), SPSS (Nie et al., 1975), and BMDP (Dixon, 1975). One or more of these packages is available at most major computer installations. These three packages are quite similar in respect to the output generated for multiple regression. The output includes R^2, the degrees of freedom, sum of squares, and mean squares due to regression and error, respectively. An F value associated with the regression sum of squares tests the null hypothesis that all of the regression parameters (except the intercept) are equal to 0. The programs present each of the estimated regression parameters (including the intercept) and their associated standard errors, t-values, and significance levels.

These regression programs can also print out the residuals, compute the first-order autocorrelation if the observations are ordered in time, and test the significance of the autocorrelation. The residuals can also be plotted against any of the independent variables or the predicted value of y. The examination of the pattern of residuals on these plots can help determine if the assumptions of the model are violated. For example, we may find that the variance of the residuals is increasing as the value of one of the independent variables increases. This would indicate the presence of heteroscedasticity. The residuals can also be examined to determine how well the model fits the data as discussed earlier in regard to nonlinear models. If the residuals indicate a lack of fit then the model could be respecified by adding additional variables, changing the functional form of the model (for example, x^2 terms), or weighting the data as in the case of heterogeneity.

Extremely large residuals referred to as "outliers," may indicate problems with certain observations. For example, an extremely large residual may indicate that something went wrong in the measurement of the dependent variable for that observation or that, perhaps, a data processing error was made. In some cases, the units associated with these outliers can be deleted from the data set and the model can be reestimated. In small data sets, even one outlier can drastically effect the estimated regression parameter values.

Many data sets have a large number of potential independent variables. This is especially true in the behavioral and social sciences. A regression model with a large number of independent variables (for example, 20 or 25) is certainly not parsimonious. It may be possible to explain virtually as much variation in the dependent variable by a handful of independent variables as it was for the complete set of independent variables. There are two basic procedures that typically have been used to select a small subset of independent variables. They are called "forward" and "backward" variable selection. These two procedures can be called by any of the three packages.

Forward selection begins by taking that single independent variable that produces the largest regression sum of squares. Then each remaining variable is examined to determine how much additional regression sum of squares it will contribute. The variable that contributes the largest additional regression sum of squares is selected as the next variable to enter the regression equation providing that its additional regression sum of squares is statistically significant at a given level. This is considered the best two-variable model. A third variable is then selected from the remaining variables, which yields the largest additional regression sum of squares. If it is significant, then it is added to the previous two-variable model for the best three-variable model. This procedure continues until no variable significantly increases the regression sum of squares. Typically, this happens after about a half dozen variables have entered the model.

Backward selection procedures begin by estimating the regression parameters and associated partial regression sum of squares for the complete set of variables. It then drops the variable with the smallest partial regression sum of squares providing that it is insignificant at a given level. The model is then reestimated and the remaining variable with the smallest partial regression sum of squares is dropped if insignificant and the model is reestimated. This procedure continues until there are no statistically insignificant variables in the regression equation. Both of these procedures should be used with caution. They should not take the place of theory building and model development. Other variable selection procedures are also available in these packages. The reader is referred to the packages for more information.

We talked earlier about testing hypotheses concerning subsets of more than one regression coefficient by running two regressions (one excluding the set of variables to be tested) and subtracting the regression sums of squares and so on for testing the null hypothesis that $\beta_i = \beta_j = \beta_k = 0$. SAS provides for a test of this or other hypotheses concerning the regression parameters in a single multiple regression run. The tests are specified by the use of **K** matrices in which the hypothesis under consideration is stated as $\mathbf{K}\boldsymbol{\beta} = \mathbf{0}$. This is called the general linear hypothesis and will be discussed in greater detail in subsequent chapters. The main point is that this hypothesis can be tested directly with the statistics generated by a single regression run. That is, the partial regression sum of squares due to this hypothesis is calculated and tested for significance. For example, the hypothesis that $\beta_1 = \beta_2 = \beta_5 = 0$ in the regression model $y = \beta_0 + \beta_1 x_1 + \beta_2 x_2 + \beta_3 x_3 + \beta_4 x_4 + \beta_5 x_5 + \epsilon$ can be stated in the general linear hypothesis form as

$$\mathbf{K}\boldsymbol{\beta} = \begin{bmatrix} 0 & 1 & 0 & 0 & 0 & 0 \\ 0 & 0 & 1 & 0 & 0 & 0 \\ 0 & 0 & 0 & 0 & 0 & 1 \end{bmatrix} \begin{bmatrix} \beta_0 \\ \beta_1 \\ \beta_2 \\ \beta_3 \\ \beta_4 \\ \beta_5 \end{bmatrix} = \begin{bmatrix} \beta_1 \\ \beta_2 \\ \beta_5 \end{bmatrix} = \begin{bmatrix} 0 \\ 0 \\ 0 \end{bmatrix}$$

SAS lets us specify various **K** matrices and have the null hypothesis associated with them tested. Other software packages may require running two separate regressions to test a general linear hypothesis such as this.

4.15 EXAMPLE

Hanushek and Jackson (1977) present an interesting application of multiple regression analysis. They cite a study by Robinson (1950), who, using 1930 state-level census data, found a regression coefficient of –.29 upon regressing state illiteracy rate (I) on percentage foreign born residing in the state. The negative regression coefficient suggests that foreign-born (F) individuals are more literate than native individuals. This finding conflicts with regression analyses using the individual as the unit of analysis where positive regression weights are typically found. Also, logically one would not expect foreign-born individuals to be more literate than natives.

Hanushek and Jackson (1977) argue that there are other state-level aggregate variables contributing to state-level literacy rates besides percentage foreign born. Some of these variables are percentage of a state's population aged 7-13 enrolled in school (E), percentage black (B), percentage Mexican (M), and percentage Indian (IND). These excluded variables would be expected to be important determiners of literacy. If they are also correlated with the independent variable, percentage foreign born (F), than the regression coefficient for F will be biased. That is, according to the authors, Robinson (1950) estimated the regression coefficient for F in the model $I = \beta_0 + \beta_1 F + \epsilon_1$ when he should have been estimating the regression parameters in the model $I = \beta_0 + \beta_1 F + \beta_2 E + \beta_3 B + \beta_4 M + \beta_5 IND + \epsilon_2$. If the second model is correctly specified, then ϵ_1 of the first model is actually $\beta_2 E + \beta_3 B + \beta_4 M + \beta_5 IND + \epsilon_2$. If any of these variables are correlated with F, then, assuming the β_i's are not zero, $\epsilon_1 = \beta_2 E + \beta_3 B + \beta_4 M + \beta_5 IND + \epsilon_2$ will be correlated with F and the ordinary least-squares estimate will be biased.

Looking at it in another way, we can see that if F is correlated with E, B, M, and IND, then F takes all of the credit for predicting I in the first equation whereas some of the credit should go to the excluded variables E, B, M, and IND.

The authors estimated the regression parameters of their multiple regression model and found

$$\underset{(6.23)}{I = .86} + \underset{(2.82)}{.12F} - \underset{(6.82)}{.88E} + \underset{(2.90)}{.10B} + \underset{(.30)}{.03M} + \underset{(.80)}{.14IND}$$

The R^2 for this model was .86, which was significant at the .01 level. The t statistic associated with each estimated regression coefficient is shown within the parentheses below the estimated coefficient. Note that F, the variable of primary interest, now has a positive sign and is significant at the .01 level. This conforms with our expectations. The regression parameters associated with E and B are also significant at the .01 level while the regression parameters associated with M and IND are not significant. For the purpose of this study, the regression parameter associated with F was of most interest. The regression parameters associated with the remaining variables were of little interest. Including these other variables in the model, however, had the effect of adjusting the estimated regression parameter associated with F. It changed from –.29 when used alone in the regression model to .12 when it was adjusted for the effects of having the additional four variables in the model. If the second model is correctly specified in terms of the variables and their functional relationship to I, then .12 is an unbiased estimate of the effect of F on I and –.29 is a biased estimate.

4.16 PROBLEMS

(1) Using the sample data in the Appendix, regress variable 12 (high school grades) on variables 1 through 6 (six ability measures). Test the overall hypothesis that $\beta_1 = \beta_2 = \beta_3 = \beta_4 = \beta_5 = \beta_6 = 0$. What is the R^2 for the full model? Which variables seem to be most important? Can a reduced model

be fit that accounts for essentially as much variation in the dependent variable as the full model?

(2) Convert the regression parameter estimates obtained for the full model in problem 1 into standardized regression coefficients.

(3) Plot the estimated residuals for the full model in problem 1. Do they appear to be normally distributed? If not, what implication does this have for the fitted model?

(4) Sometimes we find that the regression of one variable on another is nonlinear. We can then add a quadratic term (i.e., x^2) or even a cubic term (i.e., x^3) to our linear model and test whether the regression coefficients associated with these terms are statistically significant. Using Vocabulary (var. 1) as a dependent variable and SES (var. 10) as an independent variable, test the hypothesis that $\beta_2 = 0$ in the following regression equation: $y = \beta_0 + \beta_1 x + \beta_2 x^2 + \epsilon$. Plot the residuals for each of the three SES scores. Do they conform to the assumptions of the linear regression model?

(5) Assume that the following data are generated by the model $y_i = \beta_0 + \beta_1 x_{i2} + \beta_2 x_{i2} + \beta_3 x_{i3} + \epsilon_i$, where ϵ_i is normally and independently distributed with $E(\epsilon_i) = 0$ and $E(\epsilon_i) = \sigma^2$ for all i.

x_1	x_2	x_3	y
15	33	100	50
15	33	112	40
18	30	111	42
20	44	112	47
20	50	103	53
22	48	92	59
24	39	94	53
26	53	88	61
32	40	98	55
31	52	92	68

(a) Compute the normal equations.
(b) Estimate $\hat{\beta}$ and $\hat{\sigma}^2$.
(c) What is the change in the estimated expected value of y if x_2 is increased 3 units, x_3 decreased by 6 units, and x_1 remains constant?
(d) Test the hypothesis that $\beta_1 = \beta_2 = \beta_3 = 0$ with $\alpha = .05$.
(e) Test the hypothesis that $\beta_1 = \beta_2 = 0$ with $\alpha = .05$.
(f) Compute R^2.
(g) Plot the estimated residuals. Do there appear to be any extreme values? If so, what does this imply about the assumptions of the model?

(6) The following correlations were taken from Kerckhoff (1974):

	x_1	x_2	x_3	x_4	x_5
x_1: child's intelligence	1.000	.277	.250	.572	.489
x_2: father's education		1.000	.611	.294	.446
x_3: father's occupation			1.000	.248	.410
x_4: child's grades				1.000	.597
x_5: child's educational expectations					1.000

N = 767

Assume that x_5 is the dependent variable; x_1, x_2, x_3, and x_4 are the independent variables; and that the regular assumptions hold.

(a) Estimate $\boldsymbol{\beta}$, σ^2, R^2, and the estimated covariance matrix of $\hat{\boldsymbol{\beta}}$.

(b) If a child's grades are increased by one half of a standard deviation, how much will the child's educational expectations, on the average, increase in standard deviation units.

(c) Test the hypothesis that $R^2 = 0$ with $\alpha = .01$.

(d) Which independent variable seems to be most important in predicting the child's educational expectations?

(e) Is there any independent variable that appears not to be an important predictor of educational expectations? If so, test its significance with $\alpha = .01$.

NOTES

1. From our discussion in Chapter 2, we can see that

$$E(\epsilon_i) = \int_{-\infty}^{\infty} \epsilon_i f(\epsilon_i) d\epsilon_i$$

2. The population covariance between two discrete variables x_1 and x_2 having n_1 and n_2 values, respectively, can be expressed as

$$\sum_{i=1}^{n_1} \sum_{j=1}^{n_2} (x_{1i} - E(x_1))(x_{2j} - E(x_2))p(x_{1i}, x_{2j})$$

where $E(x_1)$ is the expectation or population mean of x_1, $E(x_2)$ is the population mean of x_2, and $p(x_{1i}, x_{2j})$ is the probability of the two variables simultaneously taking on the values x_{1i} and x_{2j}.

For continuous variables, the analogous convariance expression is

$$\int_{-\infty}^{\infty} \int_{-\infty}^{\infty} (x_1 - E(x_1))(x_2 - E(x_2))f(x_1, x_2)dx_1 dx_2$$

where $f(x_1, x_2)dx_1dx_2$ represents loosely the probability of particular values of x_1 and x_2 occurring jointly. This is multiplied by the cross product of deviations from the mean and summed for all values of x and y, represented by the double integral sign.

Since ϵ_i is a continuous variable, the expression for the variance of ϵ_i is

$$\int_{-\infty}^{\infty} (\epsilon_i - E(\epsilon_i))^2 f(\epsilon_i)d\epsilon_i = \int_{-\infty}^{\infty} \epsilon_i^2 f(\epsilon_i)d\epsilon_i = E(\epsilon_i^2) = \sigma^2$$

since $E(\epsilon_i) = 0$ by assumption. Using the general expression for the covariance of two continuous variables, the expression for the covariance of ϵ_i and ϵ_j is

$$\int_{-\infty}^{\infty}\int_{-\infty}^{\infty} (\epsilon_i - E(\epsilon_i))(\epsilon_j - E(\epsilon_j))f(\epsilon_i, \epsilon_j)d\epsilon_i d\epsilon_j$$

or

$$\int_{-\infty}^{\infty}\int_{-\infty}^{-\infty} \epsilon_i\epsilon_j f(\epsilon_i, \epsilon_j)d\epsilon_i d\epsilon_j = E(\epsilon_i\epsilon_j)$$

since $E(\epsilon_i) = E(\epsilon_j) = 0$. In summary, expectation refers to average values over a population.

3. We saw in Chapter 3 that the probability of a specific value of a continuous random variable occurring is defined as zero.

4. Before taking the partial derivative of $\mathbf{e'e}$ with respect to $\hat{\boldsymbol{\beta}}$, it will necessary to expand $\mathbf{e'e}$ so that terms in $\hat{\boldsymbol{\beta}}$ are identifiable. We have

$$\begin{aligned} e'e &= (y - X\hat{\beta})'(y - X\hat{\beta}) = (y' - \hat{\beta}'X')(y - X\hat{\beta}) \\ &= y'y - \hat{\beta}X'y - y'X\hat{\beta} + \hat{\beta}'X'X\hat{\beta} \\ &= y'y - 2\hat{\beta}'X'y + \hat{\beta}'X'X\hat{\beta} \end{aligned}$$

since $(\mathbf{y} - \mathbf{X}\hat{\boldsymbol{\beta}})' = \mathbf{y}' - (\mathbf{X}\hat{\boldsymbol{\beta}})' = \mathbf{y}' - \hat{\boldsymbol{\beta}}'\mathbf{X}'$ (the transpose of the product of two matrices is the transpose of each matrix multiplied in reverse order); and since $\hat{\boldsymbol{\beta}}'\mathbf{X}'\mathbf{y} = \mathbf{y}'\mathbf{X}\hat{\boldsymbol{\beta}}$ (both are scalars and one is the transpose of the other).

Before differentiating, let us examine the nature of the matrix expression

$$e'e = y'y - 2\hat{\beta}'X'y + \hat{\beta}'X'X\hat{\beta}$$

Let us first draw an analogy to scalar algebra. If $\mathbf{e'e}$ is considered the dependent variable y, $\mathbf{y'y}$ a constant a, $\mathbf{X'y}$ a constant b, $\mathbf{X'X}$ a constant c, and $\hat{\boldsymbol{\beta}}$ the scalar independent variable B, then the analogous expression in terms of scalar algebra is

$$y = a - 2bB + cB^2$$

The ordinary derivative of y in scalar algebra with respect to the variable B is given as

$$\frac{dy}{dB} = -2b + 2cB$$

It can be shown that the partial derivative of **e′e** with respect to the vector $\hat{\boldsymbol{\beta}}$ is

$$\frac{\partial e'e}{\partial \hat{\beta}} = -2X'y + 2X'X\hat{\beta}$$

Note the correspondence between the scalar expression and the matrix expression when **X′y** is mapped into b and **X′X** into c.

5. We shall subsequently see that we can meaningfully compare the magnitude of regression parameters within a regression equation only if each variable has the same scale or unit of measurement. If the standard deviations of the variables are the same, then the variables have the same unit of measurement and the regression parameters can be meaningfully compared. In our example, the standard deviations are not identical, but they are close enough to allow us to say that verbal ability is more important than quantitative ability in predicting grade point average.

6. The assumption of a fixed **X** matrix is reasonable under two conditions. First, we may be interested only in making inferences to specific schools, classrooms, or organizations. For example, an educational administrator may be interested only in the relationship between school characteristics (the independent variables) and achievement for schools under his or her jurisdiction. Second, in an experimental design we may be able to assign individuals randomly to particular fixed values of the independent variable(s). For example, we may randomly assign subjects to particular levels of drug dosage in a clinical trials experiment evaluating a new drug. The field of experimental design assumes that we fix the values of **X** and then randomly assign individuals to these fixed values, called "treatment conditions," to determine their effect on the dependent variable.

7. This matrix representation of the expectation operator E is based upon the scalar expectation of ax, where a is a scalar constant and x is a univariate random variable. In this case the expectation operator functions like a summation sign and we have E(ax) = aE(x). Using this scalar result concerning expectations, we can generalize to the matrix case. Let us demonstrate by letting the fixed matrix

$$\mathbf{A} = \begin{bmatrix} a_{11} & a_{12} \\ a_{21} & a_{22} \end{bmatrix}$$

and the random vector

$$\mathbf{x} = \begin{bmatrix} x_1 \\ x_2 \end{bmatrix}$$

then

$$E(\mathbf{Ax}) = E\begin{bmatrix} a_{11} & a_{12} \\ a_{21} & a_{22} \end{bmatrix}\begin{bmatrix} x_1 \\ x_2 \end{bmatrix} = E\begin{bmatrix} a_{11}x_1 + a_{12}x_2 \\ a_{21}x_1 + a_{22}x_2 \end{bmatrix}$$

$$= \begin{bmatrix} a_{11}E(x_1) + a_{12}E(x_2) \\ a_{21}E(x_1) + a_{22}E(x_2) \end{bmatrix}$$

since the expectation of a matrix is defined as the expectations of the individual elements contained in the matrix. Continuing,

$$\begin{bmatrix} a_{11}E(x_1) + a_{12}E(x_2) \\ a_{21}E(x_1) + a_{22}E(x_2) \end{bmatrix} = \begin{bmatrix} a_{11} & a_{12} \\ a_{21} & a_{22} \end{bmatrix} \begin{bmatrix} E(x_1) \\ E(x_2) \end{bmatrix} = \mathbf{A}E(\mathbf{x})$$

and therefore, $E(\mathbf{Ax}) = \mathbf{A}E(\mathbf{x})$.

8. The proof that $E(s^2) = \sigma^2$ and that consequently $E(s^2[\mathbf{X'X}]^{-1}) = \sigma^2[\mathbf{X'X}]^{-1}$ is briefly sketched. First, it can be shown that $\mathbf{e'e}$ can be expressed as $\boldsymbol{\epsilon}'\mathbf{M}\boldsymbol{\epsilon}$ where

$$\mathbf{M} = [\mathbf{I} - \mathbf{X}[\mathbf{X'X}]^{-1}\mathbf{X'}]$$

That is, the sum of squares of sample residuals $\mathbf{e}$ can be expressed as a quadratic form of the unknown population residuals $\boldsymbol{\epsilon}$ from the population regression plane. Next, it is obvious that

$$E(\mathbf{e'e}) = E(\boldsymbol{\epsilon}'\mathbf{M}\boldsymbol{\epsilon})$$

and it can be shown that

$$E(\boldsymbol{\epsilon}'\mathbf{M}\boldsymbol{\epsilon}) = \sigma^2 \mathrm{tr}(\mathbf{M})$$

where tr denotes the trace operation on the matrix $\mathbf{M}$. Finally,

$$\mathrm{tr}(\mathbf{M}) = \mathrm{tr}(\mathbf{I} - \mathbf{X}[\mathbf{X'X}]^{-1}\mathbf{X'}) = \mathrm{tr}\mathbf{I} - \mathrm{tr}(\mathbf{X}[\mathbf{X'X}]^{-1}\mathbf{X'}) = n - k$$

so that

$$E(\mathbf{e'e}) = (n - k)\sigma^2$$

and therefore

$$\frac{E(\mathbf{e'e})}{n - k} = \sigma^2$$

so that

$$\frac{\mathbf{e'e}}{n - k}$$

is an unbiased estimator of σ^2, the unknown residual variance.

9. The $\hat{\beta}_i$'s are normally distributed since they are linear combinations of the values of the dependent variable y, which themselves are normally and independently distributed. In Chapter 2, we saw that a linear combination of normally distributed variables is itself normally distributed.

5 Linear Regression with One Categorical Independent Variable

5.1 INTRODUCTION

This chapter is concerned with using categorical independent variables rather than continuous independent variables in a linear regression framework. The dependent variable is still assumed to be continuous. Examples of categorical variables that come to mind in a social and behavioral science setting are race, sex, occupation, religion, and so on. For example, we might want to predict some continuous attitudinal variable on the basis of these and other categorical independent variables. In this chapter we will focus upon a linear regression model with only one categorical variable. Subsequent chapters will generalize this model to two or more categorical variables and a mixture of categorical and continuous independent variables.

Section 5.2 introduces the categorical independent variable regression model. The assumptions of the model are similar to those for the multiple regression model. Section 5.3 discusses estimable functions of regression parameters. Unlike multiple regression analysis, the design matrix for the one categorical independent variable model is singular. Fortunately, we can still estimate certain meaningful linear combinations of regression parameters, the estimable functions. While the normal equations do not have a unique inverse, one of the infinite number of solutions can be found through the use of the generalized inverse. The procedure is fully illustrated in section 5.4. Like the multiple regression model, the total sum of squares can be partitioned into two components: the regression sum of squares and the error sum of squares. As in multiple regression, these two sums of squares play a key role in testing the overall global statistical hypothesis that all of the regression parameters are equal to zero. These topics are discussed in sections 5.5 and 5.6, respectively. Section 5.6 also illustrates how certain statistical hypotheses can be tested using the principle of estimable functions developed in section 5.3. The relationship between the regression framework of this chapter and the classical one-way analysis of variance is explained in section 5.7. Section 5.8 illustrates the use of constraints on the regression parameters in solving the normal equations. It also shows how the regression model can be reparameterized in terms of estimable functions of the regression parameters so that estimates of the estimable functions can be solved for directly. Section 5.9 discusses commonly available computer software packages. It also illustrates how the independent variables can be recoded for input into conventional regression programs.

5.2 THE MODEL

Let us assume that we have collected information on the socioeconomic status (SES) level (of parents) defined by three categories and the intelligence (IQ), a continuous variable, for a random sample of children. Let SES be the independent variable and IQ the dependent variable. One way that a problem like this is typically resolved is to assign 1s, 2s, and 3s to the low, medium, and high categories of SES, respectively, and conduct a bivariate regression analysis where IQ would be regressed upon SES, which takes on values of 1, 2, and 3. The scale is certainly an ordinal scale in that a 2 implies a higher level of SES than does a 1 and, likewise, 3 implies a higher level of SES than a 1 or 2. However, it is very doubtful that the scale is an interval scale. If our SES scale were an interval scale, then the difference between the low and medium in the SES attribute would be equal to the difference between the medium and high levels of the SES attribute. It is doubtful that we have an interval scale in this situation and it is furthermore doubtful whether the regression of IQ on SES is linear. This linearity could be tested by examining the difference in the regression sum of squares for a linear regression and a quadratic regression in relationship to the estimate of the error sum of squares.[1]

An approach that would be more appropriate in a situation such as this would be to construct three dummy variables, one for each of the three SES levels. A dummy variable takes the value 1 if an observation (for example, person) falls within a particular category and 0 if it does not. Let us construct three dummy variables, x_1, x_2, and x_3 (one for each SES level), each of which can take on two possible values, 0 or 1. Now let us assign a value on each dummy variable for each individual, referring to Table 5.1. The variable x_1 identifies the low SES category and takes on a value of 1 if a child falls into the low SES category, and a 0 if he or she does not. Similarly, x_2 identifies the middle SES category and takes on a value of 1 if a child falls into the middle SES category and a 0 if he or she does not. The variable x_3 is similarly defined. Each child has a value of 0 or 1 for each of the three dummy variables; one dummy variable has a value of 1 and the remaining two have a value of 0 for any one child.

In the example shown in Table 5.1, there are five children in each of the three SES levels. The model to be discussed applies equally well to categories or cells with unequal n's. Let us represent these scores as a vector **y** where each element is identified by a double subscript y_{ij}, where i denotes SES level and takes on the values of 1, 2, or 3 and j denotes the child within the SES level and takes on values from 1 to n_i where n_i is the number of children in the ith SES level. In this example, n_i is 5 for all i. The vector of IQ scores, the dependent variable, can be represented as

$$y = \begin{bmatrix} y_{11} \\ y_{12} \\ y_{13} \\ y_{14} \\ y_{15} \\ y_{21} \\ y_{22} \\ y_{23} \\ y_{24} \\ y_{25} \\ y_{31} \\ y_{32} \\ y_{33} \\ y_{34} \\ y_{35} \end{bmatrix} = \begin{bmatrix} 85 \\ 91 \\ 87 \\ 93 \\ 96 \\ 94 \\ 105 \\ 110 \\ 120 \\ 98 \\ 96 \\ 110 \\ 122 \\ 118 \\ 108 \end{bmatrix}$$

Each child also has three scores, one for each of the dummy variables x_1, x_2, and x_3. For example, child 21, the first child of the second SES category, would be assigned values of 1 for x_2 and 0 for x_1 and x_3. This child's vector of scores on the independent dummy variables would be [0, 1, 0]. Similarly, the third child of the third SES category would have the vector [0, 0, 1] associated with him or her. All children in any one SES category would have identical vectors of scores for the three dummy variables. That is, all children in SES category 1 will have the vector [1, 0, 0]; all children in SES category 2 will have the vector [0, 1, 0]; and all children in SES category 3 will have the vector [0, 0, 1]. Let us now make up an **X*** matrix of our independent ("dummy") variables. Each child has a vector of three scores, one for each of the three dummy variables.

$$\mathbf{X}^* = \begin{bmatrix} X_{111} & X_{112} & X_{113} \\ X_{121} & X_{122} & X_{123} \\ X_{131} & X_{132} & X_{133} \\ X_{141} & X_{142} & X_{143} \\ X_{151} & X_{152} & X_{153} \\ X_{211} & X_{212} & X_{213} \\ X_{221} & X_{222} & X_{223} \\ X_{231} & X_{232} & X_{233} \\ X_{241} & X_{242} & X_{243} \\ X_{251} & X_{252} & X_{253} \\ X_{311} & X_{312} & X_{313} \\ X_{321} & X_{322} & X_{323} \\ X_{331} & X_{332} & X_{333} \\ X_{341} & X_{342} & X_{343} \\ X_{351} & X_{352} & X_{353} \end{bmatrix} = \begin{bmatrix} 1 & 0 & 0 \\ 1 & 0 & 0 \\ 1 & 0 & 0 \\ 1 & 0 & 0 \\ 1 & 0 & 0 \\ 0 & 1 & 0 \\ 0 & 1 & 0 \\ 0 & 1 & 0 \\ 0 & 1 & 0 \\ 0 & 1 & 0 \\ 0 & 0 & 1 \\ 0 & 0 & 1 \\ 0 & 0 & 1 \\ 0 & 0 & 1 \\ 0 & 0 & 1 \end{bmatrix}$$

The third subscript of the elements of the n (number of children) by p (number of variables) **X*** matrix indicates the dummy variable number, while the first two subscripts indicate the child's SES level and number within the SES level, respectively. The **X*** matrix indicates that every child in a particular SES category has the same row vector and each row vector of $\mathbf{X}^*$ contains only a single 1 and two zeros. The single categorical independent variable has, in effect, been replaced by three derived dummy variables.

Like the multiple regression model, this linear model also specifies an overall effect β_0 and consequently a column vector of ones must augment the $\mathbf{X}^*$ matrix by being placed as the first column. The augmented matrix is presented below.

$$\mathbf{X} = \begin{bmatrix} 1 & 1 & 0 & 0 \\ 1 & 1 & 0 & 0 \\ 1 & 1 & 0 & 0 \\ 1 & 1 & 0 & 0 \\ 1 & 1 & 0 & 0 \\ 1 & 0 & 1 & 0 \\ 1 & 0 & 1 & 0 \\ 1 & 0 & 1 & 0 \\ 1 & 0 & 1 & 0 \\ 1 & 0 & 1 & 0 \\ 1 & 0 & 0 & 1 \\ 1 & 0 & 0 & 1 \\ 1 & 0 & 0 & 1 \\ 1 & 0 & 0 & 1 \\ 1 & 0 & 0 & 1 \end{bmatrix}$$

This augmented $\mathbf{X}$ matrix is then our score matrix and is sometimes referred to as the design matrix of the linear model. The matrix equation of this linear model can now be written as:

$$\mathrm{y} = \mathrm{X}\beta + \epsilon$$

where $\mathbf{y}$ and $\mathbf{X}$ have been defined previously, $\boldsymbol{\beta}$ is a vector of regression weights, and $\boldsymbol{\epsilon}$ is a vector of errors. The model takes the form of the multiple regression model discussed in the previous chapter.

TABLE 5.1
IQ Scores for Three Levels of SES

	x_1 *Low SES*	x_2 *Medium SES*	x_3 *High SES*
	85	94	96
	91	105	110
	87	110	122
	93	120	118
	96	98	108
$\bar{X}$	90.4	105.4	110.8
N	5	5	5

For our particular example, the model is presented below.

$$\begin{bmatrix} 85 \\ 91 \\ 87 \\ 93 \\ 96 \\ 94 \\ 105 \\ 110 \\ 120 \\ 98 \\ 96 \\ 110 \\ 122 \\ 118 \\ 108 \end{bmatrix} = \begin{bmatrix} 1 & 1 & 0 & 0 \\ 1 & 1 & 0 & 0 \\ 1 & 1 & 0 & 0 \\ 1 & 1 & 0 & 0 \\ 1 & 1 & 0 & 0 \\ 1 & 0 & 1 & 0 \\ 1 & 0 & 1 & 0 \\ 1 & 0 & 1 & 0 \\ 1 & 0 & 1 & 0 \\ 1 & 0 & 1 & 0 \\ 1 & 0 & 0 & 1 \\ 1 & 0 & 0 & 1 \\ 1 & 0 & 0 & 1 \\ 1 & 0 & 0 & 1 \\ 1 & 0 & 0 & 1 \end{bmatrix} \begin{bmatrix} \beta_0 \\ \beta_1 \\ \beta_2 \\ \beta_3 \end{bmatrix} + \begin{bmatrix} \epsilon_{11} \\ \epsilon_{12} \\ \epsilon_{13} \\ \epsilon_{14} \\ \epsilon_{15} \\ \epsilon_{21} \\ \epsilon_{22} \\ \epsilon_{23} \\ \epsilon_{24} \\ \epsilon_{25} \\ \epsilon_{31} \\ \epsilon_{32} \\ \epsilon_{33} \\ \epsilon_{34} \\ \epsilon_{35} \end{bmatrix}$$

This model could also be written as $y_{ij} = \beta_0 + \beta_i + \epsilon_{ij}$. A child's score then is assumed to be a linear function of the overall effect, β_0, the effect β_i of the SES category in which the child falls, and an error term.

In order to use significance tests based upon normal distribution theory we make the following assumptions:

(a) $E(\epsilon) = \mathbf{0}$.

(b) $Var(\epsilon) = E(\epsilon\epsilon') = \sigma^2\mathbf{I}$.

(c) Each ϵ_i is normally distributed.

(d) The **X** matrix has rank less than N and is fixed over repeated samplings of the dependent variable.

These are the same assumptions made in the multiple regression model and, in fact, are the assumptions made for all linear regression models with fixed **X** when testing hypotheses concerning the parameters is desired.[2]

5.3 ESTIMABLE FUNCTIONS OF PARAMETERS

In the multiple regression analyses of the previous chapter, we saw that we could solve for unbiased estimates of $\boldsymbol{\beta}$ and σ^2. We might assume that we could, similar to multiple regression, estimate the parameters of the present model as $[\mathbf{X'X}]^{-1}\mathbf{X'y}$. However, we run into the problem that the inverse of $\mathbf{X'X}$, $(\mathbf{X'X})^{-1}$, does not exist. The reason for this is that the rank (r) of **X** is not 4, but is 3, and that consequently the r of the 4×4 matrix $\mathbf{X'X}$ is less than 4. Since the rank of $\mathbf{X'X}$ is less than 4, $|\mathbf{X'X}|$ equals 0 and the inverse does not exist. We can easily determine that the rank of **X** is not 4 since the sum of the last three columns equals the first column vector of ones. Hence there is a linear dependency among the columns of the **X** matrix. It may seem that we are at an impasse, but it happens that although there is no inverse that yields a unique solution for $\boldsymbol{\beta}$, there is what is called a generalized inverse that yields one of an infinitely large numbers of $\hat{\boldsymbol{\beta}}^*$s that will satisfy the normal equations $\mathbf{X'X}\boldsymbol{\beta} = \mathbf{X'y}$. Although the vector $\hat{\boldsymbol{\beta}}^*$ (solution using a generalized inverse) is not really an estimator of $\boldsymbol{\beta}$, the population regression parameter vector, that we desire in our model, it has many desirable properties that will be useful for us. For example, it can be shown that any solution $\hat{\boldsymbol{\beta}}^*$ determined from a generalized inverse yields the same estimate of the error sums of squares. That is, the $(\mathbf{y} - \mathbf{X}\hat{\boldsymbol{\beta}}^*)'(\mathbf{y} - \mathbf{X}\hat{\boldsymbol{\beta}}^*)$ generated by different solutions, $\hat{\boldsymbol{\beta}}^*$, are identical. In each case

$$\frac{(y - X\hat{\beta}^*)'(y - X\hat{\beta}^*)}{N - r(X)}$$

yields an unbiased estimate of σ^2. Notice that the denominator is N – r(**X**) where r(**X**) is the rank of **X** rather than N – p where p is the number of parameters in the model. In the SES example, it turns out that the r(**X**) is 3 although 4 parameters are in the model. In the case of multiple regression, it turns out that the number of parameters estimated and the rank of **X** are identical. Multiple regression with continuous variables results in a full rank model. However, when the model is not of full rank (**X** is less than full rank), as in models with categorical independent variables such as in the present example, then the rank of **X** rather than the number of parameters must be subtracted from the number of observations to estimate the error variance.

The most important property of $\hat{\boldsymbol{\beta}}^*$ is that certain linear combinations of the elements of $\hat{\boldsymbol{\beta}}^*$ (that is, $\mathbf{k}'\hat{\boldsymbol{\beta}}^*$) are invariant to each of the infinite number of solutions, $\hat{\boldsymbol{\beta}}^*$, that satisfy the normal equations. These $\mathbf{k}'\hat{\boldsymbol{\beta}}^*$s are BLUE of $\mathbf{k}'\hat{\boldsymbol{\beta}}$. To repeat, certain $\mathbf{k}'\hat{\boldsymbol{\beta}}^*$s for certain **k**s yield the identical estimate (same numerical value) for any $\hat{\boldsymbol{\beta}}^*$ that satisfies the normal equations. These $\mathbf{k}'\boldsymbol{\beta}$s are called "estimable functions." In order for a function to be estimable, a non-null vector **t** must exist such that the following relationship holds: $\mathbf{k}'\boldsymbol{\beta} = \mathbf{t}'\mathrm{E}(\mathbf{y})$. That is, $\mathbf{k}'\boldsymbol{\beta}$ is estimable if a linear combination of the elements of E(**y**) is identically equal to a certain linear combination of the elements of $\boldsymbol{\beta}$ where E(**y**) is expressed in terms of the regression model parameters. Let us now examine some $\mathbf{k}'\boldsymbol{\beta}$s of interest and determine whether they are estimable.

(1) $k'\beta = [0,1,-1,0]\begin{bmatrix}\beta_0\\ \beta_1\\ \beta_2\\ \beta_3\end{bmatrix} = \beta_1 - \beta_2$ is estimable because if

$$\mathbf{t}' = [1,0,0,0,0,-1,0,0,0,0,0,0,0,0,0] \text{ then}$$

$$\mathbf{t}'\mathrm{E}(\mathbf{y}) = [1,0,0,0,0,-1,0,0,0,0,0,0,0,0,0] \begin{bmatrix} \beta_0 + \beta_1 \\ \beta_0 + \beta_1 \\ \beta_0 + \beta_1 \\ \beta_0 + \beta_1 \\ \beta_0 + \beta_1 \\ \beta_0 + \beta_2 \\ \beta_0 + \beta_2 \\ \beta_0 + \beta_2 \\ \beta_0 + \beta_2 \\ \beta_0 + \beta_2 \\ \beta_0 + \beta_3 \\ \beta_0 + \beta_3 \\ \beta_0 + \beta_3 \\ \beta_0 + \beta_3 \\ \beta_0 + \beta_3 \end{bmatrix} = \beta_1 - \beta_2$$

and consequently $\mathbf{k}'\boldsymbol{\beta} = \mathbf{t}'\mathrm{E}(\mathbf{y})$. Notice that **t** is not unique and that many **t**s can be found such that $\mathbf{t}'\mathrm{E}(\mathbf{y}) = \beta_1 - \beta_2$. For example, we could change the ones in $\mathbf{t}'$ from the first and sixth positions to the second and seventh positions, or to the third and eighth positions, and so on, and still generate $\mathbf{t}'\mathrm{E}(\mathbf{y}) = \beta_1 - \beta_2$. The BLUE of $\beta_1 - \beta_2$ is $\hat{\beta}_1^* - \hat{\beta}_2^*$.

$$(2)\quad \mathbf{k}'\beta = [0,0,1,-1]\begin{bmatrix}\beta_0\\ \beta_1\\ \beta_2\\ \beta_3\end{bmatrix} = \beta_2 - \beta_3 \text{ and } [0,1,0,-1]\begin{bmatrix}\beta_0\\ \beta_1\\ \beta_2\\ \beta_3\end{bmatrix} = \beta_1 - \beta_3$$

are both estimable since, as the reader can easily verify, **t**s can be found where $\beta_2 - \beta_3 = \mathbf{t}'E(\mathbf{y})$ and $\beta_1 - \beta_3 = \mathbf{t}'E(\mathbf{y})$. Therefore, the BLUE of $\beta_2 - \beta_3 = \beta_2^* - \beta_3^*$ and the BLUE of $\beta_1 - \beta_3$ is $\beta_1^* - \beta_3^*$.

$$(3)\quad \mathbf{k}'\beta = \left[0,1,-\frac{1}{2},-\frac{1}{2}\right]\begin{bmatrix}\beta_0\\ \beta_1\\ \beta_2\\ \beta_3\end{bmatrix} = \beta_1 - \frac{1}{2}(\beta_2 + \beta_3) \text{ is estimable since}$$

$$\mathbf{t}'E(\mathbf{y}) = \left[1,0,0,0,0,-\frac{1}{2},0,0,0,0,-\frac{1}{2},0,0,0,0\right]\begin{bmatrix}\beta_0+\beta_1\\ \beta_0+\beta_1\\ \beta_0+\beta_1\\ \beta_0+\beta_1\\ \beta_0+\beta_1\\ \beta_0+\beta_2\\ \beta_0+\beta_2\\ \beta_0+\beta_2\\ \beta_0+\beta_2\\ \beta_0+\beta_2\\ \beta_0+\beta_3\\ \beta_0+\beta_3\\ \beta_0+\beta_3\\ \beta_0+\beta_3\\ \beta_0+\beta_3\end{bmatrix} = \beta_1 - \frac{1}{2}(\beta_2+\beta_3)$$

$$= \mathbf{k}'\beta.$$

Therefore $\beta_1 - \frac{1}{2}(\beta_2 + \beta_3)$ is estimable and $\hat{\beta}_1^* - \frac{1}{2}(\hat{\beta}_2^* + \hat{\beta}_3^*)$ is a BLUE of $\beta_1 - \frac{1}{2}(\beta_2 + \beta_3)$.

Again, a large number of **t**s will satisfy this relationship.

$$(4)\ \ \mathbf{k}'\boldsymbol{\beta} = [1,0,0,0]\begin{bmatrix}\beta_0\\ \beta_1\\ \beta_2\\ \beta_3\end{bmatrix} = \beta_0, [0,1,0,0]\begin{bmatrix}\beta_0\\ \beta_1\\ \beta_2\\ \beta_3\end{bmatrix} = \beta_1, [0,0,1,0]\begin{bmatrix}\beta_0\\ \beta_1\\ \beta_2\\ \beta_3\end{bmatrix} = \beta_2$$

and

$$[0,0,0,1]\begin{bmatrix}\beta_0\\ \beta_1\\ \beta_2\\ \beta_3\end{bmatrix} = \beta_3$$

are not estimable since no **t**s can be found such that $\beta_0 = \mathbf{t}'\mathrm{E}(\mathbf{y})$, $\beta_1 = \mathbf{t}'\mathrm{E}(\mathbf{y})$, $\beta_2 = \mathbf{t}'\mathrm{E}(\mathbf{y})$, or $\beta_3 = \mathbf{t}'\mathrm{E}(\mathbf{y})$. We previously saw that an infinite set of $\hat{\boldsymbol{\beta}}^*$s satisfy the normal equations and, hence, we would suspect that the parameters themselves are not estimable.

Even though we cannot estimate the individual elements of $\boldsymbol{\beta}$ for a less than full rank model, we can estimate, as we saw immediately above, some interesting and useful contrasts of the elements of $\boldsymbol{\beta}$. We saw that we could estimate the difference between any two effects (for example, $\beta_1 - \beta_2$) or the difference between one effect and the average of the others (for example, $\beta_1 - 1/2(\beta_2 - \beta_3)$. These are the contrasts that are of the most interest to the researcher.

5.4 SOLVING THE NORMAL EQUATIONS

We have seen previously that the normal equations corresponding to the model $\mathbf{y} = \mathbf{X}\boldsymbol{\beta} + \boldsymbol{\epsilon}$ are $\mathbf{X}'\mathbf{X}\boldsymbol{\beta} = \mathbf{X}'\mathbf{y}$. For our example data, we have

$$\mathbf{X}'\mathbf{X} = \begin{bmatrix} 1 & 1 & 1 & 1 & 1 & 1 & 1 & 1 & 1 & 1 & 1 & 1 & 1 & 1 & 1 \\ 1 & 1 & 1 & 1 & 1 & 0 & 0 & 0 & 0 & 0 & 0 & 0 & 0 & 0 & 0 \\ 0 & 0 & 0 & 0 & 0 & 1 & 1 & 1 & 1 & 1 & 0 & 0 & 0 & 0 & 0 \\ 0 & 0 & 0 & 0 & 0 & 0 & 0 & 0 & 0 & 0 & 1 & 1 & 1 & 1 & 1 \end{bmatrix} \begin{bmatrix} 1 & 1 & 0 & 0 \\ 1 & 1 & 0 & 0 \\ 1 & 1 & 0 & 0 \\ 1 & 1 & 0 & 0 \\ 1 & 1 & 0 & 0 \\ 1 & 0 & 1 & 0 \\ 1 & 0 & 1 & 0 \\ 1 & 0 & 1 & 0 \\ 1 & 0 & 1 & 0 \\ 1 & 0 & 1 & 0 \\ 1 & 0 & 0 & 1 \\ 1 & 0 & 0 & 1 \\ 1 & 0 & 0 & 1 \\ 1 & 0 & 0 & 1 \\ 1 & 0 & 0 & 1 \end{bmatrix} = \begin{bmatrix} 15 & 5 & 5 & 5 \\ 5 & 5 & 0 & 0 \\ 5 & 0 & 5 & 0 \\ 5 & 0 & 0 & 5 \end{bmatrix}$$

Notice that $\mathbf{X}'\mathbf{X}$ is a matrix with the diagonal elements equal to the number of observations in the total sample and each of the three SES categories, respectively. Continuing, we have

$$
\mathbf{X'y} = \begin{bmatrix} 1 & 1 & 1 & 1 & 1 & 1 & 1 & 1 & 1 & 1 & 1 & 1 & 1 & 1 & 1 \\ 1 & 1 & 1 & 1 & 1 & 0 & 0 & 0 & 0 & 0 & 0 & 0 & 0 & 0 & 0 \\ 0 & 0 & 0 & 0 & 0 & 1 & 1 & 1 & 1 & 1 & 0 & 0 & 0 & 0 & 0 \\ 0 & 0 & 0 & 0 & 0 & 0 & 0 & 0 & 0 & 0 & 1 & 1 & 1 & 1 & 1 \end{bmatrix} \begin{bmatrix} 85 \\ 91 \\ 87 \\ 93 \\ 96 \\ 94 \\ 105 \\ 110 \\ 120 \\ 98 \\ 96 \\ 110 \\ 122 \\ 118 \\ 108 \end{bmatrix} = \begin{bmatrix} 1533 \\ 452 \\ 527 \\ 554 \end{bmatrix}
$$

It can easily be seen that $\mathbf{X'y}$ is a 4×1 vector whose elements are the totals of the y observations for all observations and the three SES categories, respectively.

The normal equations for our example can now be written as

$$
\begin{bmatrix} 15 & 5 & 5 & 5 \\ 5 & 5 & 0 & 0 \\ 5 & 0 & 5 & 0 \\ 5 & 0 & 0 & 5 \end{bmatrix} \begin{bmatrix} \beta_0 \\ \beta_1 \\ \beta_2 \\ \beta_3 \end{bmatrix} = \begin{bmatrix} 1533 \\ 452 \\ 527 \\ 554 \end{bmatrix}
$$

A solution for these normal equations can be found by taking the generalized inverse of **X′X** and postmultiplying this generalized inverse by **X′y**. This is analogous to the multiple regression situation, where a unique inverse existed that was postmultiplied by **X′y** to find $\hat{\boldsymbol{\beta}}$. That is, $\hat{\boldsymbol{\beta}}^* = \mathbf{GX'y}$. Let us now go through the procedure of finding the **G** of **X′X**.

As previously discussed, the generalized inverse is any matrix **G** that satisfies $\mathbf{X'XGX'X} = \mathbf{X'X}$. It can be shown that the generalized inverse of any matrix can be computed by first partitioning the matrix whose generalized inverse is desired (for example, **X′X**) in a manner such that a $k \times k$ minor (that is, submatrix) is nonsingular and equal to the rank of **X′X**. We can easily see from examining **X′X** that the minor

$$\begin{bmatrix} 5 & 0 & 0 \\ 0 & 5 & 0 \\ 0 & 0 & 5 \end{bmatrix} = [X'X]_1$$

is a 3×3 matrix of full rank (that is, 3) since the rows (columns) are linearly independent. The matrix **X′X** has three linearly independent columns. Therefore, $r[\mathbf{X'X}]_1 = r[\mathbf{X'X}] = 3$ and $r[\mathbf{X'X}]_1$ satisfies the definition of the appropriate minor or submatrix. The next step in computing the generalized inverse is to take the inverse of $[\mathbf{X'X}]_1$. The inverse of $[\mathbf{X'X}]_1$ is simple to compute since it is a diagonal matrix. We simply change the diagonal elements of $[\mathbf{X'X}]_1$ to their reciprocals and have

$$[X'X]_1^{-1} \begin{bmatrix} \frac{1}{5} & 0 & 0 \\ 0 & \frac{1}{5} & 0 \\ 0 & 0 & \frac{1}{5} \end{bmatrix}$$

The final step in computing the generalized inverse is to augment this inverse with a **0** row and column vector in order to make the dimensions of **G** equal to that of **X′X**. This gives the generalized inverse

$$\mathbf{G} = \begin{bmatrix} 0 & 0 & 0 & 0 \\ 0 & \frac{1}{5} & 0 & 0 \\ 0 & 0 & \frac{1}{5} & 0 \\ 0 & 0 & 0 & \frac{1}{5} \end{bmatrix}$$

The algorithm described above is useful for calculating generalized inverses. Let us now check to see if, indeed, we have a generalized inverse. For the above matrix to be a generalized inverse of **X′X**, it must satisfy the relationship **X′XGX′X** = **X′X**. Substituting into the above equation, it can be seen that

$$\begin{bmatrix} 15 & 5 & 5 & 5 \\ 5 & 5 & 0 & 0 \\ 5 & 0 & 5 & 0 \\ 5 & 0 & 0 & 5 \end{bmatrix} \begin{bmatrix} 0 & 0 & 0 & 0 \\ 0 & \frac{1}{5} & 0 & 0 \\ 0 & 0 & \frac{1}{5} & 0 \\ 0 & 0 & 0 & \frac{1}{5} \end{bmatrix} \begin{bmatrix} 15 & 5 & 5 & 5 \\ 5 & 5 & 0 & 0 \\ 5 & 0 & 5 & 0 \\ 5 & 0 & 0 & 5 \end{bmatrix} = \begin{bmatrix} 15 & 5 & 5 & 5 \\ 5 & 5 & 0 & 0 \\ 5 & 0 & 5 & 0 \\ 5 & 0 & 0 & 5 \end{bmatrix}$$

It can be shown that there are an infinite number of **G** matrices that will satisfy **X′XGX′X**. In other words, **G** is not unique like the regular inverse, $[\mathbf{X'X}]^{-1}$. Since we have now solved for a generalized inverse, let us now find a solution for $\hat{\boldsymbol{\beta}}^*$, remembering that the elements of the vector $\hat{\boldsymbol{\beta}}^*$ in themselves are relatively meaningless; their values depend upon the particular generalized inverse that was used to obtain a solution for the normal equations. Using our generalized inverse we can solve for $\hat{\boldsymbol{\beta}}^*$. Substituting into $\hat{\boldsymbol{\beta}}^* = \mathbf{GX'y}$, we find

$$\begin{bmatrix} \beta_0^* \\ \beta_1^* \\ \beta_2^* \\ \beta_3^* \end{bmatrix} = \begin{bmatrix} 0 & 0 & 0 & 0 \\ 0 & \frac{1}{5} & 0 & 0 \\ 0 & 0 & \frac{1}{5} & 0 \\ 0 & 0 & 0 & \frac{1}{5} \end{bmatrix} \begin{bmatrix} 1533 \\ 452 \\ 527 \\ 554 \end{bmatrix} = \begin{bmatrix} 0 \\ 90.4 \\ 105.4 \\ 110.8 \end{bmatrix}$$

This means of solving for $\hat{\boldsymbol{\beta}}^*$ yields the vector of dependent variable means for each of the three categories of the independent variable as the solution vector along with a leading zero. The reader can verify this by comparing the elements in the above solution vector to the means in Table 5.1.

5.5 PARTITIONING AND COMPUTING SUMS OF SQUARES

As in multiple regression analysis, the total sum of squares adjusted for the mean (SST_m) is $\mathbf{y'y} - N\bar{y}^2$, the error sum of squares (SSE) is $(\mathbf{y} - \mathbf{X}\hat{\boldsymbol{\beta}}^*)'(\mathbf{y} - \mathbf{X}\hat{\boldsymbol{\beta}}^*)$, and the regression sum of squares (SSR_m) about the mean is $\hat{\boldsymbol{\beta}}^*\mathbf{X'y} - N\bar{y}^2$. Note that any solution of the normal equations results in an identical partitioning of the total sum of squares and that $SST_m = SSR_m + SSE$. In our example

$$\mathbf{y'y} - N\bar{y}^2 = [85, 91, 87, 93, 96, 94, 105, 110, 120, 98, 96, 110, 122, 118, 108] \begin{bmatrix} 85 \\ 91 \\ 87 \\ 93 \\ 96 \\ 94 \\ 105 \\ 110 \\ 120 \\ 98 \\ 96 \\ 110 \\ 122 \\ 118 \\ 108 \end{bmatrix} - 15(102.3)^2 = 2021$$

This matrix equation is sometimes written in scalar algebra as $\sum_i \sum_j y_{ij}^2 - N\bar{y}^2$, where the subscripts i and j represent the categories and the cases within the categories, respectively.

The regression sums of squares corrected for the mean can be calculated by substituting into

$$SSR_m = \hat{\beta}^* X'y - N\bar{y}^2$$

$$= [0,\ 90.4,\ 105.4,\ 110.8] \begin{bmatrix} 1533 \\ 452 \\ 527 \\ 554 \end{bmatrix} - 156{,}672$$

$$= 157{,}789.8 - 156{,}672$$

$$= 1117.8$$

The error sums of squares could be, of course, obtained by subtracting the SSR_m from SST_m, but in order to illustrate more aspects of the model let us calculate it independently by using $SSE = (\mathbf{y} - \hat{\mathbf{y}})'(\mathbf{y} - \hat{\mathbf{y}})$, where **y** is the vector of observations on our dependent variable and $\hat{\mathbf{y}}$ is a vector of predicted values based upon our model. The vector of predicted values, $\hat{\mathbf{y}}$, can be obtained from $\hat{\mathbf{y}} = \mathbf{X}\boldsymbol{\beta}^*$ since $\mathbf{X}\boldsymbol{\beta}^*$ is estimable. For our example, we have

$$\hat{y} = \begin{bmatrix} \hat{y}_{11} \\ \hat{y}_{12} \\ \hat{y}_{13} \\ \hat{y}_{14} \\ \hat{y}_{15} \\ \hat{y}_{21} \\ \hat{y}_{22} \\ \hat{y}_{23} \\ \hat{y}_{24} \\ \hat{y}_{25} \\ \hat{y}_{31} \\ \hat{y}_{32} \\ \hat{y}_{33} \\ \hat{y}_{34} \\ \hat{y}_{35} \end{bmatrix} = \begin{bmatrix} 1 & 1 & 0 & 0 \\ 1 & 1 & 0 & 0 \\ 1 & 1 & 0 & 0 \\ 1 & 1 & 0 & 0 \\ 1 & 1 & 0 & 0 \\ 1 & 0 & 1 & 0 \\ 1 & 0 & 1 & 0 \\ 1 & 0 & 1 & 0 \\ 1 & 0 & 1 & 0 \\ 1 & 0 & 1 & 0 \\ 1 & 0 & 0 & 1 \\ 1 & 0 & 0 & 1 \\ 1 & 0 & 0 & 1 \\ 1 & 0 & 0 & 1 \\ 1 & 0 & 0 & 1 \end{bmatrix} \begin{bmatrix} 0 \\ 90.4 \\ 105.4 \\ 110.8 \end{bmatrix} = \begin{bmatrix} 90.4 \\ 90.4 \\ 90.4 \\ 90.4 \\ 90.4 \\ 105.4 \\ 105.4 \\ 105.4 \\ 105.4 \\ 105.4 \\ 110.8 \\ 110.8 \\ 110.8 \\ 110.8 \\ 110.8 \end{bmatrix}$$

We can see that the predicted values of y are the same for each individual in a particular category. For example, all five children in the low SES category were predicted by the model to have an IQ of 90.4. The reader should note that this is an estimate of $\beta_0 + \beta_1$, the population mean for that cell.

To find SSE, we now take the deviation of each observed score from its predicted value and sum the squares of these deviations since

$$(y - \hat{y})'(y - \hat{y}) = \sum_i \sum_j (y_{ij} - \hat{y}_{ij})^2$$

The error sum of squares turns out to be 903.2.

TABLE 5.2
Test of the Hypothesis $\beta_1 = \beta_2 = \ldots = \beta_k$

Source of Variation	*Sum of Squares*	*Degrees of Freedom*	*Mean Square*	*F Ratio*
SSR_m	$\hat{\boldsymbol{\beta}}^{*\prime}\mathbf{X}'\mathbf{y} - N\bar{y}^2$	$r - 1$	$\frac{SSR_m}{r-1}$	$\frac{SSR_m}{r-1} \Big/ \frac{SSE}{N-r}$
SSE	$\mathbf{y}'\mathbf{y} - \hat{\boldsymbol{\beta}}^{*\prime}\mathbf{X}'\mathbf{y}$	$N - r$	$\frac{SSE}{N-r}$	
SST_m	$\mathbf{y}'\mathbf{y} - N\bar{y}^2$	$N - 1$		

$r = r(X)$

TABLE 5.3
Test of the Hypothesis $\beta_1 = \beta_2 = \beta_3$ for Example Data

Source of Variation	*Sum of Squares*	*Degrees of Freedom*	*Mean Square*	*F Ratio*
SSR_m	1117.8	2	558.9	7.42
SSE	903.2	12	75.3	
SST_m	2021.0	14		

5.6 HYPOTHESIS TESTING

It can be shown under the null hypothesis $\beta_1 = \beta_2 = \ldots = \beta_k$ that the ratio of the regression sum of squares about the mean divided by $r(\mathbf{X}) - 1$ to the error sum of squares divided by $N - r(\mathbf{X})$ is distributed as F with $r - 1$ and $N - r$ degrees of freedom. The procedure for testing the hypothesis, $\beta_1 = \beta_2 = \ldots \beta_k = 0$, is summarized in Table 5.2.

Let us now fill in Table 5.3 with our calculated values following the procedures laid out in Table 5.2.

Referring to an F table with 2 degrees of freedom in the numerator and 12 degrees of freedom in the denominator, we see that the F of 7.42 is significant at the .01 level. This tells us that the parameters β_1, β_2, and β_3 in the model explain some of the variation in IQ. If the β_i's are equal, then the model explains none of the variation in the dependent variable and R^2 is equal to zero. This is because the predicted value, y, for each observation in the sample is equal to the constant $\beta_0 + \beta_1$ and hence the regression sum of squares is zero. This test is equivalent to the test that the three β_i's are equal. This in turn is equivalent to the hypothesis $\beta_1 - \beta_2 = \beta_2 - \beta_3 = 0$, which can be written as

$$\begin{bmatrix} 0 & 1 & -1 & 0 \\ 0 & 1 & 1 & -1 \end{bmatrix} \begin{bmatrix} \beta_0 \\ \beta_1 \\ \beta_2 \\ \beta_3 \end{bmatrix} = \begin{bmatrix} 0 \\ 0 \end{bmatrix}$$

Substituting our solution to $\hat{\boldsymbol{\beta}}^*$ into these equations, we find that

$$\mathbf{K}\hat{\beta}^* = \begin{bmatrix} 0 & 1 & -1 & 0 \\ 0 & 0 & 1 & -1 \end{bmatrix} \begin{bmatrix} 0 \\ 90.4 \\ 105.4 \\ 110.8 \end{bmatrix} = \begin{bmatrix} -15.0 \\ -5.4 \end{bmatrix}$$

We note that these are estimates of the two estimable functions $\beta_1 - \beta_2$ and $\beta_2 - \beta_3$. We hypothesized that they are each equal to 0, but our estimates derived from the data yielded estimates of –15.0 and –5.4, respectively. These estimable contrasts contain all of the information in the regression parameter estimates. We will see that these two contrasts account for our regression sums of squares corrected for the mean by computing

$$\hat{\beta}^{*\prime}\mathbf{K}'(\mathbf{KGK}')^{-1}\mathbf{K}\hat{\beta}^*$$

This is an alternate formula for estimating the regression sum of squares. Substituting, we find

$$\hat{\beta}^{*\prime}\mathbf{K}'(\mathbf{KGK}')^{-1}\mathbf{K}\hat{\beta}^*$$

$$= [-15.0 \quad -5.4] \left[\begin{bmatrix} 0 & 1 & -1 & 0 \\ 0 & 0 & 1 & -1 \end{bmatrix} \begin{bmatrix} 0 & 0 & 0 & 0 \\ 0 & \frac{1}{5} & 0 & 0 \\ 0 & 0 & \frac{1}{5} & 0 \\ 0 & 0 & 0 & \frac{1}{5} \end{bmatrix} \begin{bmatrix} 0 & 0 \\ 1 & 0 \\ -1 & 1 \\ 0 & -1 \end{bmatrix} \right]^{-1} \begin{bmatrix} -15.0 \\ -5.4 \end{bmatrix}$$

$$= [-15.0 \quad -5.4] \begin{bmatrix} \frac{2}{5} & \frac{-1}{5} \\ \frac{-1}{5} & \frac{2}{5} \end{bmatrix}^{-1} \begin{bmatrix} -15.0 \\ -5.4 \end{bmatrix}$$

$$= \frac{1}{3} [-15.0 \quad -5.4] \begin{bmatrix} 10 & 5 \\ 5 & 10 \end{bmatrix} \begin{bmatrix} -15.0 \\ -5.4 \end{bmatrix}$$

$$= 1117.8$$

It has been shown that the regression sum of squares can be computed by finding a 2×4 matrix **K** of rank equal to 2 and whose rows yield estimable functions when postmultiplied by the vector $\hat{\boldsymbol{\beta}}^*$. The reader can easily verify that other **K** matrices such as

$$\begin{bmatrix} 0 & 1 & -1 & 0 \\ 0 & 1 & 0 & -1 \end{bmatrix}$$

would have produced the same regression sum of squares. We can see that under the null hypothesis that $\mathbf{K}\boldsymbol{\beta} = \mathbf{0}$ large differences between the elements of $\hat{\boldsymbol{\beta}}^*$ will result in a large regression sum of squares. When the mean square for regression is substantially larger than the mean square for error, then we have the evidence needed to reject the hypothesis $\mathbf{K}\boldsymbol{\beta} = \mathbf{0}$. The matrix, **K**, must have rank equal to the degrees of freedom for regression and, in addition, the rows of **K** must involve estimable contrasts whose coefficients sum to zero.

The advantage of this formulation, as we shall see later, is that other types of hypotheses can be tested besides the overall hypothesis that $\beta_1 = \beta_2 = \beta_3$, or, equivalent, $R^2 = 0$. For example, we could test the more specific hypothesis that $\beta_1 - \beta_2 = 0$ by having **K** made up of the single row [0, 1, –1, 0]. We can even test nonzero hypotheses such as $\beta_2 - \beta_3 = 2$ with this formulation by substituting $[[0, 0, 1, -1] \hat{\boldsymbol{\beta}}^* - 2]$ into the general formula. The proper degrees of freedom and the error term will be addressed below.

5.7 ONE-WAY ANALYSIS OF VARIANCE

The regression sums of squares would be expected to be small if the β_i's in the population were equal. Testing the hypothesis that the β_i's are equal in a one-factor experiment as we have done by using a linear model and considering the general linear hypothesis is equivalent to what is commonly termed in statistics "one-way analysis of variance." A one-way analysis of variance involves partitioning the total sum of squares of deviations from the overall mean into a between-group sum of squares and a within-group sum of squares such that

$$SS_{Total} = SS_{Between} + SS_{Within}$$

or

$$\sum_i \sum_j (y_{ij} - \bar{y})^2 = \sum_i n_i(\bar{y}_{i.} - \bar{y})^2 + \sum_i \sum_j (y_{ij} - \bar{y}_{i.})^2$$

where y is the overall mean, $y_{i.}$, is the mean for subgroups i, n_i is the number of observations in the ith subgroup, and y_{ij} is the score of the jth person in the ith subgroup.

The reader can verify that, for our example,

$$\sum_i \sum_j (y_{ij} - \bar{y})^2 = 2021, \quad \sum_i n_i(\bar{y}_{i.} - \bar{y})^2 = 1117.8, \text{ and } \sum_i \sum_j (y_{ij} - \bar{y}_{i.})^2 = 903.2$$

and

$$2021 = 1117.8 + 903.2$$

We can see that the between-group sum of squares is equivalent to what we have called the regression sum of squares corrected for the mean and the within-group sum of squares is what we have called the error sum of squares. A little reflection will indicate that the between-group sum of squares would be small if the group means were of a similar magnitude. This is the same as saying that the various contrasts involving the β_i for our linear model would yield small values. Since the estimated predicted value, $\hat{y}_i$, of our linear model for an observation from a particular group is the mean of that cell, we can easily see that the within-group sum of squares is equivalent to the error sum of squares, $(\mathbf{y} - \hat{\mathbf{y}})'(\mathbf{y} - \hat{\mathbf{y}})$, of our linear model. The remaining computations and tests for an analysis of variance are identical to those used for our linear model with one categorical independent variable. The only thing that we would need to do to our linear model table to change it into an analysis of variance table is to change the table labels from "SSR_m" to "between-group sums of squares" and "SSE" to "within-group sums of squares."

5.8 OTHER WAYS TO SOLVE THE NORMAL EQUATIONS

The method of generalized inverses was chosen to solve the normal equations in section 5.4. There are also two other approaches that are commonly used to solve the normal equations: constraining the values of the parameters and reparameterization. Before discussing these methods, it might be worthwhile to make a few remarks concerning why I chose to concentrate on the generalized inverse approach. First, the generalized inverse approach is conceptually appealing since it models the dependent variable in terms of all the necessary parameters whether they are estimable or not. Second, the regression sum of squares itself does not depend upon the particular solution to the normal equations. Third, it forces the user to define parameter contrasts that are both estimable and of interest to the researcher since the solution vector to the normal equations is in itself meaningless.

One typical constraint[3] used in solving the normal equations is

$$\sum_{i=1}^{k} \beta_i = 0$$

In our example with three categories or levels of the independent variable we would have $\beta_1 + \beta_2 + \beta_3 = 0$. Let us see how this helps us determine a unique solution for the normal equations. We previously found the normal equations to be

$$15\,\hat{\beta}_0^* + 5\,\hat{\beta}_1^* + 5\,\hat{\beta}_2^* + 5\,\hat{\beta}_3^* = 1533$$

$$5\,\hat{\beta}_0^* + 5\,\hat{\beta}_1^* + 0\,\hat{\beta}_2^* + 0\,\hat{\beta}_3^* = 452$$

$$5\,\hat{\beta}_0^* + 0\,\hat{\beta}_1^* + 5\,\hat{\beta}_2^* + 0\,\hat{\beta}_3^* = 527$$

$$5\,\hat{\beta}_0^* + 0\,\hat{\beta}_1^* + 0\,\hat{\beta}_2^* + 5\,\hat{\beta}_3^* = 554$$

We also saw that the first equation was redundant since it is the sum of the other three equations. Hence we can drop it and are left with the remaining three equations with four unknowns. Because we had more unknowns than equations, the generalized inverse approach yielded an infinite number of solutions. The constraint, $\hat{\beta}_1^* + \hat{\beta}_2^* + \hat{\beta}_3^* = 0$, added to this set of three equations yields a set of 4 independent equations in 4 unknowns and hence a unique solution for $\hat{\beta}_0^*$, $\hat{\beta}_1^*$, $\hat{\beta}_2^*$ and $\hat{\beta}_3^*$exists. The new set of equation is

$$\begin{bmatrix} 5 & 5 & 0 & 0 \\ 5 & 0 & 5 & 0 \\ 5 & 0 & 0 & 5 \\ 0 & 1 & 1 & 1 \end{bmatrix} \begin{bmatrix} \hat{\beta}_0^* \\ \hat{\beta}_1^* \\ \hat{\beta}_2^* \\ \hat{\beta}_3^* \end{bmatrix} = \begin{bmatrix} 452 \\ 527 \\ 554 \\ 0 \end{bmatrix}$$

In order for a unique solution to exist, the inverse of the coefficient matrix on the left side must exist so that

$$\hat{\beta}^* = \begin{bmatrix} \hat{\beta}_0^* \\ \hat{\beta}_1^* \\ \hat{\beta}_2^* \\ \hat{\beta}_3^* \end{bmatrix} = \begin{bmatrix} 5 & 5 & 0 & 0 \\ 5 & 0 & 5 & 0 \\ 5 & 0 & 0 & 5 \\ 0 & 1 & 1 & 1 \end{bmatrix}^{-1} \begin{bmatrix} 452 \\ 527 \\ 554 \\ 0 \end{bmatrix}$$

The inverse can easily be found by performing a series of elementary transformations simultaneously on the coefficient and **I** matrix as demonstrated in Chapter 3. Doing this, we find

$$\begin{bmatrix} \hat{\beta}_0^* \\ \hat{\beta}_1^* \\ \hat{\beta}_2^* \\ \hat{\beta}_3^* \end{bmatrix} = \begin{bmatrix} .06667 & .06667 & .06667 & -.33333 \\ .13333 & -.06667 & -.06667 & .33333 \\ -.06667 & .13333 & -.06667 & .33333 \\ -.06667 & -.06667 & .13333 & .33333 \end{bmatrix} \begin{bmatrix} 452 \\ 527 \\ 554 \\ 0 \end{bmatrix} = \begin{bmatrix} 102.2 \\ -11.8 \\ 3.2 \\ 8.6 \end{bmatrix}$$

It can be easily verified that the estimable functions of the parameters are identical to those found using the generalized inverse approach. For example, $\widehat{\beta_0 + \beta_1} = \hat{\beta}_0^* + \hat{\beta}_1^* = 102.2 - 11.8 = 90.4$; $\widehat{\beta_1 - \beta_2} = \hat{\beta}_1^* - \hat{\beta}_2^* = -11.8 - 3.2 = -15$; and so on. The advantage of the constraint $\Sigma\beta_i = 0$ now becomes apparent. Since $\Sigma\hat{\beta}_i^* = 0$, $\hat{\beta}_i^* = \hat{\beta}_i^* - 1/3\,(\hat{\beta}_1^* + \hat{\beta}_2^* + \hat{\beta}_3^*)$ and therefore $\hat{\beta}_i^*$ is an estimate of the estimable function $\beta_i - 1/3\,(\beta_1 + \beta_1 + \beta_3)$. This estimable function makes sense. It is the difference of an effect for a level of the categorical variable and the average of all of the effects. The constraints on the parameters can be used solely for the purpose of finding a solution of the normal equations or they can be used to solve directly for estimable functions. If the constraints on the parameters are actually considered as restrictions, then the individual parameters themselves are estimable as well as the estimable functions under the unrestricted model. That is, if we assume that the restriction $\beta_1 + \beta_2 + \beta_3 = 0$ is a part of the model rather than a convenient constraint for solving the normal equations, then β_0, β_1, β_2, and β_3 are themselves estimable; the estimates in the present example are $\beta_0 = 102.2$, $\beta_1 = 11.8$, $\beta_2 = 3.2$, and $\beta_3 = 8.6$.

The remaining method, reparameterization, involves writing the model in terms of estimable functions of the original parameters and solving the modified full rank normal equations directly for these new parameters, the estimable functions. Let us see how this can be done. For the original model, the dependent variable for each of the three categories of the independent variable are expressed as

$$y_{1j} = \beta_0 + \beta_1 + \epsilon_{1j}$$

$$y_{2j} = \beta_0 + \beta_2 + \epsilon_{2j}$$

$$y_{3j} = \beta_0 + \beta_3 + \epsilon_{3j}$$

where the first subscript of y refers to the category of the independent variable and the second subscript, j, refers to the particular observation within a category. We could have just as easily expressed the model as

$$y_{1j} = (\beta_0 + \beta_1) + \epsilon_{1j}$$

$$y_{2j} = (\beta_0 + \beta_1) + (\beta_2 - \beta_1) + \epsilon_{2j}$$

$$y_{3j} = (\beta_0 + \beta_1) + (\beta_3 - \beta_1) + \epsilon_{3j}$$

The latter model is the reparameterized model. (Note that it is algebraically equivalent to the original model.) However, it can now be considered as a model written in three estimable functions of the original parameters ($\beta_0 + \beta_1$, $\beta_2 - \beta_1$, and $\beta_3 - \beta_1$) rather than the four unestimable parameters (β_0, β_1, β_2, and β_3) of the original model. It can easily be seen that the design matrix under the reparameterized model for our example is

$$\mathbf{X}_r = \begin{bmatrix} 1 & 0 & 0 \\ 1 & 0 & 0 \\ 1 & 0 & 0 \\ 1 & 0 & 0 \\ 1 & 0 & 0 \\ 1 & 1 & 0 \\ 1 & 1 & 0 \\ 1 & 1 & 0 \\ 1 & 1 & 0 \\ 1 & 1 & 0 \\ 1 & 0 & 1 \\ 1 & 0 & 1 \\ 1 & 0 & 1 \\ 1 & 0 & 1 \\ 1 & 0 & 1 \end{bmatrix}$$

since the reparameterized model can be written as

$$\mathbf{y} = \mathbf{X}_r \begin{bmatrix} \beta_0 + \beta_1 \\ \beta_2 - \beta_1 \\ \beta_3 - \beta_1 \end{bmatrix} + \epsilon$$

The matrix $\mathbf{X}'_r\mathbf{X}_r$ is clearly nonsingular and consequently $[\mathbf{X}'_r\mathbf{X}_r]^{-1}$ exists. It follows that the normal equations can be written as

$$\mathbf{X}'_r\mathbf{X}_r\beta_r = \mathbf{X}'_r\mathbf{y}$$

where

$$\beta_r = \begin{bmatrix} \beta_0 + \beta_1 \\ \beta_2 - \beta_1 \\ \beta_3 - \beta_1 \end{bmatrix}; \mathbf{X}_r'\mathbf{X}_r = \begin{bmatrix} 15 & 5 & 5 \\ 5 & 5 & 0 \\ 5 & 0 & 5 \end{bmatrix}; \text{ and } \mathbf{X}_r'\mathbf{y} = \begin{bmatrix} 1533 \\ 527 \\ 554 \end{bmatrix}$$

Solving the normal equation, we find

$$\hat{\beta}_r = \begin{bmatrix} \widehat{\beta_0 + \beta_1} \\ \widehat{\beta_2 - \beta_1} \\ \widehat{\beta_3 - \beta_1} \end{bmatrix} = \begin{bmatrix} 90.4 \\ 15.0 \\ 20.4 \end{bmatrix}$$

If the researcher is interested in an estimate of $\beta_2 - \beta_3$, it can be found as $(\widehat{\beta_2 - \beta_1}) - (\widehat{\beta_3 - \beta_1})$ since it is a linear contrast of two estimable functions.

The regression sums of squares for all three models are identical and consequently so are the error sums of squares. If $\hat{\sigma}^2$ is an estimate of the error variance, then, generalizing from the multiple regression model, the covariance matrix of the estimate β_r is

$$\text{Cov } \hat{\beta}_r = \hat{\sigma}^2 [\mathbf{X}_r'\mathbf{X}_r]^{-1}$$

The diagonal elements of this matrix are the estimated variances of the estimable functions $\beta_0 + \beta_1$, $\beta_2 - \beta_1$, and $\beta_3 - \beta_1$, respectively. The null hypothesis that any particular estimable function is zero can be tested directly by a t-test.

5.9 USE OF COMPUTERS

The general linear model (GLM) procedure of SAS is consistent with the approach taken in this book. SAS does not require a full rank design matrix and solves the normal equations through the use of a generalized inverse. The program prints out the sums of squares due to regression and error and tests the statistical significance of the regression sum of squares. This is equivalent to testing the null hypothesis that the effect parameters corresponding to the different levels of the single categorical variable are equal to each other. The program also calculates estimable contrasts among the parameters and tests various hypotheses concerning them. That is, we can request the test of any admissible hypothesis, $\mathbf{K}\boldsymbol{\beta}$.

Linear model procedures in other software packages may require a full rank design matrix. Two possible full rank design matrices follow directly from the discussion in the previous section. One full rank design matrix was already given as

$$\mathbf{X} = \begin{bmatrix} 1 & 0 & 0 \\ 1 & 0 & 0 \\ 1 & 0 & 0 \\ 1 & 0 & 0 \\ 1 & 0 & 0 \\ 1 & 1 & 0 \\ 1 & 1 & 0 \\ 1 & 1 & 0 \\ 1 & 1 & 0 \\ 1 & 1 & 0 \\ 1 & 0 & 1 \\ 1 & 0 & 1 \\ 1 & 0 & 1 \\ 1 & 0 & 1 \\ 1 & 0 & 1 \end{bmatrix}$$

We saw that the estimable function of the parameters associated with this matrix were $\beta_0 + \beta_1$, $\beta_2 - \beta_1$, and $\beta_3 - \beta_1$. This is called dummy variable coding. This matrix resembles the original design matrix except that one column representing one level of the categorical variable is deleted. We can leave out any dummy variable we choose. The effect contrasts we are estimating, then, are the differences in the effects of the remaining levels with the level whose associated dummy variable was deleted. In our example we have removed column two of the original design matrix. We could have removed column three of the original design matrix. The reader can verify that, in this case, the estimable functions associated with the full rank design matrix are $\beta_0 + \beta_2$, $\beta_3 - \beta_2$, and $\beta_3 - \beta_2$.

Our example involved a categorical variable with three levels. As the reader might suspect, this approach can be generalized to a one-factor design with an arbitrary number of levels, k. Delete one of the dummy variables from the original design matrix associated with a level of the categorical variable. The estimable contrasts associated with this design matrix will then be the differences in the effect of the remaining levels with the level whose corresponding column was deleted.

If we removed column one of the original design matrix, the column vector of ones, then the design matrix would be of full rank. The estimable functions, however, would be $\beta_0 + \beta_1$, $\beta_0 + \beta_2$, . . , $\beta_0 + \beta_k$, as the reader can verify. These estimable functions are the expected values of the observations for the k levels of the categorical variable. Depending upon the purpose of the analysis, these estimable functions may or may not be of interest to the researcher.

When the full rank design matrix associated with a particular reparameterization and the vector of dependent variable values is fed into the linear model or regression package, the resulting output will include estimates of the estimable functions, their associated standard error, and their levels of statistical significance.

A second full rank design matrix can be associated with the restricted model in the previous section. If $\beta_1 + \beta_2 + \beta_3 = 0$, then $\beta_3 = -\beta_1 - \beta_2$ and the model can be reexpressed as

$$y_{1j} = \beta_0 + \beta_1 + \epsilon_{1j}.$$

$$y_{2j} = \beta_0 + \beta_2 + \epsilon_{2j}$$

$$y_{3j} = \beta_0 - \beta_2 - \beta_1 + \epsilon_{3j}$$

where y_{1j} is the jth observation in the first SES level, y_{2j} is the jth observation in the second SES level, and y_{3j} is the jth observation in the third SES level. Expressed in matrix algebra, the restricted model becomes

$$\begin{bmatrix} y_{1j} \\ y_{2j} \\ y_{3j} \end{bmatrix} = \begin{bmatrix} 1 & 1 & 0 \\ 1 & 0 & 1 \\ 1 & -1 & -1 \end{bmatrix} \begin{bmatrix} \beta_0 \\ \beta_1 \\ \beta_2 \end{bmatrix} + \begin{bmatrix} \epsilon_{1j} \\ \epsilon_{2j} \\ \epsilon_{3j} \end{bmatrix}$$

so that the model for our 15 observation data set becomes

$$
y = \begin{bmatrix} 1 & 1 & 0 \\ 1 & 1 & 0 \\ 1 & 1 & 0 \\ 1 & 1 & 0 \\ 1 & 1 & 0 \\ 1 & 0 & 1 \\ 1 & 0 & 1 \\ 1 & 0 & 1 \\ 1 & 0 & 1 \\ 1 & 0 & 1 \\ 1 & -1 & -1 \\ 1 & -1 & -1 \\ 1 & -1 & -1 \\ 1 & -1 & -1 \\ 1 & -1 & -1 \end{bmatrix} \begin{bmatrix} \beta_0 \\ \beta_1 \\ \beta_2 \end{bmatrix} + \epsilon
$$

This design matrix is produced by what is called "effects coding" since, if the restriction holds, the parameters estimated are all of the effects except one. The effect that is left out can be estimated by substitution into the restriction, that is, $\hat{\beta}_3 = -\hat{\beta}_2 - \hat{\beta}_1$. If the restriction is not assumed to hold, then $\hat{\beta}_1$ and $\hat{\beta}_2$ are no longer estimates of effects. They are, however, estimates of the estimable functions $\beta_1 - 1/3(\beta_1 + \beta_2 + \beta_3)$ and $\beta_2 - 1/3(\beta_1 + \beta_2 + \beta_3)$, respectively. That is, they are estimates of the difference between the effect of a particular level and the average of all effects. They are still useful estimable functions of the regression parameters.

This type of design matrix can be generalized to any number of levels and numbers of observations within levels. If this design matrix along with the vector **y** is fed into a standard linear model or regression package, then the resulting output will include estimates of the effects (or the difference between a particular effect and the average of the effects), their associated standard errors, and their levels of statistical significance.

We can now see more clearly the advantages of a procedure such as SAS's GLM. First, we do not have the extra work associated with recoding our independent variables. Second, we can test as many different hypotheses concerning the regression parameters as desired in a single regression run. A particular recoded full design matrix results in only one type of hypothesis being tested. If more than one type of hypothesis needs to be tested, then a separate regression analysis needs to be run for each type of hypothesis. For example, GLM could in one run test the hypothesis that

$$\beta_0 + \beta_1 = 0,\ \beta_2 - \beta_1 = \beta_3 - \beta_4,\ \text{and}\ \beta_2 - \frac{1}{k}\sum_{i=1}^{k} \beta_i = 0$$

We would have to use a different full rank matrix to test each of these types of hypotheses using some standard regression packages.

5.10 PROBLEMS

(1) Using the sample data in the Appendix, consider variable 5 (math aptitude) as the dependent variable and variable 10 (SES) as the independent variable. Test the hypothesis that $\alpha_1 = \alpha_2 = \alpha_3$ where α_1, α_2, and α_3 are the effects of the levels 1, 2, and 3 of SES, respectively. What are the parameter estimates μ_1, α_1, α_2, and α_3 under the model restrictions that $\alpha_1 + \alpha_2 + \alpha_3 = 0$?

(2) If the hypothesis $\alpha_1 = \alpha_2 = \alpha_3$ is rejected, test the hypothesis that $\alpha_1 - \alpha_2 = \alpha_2 - \alpha_3$. What does this test tell us about the relationship of the mean math scores with SES? How do you think these results would compare to a model where SES was treated as a continuous variable with values 1, 2, and 3?

(3) Plot the residuals for each of the three levels of SES. Do they appear to conform to the assumptions of the regression model?

(4) A group of 21 psychiatric patients were randomly assigned to one of three drug treatments, as shown below. The data elements are the changes in behavior over a six week interval.

	Drug Treatment	
A	*B*	*C*
3	1	0
5	2	0
3	1	0
3	2	1
2	2	2
4	2	2
4	0	1

(a) Summarize the regression analysis in a one-way analysis of variance table.
(b) Reparameterize the model in terms of estimable functions of the parameters, set up the normal equations and solve for the estimable functions of the parameters.
(c) Test the hypothesis that the effects of the three drugs are equal with $\alpha = .01$.
(d) Test the following additional hypotheses with $\alpha = .01$:
   (1) The effect of drug A is equal to the effect of drug B.
   (2) The effect of drug B is equal to the effect of drug C.
(e) Set up and test the hypothesis that the effect of drug A is equal to the average of the effects of drugs B and C.

(5) During World War II a general intelligence test was given to 18,782 white Army Air Force enlisted men (Harrell and Harrell, 1945). The means, standard deviations, and sample sizes for four of these groups are presented below.

Occupation	*N*	$\bar{X}$	*S.D.*
Engineer	39	126.6	11.7
Pharmacist	58	120.5	15.2
Production manager	34	118.1	16.0
Artist	48	114.9	11.2

(a) Test the overall hypothesis that the four occupational effects are equal with $\alpha = .05$.

(b) Reparameterize the model in terms of estimable functions of the parameters, set up the normal equations, and solve for them.

(c) Test the following two specific hypotheses:

(1) $\mu_A - \mu_B = \mu_C - \mu_D$ with $\alpha = .05$.

(2) The engineer effect is equal to the average of the other three effects with $\alpha = .05$.

(d) What assumptions of the regression model might possibly be violated?

(e) Can you think of any problems of making inferences to these four populations?

NOTES

1. Equivalently, we would estimate the parameters of the model $y = \beta_0 + \beta_1 x + \beta_2 x^2 + \epsilon$, where x is a continuous measure of SES, and test the hypothesis that $\beta_2 = 0$. The parameter β_2 indicates the degree of nonlinearity in the relationship between x and y.

2. If $\mathbf{X}$ is stochastic, then we must assume that $\mathbf{X}$ and ϵ are independent.

3. Other constraints such as setting β_0 or one of the β_i's to zero could also be used to yield a unique solution to the normal equations, but the constraint

$$\sum_{i=1}^{k} \beta_i = 0$$

has some conceptual advantages, which we will see later.

6 Linear Regression with Two Categorical Independent Variables

6.1 INTRODUCTION

The reason that we went through a rather detailed discussion of a linear model applicable to a one-way classification is that it generalizes neatly to more complex cases where we have more than one way of classifying an observation (that is, more than one categorical independent variable) and where in addition the data are not distributed equally or proportionately among the cells formed by classifying observations in two or more ways. If the data are balanced, then we will see that we can partition the total sums of squares into various components and use the analysis of variance paradigm to analyze our data and make tests of hypotheses as we did for the case of one categorical independent variable. When the data are unbalanced or the classification variables are not independent of one another, then the partitioning of the total sums of squares using analysis of variance breaks down because the component sums of squares do not add up to the total sums of squares. However, the linear model approach used with balanced data turns out to be equivalent to the analysis of variance approach.

We could simplify data analysis immensely if we could always conduct an experiment with an equal number of cases in each cell. However, even if we began with an equal number of subjects in each treatment combination we might lose cases in the various treatment cells at a differential rate. For example, in a maze experiment with rats under various conditions of food deprivation, some rats may die in some of the treatment conditions and the end result for the analyst would be different numbers of rats in the various treatment combinations or cells.

Another more common problem is that much of the data collected and analyzed by social scientists are survey-type data collected through questionnaires given to people selected on a probability basis. In many instances the independent variables of interest are naturally confounded or correlated in the population and hence the data will be unbalanced.

Examples of unbalanced data can be found in survey investigations concerning the "effects" of the home and school on children's academic achievement. Up to the present, there has been a substantial positive relationship between the socioeconomic status of the children's parents and the quality of the school the children attends. Poor ghetto childen have attended poor-quality schools, while upper-class suburban children have attended good-quality schools. Consequently, if we collected data to measure the effects of schools and home environment on achievement and cross-classified children on the basis of both home and school environment, we might find for a probability sample that the children were distributed as in Table 6.1.

This table is based upon a hypothetical sample of 500 and shows that the quality of the school that the child attends and the SES of the child's household are by no means independent. Specifically, 80 of the 100 low SES children attend poor schools, while only 5 of the high SES children attend poor schools. Table 6.1 is an example of what is called a two-way table. Children are cross-classified by two factors: quality of school and socioeconomic level of child's household. The distribution of these children in Table 6.1 is an example of unbalanced data. An example of balanced data involving the same two classifications is presented in Table 6.2.

While the numbers of cases in the cells are not equal in Table 6.2, the cell numbers in the rows and columns are proportional to each other. For example, 20 percent of low, medium, and high SES children go to poor schools; 50 percent of low, medium, and high SES children go to average schools; and 30 percent of low, medium, and high SES children go to good schools. When data are distributed like this we will see that we can partition the total sums of squares of the dependent variable around the mean into a sum of squares for rows (quality of school), a sum of squares for columns (socioeconomic level of child's household), a sum of squares due to interactions, and a within-group sum of squares. These sums of squares add up to the total sum of squares about the mean. Interaction will be defined in detail later, but can roughly be described in the case of balanced data as the sum of squares between cells that is not accounted for by the row and column sums of squares. This means that it is necessary to specify additional parameters beyond row and column parameters to account for the variation in the cell means. (When presenting means,

TABLE 6.1
Unbalanced Data for a Two-Way Classification

	Socioeconomic Status of Child's Household			
Quality of School	*Low*	*Medium*	*High*	*Total*
Poor	80	15	5	100
Average	10	220	20	250
Good	10	65	75	150
Total	100	300	100	500

TABLE 6.2
Balanced Data for a Two-Way Classification

	Socioeconomic Status of Child's Household			
Quality of School	*Low*	*Medium*	*High*	*Total*
Poor	20	60	20	100
Average	50	150	50	250
Good	30	90	30	150
Total	100	300	100	500

sample sizes, or any other data characterized by two categorical independent variables in a two-way table such as Table 6.2, one factor is associated with the rows and the other factor with the columns of the table.) When data are balanced we can compute these various sums of squares and test various hypotheses in a simple analysis of variance fashion. However, when the data are unbalanced, the same analysis of variance computation would lead to erroneous results. When one proceeds in a linear model-building fashion analogous to that previously used in describing a one-way classification, one always obtains the correct results.

A word of caution concerning the interpretation of "effects" of a variable is in order. For example, in the one-factor linear model we cannot say that SES *causes* achievement. We can only say that SES is *significantly related to* achievement. This is especially true of survey-type data where people are not allocated randomly to the various levels of the factor of interest. We did not randomly allocate the children to the three SES levels, they were selected through life circumstances to be in these categories. Aside from SES, these children in the different SES categories differ in many significant ways that are related to academic achievement. For example, they also attend different quality schools. The achievement of these children could be due in part to the schools that they attend. We would feel more comfortable attributing "cause" to a factor if the children were randomly assigned to the various levels of the factor because we would expect less confounding with other potentially important factors that might contribute to achievement. In order to be able to make relatively confident causal statements concerning the relative effects of the home environment and the school environment, we would have to allocate children randomly at birth to the various cells of the two-way table. Ideally, we would allocate an equal number of children randomly to each of the nine cells. Social manipulations of this type are either impossible or undesirable from a number of points of view. The only recourse left to the researcher is to sample children already found in these life situations and interpret relationships found between the independent variables and dependent variables with extreme caution.

The linear model approach applied to these real-life situations where the children are distributed neither randomly nor proportionately among the cells yields estimates of "effects" that are adjusted for the "effects" of other factors in the model. In our home versus school example, we can estimate the effects of the home environment adjusted for the effects of school quality. If the factors are highly confounded or related, as they are in our example, then we will see that our estimates of various contrasts or estimable functions of the parameters will have large standard errors associated with them. We have seen previously in the case of multiple regression that if the independent variables are highly intercorrelated, then each of the regression coefficients has a large standard error. Many examples can be found in the literature in which all regression coefficients are found not to be significantly different from zero, even though the regression sum of squares that reflects the joint influence of all variables simultaneously is highly significant. This problem was earlier referred to as "multicolinearity." The same basic problem arises when dealing with categorical variables, as in the present situation.

The two-factor categorical regression model is developed in section 6.2. It is an extension of regression models that were previously discussed. It is illustrated on an unbalanced data set in order to illustrate its generality. However, it is equally applicable to a balanced data set. Section 6.3 illustrates, once again, the use of the generalized inverse for solving the normal equations. As before, we have the problem of nonuniqueness of the solution vector to the normal equations and must again rely upon estimable functions of the regression parameters. This is discussed in section 6.4. The partitioning of the total sum of squares and its relationship to hypothesis testing is discussed in section

6.5. A more detailed discussion of the testing of specific hypotheses is presented in section 6.6. Section 6.7 presents a general procedure that can be followed step by step in order to test any admissible hypothesis. This procedure can be applied to any linear model whatsoever. Section 6.8 discusses considerations in using the computer to generate the regression analyses for the types of models discussed in this chapter. Section 6.9 concludes with an example using dummy variable codings.

6.2 TWO-FACTOR MODEL WITH UNBALANCED DATA

For demonstrating a two-factor linear models, we shall use a small set of hypothetical data consisting of two types of communities (urban and suburban) and two types of schools (poor and good). The hypothetical achievement scores for fifteen students are presented in Table 6.3. The row, column, and cell means, as well as sample sizes, are presented in Table 6.4. These data are clearly unbalanced in that children in good schools are more likely to be found in suburban communities.

The linear model proposed to fit this model is similar to those already discussed. The model can be expressed as $\mathbf{y} = \mathbf{X}\boldsymbol{\beta} + \boldsymbol{\epsilon}$, where $\mathbf{y}$ is the vector of observations on the dependent variable, $\mathbf{X}$ is an $N \times p$ matrix of the values of the independent variables, $\boldsymbol{\beta}$ is a $p \times 1$ vector of regression parameters, and $\boldsymbol{\epsilon}$ is a vector of residuals that is assumed to be normally distributed with mean equal to $\mathbf{0}$ and variance equal to $\sigma^2\mathbf{I}$. We will see that the $\mathbf{X}$ matrix is not of full rank and hence $\boldsymbol{\beta}$ itself is not estimable. However, certain contrasts among the elements of $\boldsymbol{\beta}$ are estimable.

In our example we have two independent variables: type of community and quality of school. We will create dummy variables for each of these two independent variables exactly as we did for the previous model that had one independent variable. Each child will have two scores for type of community and two scores for quality of school, as well as a score on the dependent variable, academic achievement.

TABLE 6.3
Achievement Scores Classified by Type of Community and Quality of School

	Quality of School	
Type of Community	*Poor*	*Good*
Urban	5,5,6,7,7	6,7,8
Suburban	7,8	7,8,8,9,9

The model $\mathbf{y} = \mathbf{X}\boldsymbol{\beta} + \epsilon$ for our example can be expressed as

$$\begin{bmatrix} y_{111} \\ y_{112} \\ y_{113} \\ y_{114} \\ y_{115} \\ y_{121} \\ y_{122} \\ y_{123} \\ y_{211} \\ y_{212} \\ y_{221} \\ y_{222} \\ y_{223} \\ y_{224} \\ y_{225} \end{bmatrix} = \begin{bmatrix} 1 & X_{111(1)} & X_{111(2)} & X_{111(3)} & X_{111(4)} \\ 1 & X_{112(1)} & X_{112(2)} & X_{112(3)} & X_{112(4)} \\ 1 & X_{113(1)} & X_{113(2)} & X_{113(3)} & X_{113(4)} \\ 1 & X_{114(1)} & X_{114(2)} & X_{114(3)} & X_{114(4)} \\ 1 & X_{115(1)} & X_{115(2)} & X_{115(3)} & X_{115(4)} \\ 1 & X_{121(1)} & X_{121(2)} & X_{121(3)} & X_{121(4)} \\ 1 & X_{122(1)} & X_{122(2)} & X_{122(3)} & X_{122(4)} \\ 1 & X_{123(1)} & X_{123(2)} & X_{123(3)} & X_{123(4)} \\ 1 & X_{211(1)} & X_{211(2)} & X_{211(3)} & X_{211(4)} \\ 1 & X_{212(1)} & X_{212(2)} & X_{212(3)} & X_{212(4)} \\ 1 & X_{221(1)} & X_{221(2)} & X_{221(3)} & X_{221(4)} \\ 1 & X_{222(1)} & X_{222(2)} & X_{222(3)} & X_{222(4)} \\ 1 & X_{223(1)} & X_{223(2)} & X_{223(3)} & X_{223(4)} \\ 1 & X_{224(1)} & X_{224(2)} & X_{224(3)} & X_{224(4)} \\ 1 & X_{225(1)} & X_{225(2)} & X_{225(3)} & X_{225(4)} \end{bmatrix} \begin{bmatrix} \mu \\ \alpha_1 \\ \alpha_2 \\ \beta_1 \\ \beta_2 \end{bmatrix} = \begin{bmatrix} \epsilon_{111} \\ \epsilon_{112} \\ \epsilon_{113} \\ \epsilon_{114} \\ \epsilon_{115} \\ \epsilon_{121} \\ \epsilon_{122} \\ \epsilon_{123} \\ \epsilon_{211} \\ \epsilon_{212} \\ \epsilon_{221} \\ \epsilon_{222} \\ \epsilon_{223} \\ \epsilon_{224} \\ \epsilon_{225} \end{bmatrix}$$

The first subscript indicates type of community, the second subscript indicates quality of school, and the third subscript indicates the child within a particular cell formed by these two classification variables. The fourth subscript in the **X** matrix is simply the dummy variable number. The first two dummy variables reflect type of community ($x_1 = 1$ if child is in urban category, 0 otherwise; and $x_2 = 1$ if child is in suburban category, 0 otherwise); the second two dummy variables reflect quality of school ($x_3 = 1$ if child is in poor quality

TABLE 6.4
Mean Achievement Scores

	Quality of School					
	Poor		*Good*		*Row Means and Sample Sizes*	
Type of Community	$\bar{x}$	*n*	$\bar{x}$	*n*		
Urban	6	5	7	3	6.37	8
Suburban	7.5	2	8.2	5	8.00	7
Column means and sample sizes	6.43	7	7.75	8	—	—

school, 0 otherwise; and $x_4 = 1$ if child is in good quality school, 0 otherwise). Let us now write the model in terms of the particular observations that we have for our hypothetical example.

$$\begin{bmatrix} 5 \\ 5 \\ 6 \\ 7 \\ 7 \\ 6 \\ 7 \\ 8 \\ 7 \\ 8 \\ 7 \\ 8 \\ 8 \\ 9 \\ 9 \end{bmatrix} = \begin{bmatrix} 1 & 1 & 0 & 1 & 0 \\ 1 & 1 & 0 & 1 & 0 \\ 1 & 1 & 0 & 1 & 0 \\ 1 & 1 & 0 & 1 & 0 \\ 1 & 1 & 0 & 1 & 0 \\ 1 & 1 & 0 & 0 & 1 \\ 1 & 1 & 0 & 0 & 1 \\ 1 & 1 & 0 & 0 & 1 \\ 1 & 0 & 1 & 1 & 0 \\ 1 & 0 & 1 & 1 & 0 \\ 1 & 0 & 1 & 0 & 1 \\ 1 & 0 & 1 & 0 & 1 \\ 1 & 0 & 1 & 0 & 1 \\ 1 & 0 & 1 & 0 & 1 \\ 1 & 0 & 1 & 0 & 1 \end{bmatrix} \begin{bmatrix} \mu \\ \alpha_1 \\ \alpha_2 \\ \beta_1 \\ \beta_2 \end{bmatrix} + \epsilon$$

From the above we can see that the first child falls in the urban category ($x_1 = 1$, $x_2 = 0$) and a poor quality school ($x_3 = 1$, $x_4 = 0$).

6.3 NORMAL EQUATIONS

The normal equations corresponding to our model are

$$\mathbf{X}'\mathbf{X}\beta = \mathbf{X}'\mathbf{y}$$

or

$$\begin{bmatrix} 1&1&1&1&1&1&1&1&1&1&1&1&1&1&1 \\ 1&1&1&1&1&1&1&1&0&0&0&0&0&0&0 \\ 0&0&0&0&0&0&0&0&1&1&1&1&1&1&1 \\ 1&1&1&1&1&0&0&0&1&1&0&0&0&0&0 \\ 0&0&0&0&0&1&1&1&0&0&1&1&1&1&1 \end{bmatrix} \begin{bmatrix} 1&1&0&1&0 \\ 1&1&0&1&0 \\ 1&1&0&1&0 \\ 1&1&0&1&0 \\ 1&1&0&1&0 \\ 1&1&0&0&1 \\ 1&1&0&0&1 \\ 1&1&0&0&1 \\ 1&0&1&1&0 \\ 1&0&1&1&0 \\ 1&0&1&0&1 \\ 1&0&1&0&1 \\ 1&0&1&0&1 \\ 1&0&1&0&1 \\ 1&0&1&0&1 \end{bmatrix} \begin{bmatrix} \mu \\ \alpha_1 \\ \alpha_2 \\ \beta_1 \\ \beta_2 \end{bmatrix}$$

$$= \begin{bmatrix} 1 & 1 & 1 & 1 & 1 & 1 & 1 & 1 & 1 & 1 & 1 & 1 & 1 & 1 & 1 \\ 1 & 1 & 1 & 1 & 1 & 1 & 1 & 1 & 0 & 0 & 0 & 0 & 0 & 0 & 0 \\ 0 & 0 & 0 & 0 & 0 & 0 & 0 & 0 & 1 & 1 & 1 & 1 & 1 & 1 & 1 \\ 1 & 1 & 1 & 1 & 1 & 0 & 0 & 0 & 1 & 1 & 0 & 0 & 0 & 0 & 0 \\ 0 & 0 & 0 & 0 & 0 & 1 & 1 & 1 & 0 & 0 & 1 & 1 & 1 & 1 & 1 \end{bmatrix} \begin{bmatrix} 5 \\ 5 \\ 6 \\ 7 \\ 7 \\ 6 \\ 7 \\ 8 \\ 7 \\ 8 \\ 7 \\ 8 \\ 8 \\ 9 \\ 9 \end{bmatrix}$$

which yields

$$\begin{bmatrix} 15 & 8 & 7 & 7 & 8 \\ 8 & 8 & 0 & 5 & 3 \\ 7 & 0 & 7 & 2 & 5 \\ 7 & 5 & 2 & 7 & 0 \\ 8 & 3 & 5 & 0 & 8 \end{bmatrix} \begin{bmatrix} \mu \\ \alpha_1 \\ \alpha_2 \\ \beta_1 \\ \beta_2 \end{bmatrix} = \begin{bmatrix} 107 \\ 51 \\ 56 \\ 45 \\ 62 \end{bmatrix}$$

The vector on the right-hand side of the equation gives the sum of the values of the dependent variables for all children, urban, suburban, poor, and good-quality schools, respectively. Each row of the matrix on the left side of the equation indicates the number μ's, α_1's, α_2's, β_1's, and β_2's respectively involved in each one of these totals. For example, there are 8 μ's, 8 α_1's, 0 α_2's, 5 β_1's, and 3 β_2's involved in the observations that total 51. These are the observations in cells 11 and 12, the urban schools.

We know from our previous discussions that **X′X** is not of full rank; consequently **X′X** has no unique inverse and there is no unique solution for $\hat{\beta}^*$. We can, however, solve for a generalized inverse of **X′X** that will yield one of an infinite number of solutions for $\hat{\beta}^*$. We know that the elements of $\hat{\beta}^*$ themselves are not estimable, but that certain contrasts among the elements of

$\hat{\beta}^*$ are estimable. A solution for $\hat{\beta}^*$ is given by $\mathbf{GX'y}$ where $\mathbf{G}$ is a generalized inverse of $\mathbf{X'X}$.

We previously found a generalized inverse for a one-factor linear model by finding the inverse of a nonsingular minor of the matrix whose rank is equal to that of the full matrix and augmenting this matrix by rows and columns of zeros to obtain the proper dimension for the generalized inverse. Cursory examination of the $\mathbf{X'X}$ matrix indicates that rows 2 and 3 sum to row 1 and likewise rows 4 and 5 sum to row 1, so that there are two linear dependencies and two vectors need to be removed from the set in order to have a linearly independent set of vectors. Consequently, the rank of $\mathbf{X'X}$ is 3.

A 3×3 nonsingular minor of $\mathbf{X'X}$ is

$$\mathbf{A} = \begin{bmatrix} 7 & 2 & 5 \\ 2 & 7 & 0 \\ 5 & 0 & 8 \end{bmatrix}$$

The inverse[1] of $\mathbf{A}$ is

$$\frac{1}{185}\begin{bmatrix} 56 & -16 & -35 \\ -16 & 31 & 10 \\ -35 & 10 & 45 \end{bmatrix}$$

We can now form a generalized inverse of $\mathbf{X'X}$ by taking our unique inverse of the 3×3 minor and augmenting it with 2 rows of zeros and 2 columns of zeros. This gives the generalized inverse

$$\mathbf{G} = \frac{1}{185}\begin{bmatrix} 0 & 0 & 0 & 0 & 0 \\ 0 & 0 & 0 & 0 & 0 \\ 0 & 0 & 56 & -16 & -35 \\ 0 & 0 & -16 & 31 & 10 \\ 0 & 0 & -35 & 10 & 45 \end{bmatrix}$$

We can verify that $\mathbf{G}$ is a generalized inverse of $\mathbf{X'X}$ by noting that it satisfies

$$\mathbf{X'XGX'X} = \mathbf{X'X}$$

since

$$\frac{1}{185}\begin{bmatrix} 15 & 8 & 7 & 7 & 8 \\ 8 & 8 & 0 & 5 & 3 \\ 7 & 0 & 7 & 2 & 5 \\ 7 & 5 & 2 & 7 & 0 \\ 8 & 3 & 5 & 0 & 8 \end{bmatrix}\begin{bmatrix} 0 & 0 & 0 & 0 & 0 \\ 0 & 0 & 0 & 0 & 0 \\ 0 & 0 & 56 & -16 & -35 \\ 0 & 0 & -16 & 31 & 10 \\ 0 & 0 & -35 & 10 & 45 \end{bmatrix}\begin{bmatrix} 15 & 8 & 7 & 7 & 8 \\ 8 & 8 & 0 & 5 & 3 \\ 7 & 0 & 7 & 2 & 5 \\ 7 & 5 & 2 & 7 & 0 \\ 8 & 3 & 5 & 0 & 8 \end{bmatrix}$$

$$= \begin{bmatrix} 15 & 8 & 7 & 7 & 8 \\ 8 & 8 & 0 & 5 & 3 \\ 7 & 0 & 7 & 2 & 5 \\ 7 & 5 & 2 & 7 & 0 \\ 8 & 3 & 5 & 0 & 8 \end{bmatrix}$$

Since we have verified that **G** is a generalized inverse of **X′X**, let us now find a solution to $\hat{\boldsymbol{\beta}}^*$ by substituting into the right side of $\hat{\boldsymbol{\beta}}^* = \mathbf{GX'y}$.

Substituting, we find

$$\begin{bmatrix} \hat{\mu}^* \\ \hat{\alpha}_1^* \\ \hat{\alpha}_2^* \\ \hat{\beta}_1^* \\ \hat{\beta}_2^* \end{bmatrix} = \frac{1}{185}\begin{bmatrix} 0 & 0 & 0 & 0 & 0 \\ 0 & 0 & 0 & 0 & 0 \\ 0 & 0 & 56 & -16 & -35 \\ 0 & 0 & -16 & 31 & 10 \\ 0 & 0 & -35 & 10 & 45 \end{bmatrix}\begin{bmatrix} 1&1&1&1&1&1&1&1&1&1&1&1&1&1&1 \\ 1&1&1&1&1&1&1&1&0&0&0&0&0&0&0 \\ 0&0&0&0&0&0&0&0&1&1&1&1&1&1&1 \\ 1&1&1&1&1&0&0&0&1&1&0&0&0&0&0 \\ 0&0&0&0&0&1&1&1&0&0&1&1&1&1&1 \end{bmatrix}\begin{bmatrix} 5 \\ 5 \\ 6 \\ 7 \\ 7 \\ 6 \\ 7 \\ 8 \\ 7 \\ 8 \\ 7 \\ 8 \\ 8 \\ 9 \\ 9 \end{bmatrix}$$

and

$$\begin{bmatrix} \hat{\mu}^* \\ \hat{\alpha}_1^* \\ \hat{\alpha}_2^* \\ \hat{\beta}_1^* \\ \hat{\beta}_2^* \end{bmatrix} = \begin{bmatrix} 0 \\ 0 \\ 1.330 \\ 6.049 \\ 6.919 \end{bmatrix}$$

We could also solve the normal equations by constraining the parameters or reparameterizing. There are five normal equations in five unknowns. However, two of the equations are linearly dependent on the remaining three equations. Removing these two redundant equations from the set of equations, we have three remaining equations in five unknowns. In order to obtain a unique solution, we need to add two more independent equations. These two independent equations each involve constraints on the parameters. The constraints typically are $\alpha_1 + \alpha_2 = 0$ and $\beta_1 + \beta_2 = 0$. Adding these two equations to the three linearly independent equations result in a set of five linearly independent equations in five unknowns. As an exercise, the reader can solve for $\hat{\boldsymbol{\beta}}^*$ using this method.

6.4 ESTIMABLE FUNCTIONS OF PARAMETERS

Once again it should be emphasized that these elements, themselves, are not estimates of the parameters in the model. Certain contrasts or linear combinations of these parameters, however, are estimable. Two contrasts of particular interest that are estimable are $\alpha_2 - \alpha_1$ and $\beta_2 - \beta_1$. They are estimable because **t**'s can be found such that $\alpha_2 - \alpha_1 = \mathbf{k}'\boldsymbol{\beta} = \mathbf{t}'\mathrm{E}(\mathbf{y})$ and $\beta_2 - \beta_1 = \mathbf{k}'\boldsymbol{\beta} = \mathbf{t}'\mathrm{E}(\mathbf{y})$ where $\mathrm{E}(\mathbf{y})$ is expressed in terms of the regression parameters. In the first case $\mathbf{t}'$ could equal $[-1,0,0,0,0,0,0,0,1,0,0,0,0,0,0]$ and in the second case $\mathbf{t}'$ could equal $[0,0,0,0,0,0,0,0,0,-1,1,0,0,0,0]$. For example,

$$
E(\mathbf{y}) = \mathbf{X}\boldsymbol{\beta} = \begin{bmatrix} 1 & 1 & 0 & 1 & 0 \\ 1 & 1 & 0 & 1 & 0 \\ 1 & 1 & 0 & 1 & 0 \\ 1 & 1 & 0 & 1 & 0 \\ 1 & 1 & 0 & 1 & 0 \\ 1 & 1 & 0 & 0 & 1 \\ 1 & 1 & 0 & 0 & 1 \\ 1 & 1 & 0 & 0 & 1 \\ 1 & 0 & 1 & 1 & 0 \\ 1 & 0 & 1 & 1 & 0 \\ 1 & 0 & 1 & 0 & 1 \\ 1 & 0 & 1 & 0 & 1 \\ 1 & 0 & 1 & 0 & 1 \\ 1 & 0 & 1 & 0 & 1 \\ 1 & 0 & 1 & 0 & 1 \end{bmatrix} \begin{bmatrix} \mu \\ \alpha_1 \\ \alpha_2 \\ \beta_1 \\ \beta_2 \end{bmatrix} = \begin{bmatrix} \mu + \alpha_1 + \beta_1 \\ \mu + \alpha_1 + \beta_1 \\ \mu + \alpha_1 + \beta_1 \\ \mu + \alpha_1 + \beta_1 \\ \mu + \alpha_1 + \beta_1 \\ \mu + \alpha_1 + \beta_2 \\ \mu + \alpha_1 + \beta_2 \\ \mu + \alpha_1 + \beta_2 \\ \mu + \alpha_2 + \beta_1 \\ \mu + \alpha_2 + \beta_1 \\ \mu + \alpha_2 + \beta_2 \\ \mu + \alpha_2 + \beta_2 \\ \mu + \alpha_2 + \beta_2 \\ \mu + \alpha_2 + \beta_2 \\ \mu + \alpha_2 + \beta_2 \end{bmatrix}
$$

and consequently,

$$
\beta_2 - \beta_1 = [0,0,0,-1,1] \begin{bmatrix} \mu \\ \alpha_1 \\ \alpha_2 \\ \beta_1 \\ \beta_2 \end{bmatrix}
$$

$$= [0,0,0,0,0,0,0,0,0,0-1,1,0,0,0,0]\begin{bmatrix} \mu+\alpha_1+\beta_1 \\ \mu+\alpha_1+\beta_1 \\ \mu+\alpha_1+\beta_1 \\ \mu+\alpha_1+\beta_1 \\ \mu+\alpha_1+\beta_1 \\ \mu+\alpha_1+\beta_2 \\ \mu+\alpha_1+\beta_2 \\ \mu+\alpha_1+\beta_2 \\ \mu+\alpha_2+\beta_1 \\ \mu+\alpha_2+\beta_1 \\ \mu+\alpha_2+\beta_2 \\ \mu+\alpha_2+\beta_2 \\ \mu+\alpha_2+\beta_2 \\ \mu+\alpha_2+\beta_2 \\ \mu+\alpha_2+\beta_2 \end{bmatrix}$$

or

$$\beta_2-\beta_1=\mu+\alpha_2+\beta_2-(\mu+\alpha_2+\beta_1)=\beta_2-\beta_1$$

In our case, $\alpha_2-\alpha_1$ equals 1.329 and $\beta_2-\beta_1$ equals .870. Other **t**'s will also satisfy these relationships. Also, note that any row of **X** forms a vector that when postmultiplied by $\boldsymbol{\beta}$ results in an estimable function of the parameters.

Consequently, the vector E(**y**) is estimable and, in our example, it is estimated as

$$
\widehat{E(\mathbf{y})} = \begin{bmatrix} 1 & 1 & 0 & 1 & 0 \\ 1 & 1 & 0 & 1 & 0 \\ 1 & 1 & 0 & 1 & 0 \\ 1 & 1 & 0 & 1 & 0 \\ 1 & 1 & 0 & 1 & 0 \\ 1 & 1 & 0 & 0 & 1 \\ 1 & 1 & 0 & 0 & 1 \\ 1 & 1 & 0 & 0 & 1 \\ 1 & 0 & 1 & 1 & 0 \\ 1 & 0 & 1 & 1 & 0 \\ 1 & 0 & 1 & 0 & 1 \\ 1 & 0 & 1 & 0 & 1 \\ 1 & 0 & 1 & 0 & 1 \\ 1 & 0 & 1 & 0 & 1 \\ 1 & 0 & 1 & 0 & 1 \end{bmatrix} \begin{bmatrix} 0 \\ 0 \\ 1.330 \\ 6.049 \\ 6.919 \end{bmatrix} = \begin{bmatrix} 6.049 \\ 6.049 \\ 6.049 \\ 6.049 \\ 6.049 \\ 6.919 \\ 6.919 \\ 6.919 \\ 7.379 \\ 7.379 \\ 8.249 \\ 8.249 \\ 8.249 \\ 8.249 \\ 8.249 \end{bmatrix}
$$

This vector is nothing more than the predicted cell means based upon the regression model. Note that all children in a particular cross-classification (cell) are predicted to have the same achievement, but that children in different cells are predicted to have different achievement levels.

6.5 COMPUTING SUMS OF SQUARES

We can now easily find the residual sums of squares by squaring the deviations of the observed scores from the predicted scores, the cell means. In matrix notation, the residual sum of squares is equal to $(\mathbf{y} - \hat{\mathbf{y}})'(\mathbf{y} - \hat{\mathbf{y}})$. In our example, the residual sum of squares ($SS_{Residual}$) equals

$$[-1.049, -1.049, -.049, .951, .951, -.919, .081, 1.081, -.379, .621, -1.249, -.249, .751, .751] \begin{bmatrix} -1.049 \\ -1.049 \\ -.049 \\ .951 \\ .951 \\ -.919 \\ .081 \\ 1.081 \\ -.379 \\ .621 \\ -1.249 \\ -.249 \\ -.249 \\ .751 \\ .751 \end{bmatrix} = 9.373$$

The least-squares fit also assures us that the sum of the residuals equals 0. This can easily be verified by adding up the residuals in our example. The sum of the residuals

$$\sum_{i=1}^{n} e_i$$

can be expressed in matrix notation as $\mathbf{1}'\mathbf{e}$ where $\mathbf{1}'$ is a row vector of ones and $\mathbf{e}$ is the column vector of residuals.

The reduction in sum of squares about zero for fitting our model is

$$\boldsymbol{\beta}'\mathbf{X}'\mathbf{y}$$

which, in our example, is

$$[0, 0, 1.330, 6.049, 6.919] \begin{bmatrix} 107 \\ 51 \\ 56 \\ 45 \\ 62 \end{bmatrix} = 775.627$$

The total sum of squares for our data is 785 and consequently we can see that the total sum of squares (785) equals the sum of squares due to the model (775.627) plus the error sum of squares (9.373). Normally, we would first obtain the sum of squares due to the model (regression) and subtract it from the total sum of squares to obtain the residual or error sums of squares.

We could test our model for significance, but we know that our overall effect, μ, accounts for a large proportion of the regression sum of squares. In our example, we know from psychological scaling considerations that μ is sigificantly different from zero and we are not interested in the contribution of μ to the regression sum of squares. What we are really interested in is the sum of squares due to regression beyond that due to fitting μ. The regression sum of squares due to μ (fitting the mean) is simply $N\bar{y}^2$ where N is the total number of observations and y is the overall mean of the dependent variable. In our example

$$N\bar{y}^2 = \frac{(\Sigma y)^2}{N} = 763.267$$

This is the same type of correction that was used to correct the regression sum of squares in our earlier discussion of multiple regression.

The regression sum of squares for our example can be partitioned into two sums of squares: a sum of squares for fitting the mean (R_μ) and a sum of squares for fitting the α_i and β_j parameters after the mean $R(\alpha_i, \beta_j | \mu)$ which is given by

$$R(\alpha_i, \beta_j | \mu) = R(\alpha_i, \beta_j, \mu) - R(\mu)$$

where $R(\alpha_i, \beta_j, \mu)$ is the regression sum of squares attributable to the full model $y_{ijk} = \mu + \alpha_i + \beta_j + \epsilon_{ijk}$. For our example, we would obtain 775.627 – 763.267 = 12.36 for $R(\alpha_i, \beta_j | \mu)$. This regression sum of squares can be interpreted as the additional sum of squares that our model $y_{ijk} = \mu + \alpha_i + \beta_j + \epsilon_{ijk}$ can account for beyond the simple model $y_{ijk} = \mu + \epsilon_{ijk}$. In essence, the regression sum of squares due to $\mu(R(\mu))$ in the simple model is

$$\frac{(\Sigma y)^2}{N}$$

since the estimate of μ for this simple model is the overall mean ($\bar{y}$). We can set up an analysis of variance (see Table 6.5) to determine if our full model explains the data better than the simple overall effect model, $y_{ijk} = \mu + \epsilon_{ijk}$.

Both F tests are significant at the .01 level. As mentioned previously, we suspected that the mean would be significantly different from zero. What we are really interested in is whether our full model fits the data better than a model with only an overall effect μ. The significant F of 7.913 indicates that the addition of the α_i and β_j parameters adds explanatory power to the model over just fitting an overall effect.

The degrees of freedom in Table 6.5 were obtained by observing that there are 15 degrees of freedom for the 15 observations: 3 degrees of freedom for regression because the rank of the **X** matrix is 3, and 12 degrees of freedom for error because the degrees of freedom for error is the number of observations minus the rank of **X**. We further partitioned the regression degrees of freedom by noting that 1 degree of freedom must be attributed to the mean and the remaining 2 degrees of freedom due to regression must be attributed to the α_i and β_j parameters after fitting μ.

6.6 TESTING SPECIFIC HYPOTHESES

Let us further examine our regression model. We found that $E(y_{ijk}) = \mu + \alpha_i + \beta_j$ was a better model than $E(y_{ijk}) = \mu$ in explaining the variation in the dependent variable. We shall now be interested to see if we need both sets of parameters in the model. For example, a model such as $E(y_{ijk}) = \mu + \alpha_i$ or $E(y_{ijk}) = \mu + \beta_j$ may fit the data essentially as well as our full model. We can test these two models by examining the differences in the regression sums of squares due to each of these reduced models and the full model. The ratio of this difference in regression sums of squares divided by its degrees of freedom to the error mean square is distributed as F. If the F is not significant, then we may consider dropping out a set of parameters from the model. In other words, what we are trying to do here is to drop out a set of parameters and determine if this reduced model has about as much explanatory power as the full model. In our example, we have two sets of parameters, the α_i's and the β_j's. The contribution of the α_i's to the explanatory power of the model is determined by fitting the model $E(y_{ijk}) = \mu + \beta_j$ and seeing how well this model performs in relation to $E(y_{ijk}) = \mu + \alpha_i + \beta_j$. Likewise, the contribution of the β_j's to the explanatory power of the model is determined by fitting the model $E(y_{ijk}) = \mu + \alpha_i$ and seeing how well this model performs in relation to $E(y_{ijk}) = \mu + \alpha_i + \beta_j$. This source of

TABLE 6.5
Sums of Squares, Mean Squares, and Tests of Significance

Source of Variance	*Sum of Squares*	*Degrees of Freedom*	*Mean Square*	*F*
Mean	763.267	1	763.267	977.29
α_i's and β_j's after fitting μ	12.360	2	6.180	7.913
Error	9.373	12	.781	—
Total	785.0	15	—	—

variation is sometimes referred to as the effects of the β_j adjusted for μ and the α_i or as the effect of the β_j after fitting μ and α_i. The difference in the regression sums of squares due to $E(y_{ijk}) = \mu + \alpha_i + \beta_j$ and $E(y_{ijk}) = \mu + \alpha_i$ divided by σ is distributed as a χ^2 with the degrees of freedom equal to the difference in degrees of freedom associated with the respective regression sums of squares. If σ^2 was known, we could directly test this hypothesis by referring the calculated value of χ^2 to a χ^2 table. However, σ^2 has to be estimated and this forces us to rely on the F distribution.

Let us now calculate the regression sums of squares for the model $E(y_{ijk}) = \mu + \beta_j + \epsilon_{ijk}$ so that we can test the effects of α_i after adjusting for μ and β_j. The reduced model for our example is

$$\begin{bmatrix} 5 \\ 5 \\ 6 \\ 7 \\ 7 \\ 6 \\ 7 \\ 8 \\ 7 \\ 8 \\ 7 \\ 8 \\ 8 \\ 9 \\ 9 \end{bmatrix} = \begin{bmatrix} 1 & 1 & 0 \\ 1 & 1 & 0 \\ 1 & 1 & 0 \\ 1 & 1 & 0 \\ 1 & 1 & 0 \\ 1 & 0 & 1 \\ 1 & 0 & 1 \\ 1 & 0 & 1 \\ 1 & 1 & 0 \\ 1 & 1 & 0 \\ 1 & 0 & 1 \\ 1 & 0 & 1 \\ 1 & 0 & 1 \\ 1 & 0 & 1 \\ 1 & 0 & 1 \end{bmatrix} \begin{bmatrix} \mu \\ \beta_1 \\ \beta_2 \end{bmatrix} + \epsilon$$

A solution for $\hat{\beta}$ can be found from $\mathbf{GX'y}$ where $\mathbf{G}$ is the generalized inverse of $\mathbf{X'X}$. This model is in essence a one-factor model similar to the one discussed in the previous chapter. The matrix $\mathbf{X'X}$ equals

$$\begin{bmatrix} 15 & 7 & 8 \\ 7 & 7 & 0 \\ 8 & 0 & 8 \end{bmatrix}$$

The rank of **X′X** is 2 since the sum of the last 2 rows equals the first row. The inverse of the 2 × 2 nonsingular minor is

$$\begin{bmatrix} \frac{1}{7} & 0 \\ 0 & \frac{1}{8} \end{bmatrix}$$

and consequently

$$\mathbf{G} = \begin{bmatrix} 0 & 0 & 0 \\ 0 & \frac{1}{7} & 0 \\ 0 & 0 & \frac{1}{8} \end{bmatrix}$$

The vector **X′y** for our example is

$$\begin{bmatrix} 107 \\ 45 \\ 62 \end{bmatrix}$$

and so

$$\hat{\beta}^* = \begin{bmatrix} 0 & 0 & 0 \\ 0 & \frac{1}{7} & 0 \\ 0 & 0 & \frac{1}{8} \end{bmatrix} \begin{bmatrix} 107 \\ 45 \\ 62 \end{bmatrix} = \begin{bmatrix} 0 \\ 6\frac{3}{7} \\ 7\frac{3}{4} \end{bmatrix}$$

The regression sum of squares for our model is

$$\hat{\beta}^{*\prime}\mathbf{X}'\mathbf{y} = \begin{bmatrix} 0 & 6\frac{3}{7} & 7\frac{3}{4} \end{bmatrix} \begin{bmatrix} 107 \\ 45 \\ 62 \end{bmatrix} = 769.787$$

The regression sum of squares for a one-factor linear model can also be calculated more easily by noting that

$$769.787 = \sum_j n_j \bar{y}_j^2 = 7(6.4286)^2 + 8(7.75)^2$$

where n_j is the number of observations in level j of the factor of interest and $\bar{y}_j$ is the corresponding mean for that level. The difference between the sum of squares for the full model and the reduced model $y_{jik} = \mu + \beta_j + \epsilon_{jik}$ is

$$R(\mu,\alpha_i,\beta_j) - R(\mu,\beta_j) = R(\alpha_i|\mu,\beta_j)$$

For our example

$$R(\alpha_i|\mu,\beta_j) = 775.627 - 769.787 = 5.84$$

It can also be shown that

$$\frac{R(\alpha_i|\mu,\beta_j)}{\sigma^2}$$

is distributed as a χ^2 with degrees of freedom equal to the difference in the degrees of freedom associated with $R(\mu,\alpha_i,\beta_j)$ and $R(\mu,\beta_j)$. It is also independently distributed of the χ^2 associated with the error sums of squares. If we divide each of these χ^2's by their respective degrees of freedom, their ratio is distributed as F with df_1 and df_2 degrees of freedom. In our example, $df_1 = 1$ and $df_2 = 12$ so that

$$F = \frac{5.48}{1} \Big/ \frac{9.373}{12} = 7.477$$

which is significant at the .01 level. The α_i parameters add explanatory power to the model over and above the model $y_{ijk} = \mu + \beta_j + \epsilon_{ijk}$.

Let us now look at the effects of the β_j's adjusting for μ and the α_i's. The adjusted sum of squares for the β_j adjusted for μ and the α_i's is given as

$$R(\beta_j|\mu,\alpha_i) = R(\mu,\alpha_i,\beta_j) - R(\mu,\alpha_i)$$

The regression sum of squares due to the model $y_{ijk} = \mu + \alpha_i + \epsilon_{ijk}$ is calculated in exactly the same way as the regression sum of squares previously calculated for $y_{ijk} = \mu + \beta_j + \epsilon_{ijk}$. For our example, $R(\beta_j | \mu, \alpha_i) = 775.627 - 773.125 = 2.502$. The F ratio is 3.204 and when referring to the F table with 1 and 12 degrees of freedom we find that the F is not significant at the .05 level. These tests are summarized in Table 6.6.

Table 6.6 indicates that a model including both the α_i and β_j parameters does better than a model that only includes an overall effect (μ). However, the

TABLE 6.6
Sources of Variation for Two-Factor Model

Source of Variance		*Sum of Squares*	*Degrees of Freedom*	*Mean Squares*	*F*
Type of community (adjusted for quality of schools)	α_i adjusting for μ and β_j $(\alpha_i \mid \mu, \beta_j)$	5.84	1	5.840	7.447
Schools (adjusted for type of community)	β_j adjusting for μ and α_i $(\beta_j \mid \mu, \alpha_i)$	2.502	1	2.502	3.204
Quality of schools and type of community (adjusted for overall effect)	α_i and β_j adjusting for $\mu (\alpha_i, \beta_j \mid \mu)$	12.360	2	6.180	7.913
Error	deviations from predicted values based upon the full model $E(y_{ijk}) = \mu + \alpha_i + \beta_j$	9.373	12	.781	—

table also indicates that maybe we can do almost as well using the model $y_{ijk} = \mu + \alpha_i + \epsilon_{ijk}$ instead of $y_{ijk} = \mu + \alpha_i + \beta_j + \epsilon_{ijk}$ because the adjusted α_i sums of squares were significant while the adjusted β_j sums of squares were not significant.

These adjusted sums of squares can be considered as sums of squares due to contrasts and their associated F tests can be considered as testing hypotheses of the form $\mathbf{K}\boldsymbol{\beta} = \mathbf{0}$ where $\mathbf{K}$ is a matrix with full row rank whose elements within a row sum to one. The hypotheses that $\alpha_1 = \alpha_2$ and $\beta_1 = \beta_2$ can be expressed as

$$\mathbf{K}\boldsymbol{\beta} = \begin{bmatrix} 0 & 1 & -1 & 0 & 0 \\ 0 & 0 & 0 & 1 & -1 \end{bmatrix} \begin{bmatrix} \mu \\ \alpha_1 \\ \alpha_2 \\ \beta_1 \\ \beta_2 \end{bmatrix} = \begin{bmatrix} 0 \\ 0 \end{bmatrix} = \mathrm{m}$$

This hypothesis can be tested by calculating the quadratic form

$$Q = [\mathbf{K}\hat{\boldsymbol{\beta}}^* - \mathbf{m}]' [\mathbf{K}\mathbf{G}\mathbf{K}']^{-1} [\mathbf{K}\hat{\boldsymbol{\beta}} - \mathbf{m}]$$

which, when divided by σ^2, is distributed as χ^2 with degrees of freedom equal to the rank of **K**. This χ^2 is distributed independently of the χ^2 based upon the error sum of squares. Consequently, the ratio

$$\frac{\dfrac{Q}{\text{rank of k}}}{\dfrac{\text{error sum of squares}}{\text{degrees of freedom for error}}}$$

is distributed as F with degrees of freedom equal to the rank of **K** and degrees of freedom for error, respectively.

Let us now proceed to calculate Q. For the hypothesis that

$$\alpha_1 = \alpha_2 \text{ and } \beta_1 = \beta_2, \mathbf{m} \text{ must be equal to } \begin{bmatrix} 0 \\ 0 \end{bmatrix}$$

For our example,

$$\mathbf{K}\hat{\beta}^* = \begin{bmatrix} 0 & 1 & -1 & 0 & 0 \\ 0 & 0 & 0 & 1 & -1 \end{bmatrix} \begin{bmatrix} 0 \\ 0 \\ 1.330 \\ 6.049 \\ 6.919 \end{bmatrix} = \begin{bmatrix} -1.330 \\ -.870 \end{bmatrix}$$

so that

$$[\mathbf{K}\hat{\beta}^* - \mathbf{m}] = \begin{bmatrix} -1.330 \\ -.870 \end{bmatrix} - \begin{bmatrix} 0 \\ 0 \end{bmatrix} = \begin{bmatrix} -1.330 \\ -.870 \end{bmatrix}$$

The vector

$$\begin{bmatrix} -1.330 \\ -.870 \end{bmatrix}$$

reflects the deviation of our sample estimates of the differences between parameter values and our hypothesis that the differences are

$$\begin{bmatrix} 0 \\ 0 \end{bmatrix}$$

In general, the larger in absolute value the elements in the vector, the larger will be the value of Q. Q can now be calculated as

$$Q = [-1.330, -.870]\left[\frac{1}{185}\begin{bmatrix}0 & 1 & -1 & 0 & 0\\ 0 & 0 & 0 & 1 & -1\end{bmatrix}\begin{bmatrix}0 & 0 & 0 & 0 & 0\\ 0 & 0 & 0 & 0 & 0\\ 0 & 0 & 56 & -16 & -35\\ 0 & 0 & -16 & 31 & 10\\ 0 & 0 & -35 & 10 & 45\end{bmatrix}\begin{bmatrix}0 & 0\\ 1 & 0\\ -1 & 0\\ 0 & 1\\ 0 & -1\end{bmatrix}\right]^{-1}\begin{bmatrix}-1.330\\ -.870\end{bmatrix}$$

$$= [-1.330, -.870]\left[\frac{1}{185}\begin{bmatrix}56 & -19\\ -19 & 56\end{bmatrix}\right]^{-1}\begin{bmatrix}-1.330\\ -.870\end{bmatrix}$$

$$= [-1.330, -.870]\begin{bmatrix}3.7330 & 1.2664\\ 1.2664 & 3.7330\end{bmatrix}\begin{bmatrix}-1.330\\ -.870\end{bmatrix} = 12.360$$

We can see that the value of Q(12.360) is identical to the sum of squares due to α_i and β_j after adjusting for μ. In this manner, any hypotheses that are composed of estimable functions of the parameters may be tested. We could, for example, have set **m** equal to

$$\begin{bmatrix}3\\ 5\end{bmatrix}$$

or any other vector if we were interested in testing a particular hypothesis besides the one that was tested in the present example. All of these tests are called tests of the general linear hypothesis.

To see how useful tests of the general linear hypothesis are, let us test the hypothesis that $\alpha_1 = \alpha_2$. The Q associated with this hypothesis can be computed as

$$(\mathbf{K}\hat{\beta}^* - \mathbf{m})'\,(\mathbf{KGK}')^{-1}\,(\mathbf{K}\hat{\beta}^* - \mathbf{m}) = (-1.330)\,(3.303)\,(-1.330) = 5.84$$

where

$$[\mathbf{K}\hat{\beta}^* - \mathbf{m}] = [0, 1, -1, 0, 0]\begin{bmatrix}0\\ 0\\ 1.330\\ 6.049\\ 6.919\end{bmatrix} - 0 = -1.330$$

and

$$[\mathbf{KGK'}]^{-1} = \left[\frac{1}{185}[0\ 1\ -1\ 0\ 0]\begin{bmatrix} 0 & 0 & 0 & 0 & 0 \\ 0 & 0 & 0 & 0 & 0 \\ 0 & 0 & 56 & -16 & -35 \\ 0 & 0 & -16 & 31 & 10 \\ 0 & 0 & -35 & 10 & 45 \end{bmatrix}\begin{bmatrix} 0 \\ 1 \\ -1 \\ 0 \\ 0 \end{bmatrix}\right]^{-1}$$

$$= \left[\frac{56}{185}\right]^{-1} = 3.303$$

We see that Q is equal to the sum of squares associated with the effects of α_i adjusting for the β_j and μ (that is, $R(\alpha_i | \mu, \beta_j)$ previously computed as the difference, $R(\alpha_i, \beta_j, \mu) - R(\beta_j, \mu)$. The effect of β_j adjusting for μ and α_i could also be tested in a similar fashion using this test of the general linear hypothesis.

6.7 GENERAL PROCEDURES FOR TESTING HYPOTHESES

We are now ready to make some general observations concerning tests of hypotheses for the general linear model. These observations will be formulated as a series of steps that have to be taken in order to test general linear hypotheses.

(1) Write out the full model and obtain the normal equations, $\mathbf{X'X}\boldsymbol{\beta} = \mathbf{X'y}$.
(2) Solve for $\hat{\boldsymbol{\beta}}^*$ by finding a generalized inverse (**G**) of **X′X** and computing **GX′y**.
(3) Express the hypotheses of interest concerning the parameters in the form $\mathbf{K}\boldsymbol{\beta} = \mathbf{m}$, making certain that the rows of **K** are linearly independent and yield estimable contrasts. If the rows of **K** are not independent, then $(\mathbf{KGK'})^{-1}$ will not exist and the hypothesis of interest will be untestable. We can make certain that $\mathbf{K}\boldsymbol{\beta}$ is estimable by finding a matrix **T** such that $\mathbf{K}\boldsymbol{\beta} = \mathbf{T}(E(\mathbf{y}))$.
(4) Calculate $Q = (\mathbf{K}\hat{\boldsymbol{\beta}}^* - \mathbf{m})'(\mathbf{KGK'})^{-1}(\mathbf{K}\hat{\boldsymbol{\beta}}^* - \mathbf{m})$ for the hypothesis of interest and divide by the rank of **K**, r(**K**).
(5) Calculate the error sums of squares for the full model involving all the parameters, which equals $\mathbf{y'y} - \hat{\boldsymbol{\beta}}^*\mathbf{X'y}$, and divide by the degrees of freedom associated with this error sum of squares, which equals $N - r(\mathbf{X})$ where N is the total number of observations and r(**X**) is the rank of **X**.
(6) Form the ratio

$$\frac{\dfrac{Q}{r(\mathbf{K})}}{\dfrac{\mathbf{y'y} - \hat{\boldsymbol{\beta}}^*\mathbf{X'y}}{N - r(\mathbf{X})}}$$

which is distributed as F with r(**K**) and [N – r(**X**)] degrees of freedom, respectively.

(7) Refer to an F table and if F exceeds the value given for the appropriate numerator and denominator degrees of freedom, then the hypothesis, $\mathbf{K}\boldsymbol{\beta} = \mathbf{m}$, can be rejected at the significance level indicated by the F table.

These steps summarize a convenient way to test hypotheses concerning linear models. They are applicable to many situations that are to be discussed later in this book. They are also applicable to multiple regression analysis, which was discussed previously.

It should be noted that this method is equivalent to running two regression models, one with the parameters under test excluded, subtracting the regression sums of squares and dividing by the number of excluded parameters. The advantage of the Q approach is that we can test as many hypotheses as we wish by a single computer run in some linear model software packages.

In multiple regression, we saw that $E(\hat{\boldsymbol{\beta}}) = \boldsymbol{\beta}$ and that consequently the individual elements of the vector $\boldsymbol{\beta}$ are estimable. Also, any linear functions of these elements are estimable. Consequently, we could express the hypothesis that all of the elements of $\boldsymbol{\beta}$ except for the intercept are zero by $\mathbf{K}\boldsymbol{\beta} = \mathbf{0}$. In the case of three independent variables, this hypothesis would be expressed as

$$\mathbf{K}\beta = \begin{bmatrix} 0 & 1 & 0 & 0 \\ 0 & 0 & 1 & 0 \\ 0 & 0 & 0 & 1 \end{bmatrix} \begin{bmatrix} \beta_0 \\ \beta_1 \\ \beta_2 \\ \beta_3 \end{bmatrix} = \begin{bmatrix} 0 \\ 0 \\ 0 \end{bmatrix}$$

In many cases we are not interested in testing the hypothesis that β_0, the intercept parameter, is zero. In the behavioral and social sciences we know that β_0 is not zero because it is a function of the arbitrary scaling procedure used to generate the independent and/or dependent variables. The test of the general linear hypothesis that $\mathbf{K}\boldsymbol{\beta} = \mathbf{0}$ for multiple regression follows directly from our previous discussion and first involves computing Q where

$$Q = [\mathbf{K}\hat{\beta}]' \, [\mathbf{K}(\mathbf{X}'\mathbf{X})^{-1} \mathbf{K}']^{-1} \, [\mathbf{K}\hat{\beta}]$$

and $\hat{\boldsymbol{\beta}}$ is the estimate of $\boldsymbol{\beta}$. This equation has the same form as the less than full rank case for categorical independent variables, except that $(\mathbf{X}'\mathbf{X})^{-1}$ is substituted for **G**. The vector $[\mathbf{K}\hat{\boldsymbol{\beta}}]$ could have been written as $[\mathbf{K}\hat{\boldsymbol{\beta}} - \mathbf{m}]$ to be more general, but in our case we were interested in hypotheses of the form $\mathbf{K}\boldsymbol{\beta} = \mathbf{0}$ so that **m** becomes **0**. Again, **K** must be of full row rank, but we do not have to worry about whether the rows of **K** yield estimable functions of the parameters as we do in the less than full rank case. If $\mathbf{K\beta}$ in the population equals **0**, then it can be shown that Q/σ^2 is distributed as χ^2 with degrees of freedom equal to the rank of **K**. In the current example, **K** has rank 3. It can also be shown that this χ^2 is distributed independently of the χ^2 associated with the residual sum of squares. The residual sum of squares, $(\mathbf{y} - \mathbf{X}\hat{\boldsymbol{\beta}})'(\mathbf{y} - \mathbf{X}\hat{\boldsymbol{\beta}})$, divided by σ^2, is distributed as χ^2 with $N - r(\mathbf{X})$ degrees of freedom. In the full rank cases, $r(\mathbf{X})$ is simply the number of columns of **X** or, equivalently, the number of parameters to be estimated. The ratio

$$\frac{\dfrac{\dfrac{Q}{\sigma^2}}{r(\mathbf{K})}}{\dfrac{\dfrac{\text{SS residual}}{\sigma^2}}{N - r(\mathbf{X})}} = \frac{\dfrac{Q}{r(\mathbf{K})}}{\hat{\sigma}^2}$$

where

$$\hat{\sigma}^2 = \frac{(\mathbf{y} - \mathbf{X}\hat{\beta})'\,(\mathbf{y} - \mathbf{X}\hat{\beta})}{N - r(\mathbf{X})}$$

is the unbiased estimate of σ^2 and is distributed as F with $r(\mathbf{K})$ and $N - r(\mathbf{X})$ degrees of freedom, respectively. We then refer to an F table to determine whether to accept or reject this hypothesis at a selected level of significance.

If we are just interested in testing the hypothesis that $\beta_3 = 0$, then Q would be

$$Q = \left[[0, 0, 0, 1] \begin{bmatrix} \hat{\beta}_0 \\ \hat{\beta}_1 \\ \hat{\beta}_2 \\ \hat{\beta}_3 \end{bmatrix} \right] \left[[0, 0, 0, 1]\ [\mathbf{X}'\mathbf{X}]^{-1} \begin{bmatrix} 0 \\ 0 \\ 0 \\ 1 \end{bmatrix} \right]^{-1} \left[[0, 0, 0, 1] \begin{bmatrix} \hat{\beta}_0 \\ \hat{\beta}_1 \\ \hat{\beta}_2 \\ \hat{\beta}_3 \end{bmatrix} \right]$$

$$= \hat{\beta}_3\, [(\mathbf{X}'\mathbf{X})^{-1}_{4,4}]^{-1}\, \hat{\beta}_3$$

$$= \frac{\hat{\beta}_3^2}{(\mathbf{X}'\mathbf{X})^{-1}_{4,4}}$$

where $(\mathbf{X'X})^{-1}_{4,4}$ signifies the element in the fourth row and fourth column of $(\mathbf{X'X})^{-1}$. In this situation, **K** has rank 1 and consequently Q/σ^2 is distributed as a χ^2 with 1 degree of freedom under the null hypothesis. Q is also distributed independently of

$$\frac{\text{SS residual}}{\sigma^2}$$

which is distributed with N – r(**X**) degrees of freedom or N – 4 for the present example. To test this hypothesis that $\beta_3 = 0$, the F ratio

$$\frac{Q}{1} \Big/ \hat{\sigma}^2 = \frac{Q}{\hat{\sigma}^2}$$

is formed and the F value is referred to the appropriate F table with 1 and N – r(**X**) degrees of freedom. If the F value exceeds the appropriate value in the table, then the hypothesis that $\beta_3 = 0$ is rejected at the selected level of significance. Since $F = t^2 = \sqrt{F}$ when there is 1 degree of freedom for the numerator, this test can be transformed to a t test with N – r(**X**) degrees of freedom by

$$t = \sqrt{F} = \sqrt{\frac{\dfrac{\hat{\beta}_3^2}{(X'X)^{-1}_{4,4}}}{\hat{\sigma}^2}} = \frac{\hat{\beta}_3}{\hat{\sigma}\sqrt{(X'X)^{-1}_{4,4}}}$$

But this is exactly the test of the hypothesis $\beta_3 = 0$ discussed in the multiple regression chapter and derived in a different manner. In general, we can test whether any element of $\boldsymbol{\beta}$ equals 0 by forming the t ratio

$$t = \frac{\hat{\beta}_i}{\hat{\sigma}\sqrt{(X'X)^{-1}_{i,i}}}$$

which has N – r(**X**) degrees of freedom. We can look at these individual tests of $\beta_i = 0$ as testing the effect of β_i in the presence of the remaining β_i's or examining the effect of β_i after adjusting for the remaining β_i's. This interpretation is analogous to the less than full rank design matrix situation.

In most applied research situations we are interested in various tests where **m** equals **0**, but we can just as easily apply tests where **m** does not equal **0**. For example, we could test whether two regression coefficients are equal by setting **k** equal to [0 . . . 1 . . . –1 . . . 0] where 1 and –1 correspond to the elements of $\boldsymbol{\beta}$ whose contrast is desired.

6.8 USE OF COMPUTERS

The model that we have been discussing easily generalizes to three or more categorical independent variables with an arbitrary number of levels for each categorical variable. The GLM procedure of SAS, as mentioned previously, does not require a full rank matrix since it uses the generalized inverse approach. The computer output of the GLM procedure includes, among other things, the total sum of squares due to regression and a test of its significance. It also includes the regression sum of squares due to each factor adjusted for the remaining factors in the model and a test of their significance. For example, in the case of three factors α, β, and δ, $R(\alpha_i | \mu, \beta_j, \delta_k)$, $R(\beta_j | \mu, \alpha_i, \delta_k)$, and $R(\delta_k | \mu, \alpha_i, \beta_j)$ would be estimated and tested for significance. Estimable functions of the parameters can also be estimated routinely and tested for significance. As mentioned earlier, the GLM procedure is compatible with the approach taken in this book.

Other software packages may require a full rank matrix. The two ways of creating a full rank matrix discussed at the end of Chapter 5 can also be generalized and applied to the use of two or more categorical variables. Let us examine each of the two full rank design matrices for the cases of two categorical variables with three levels of each factor. For simplicity, let us assume that there is only one observation per cell.

The model, expressed in terms of expected cell values, is $E(y_{ij}) = \mu + \alpha_i + \beta_j$ where i and j takes the values 1, 2, and 3. Expressed in terms of matrix algebra, the model is

Column Number

$$
\begin{array}{c}
\quad\quad\quad\quad 1 \;\; \overbrace{2 \;\; 3 \;\; 4}^{\alpha} \;\; \overbrace{5 \;\; 6 \;\; 7}^{\beta}
\end{array}
$$

$$
E\begin{bmatrix} y_{11} \\ y_{12} \\ y_{13} \\ y_{21} \\ y_{22} \\ y_{23} \\ y_{31} \\ y_{32} \\ y_{33} \end{bmatrix} = \begin{bmatrix} 1 & 1 & 0 & 0 & 1 & 0 & 0 \\ 1 & 1 & 0 & 0 & 0 & 1 & 0 \\ 1 & 1 & 0 & 0 & 0 & 0 & 1 \\ 1 & 0 & 1 & 0 & 1 & 0 & 0 \\ 1 & 0 & 1 & 0 & 0 & 1 & 0 \\ 1 & 0 & 1 & 0 & 0 & 0 & 1 \\ 1 & 0 & 0 & 1 & 1 & 0 & 0 \\ 1 & 0 & 0 & 1 & 0 & 1 & 0 \\ 1 & 0 & 0 & 1 & 0 & 0 & 1 \end{bmatrix} \begin{bmatrix} \mu \\ \alpha_1 \\ \alpha_2 \\ \alpha_3 \\ \beta_1 \\ \beta_2 \\ \beta_3 \end{bmatrix}
$$

Let us first use the dummy variable approach to creating a full rank design matrix from the above less than full rank design matrix. In order to do this, one column associated with each of the two factors must be deleted from the design matrix. This is because column 1 equals the sum of columns 2, 3, and 4 and the sum of columns 5, 6, and 7. Any combination of two columns, one from each factor set, can be deleted. For example, columns 2 and 5, 3 and 6, or 4 and 7, as well as other combinations, can be deleted. The column deleted for a particular factor becomes the base level against which the effects of the other levels are contrasted. The procedure is an extension of that used for the single categorical variable case. We simply repeat the process for each set of columns representing a factor. The procedure can be extended to any number of categorical variables with any number of levels. If columns 2 and 5 are deleted, the full rank model is

$$E(y) = \begin{bmatrix} 1 & 0 & 0 & 0 & 0 \\ 1 & 0 & 0 & 1 & 0 \\ 1 & 0 & 0 & 0 & 1 \\ 1 & 1 & 0 & 0 & 0 \\ 1 & 1 & 0 & 1 & 0 \\ 1 & 1 & 0 & 0 & 1 \\ 1 & 0 & 1 & 0 & 0 \\ 1 & 0 & 1 & 1 & 0 \\ 1 & 0 & 1 & 0 & 1 \end{bmatrix} \begin{bmatrix} \theta_1 \\ \theta_2 \\ \theta_3 \\ \theta_4 \\ \theta_5 \end{bmatrix}$$

The reader can verify that the new parameters θ_1, θ_2, θ_3, θ_4, and θ_5 are estimable functions of the original parameters μ, α_1, α_2, α_3, β_1, β_2, and β_3. They are $\theta_1 = \mu + \alpha_1 + \beta_1$, $\theta_2 = \alpha_2 - \alpha_1$, $\theta_3 = \alpha_3 - \alpha_1$, $\theta_4 = \beta_2 - \beta_1$, and $\theta_5 = \beta_3 - \beta_1$. Thus, if a full rank design matrix was created in this manner and used along with **y** as input to a linear regression procedure, the program would output the estimates $\hat{\theta}_1$, $\hat{\theta}_2$, $\hat{\theta}_3$, $\hat{\theta}_4$, and $\hat{\theta}_5$, their associated standard errors and separate tests of the hypothesses that $\theta_1 = 0$, $\theta_2 = 0$, $\theta_3 = 0$, $\theta_4 = 0$, and $\theta_5 = 0$, respectively. Note that the test of the hypothesis that $\theta_1 = \mu + \alpha_1 + \beta_1 = 0$ is usually of no interest. The regression program would also test the joint hypothesis that $\theta_2 = \theta_3 = \theta_4 = \theta_5 = 0$ by examining the sum of squares due to regression. The program will not test the hypothesis that $\theta_2 = \theta_3 = 0$ or $\theta_4 = \theta_5 = 0$. In order to test each of these hypotheses the regression analysis must be run again with the parameters being tested excluded from the model. The difference in the regression sum of squares with and without the parameters would be used to test each of the above hypotheses.

We will now illustrate how to create a full rank design matrix using effect coding. As in the previous dummy variable case, we begin by deleting one column from each set of columns representing a particular factor. Then, for each set of remaining columns representing a particular factor, there will be rows within that set of columns that contain all zeros. The next step is to change these zeros to –1's. The process is repeated for each factor. This is a generalization of the effects coding process discussed in the previous chapter for one categorical variable. We can begin with the previous full rank design matrix where columns 2 and 5 are deleted. The second and third columns of this design matrix are associated with factor α. The first three rows of columns 2 and 3 contain all zeros. These are changed to –1. Similarly, columns 4 and 5 are associated with factor β. Rows 1, 4, and 7 of these two columns contain all zeros. These are changed to –1. The linear model using this full rank design matrix is

$$E(y) = \begin{bmatrix} 1 & -1 & -1 & -1 & -1 \\ 1 & -1 & -1 & 1 & 0 \\ 1 & -1 & -1 & 0 & 1 \\ 1 & 1 & 0 & -1 & -1 \\ 1 & 1 & 0 & 1 & 0 \\ 1 & 1 & 0 & 0 & 1 \\ 1 & 0 & 1 & -1 & -1 \\ 1 & 0 & 1 & 1 & 0 \\ 1 & 0 & 1 & 0 & 1 \end{bmatrix} \begin{bmatrix} \delta_1 \\ \delta_2 \\ \delta_3 \\ \delta_4 \\ \delta_5 \end{bmatrix}$$

This full rank design matrix is based on the restrictions that $\alpha_1 + \alpha_2 + \alpha_3 = 0$ and $\beta_1 + \beta_2 + \beta_3 = 0$. If they are assumed to hold, then $\delta_1 = \mu$, $\delta_2 = \alpha_2$, $\delta_3 = \alpha_3$, $\delta_4 = \beta_2$, and $\delta_5 = \beta_3$. If they are not assumed to hold, then $\delta_2 = \alpha_2 - 1/3(\alpha_1 + \alpha_2 + \alpha_3)$, $\delta_3 = \alpha_3 - 1/3(\alpha_1 + \alpha_2 + \alpha_3)$, $\delta_4 = \beta_2 - 1/3(\beta_1 + \beta_2 + \beta_3)$, $\delta_5 = \beta_3 - 1/3(\beta_1 + \beta_2 + \beta_3)$, and δ_1 is a complicated function of the original parameters that is of no interest.

If this design matrix and **y** are used as input to a linear regression program, then the output will consist of the estimates $\hat{\delta}_1$, $\hat{\delta}_2$, $\hat{\delta}_3$, $\hat{\delta}_4$, and $\hat{\delta}_5$, their associated standard errors, and separate tests of the hypotheses that $\delta_1 = 0$, $\delta_2 = 0$, $\delta_3 = 0$, $\delta_4 = 0$, and $\delta_5 = 0$. The regression program would also test the joint hypothesis that $\delta_2 = \delta_3 = \delta_4 = \delta_5 = 0$ by examining the sum of squares due to regression. The program will not test the hypothesis that $\delta_2 = \delta_3 = 0$ or $\delta_4 = \delta_5 = 0$. Separate regressions must be run and compared in order to test these hypotheses.

6.9 EXAMPLE

Hanushek and Jackson (1977) used dummy variable coding in developing a linear model to predict annual income (1), a continuous variable, from work experience (E) and amount of schooling (S), two categorical variables. (As we have seen, creating a full rank matrix using dummy variables allows the researcher to use a regular multiple regression program to generate estimates of contrasts among regression parameters, their standard errors, and their statistical significance level.) The sample consisted of 105 full-time black workers residing in Boston during 1969.

Work experience (E) had three levels: less than 10 years, 10-30 years, and more than 30 years. Schooling (S) had four levels: less than high school, high school only, college degree but no advanced degree, and advanced degree. Two dummy variables were used to represent the three levels of experience: $E_1 = 1$ for people with 10-30 years of experience, 0 otherwise; and $E_2 = 1$ for people with more than 30 years of experience, 0 otherwise. This is equivalent to deleting the dummy variable associated with less than 10 years of experience from the less than full rank design matrix. Three dummy variables were used to represent the four levels of schooling: $S_1 = 1$ for people with high school only, 0 otherwise; $S_2 = 1$ for people with a college degree but no advanced degree, 0 otherwise; $S_3 = 1$ for people with an advanced degree, 0 otherwise. This is equivalent to deleting the dummy variable associated with less than high school from the full rank design matrix. The expected annual income can then be expressed as

$$E(I) = \beta_0 + \beta_1 E_1 + \beta_2 E_2 + \beta_3 S_1 + \beta_4 S_2 + \beta_5 S_3$$

where β_0 represents the income of workers with less than a high school diploma and less than 10 years of experience since the dummy variables associated with these two levels, the base levels, were deleted from the full rank design matrix. β_1 and β_2 are the differences in income between workers with 10-30 years of experience and over 30 years of experience and the base level of less than 10 years of experience, respectively. β_3, β_4, and β_5 are the differences in income between the three higher levels of schooling and the base level of less than high school.

A multiple regression program produced the following regression equation

$$\hat{I} = 4212 + \underset{(2.0)}{586\, E_1} + \underset{(2.6)}{817\, E_2} + \underset{(1.5)}{1950\, S_1} + \underset{(3.5)}{5325\, S_2} + \underset{(4.5)}{7405\, S_3}$$

The t values of the tests that $\beta_i = 0$ are shown in parentheses below each coefficient. All of the coefficients are statistically significant except the one associated with S_1. The size of the estimated regression parameters indicates that schooling appears to be more important than experience in predicting income. Workers with advanced degrees (S_3) earn \$7,405 more than workers with less than a high school education, while workers with over 30 years experience (E_2) earn only \$817 more than workers with less than 10 years experience.

Since there are three levels of experience and four levels of schooling, 4×3, or 12, categories of workers can be defined. The expected income of each of these categories can be estimated by adding the appropriate coefficients in the equation. For example, the estimated expected income of workers with more than 30 years of experience and an advanced degree can be found by setting E_2 and S_3 equal to one and the remaining variable to zero in the regression equation. Upon doing this we find that the estimated expected income for this group is \$4,212 + \$817 + \$7,405, or \$12,434. Estimates for other cells can be estimated accordingly.

It may seem more straightforward simply to calculate the mean income for a particular category of workers. However, the modeling approach has advantages over this simpler approach. Specifically, if the mean income is based upon a small cell frequency, then the estimate will be unreliable. The estimate based upon the model uses information from all the data, not just data from the cell itself, to generate a cell estimate. Consequently, this estimate could be more reliable than the simpler estimate based upon the cell mean.

This example shows that a linear model may be used for two purposes: testing hypotheses about regression parameters and predicting values of the dependent variable for certain values of the independent variables.

6.10 PROBLEMS

(1) Add sex to the model developed in problem 1 of Chapter 5. Test the hypothesis that $\beta_1 = \beta_2 = 0$ where β_1 is the effect parameter associated with males and β_2 is the effect parameter associated with females. How much more variation in math ability is accounted for by adding sex to the model?

(2) Compare the estimated expected cell values with the cell means. On the basis of this do you think the model fits the data rather well? Plot the distribution of residuals for each of the six cells. Do they appear to meet the assumptions of the linear regression model?

(3) Using restrictions on the parameters, write out the equation that would yield a unique solution for the estimated parameters; solve for them.

(4) Reparameterize the model in terms of estimable functions; solve for them.

(5) Using the data presented below, answer the following questions or address the statements (note that cell 3,3 is empty).

Levels of Factor B	*Levels of Factor A* 1	2	3
1	2, 6, 5	1, 0, 2	1, 2
2	5	2, 3	3, 4
3	4, 3	1	

(a) Set up the normal equations in the original parameters; solve the normal equations.

(b) Set up the normal equations in terms of estimable functions of the parameters; solve the normal equations.

(c) Set up the normal equations for the restricted model that would yield a solution for the restricted parameters; solve the normal equations.

(d) Set up an analysis of variance table like Table 6.6 and indicate which sources of variation are significant at the .05 level.

(e) Let α_i represent the effect of level i of Factor A and β_j represent the effect of level j of Factor B.

(i) Compute unbiased estimates of $\alpha_i - \bar{\alpha}_i$ where $\bar{\alpha}_i$ indicates the average of the α_i for i = 1,2,3; test each for significance at the .05 level.

(ii) Compute unbiased estimates of $\beta_1 - \beta_2$ and $\beta_2 - \beta_3$; test each for significance at the .05 level.

(f) Generate the estimated expected cell means for all 9 cells.

(6) Even though cell 3,3 was empty, we could still estimate all estimable functions of the parameters. Such a design is connected. A design is connected if all contrasts among the α_i and among the β_j are estimable. We can tell if a design is connected by examining the pattern of empty cells and determining if there are unbiased, though not necessarily best, estimates of each contrast. For example, an estimate of $\alpha_1 - \alpha_2$, though not efficient, would be the difference between a randomly selected observation in cell 11 and cell 12 (e.g., 2 – 1, 5 – 0, etc.); an estimate of $\beta_1 - \beta_3$ would be the difference between an observation in cell 12 and cell 32 (e.g., 2 – 1) or between an observation in cell 11 and cell 31.

(a) Show that there is at least one estimate of $\alpha_1 - \alpha_3$, $\alpha_2 - \alpha_3$, $\beta_1 - \beta_2$, and $\beta_2 - \beta_3$ verifying that the design is connected.

(b) Are all 3×3 designs with two empty cells connected?

(c) Give some examples (i.e., empty cell configurations) of 3×3 designs with three empty cells that are connected and that are not connected.

(d) Give some examples of 3×3 designs with four empty cells that are connected and that are not connected.
(e) Are all 3×3 designs with five empty cells unconnected?
(f) For a 4×4 design, what is the maximum number of empty cells for which a design is always connected? What is the minimum number of empty cells for which a design is always unconnected?

NOTE

1. There are many ways to find inverses and most large inverses have to be solved by electronic computer algorithms. One method was demonstrated in previous chapters. In order to develop our facility with matrix algebra, we shall demonstrate another method of finding the inverse of a matrix, the method of cofactors. This method involves finding the adjoint of **A**. The adjoint of **A** is the transpose of the matrix of cofactors of the elements of **A**. The inverse of $\mathbf{A}^{-1}$ is then $|\mathbf{A}|^{-1}$ adj (**A**) where $|\mathbf{A}|$ is the determinant of the matrix **A**. The matrix of the cofactors of **A** is

$$C = \begin{bmatrix} 56 & -16 & -35 \\ -16 & 31 & 10 \\ -35 & 10 & 45 \end{bmatrix}$$

The cofactor for any arbitrary element is found by deleting the row and column containing the element, finding the determinant of the remaining matrix and then multiplying the value of the determinant by $(-1)^{i+j}$ where i and j indicate respectively the row and column location of the element. For example, the cofactor for the element in row 1, column 1, of **A** is $(-1)^{1+1}[(7 \times 8) - (0 \times 0)] = 56$ where the determinant of the 2×2 matrix

$$\begin{bmatrix} 7 & 0 \\ 0 & 8 \end{bmatrix}$$

is $[(7 \times 8) - (0 \times 0)]$ or 56. The cofactors for the remaining eight elements are found in the same manner. The transpose of **C** will give us the adjoint of **A**

$$\text{adj}(\mathbf{A}) = \mathbf{C}' = \begin{bmatrix} 56 & -16 & -35 \\ -16 & 31 & 10 \\ -35 & 10 & 45 \end{bmatrix}$$

Since our matrix is symmetric, the transpose equals the original matrix or adj(**A**) = **C**. The next step in finding the inverse of **A** is to find the determinant of **A**.

The determinant of **A** can be found by arbitrarily selecting one row of **A** and multiplying each element in the row by its corresponding cofactor and then summing these products. In our example, using the first row, we have $|\mathbf{A}| = 7(56) + 2(-16) +$

5(−35) = 185. It, of course, could also be computed, using elements of the second row, as 2(−16) + 7(31) + 0(10) = 185.

The inverse of **A** is now easily found as

$$\mathbf{A}^{-1} = |\mathbf{A}|^{-1}\ \text{adj}[\mathbf{A}] = \frac{1}{185}\begin{bmatrix} 56 & -16 & -35 \\ -16 & 31 & 10 \\ -35 & 10 & 45 \end{bmatrix}$$

We can invert any size matrix by the successive application of these principles whereby higher-order determinants are defined on the basis of lower-order determinants through the cofactor approach.

7 Regression Models with Interaction

7.1 INTRODUCTION

In this chapter we extend both the multiple regression model with continuous independent variables and the less than full rank categorical independent variable model to include interaction parameters. Primary emphasis is on the less than full rank models.

Section 7.2 illustrates how the multiple regression model can be modified to include interaction terms. Briefly, interaction exists when the relationship of one or more independent variables with the dependent variable varies across the levels of one or more of the remaining independent variables.

For example, ability and motivation may be important in predicting job performance, but we may find that ability is related to job performance only if motivation is at a sufficiently high level. If a person is not motivated, then we would not expect him or her to apply his or her ability on the job and, hence, ability and job performance would be relatively independent. We say that ability and motivation interact with each other in producing job performance. We shall see that an interaction between two variables is incorporated into a linear regression model by constructing an interaction variable that is the cross product of the two variables entering into the interaction. The estimated regression parameter associated with this derived variable can be interpreted and tested in the same way as any other regression coefficient. Section 7.3 discusses the extension of the categorical independent variable model to include interaction parameters. The purpose of both of these sections is to familiarize the reader with the general concept of interaction. Section 7.4 discusses the estimation of estimable contrasts and hypothesis testing for a two-factor model with interaction. The procedures are illustrated on a small data set. In the case of a balanced data set, the sum of squares can be partitioned into various sources of variation, including interaction. This is an analysis of variance-type partition that we have addressed earlier and is discussed in section 7.5. Section 7.6 illustrates the use of constraints or restrictions for generating a revised set of normal equations that has a unique solution vector. The basic ideas are familiar since we discussed earlier the use of constraints in solving the normal equations for a one-factor design.

Section 7.7 illustrates the application of the model on an unbalanced data set. The last section, section 7.8, discusses the use of computers in analyzing models of this type. It also discusses recoding the independent variables so that conventional linear regression routines can be used.

7.2 THE CONCEPT OF INTERACTION IN MULTIPLE REGRESSION

An interaction term can be added to the regression model in the chapter on multiple regression where verbal (X_1) and quantitative scores (X_2) were used to predict college grade point average (Y) by deriving a new variable defined as the cross product between the variables X_1 and X_2. In our example, this would mean generating the cross products of verbal and quantitative aptitude and labeling this variable X_3. We could then write our model as $\hat{Y}_i = \beta_0 + \beta_1 X_{1i} + \beta_2 X_{2i} + \beta_3 X_{3i}$, where β_3 is the interaction parameter and X_3 is defined as the cross product, $X_1 X_2$.

The estimation of β and the various tests of hypotheses are identical to those already discussed. The 3×3 **X′X** matrix becomes a 4×4 matrix with the following elements

$$\begin{bmatrix} N & \Sigma X_1 & \Sigma X_2 & \Sigma(X_1 X_2) \\ \Sigma X_1 & \Sigma X_1^2 & \Sigma X_1 X_2 & \Sigma X_1(X_1 X_2) \\ \Sigma X_2 & \Sigma X_2 X_1 & \Sigma X_2^2 & \Sigma X_2(X_1 X_2) \\ \Sigma(X_1 X_2) & \Sigma(X_1 X_2)X_1 & \Sigma(X_1 X_2)X_2 & \Sigma(X_1 X_2)^2 \end{bmatrix}$$

The 4×4 matrix was constructed by adding a row and column containing the approximate sum, sum of squares, and sums of cross products of $X_1 X_2$ with the remaining 2 variables. The regression weight or interaction parameter, β_3, can be testing for significance in the same manner as any other regression weight.

We saw earlier that an equation such as $Y_i = \beta_0 + \beta_1 X_{1i} + \beta_2 X_{2i}$ represents a plane in three-dimensional space, that is, the space formed by the three perpendicular axes, X_1, X_2, and Y. If a plane fits the data points adequately from a least-squares standpoint, then we would find that adding an interaction term to this simple model would not significantly improve upon the fit of the simple planar model. Adding an interaction term such as $\beta_3 X_1 X_2$ to the planar model $\beta_0 + \beta_1 X_1 + \beta_2 X_1$ results in a two-dimensional surface that resembles a twisted plane. The plane is twisted in a manner that minimizes the error sum of squares. If the coefficient β_3 turns out to be statistically significant, then it could be said that the predicted value of the dependent variable, Y, is not just an additive function of a contribution from X_1 and X_2, but also depends upon the particular values of X_1 and X_2.

We can see why the regression surface resembles a twisted plane if we rewrite the original equation as $\beta_0 + \beta_1 X_1 + (\beta_2 + \beta_3 X_1)(X_2)$. The third term contains a "regression parameter," $\beta_2 + \beta_3 X_1$, whose magnitude depends upon the size of X_1. As X_1 increases, the parameters for X_2 increase and, hence, the slope for X_2 increases for increasing values of X_1. In effect the regression plane becomes twisted since the slope of the regression surface in the direction of X_2 increases as X_1 increases. As previously mentioned, an example of two independent variables that might behave in this interactive fashion are motivation and ability, when a researcher is trying to predict job performance. If the regression weight for the cross product of the ability and the motivation score were relatively large, this would indicate that individuals who score high both in ability and motivation would be expected to perform at a higher level than what would be predicted by a simple additive function of ability and motivation. For example, if our equation were $\hat{Y} = 10 + 5X_1 + 5X_2 + 4X_1X_2$, then the vector of scores (10, 10) would yield a higher predicted value than the vector of scores (18, 2), even though the elements of both of these vectors sum to 20. The predicted value for the first vector would be $10 + 5(10) + 5(10) + 4(10)(10)$, or 510, while the predicted value for the second vector would be $10 + 5(18) + 5(2) + 4(18)(2)$, or 254. The predicted value in the first instance is over twice the size of the predicted value in the second instance. If we examined these two predictions from the linear additive parts of this model, $10 + 5X_1 + 5X_2$, we would find that the model would yield the exact same predictions for both vectors, 110. As an exercise the reader should add the interaction term to the basic GPA model illustrated in Chapter 4 and test the significance of the interaction parameter.

7.3 INTERACTION IN THE CASE OF CATEGORICAL INDEPENDENT VARIABLES

The concept of interaction might become clearer if we examine another example of interaction from a factorial experiment with two levels for each of two factors. For our hypothetical example, let us say that we are conducting an experiment to determine the effects of intensity and type of reading program on reading comprehension. Factor A involves two types of reading programs, A_1 and A_2, while Factor B involves two levels of intensity (for example, number of hours per week), B_1 and B_2. An educational researcher randomly assigns an equal number of third-grade children to each of the four cells defined by cross-classifying these two factors (hence, the name "factorial experiment"). The mean scores in reading comprehension for each cell, row, column, and total are presented in Table 7.1.

For this example, we will assume that the size of the cell samples are so large that we are, in effect, dealing with population parameters. That is, there is no sampling error of which to speak. A linear additive model for this balanced experiment can be written as

$$y_{ijk} = \mu + \alpha_i + \beta_j + \epsilon_{ijk}$$

where μ is the overall effect, α_i is the regression parameter associated with i^{th} level of Factor A, β_j is the regression parameter associated with the jth level of Factor B, k represents the child in a particular cross classification of Factors A and B, and ϵ_{ijk} is the error for child k in the ij^{th} cross classification.

The predicted value for a child in level A_1 of A and level B_1 of B is

$$\hat{y}_{11k} = \mu + \alpha_1 + \beta_1$$

and the predicted values for the remaining three cells are

$$\hat{y}_{12k} = \mu + \alpha_1 + \beta_2, \ \hat{y}_{21k} = \mu + \alpha_2 + \beta_1, \text{ and } \hat{y}_{22k} = \mu + \alpha_2 + \beta_2$$

for cells A_1B_2, A_2B_1, and A_2B_2, respectively.

From this model, it is clear that we can predict the performance of a child in a particular cross classification of Factors A and B by adding to an overall effect μ, an effect for the level of A that the child is in and an effect for the level of B that the child is in. This is a simple additive regression model where the cell mean or predicted value of an observation is assumed to be a linear function of the effects associated with Factors A and B. A model such as this is commonly termed a "main effects model."

Since there are equal numbers of observations in each of the four cells (that is, balanced data), it can easily be shown that one solution to the normal equations is $\alpha_1 = \overline{X}_{A_1} - \overline{X}_T$, $\alpha_2 = \overline{X}_{A_2} - \overline{X}_T$, $\beta_1 = \overline{X}_{B_1} - \overline{X}_T$, $\beta_2 = \overline{X}_{B_2} - \overline{X}_T$, and $\mu = \overline{X}_T$. In our example, $\alpha_1 = 10 - 15 = -5$, $\alpha_2 = 20 - 15 = 5$, $\beta_1 = 10 - 15 = -5$, $\beta_2 = 20 - 15 = 5$, and $\mu = 15$. We have seen previously that these five values are not unique solutions to the normal equations unless certain restrictions are incorporated into the model and therefore are not estimable. However, we know that $\mu + \alpha_1$, $\mu + \alpha_2$, $\mu + \beta_1$, $\mu + \beta_2$, $\mu + \alpha_1 + \beta_1$, $\mu + \alpha_1 + \beta_2$, $\mu + \alpha_2 + \beta_1$, $\mu + \alpha_2 + \beta_2$, $\alpha_1 - \alpha_2$, and $\beta_1 - \beta_2$ are estimable.

TABLE 7.1
Means for Hypothetical Reading Experiment

	Factor A *Reading Program*		
Factor B Intensity	*Program* A_1	*Program* A_2	*Row Means*
Low intensity B_1	5	15	10
High intensity B_2	15	25	20
Column means	10	20	15 (total)

The predicted value of an observation in cell AB_{11} is $\mu + \alpha_1 + \beta_1 = 15 - 5 - 5 = 5$. The predictions for the remaining three cells, AB_{12}, AB_{21}, and AB_{22}, are $\mu + \alpha_1 + \beta_2 = 15 - 5 + 5 = 15$, $\mu + \alpha_2 + \beta_1 = 15 + 5 - 5 = 15$, and $\mu + \alpha_2 + \beta_2 = 15 + 5 + 5 = 25$, respectively. It is easy to see that the means of the cells for this hypothetical data can be predicted perfectly by adding the appropriate "row" and "column" effects. It is not necessary to add other terms to the model to precisely fit the cell means. This simple model yields the smallest residual sum of squares since it fits the cell means exactly, and the sum of squares of deviation of the observations is smallest when taken from the mean. This model is a simple row and column effects model with no interaction terms.

It frequently happens that a model such as this does not adequately fit the data. That is, if we estimate effects for A and B and add these effects to μ to estimate a particular cell mean, the observed cell mean deviates significantly from that predicted by the model, $\mu + \alpha_i + \beta_j$. In these cases, we need to add what is called an interaction effect $\alpha\beta_{ij}$ to the model to predict the cell mean adequately. This model can be written as $y_{ijk} = \mu + \alpha_1 + \beta_j + \alpha\beta_{ij} + \epsilon_{ijk}$, where $\alpha\beta_{ij}$ is an interaction parameter associated with the ij^{th} cell.

Let us now look at another large set of hypothetical balanced data where the factors are identical but in which we have changed the cell means as in Table 7.2.

First let us fit the main effects model $\mu + \alpha_i + \beta_j$ to these data. A solution for μ, α_1, α_2, β_1, and β_2 can easily be found to be 20, –10, 10, –10, and 10, respectively, by the same method used previously when the data are balanced. Let us now see how well we can predict the cell means using this simple model. The predictions for cells AB_{11}, AB_{12}, AB_{21}, and AB_{22} are $\mu + \alpha_1 + \beta_1 = 20 - 10 - 10 = 0$, $\mu + \alpha_1 + \beta_2 = 20 - 10 + 10 = 20$, $\mu + \alpha_2 + \beta_1 = 20 + 10 - 10 = 20$, and $\mu + \alpha_2 + \beta_2 = 20 + 10 + 10 = 40$, respectively. Since we assume little or no sampling error, we can see that this simple model does not adequately fit the cell means. In fact, the predicted and observed cell means differ in each instance by an absolute value of 5. This is substantial when compared to the main effect parameters. They are about one-half the size of the main effect parameters in absolute

TABLE 7.2
Means for Revised "Reading" Data

	Factor A		
Factor B	A_1	A_2	*Row Means*
B_1	5	15	10
B_2	15	45	30
Column means	10	30	20 (total)

value. It would appear that we have to add a term to the model in order for the model to fit the cell means. These are the $\alpha\beta_{ij}$ terms, the interaction terms, discussed above. In this simple two-factor experiment with balanced data, the $\alpha\beta_{ij}$ terms are estimated by taking the deviation of the cell mean from the cell mean predicted on the basis of the two main effects. That is, we fit a main effects model, use this model to predict the cell means, and then subtract the observed cell mean from the predicted cell mean to obtain the interaction parameters. We found above that a main effects model yielded predictions of the cell means that differed from the observed cell means by 5 absolute units. These deviations, along with their signs, are the estimated interaction effects. If we add these effects to the main effects model, then the model yields a perfect fit to the cell means and the error sum of squares will be smaller than for the main effects model since the errors or residuals are deviations from the cell means. The model $E(y_{ijk}) = \mu + \alpha_i + \beta_j + \alpha\beta_{ij}$ applied to the reading data has the following solution:

$$\mu = 20$$

$$\alpha_1 = -10 \qquad \alpha\beta_{11} = 5$$

$$\alpha_2 = 10 \qquad \alpha\beta_{12} = -5$$

$$\beta_1 = -10 \qquad \alpha\beta_{21} = -5$$

$$\beta_2 = 10 \qquad \alpha\beta_{22} = 5$$

This solution is not unique unless certain restrictions are incorporated into the model, as we shall see subsequently. The restrictions that we, in effect, used to obtain these parameters were $\alpha_1 + \alpha_2 = 0$, $\beta_1 + \beta_2 = 0$, $\alpha\beta_{11} + \alpha\beta_{12} = 0$, $\alpha\beta_{21} + \alpha\beta_{22} = 0$, $\alpha\beta_{11} + \alpha\beta_{21} = 0$, and $\alpha\beta_{12} + \alpha\beta_{22} = 0$. The problem is that we are estimating nine parameters to fit only four cell means. The reader can verify that the above solution satisfies all of these constraints.

We can easily verify that this model will yield a perfect fit to the observed cell means since

$$\bar{X}_{AB_{11}} = \mu^* + \alpha_1^* + \beta_1^* + \alpha\beta_{11}^* = 20 - 10 - 10 + 5 = 5$$

$$\bar{X}_{AB_{12}} = \mu^* + \alpha_1^* + \beta_2^* + \alpha\beta_{12}^* = 20 - 10 + 10 - 5 = 15$$

$$\bar{X}_{AB_{21}} = \mu^* + \alpha_2^* + \beta_1^* + \alpha\beta_{21}^* = 20 + 10 - 10 - 5 = 15$$

$$\bar{X}_{AB_{22}} = \mu^* + \alpha_2^* + \beta_2^* + \alpha\beta_{22}^* = 20 + 10 + 10 + 5 = 45$$

The asterisks attached to the effects indicate that the values solved for are one of an infinite number of solutions to the normal equations and are not estimates of these parameters because they are not estimable unless the above restrictions are incorporated into the model. The following contrasts of interest are, however, estimable, under certain restrictions that will subsequently be discussed. They are $\alpha_1 - \alpha_2$, $\beta_1 - \beta_2$ and $(\alpha\beta_{11} - \alpha\beta_{12}) - (\alpha\beta_{21} - \alpha\beta_{22})$, and their estimates are

$$\widehat{\alpha_1 - \alpha_2} = -10 - 10 = -20$$

$$\widehat{\beta_1 - \beta_2} = -10 - 10 = -20$$

$$\widehat{(\alpha\beta_{11} - \alpha\beta_{12}) - (\alpha\beta_{21} - \alpha\beta_{22})} = (5 + 5) - (-5 - 5) = 20$$

The interpretation of the first two contrasts is that the parameter for level A_2 is 20 units greater than the parameter for A_1 and, similarly, the parameter for B_2 is 20 units greater than the parameter for B_1. However, the relatively large value for the third contrast indicates that substantial interaction is taking place. The differences in the effects for A_1 and A_2 depend upon the level of Factor B. The difference between the means of A_1 and A_2 for level B_1 is $5 - 15 = 10$, while the difference between the means of A_1 and A_2 for level $B_2 = 15 - 45 = 30$. The difference between these differences, the interaction, is 20. That is, the contrast $(\alpha\beta_{11} - \alpha\beta_{12}) - (\alpha\beta_{21} - \alpha\beta_{22})$ can be estimated from $(\bar{X}_{AB_{11}} - \bar{X}_{AB_{12}}) - (\bar{X}_{AB_{21}} - \bar{X}_{AB_{22}})$ as $(5 - 15) - (15 - 45) = 20$. Treatment A_2 is relatively more effective than treatment A_1 under condition B_2 than under condition B_1. A model based upon adding the row and column effects would underestimate the effectiveness of treatment A_2 under condition B_2 by 5 units and would either under- or overestimate the remaining three cell means.

Sometimes it is helpful to plot the cell means as illustrated in Figure 7.1 in order to gauge the presence and magnitude of interaction between two factors.

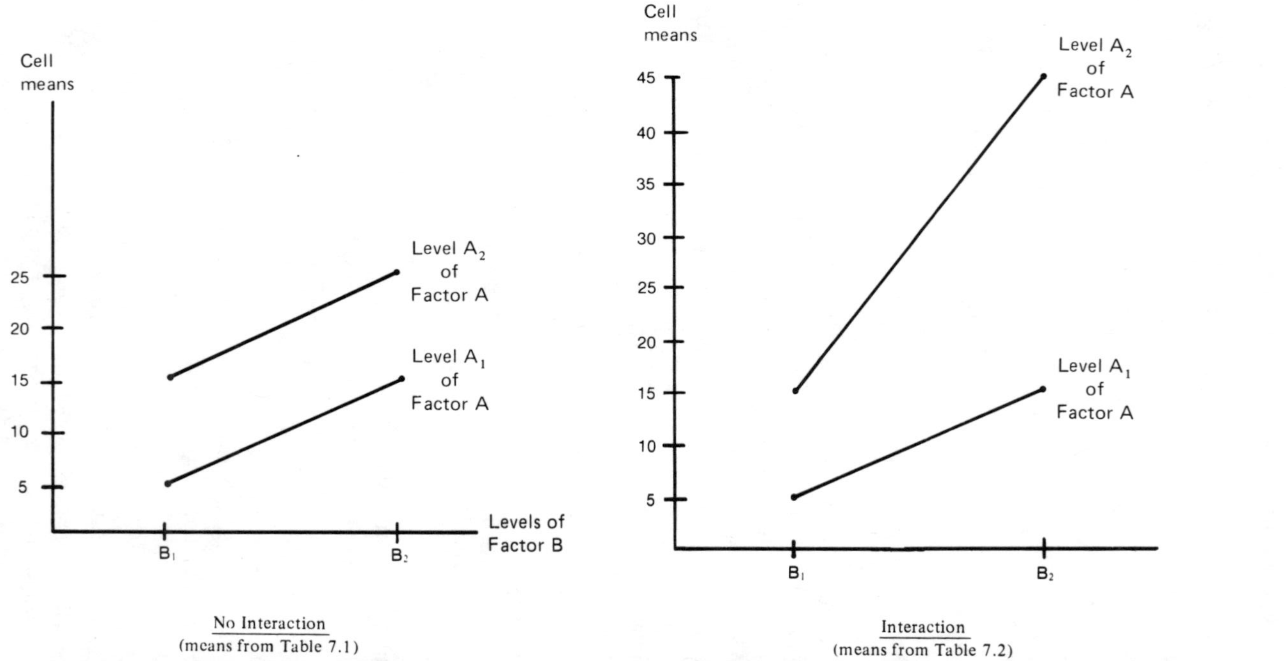

Figure 7.1 Graph of Cell Means from Tables 7.1 and 7.2 Illustrating the Absence and Presence of Interaction

Parallel lines indicate no interaction and nonparallel lines indicate the presence of interaction. The larger the difference in the slope of the lines, the greater the interaction. Of course, for sample data, the presence of interaction must be statistically tested.

7.4 A BALANCED FACTORIAL DESIGN WITH INTERACTIONS

Now that we have familiarized ourselves with the concept of interaction and the simple manner of deriving estimable functions for the balanced data case, let us work through a hypothetical example of a more complex design employing balanced data. We will write the model and obtain and solve the normal equations. In so doing we will see how the normal equations simplify when we have an equal number of observations in each cell.

Let us extend our reading comprehension example so that we have three types of reading programs—A_1, A_2, and A_3—and three levels of exposure—B_1, B_2, and B_3. Assume that we have randomly assigned 5 children to each of the possible combinations of Factors A and B and that the distribution of reading comprehension scores is presented in Table 7.3. The cell, row, column, and total means are presented in Table 7.4.

As we have seen, the model for this design can be written as

$$y_{ijk} = \mu + \alpha_i + \beta_j + \alpha\beta_{ij} + \epsilon_{ijk}$$

where α_i is the effect for the ith level of Factor A, β_j is the effect for the jth level of Factor B, $\alpha\beta_{ij}$ is an interaction effect for the cell obtained by crossing level i of A and j of B, and ϵ_{ijk} is the error for the kth individual in cell AB_{ij}. In order to obtain the normal equations necessary for obtaining a solution for $\hat{\alpha}_i^*$, $\hat{\beta}_j^*$ and $\widehat{\alpha\beta}^*_{ij}$, it is necessary to write out the model in terms of dummy or 0, 1 variables. Doing so we find

$$y_{ijk} = \mu + \alpha_1 X_1 + \alpha_2 X_2 + \alpha_3 X_3 + \beta_1 X_4 + \beta_2 X_5 + \beta_3 X_6$$
$$+ \alpha\beta_{11} X_7 + \alpha\beta_{12} X_8 + \alpha\beta_{13} X_9 + \alpha\beta_{21} X_{10} + \alpha\beta_{22} X_{11}$$
$$+ \alpha\beta_{23} X_{12} + \alpha\beta_{31} X_{13} + \alpha\beta_{32} X_{14} + \alpha\beta_{33} X_{15} + \epsilon_{ijk}$$

where the Xs are 15 dummy variables.

We can find this 45×15 matrix of dummy variables by constructing a table with the 15 effects as columns and the 45 observations as rows and filling in ones or zeros to indicate whether or not the particular effect influences the y observation.

Since each observation is a function of μ, a column of ones needs to be added as the leading column of the dummy variable matrix. The resulting 45×16 matrix is the **X** matrix for the model. The model can now be written as

$$y = X\beta + \epsilon$$

and for the present data set takes the form

$$
y = \begin{bmatrix} 1 \\ 2 \\ 2 \\ 3 \\ \underline{3} \\ 2 \\ 3 \\ 3 \\ 4 \\ \underline{4} \\ 3 \\ 4 \\ 5 \\ 5 \\ \underline{6} \\ 2 \\ 2 \\ 2 \\ 3 \\ \underline{3} \\ 4 \\ 4 \\ 5 \\ 5 \\ \underline{6} \\ 4 \\ 5 \\ 5 \\ 6 \\ \underline{7} \\ 3 \\ 3 \\ 4 \\ 4 \\ \underline{5} \\ 3 \\ 6 \\ 7 \\ 7 \\ \underline{8} \\ 7 \\ 8 \\ 8 \\ 9 \\ 9 \end{bmatrix}
=
\begin{bmatrix}
1&1&0&0&1&0&0&1&0&0&0&0&0&0&0&0\\
1&1&0&0&1&0&0&1&0&0&0&0&0&0&0&0\\
1&1&0&0&1&0&0&1&0&0&0&0&0&0&0&0\\
1&1&0&0&1&0&0&1&0&0&0&0&0&0&0&0\\
1&1&0&0&1&0&0&1&0&0&0&0&0&0&0&0\\
1&1&0&0&0&1&0&0&1&0&0&0&0&0&0&0\\
1&1&0&0&0&1&0&0&1&0&0&0&0&0&0&0\\
1&1&0&0&0&1&0&0&1&0&0&0&0&0&0&0\\
1&1&0&0&0&1&0&0&1&0&0&0&0&0&0&0\\
1&1&0&0&0&1&0&0&1&0&0&0&0&0&0&0\\
1&1&0&0&0&0&1&0&0&1&0&0&0&0&0&0\\
1&1&0&0&0&0&1&0&0&1&0&0&0&0&0&0\\
1&1&0&0&0&0&1&0&0&1&0&0&0&0&0&0\\
1&1&0&0&0&0&1&0&0&1&0&0&0&0&0&0\\
1&1&0&0&0&0&1&0&0&1&0&0&0&0&0&0\\
1&0&1&0&1&0&0&0&0&0&1&0&0&0&0&0\\
1&0&1&0&1&0&0&0&0&0&1&0&0&0&0&0\\
1&0&1&0&1&0&0&0&0&0&1&0&0&0&0&0\\
1&0&1&0&1&0&0&0&0&0&1&0&0&0&0&0\\
1&0&1&0&1&0&0&0&0&0&1&0&0&0&0&0\\
1&0&1&0&0&1&0&0&0&0&0&1&0&0&0&0\\
1&0&1&0&0&1&0&0&0&0&0&1&0&0&0&0\\
1&0&1&0&0&1&0&0&0&0&0&1&0&0&0&0\\
1&0&1&0&0&1&0&0&0&0&0&1&0&0&0&0\\
1&0&1&0&0&1&0&0&0&0&0&1&0&0&0&0\\
1&0&1&0&0&0&1&0&0&0&0&0&1&0&0&0\\
1&0&1&0&0&0&1&0&0&0&0&0&1&0&0&0\\
1&0&1&0&0&0&1&0&0&0&0&0&1&0&0&0\\
1&0&1&0&0&0&1&0&0&0&0&0&1&0&0&0\\
1&0&1&0&0&0&1&0&0&0&0&0&1&0&0&0\\
1&0&0&1&1&0&0&0&0&0&0&0&0&1&0&0\\
1&0&0&1&1&0&0&0&0&0&0&0&0&1&0&0\\
1&0&0&1&1&0&0&0&0&0&0&0&0&1&0&0\\
1&0&0&1&1&0&0&0&0&0&0&0&0&1&0&0\\
1&0&0&1&1&0&0&0&0&0&0&0&0&1&0&0\\
1&0&0&1&0&1&0&0&0&0&0&0&0&0&1&0\\
1&0&0&1&0&1&0&0&0&0&0&0&0&0&1&0\\
1&0&0&1&0&1&0&0&0&0&0&0&0&0&1&0\\
1&0&0&1&0&1&0&0&0&0&0&0&0&0&1&0\\
1&0&0&1&0&1&0&0&0&0&0&0&0&0&1&0\\
1&0&0&1&0&0&1&0&0&0&0&0&0&0&0&1\\
1&0&0&1&0&0&1&0&0&0&0&0&0&0&0&1\\
1&0&0&1&0&0&1&0&0&0&0&0&0&0&0&1\\
1&0&0&1&0&0&1&0&0&0&0&0&0&0&0&1\\
1&0&0&1&0&0&1&0&0&0&0&0&0&0&0&1
\end{bmatrix}
\begin{bmatrix} \mu \\ \alpha_1 \\ \alpha_2 \\ \alpha_3 \\ \beta_1 \\ \beta_2 \\ \beta_3 \\ \alpha\beta_{11} \\ \alpha\beta_{12} \\ \alpha\beta_{13} \\ \alpha\beta_{21} \\ \alpha\beta_{22} \\ \alpha\beta_{23} \\ \alpha\beta_{31} \\ \alpha\beta_{32} \\ \alpha\beta_{33} \end{bmatrix}
+ \epsilon
$$

where ϵ is a column vector with 45 errors corresponding to the observations.

The normal equations can be written as

$$\mathbf{X'X}\beta = \mathbf{X'y}$$

where $\boldsymbol{\beta}$ is the vector of parameters. The **X′X** matrix and **X′y** vector are presented below.

X′X =

	μ	α_1	α_2	α_3	β_1	β_2	β_3	$\alpha\beta_{11}$	$\alpha\beta_{12}$	$\alpha\beta_{13}$	$\alpha\beta_{21}$	$\alpha\beta_{22}$	$\alpha\beta_{23}$	$\alpha\beta_{31}$	$\alpha\beta_{32}$	$\alpha\beta_{33}$
1	45	15	15	15	15	15	15	5	5	5	5	5	5	5	5	5
2	15	15	0	0	5	5	5	5	5	5	0	0	0	0	0	0
3	15	0	15	0	5	5	5	0	0	0	5	5	5	0	0	0
4	15	0	0	15	5	5	5	0	0	0	0	0	0	5	5	5
5	15	5	5	5	15	0	0	5	0	0	5	0	0	5	0	0
6	15	5	5	5	0	15	0	0	5	0	0	5	0	0	5	0
7	15	5	5	5	0	0	15	0	0	5	0	0	5	0	0	5
8	5	5	0	0	5	0	0	5	0	0	0	0	0	0	0	0
9	5	5	0	0	0	5	0	0	5	0	0	0	0	0	0	0
10	5	5	0	0	0	0	5	0	0	5	0	0	0	0	0	0
11	5	0	5	0	5	0	0	0	0	0	5	0	0	0	0	0
12	5	0	5	0	0	5	0	0	0	0	0	5	0	0	0	0
13	5	0	5	0	0	0	5	0	0	0	0	0	5	0	0	0
14	5	0	0	5	5	0	0	0	0	0	0	0	0	5	0	0
15	5	0	0	5	0	5	0	0	0	0	0	0	0	0	5	0
16	5	0	0	5	0	0	5	0	0	0	0	0	0	0	0	5

and

$$\mathbf{X'y} = \begin{bmatrix} 204 \\ 50 \\ 63 \\ 91 \\ 42 \\ 71 \\ 91 \\ 11 \\ 16 \\ 23 \\ 12 \\ 24 \\ 27 \\ 19 \\ 31 \\ 41 \end{bmatrix} = \begin{bmatrix} \text{Total} \\ A_1 \\ A_2 \\ A_3 \\ B_1 \\ B_2 \\ B_3 \\ AB_{11} \\ AB_{12} \\ AB_{13} \\ AB_{21} \\ AB_{22} \\ AB_{23} \\ AB_{31} \\ AB_{32} \\ AB_{33} \end{bmatrix}$$

TABLE 7.3
Reading Scores for Hypothetical Reading Experiment

	Factor A Reading Programs		
Factor B Intensity	*Program A_1*	*Program A_2*	*Program A_3*
	1	2	3
	2	2	3
Low B_1	2	2	4
	3	3	3
	3	3	5
	2	4	3
	3	4	6
Medium B_2	3	5	7
	4	5	7
	4	6	8
	3	4	7
	4	5	8
High B_3	5	5	8
	5	6	9
	6	7	9

TABLE 7.4
Means for Hypothetical Reading Experiment

	Factor A Reading Program			
Factor B Intensity	*Program A_1*	*Program A_2*	*Program A_3*	*Row Means*
Low B_1	2.20	2.40	3.80	2.80
Medium B_2	3.20	4.80	6.20	6.07
High B_3	4.60	5.40	8.20	6.07
Column means	3.33	4.20	6.07	4.53 (total)

In order to facilitate the examination of this relationship, the vector of parameters has been placed over $\mathbf{X'X}$ and a corresponding total indicator has been placed next to $\mathbf{X'y}$.

The $\mathbf{X'X}$ matrix is symmetric and of less than full rank. If we look at each of the rows of $\mathbf{X'X}$ and the corresponding element from $\mathbf{X'y}$, then we can see a relationship indicating the number of times certain parameters are involved in particular totals. The first element of $\mathbf{X'y}$ is 204, and this is the total of all 45 observations. The first row of $\mathbf{X'X}$ indicates that if we added up all 45 observations that were defined in terms of parameters, then the total would involve 45 μ's, 15 α_1's, 15 α_2's, 15 α_3's, 15 β_1's, 15 β_2's, 15 β_3's, 5 $\alpha\beta_{11}$'s, 5 $\alpha\beta_{12}$'s, 5

$\alpha\beta_{13}$'s, 5 $\alpha\beta_{21}$'s, 5 $\alpha\beta_{22}$'s, 5 $\alpha\beta_{23}$'s, 5 $\alpha\beta_{31}$'s, 5 $\alpha\beta_{32}$'s, and 5 $\alpha\beta_{33}$'s. Likewise, the second element of **X′y**, which is 50, equals the total of all observations under treatment A_1 and the corresponding row (second) of **X′X** indicates that 15 μ's, 15 α_1's, 5 β_1's, 5 β_2's, 5 β_3's, 5 $\alpha\beta_{11}$'s, 5 $\alpha\beta_{12}$'s, and 5 $\alpha\beta_{13}$'s are involved in this total. The same relations exist for the remaining 14 rows of **X′X** and the corresponding elements of **X′y**.

It is easy to verify that **X′X** is less than full rank. Rows 2, 3, and 4 sum to row 1 and therefore there is a linear dependency among the rows of **X′X**. If we examine this matrix closely we can find other linear dependencies among the rows of **X′X** as follows:

(1) row 8 + row 9 + row 10 = row 2
(2) row 11 + row 12 + row 13 = row 3
(3) row 14 + row 15 + row 16 = row 4
(4) row 8 + row 11 + row 14 = row 5
(5) row 9 + row 12 + row 15 = row 6
(6) row 10 + row 13 + row 16 = row 7

Altogether, then, there are 7 independent linear dependencies and it can be verified that the rank of **X′X** is 16 – 7 + 9. It should be noted that the rank of this **X′X** matrix is equal to the number of cells into which the data can be classified, which is 9. If we delete the first 7 rows and columns of **X′X** we will have the following full rank matrix of rank 9. (The first 7 rows can be deleted because each is linearly dependent on the last 9 rows.)

$$\begin{bmatrix} 5 & 0 & 0 & 0 & 0 & 0 & 0 & 0 & 0 \\ 0 & 5 & 0 & 0 & 0 & 0 & 0 & 0 & 0 \\ 0 & 0 & 5 & 0 & 0 & 0 & 0 & 0 & 0 \\ 0 & 0 & 0 & 5 & 0 & 0 & 0 & 0 & 0 \\ 0 & 0 & 0 & 0 & 5 & 0 & 0 & 0 & 0 \\ 0 & 0 & 0 & 0 & 0 & 5 & 0 & 0 & 0 \\ 0 & 0 & 0 & 0 & 0 & 0 & 5 & 0 & 0 \\ 0 & 0 & 0 & 0 & 0 & 0 & 0 & 5 & 0 \\ 0 & 0 & 0 & 0 & 0 & 0 & 0 & 0 & 5 \end{bmatrix}$$

The inverse of this 9 × 9 diagonal matrix is simply

$$\begin{bmatrix} \frac{1}{5} & 0 & 0 & 0 & 0 & 0 & 0 & 0 & 0 \\ 0 & \frac{1}{5} & 0 & 0 & 0 & 0 & 0 & 0 & 0 \\ 0 & 0 & \frac{1}{5} & 0 & 0 & 0 & 0 & 0 & 0 \\ 0 & 0 & 0 & \frac{1}{5} & 0 & 0 & 0 & 0 & 0 \\ 0 & 0 & 0 & 0 & \frac{1}{5} & 0 & 0 & 0 & 0 \\ 0 & 0 & 0 & 0 & 0 & \frac{1}{5} & 0 & 0 & 0 \\ 0 & 0 & 0 & 0 & 0 & 0 & \frac{1}{5} & 0 & 0 \\ 0 & 0 & 0 & 0 & 0 & 0 & 0 & \frac{1}{5} & 0 \\ 0 & 0 & 0 & 0 & 0 & 0 & 0 & 0 & \frac{1}{5} \end{bmatrix}$$

We have previously shown that a generalized inverse of $\mathbf{X'X}$ can be found by replacing the rows and columns of $\mathbf{X'X}$ that had to be deleted to form a full rank matrix by zeros and replacing the full rank matrix by its inverse. In this case, the generalized inverse of $\mathbf{X'X}$ is

$$\mathbf{G} = \begin{bmatrix} 0 & 0 & 0 & 0 & 0 & 0 & 0 & 0 & 0 & 0 & 0 & 0 & 0 & 0 & 0 & 0 \\ 0 & 0 & 0 & 0 & 0 & 0 & 0 & 0 & 0 & 0 & 0 & 0 & 0 & 0 & 0 & 0 \\ 0 & 0 & 0 & 0 & 0 & 0 & 0 & 0 & 0 & 0 & 0 & 0 & 0 & 0 & 0 & 0 \\ 0 & 0 & 0 & 0 & 0 & 0 & 0 & 0 & 0 & 0 & 0 & 0 & 0 & 0 & 0 & 0 \\ 0 & 0 & 0 & 0 & 0 & 0 & 0 & 0 & 0 & 0 & 0 & 0 & 0 & 0 & 0 & 0 \\ 0 & 0 & 0 & 0 & 0 & 0 & 0 & 0 & 0 & 0 & 0 & 0 & 0 & 0 & 0 & 0 \\ 0 & 0 & 0 & 0 & 0 & 0 & 0 & 0 & 0 & 0 & 0 & 0 & 0 & 0 & 0 & 0 \\ 0 & 0 & 0 & 0 & 0 & 0 & 0 & \frac{1}{5} & 0 & 0 & 0 & 0 & 0 & 0 & 0 & 0 \\ 0 & 0 & 0 & 0 & 0 & 0 & 0 & 0 & \frac{1}{5} & 0 & 0 & 0 & 0 & 0 & 0 & 0 \\ 0 & 0 & 0 & 0 & 0 & 0 & 0 & 0 & 0 & \frac{1}{5} & 0 & 0 & 0 & 0 & 0 & 0 \\ 0 & 0 & 0 & 0 & 0 & 0 & 0 & 0 & 0 & 0 & \frac{1}{5} & 0 & 0 & 0 & 0 & 0 \\ 0 & 0 & 0 & 0 & 0 & 0 & 0 & 0 & 0 & 0 & 0 & \frac{1}{5} & 0 & 0 & 0 & 0 \\ 0 & 0 & 0 & 0 & 0 & 0 & 0 & 0 & 0 & 0 & 0 & 0 & \frac{1}{5} & 0 & 0 & 0 \\ 0 & 0 & 0 & 0 & 0 & 0 & 0 & 0 & 0 & 0 & 0 & 0 & 0 & \frac{1}{5} & 0 & 0 \\ 0 & 0 & 0 & 0 & 0 & 0 & 0 & 0 & 0 & 0 & 0 & 0 & 0 & 0 & \frac{1}{5} & 0 \\ 0 & 0 & 0 & 0 & 0 & 0 & 0 & 0 & 0 & 0 & 0 & 0 & 0 & 0 & 0 & \frac{1}{5} \end{bmatrix}$$

As an exercise, the reader can verify that the above matrix is a generalized inverse of **X′X**. We can now solve for $\hat{\boldsymbol{\beta}}^* = \mathbf{G}\mathbf{X}'\mathbf{y}$ where $\hat{\boldsymbol{\beta}}^*$ is a solution to the normal equations $\mathbf{X}'\mathbf{X}\boldsymbol{\beta} = \mathbf{X}'\mathbf{y}$. In our example

$$\beta^* = \begin{bmatrix} \hat{\mu}^* \\ \hat{\alpha}_1^* \\ \hat{\alpha}_2^* \\ \hat{\alpha}_3^* \\ \hat{\beta}_1^* \\ \hat{\beta}_2^* \\ \hat{\beta}_3^* \\ \hat{\alpha\beta}_{11}^* \\ \hat{\alpha\beta}_{12}^* \\ \hat{\alpha\beta}_{13}^* \\ \hat{\alpha\beta}_{21}^* \\ \hat{\alpha\beta}_{22}^* \\ \hat{\alpha\beta}_{23}^* \\ \hat{\alpha\beta}_{31}^* \\ \hat{\alpha\beta}_{32}^* \\ \hat{\alpha\beta}_{33}^* \end{bmatrix} = \begin{bmatrix}
0&0&0&0&0&0&0&0&0&0&0&0&0&0&0&0 \\
0&0&0&0&0&0&0&0&0&0&0&0&0&0&0&0 \\
0&0&0&0&0&0&0&0&0&0&0&0&0&0&0&0 \\
0&0&0&0&0&0&0&0&0&0&0&0&0&0&0&0 \\
0&0&0&0&0&0&0&0&0&0&0&0&0&0&0&0 \\
0&0&0&0&0&0&0&0&0&0&0&0&0&0&0&0 \\
0&0&0&0&0&0&0&0&0&0&0&0&0&0&0&0 \\
0&0&0&0&0&0&0&\frac{1}{5}&0&0&0&0&0&0&0&0 \\
0&0&0&0&0&0&0&0&\frac{1}{5}&0&0&0&0&0&0&0 \\
0&0&0&0&0&0&0&0&0&\frac{1}{5}&0&0&0&0&0&0 \\
0&0&0&0&0&0&0&0&0&0&\frac{1}{5}&0&0&0&0&0 \\
0&0&0&0&0&0&0&0&0&0&0&\frac{1}{5}&0&0&0&0 \\
0&0&0&0&0&0&0&0&0&0&0&0&\frac{1}{5}&0&0&0 \\
0&0&0&0&0&0&0&0&0&0&0&0&0&\frac{1}{5}&0&0 \\
0&0&0&0&0&0&0&0&0&0&0&0&0&0&\frac{1}{5}&0 \\
0&0&0&0&0&0&0&0&0&0&0&0&0&0&0&\frac{1}{5}
\end{bmatrix} \begin{bmatrix} 204 \\ 50 \\ 63 \\ 91 \\ 42 \\ 71 \\ 91 \\ 11 \\ 16 \\ 23 \\ 12 \\ 24 \\ 27 \\ 19 \\ 31 \\ 41 \end{bmatrix} = \begin{bmatrix} 0 \\ 0 \\ 0 \\ 0 \\ 0 \\ 0 \\ 0 \\ 2.2 \\ 3.2 \\ 4.6 \\ 2.4 \\ 4.8 \\ 5.4 \\ 3.8 \\ 6.2 \\ 8.2 \end{bmatrix}$$

The regression sum of squares can be estimated as $\hat{\boldsymbol{\beta}}^{*\prime}\mathbf{X}'\mathbf{y}$, which for our example is

$$[0, 0, 0, 0, 0, 0, 0, 2.2, 3.2, 4.6, 2.4, 4.8, 5.4, 3.8, 6.2, 8.2] \begin{bmatrix} 204 \\ 50 \\ 63 \\ 91 \\ 42 \\ 71 \\ 91 \\ 11 \\ 16 \\ 23 \\ 12 \\ 24 \\ 27 \\ 19 \\ 31 \\ 41 \end{bmatrix} = 1071.6$$

and is invariant to the particular solution of the normal equations.

The total sum of squares $\mathbf{y}'\mathbf{y}$ is

$$[12233 \vdots 23344 \vdots 34556 \vdots 22233 \vdots 44556 \vdots 45567 \vdots 33445 \vdots 36778 \vdots 78899] \left[\begin{array}{c} 1 \\ 2 \\ 2 \\ 3 \\ 3 \\ \hdashline 2 \\ 3 \\ 3 \\ 4 \\ 4 \\ \hdashline 3 \\ 4 \\ 5 \\ 5 \\ 6 \\ \hdashline 2 \\ 2 \\ 2 \\ 3 \\ 3 \\ \hdashline 4 \\ 4 \\ 5 \\ 5 \\ 6 \\ \hdashline 4 \\ 5 \\ 5 \\ 6 \\ 7 \\ \hdashline 3 \\ 3 \\ 4 \\ 4 \\ 5 \\ \hdashline 3 \\ 6 \\ 7 \\ 7 \\ 8 \\ \hdashline 7 \\ 8 \\ 8 \\ 9 \\ 9 \end{array}\right] = 1112.0$$

The error sum of squares is $\mathbf{y}'\mathbf{y} - \hat{\boldsymbol{\beta}}^{*\prime}\mathbf{X}'\mathbf{y}$, which equals 1112.0 – 1071.6, or 40.4. We are not really interested in the contribution of μ to the regression sum of squares, so let us correct the regression sum of squares for μ by subtracting $N\bar{y}^2$ from $\hat{\boldsymbol{\beta}}^{*\prime}\mathbf{X}'\mathbf{y}$ to obtain the regression sum of squares corrected or adjusted for μ, which is

$$R(\alpha_i, \beta_j, \alpha\beta_{ij} | \mu) = 1071.6 - 45(4.533)^2 = 146.8$$

We can now perform a statistical test to see if including the α_i, β_j, and $\alpha\beta_{ij}$ terms in our model better explains the variation in the dependent variable than the simple and, for our purposes, trivial model, $y_{ijk} = \mu + \epsilon_{ijk}$. Under the null hypothesis that the α_i, β_j, and $\alpha\beta_{ij}$ are not needed in the model, it can be shown that the corrected regression sum of squares divided by σ^2 is distributed as a χ^2 variable with $r(\mathbf{X}) - 1$ or 8 degrees of freedom and is furthermore distributed independently of the error sum of squares divided by σ^2 which is distributed as a χ^2 variable with $N - r(\mathbf{X})$ or $45 - 9 = 36$ degrees of freedom. Consequently, the ratio of these two χ^2's divided by their respective degrees of freedom is distributed as F with 8 and 36 degrees of freedom, respectively. The F for our example is

$$F = \frac{\frac{146.8}{8}}{\frac{40.4}{36}} = \frac{18.35}{1.122} = 16.5$$

This F is significant at the .01 level and indicates that the full model $y_{ijk} = \mu + \alpha_i + \beta_j + \alpha\beta_{ij} + \epsilon_{ijk}$ explains the variation in y better than the model $y_{ijk} = \mu + \epsilon_{ijk}$. Although the inclusion of these main effect and interaction parameters jointly adds to the model, this does not tell us anything concerning the relative importance of the parameter sets. Consequently, we would like to test separate hypotheses involving various contrasts among the α_i parameters, the β_j parameters, and the $\alpha\beta_{ij}$ parameters. If we look back at the solution to the normal equations, we can see that the solution for $\hat{\boldsymbol{\beta}}^*$ yielded zero values for $\hat{\mu}^*$, $\hat{\alpha}_1^*$, $\hat{\alpha}_2^*$, $\hat{\alpha}_3^*$, $\hat{\beta}_1^*$, $\hat{\beta}_2^*$ and $\hat{\beta}_3^*$ and that the remaining positive elements corresponding to the $\hat{\alpha}\hat{\beta}_{ij}^*$ are simply the corresponding cell means. For example, $\alpha\beta_{11}$ equals 2.2, which is the mean of the 5 observations in cell AB_{11}. We have previously seen that in main effects models with no interaction terms contrasts such as $\alpha_1 - \alpha_2$ and $\beta_1 - \beta_2$ are estimable, although the parameters themselves are not estimable. Of course, in the present model, the individual parameters are not estimable, but neither are contrasts such as $\alpha_1 - \alpha_2$ and $\beta_1 - \beta_2$. If we tried to calculate them we would find that they are all zero, as the reader can verify. Intuitively, we would not expect all of these contrasts to be exactly equal to zero. However, it turns out that these contrasts are non-estimable unless certain restrictions are placed upon the parameters. We previously pointed out that a linear function of the parameters $\mathbf{K}'\boldsymbol{\beta}$ was estimable if we would find a $\mathbf{t}$ such that $\mathbf{K}'\boldsymbol{\beta} = \mathbf{t}'E(\mathbf{y})$ when $\mathbf{y}$ is expressed in terms of the parameters of the model. If we write $E(\mathbf{y})$ in terms of the parameters, we can easily see that the above contrasts or linear functions of the parameters are not estimable. Let us write the expected value of y for each of the nine cells in terms of our parameters.

$$E(y_{11}) = \mu + \alpha_1 + \beta_1 + \alpha\beta_{11}$$

$$E(y_{12}) = \mu + \alpha_1 + \beta_2 + \alpha\beta_{12}$$

$$E(y_{13}) = \mu + \alpha_1 + \beta_3 + \alpha\beta_{13}$$

$$E(y_{21}) = \mu + \alpha_2 + \beta_1 + \alpha\beta_{21}$$

$$E(y_{22}) = \mu + \alpha_2 + \beta_2 + \alpha\beta_{22}$$

$$E(y_{23}) = \mu + \alpha_2 + \beta_3 + \alpha\beta_{23}$$

$$E(y_{31}) = \mu + \alpha_3 + \beta_1 + \alpha\beta_{31}$$

$$E(y_{32}) = \mu + \alpha_3 + \beta_2 + \alpha\beta_{32}$$

$$E(y_{33}) = \mu + \alpha_3 + \beta_3 + \alpha\beta_{33}$$

From these equations, we can easily see that there is no $\mathbf{t}$ such that $\mathbf{t}'E(\mathbf{y})$ will equal either an individual parameter or a main effect contrast. The most useful contrasts that involve main effect parameters will also contain interaction parameters. That is, although we cannot estimate $\alpha_1 - \alpha_2$, we can estimate

$$\alpha_1 + \frac{1}{3}(\alpha\beta_{11} + \alpha\beta_{12} + \alpha\beta_{13}) - \left[\alpha_2 + \frac{1}{3}(\alpha\beta_{21} + \alpha\beta_{22} + \alpha\beta_{23})\right]$$

because

$$\frac{1}{3}E(y_{11}) + \frac{1}{3}E(y_{12}) + \frac{1}{3}E(y_{13}) - \frac{1}{3}E(y_{21}) - \frac{1}{3}E(y_{22}) - \frac{1}{3}E(y_{23})$$

$$= \frac{1}{3}(3\mu + 3\alpha_1 + \sum_j \beta_j + \sum_j \alpha\beta_{1j}) - \frac{1}{3}(3\mu + 3\alpha_2 + \sum_j \beta_j + \sum_j \alpha\beta_{2j})$$

$$= \alpha_1 + \frac{1}{3}(\alpha\beta_{11} + \alpha\beta_{12} + \alpha\beta_{13}) - \left[\alpha_2 + \frac{1}{3}(\alpha\beta_{21} + \alpha\beta_{22} + \alpha\beta_{23})\right]$$

We can see from above that if the model included restriction such as $\sum_i \alpha\beta_{ij} = 0$ and $\sum_j \alpha\beta_{ij} = 0$, then $\alpha_1 - \alpha_2$ would be estimable. In any event the above contrast is meaningful in that it is a contrast between the sum of one main effect parameter and the average of its associated interaction parameters and the sum of another main effect parameter and the average of its associated interaction parameters. It makes sense conceptually to contrast the parameters associated with one level of a factor with the parameters associated with another level of the same factor even if interaction parameters are involved in this contrast since the interaction parameters still reflect the contribution of that level. For example, the parameters $\alpha\beta_{11}$, $\alpha\beta_{12}$, and $\alpha\beta_{13}$ are all linked, tied, or associated with level 1 or A, whose main effect parameter is α_1 so that

$$\alpha_1 + \frac{1}{3}(\alpha\beta_{11} + \alpha\beta_{12} + \alpha\beta_{13})$$

is a reasonable function with which to be concerned and contrasts between linear functions such as this are also reasonable from a conceptual viewpoint.

Let us now estimate this contrast from the data and test the hypothesis that

$$\alpha_1 + \frac{1}{3}(\alpha\beta_{11} + \alpha\beta_{12} + \alpha\beta_{13}) - \left(\alpha_2 + \frac{1}{3}(\alpha\beta_{21} + \alpha\beta_{22} + \alpha\beta_{23})\right) = 0$$

The sample estimate is

$$\hat{\alpha}_1^* + \frac{1}{3}(\widehat{\alpha\beta}_{11}^* + \widehat{\alpha\beta}_{12}^* + \widehat{\alpha\beta}_{13}^*) - \left(\hat{\alpha}_2^* + \frac{1}{3}(\widehat{\alpha\beta}_{21}^* + \widehat{\alpha\beta}_{22}^* + \widehat{\alpha\beta}_{23})\right)$$

$$= 0 + \frac{1}{3}(2.2 + 3.2 + 4.6) - \left(0 + \frac{1}{3}(2.4 + 4.8 + 5.4)\right) = 3.33 - 4.20$$

$$= -.87$$

It is interesting to observe that for balanced data $-.87$ is simply the difference, $\bar{y}_{A_1} - \bar{y}_{A_2}$, where $\bar{y}_{A_1}$ is the mean for the 15 observations in level 1 of A and $\bar{y}_{A_2}$ is the mean for the 15 observations in level 2 of A. It turns out that if we restrict the interaction parameters so that $\sum_j \alpha\beta_{ij} = 0$ for all i then the estimate of the estimable function $\alpha_1 - \alpha_2$ is also $-.87$ or $\bar{y}_{A_1} - \bar{y}_{A_2}$. The restrictions would give us a different solution for $\boldsymbol{\beta}^*$. In particuar, $\hat{\alpha}_1^*$ and $\hat{\alpha}_2^*$ would be nonzero and their difference would be .87.

From our data, let us test the null hypothesis that the set of parameters associated with Factor A are jointly not a significant part of the model. This null hypothesis can be expressed as

$$\alpha_1 + \frac{1}{3}(\alpha\beta_{11} + \alpha\beta_{12} + \alpha\beta_{13}) = \alpha_2 + \frac{1}{3}(\alpha\beta_{21} + \alpha\beta_{22} + \alpha\beta_{23})$$

$$= \alpha_3 + \frac{1}{3}(\alpha\beta_{31} + \alpha\beta_{32} + \alpha\beta_{33})$$

This would be expressed for hypothesis-testing purposes as

$$\alpha_1 + \frac{1}{3}(\alpha\beta_{11} + \alpha\beta_{12} + \alpha\beta_{13}) - \left(\alpha_3 + \frac{1}{3}(\alpha\beta_{31} + \alpha\beta_{32} + \alpha\beta_{33})\right) = 0$$

and

$$\alpha_2 + \frac{1}{3}(\alpha\beta_{21} + \alpha\beta_{22} + \alpha\beta_{23}) - \left(\alpha_3 + \frac{1}{3}(\alpha\beta_{31} + \alpha\beta_{32} + \alpha\beta_{33})\right) = 0$$

This hypothesis could also be stated in other ways, as the reader can verify.

To test this hypothesis, we compute from our data the appropriate

$$Q = (\mathbf{K}'\hat{\beta}^* - \mathbf{m})'(\mathbf{K}'\mathbf{G}\mathbf{K})^{-1}(\mathbf{K}'\beta^* - \mathbf{m})$$

where

$$\mathbf{K}'\hat{\beta}^* = \begin{bmatrix} 0 & 1 & 0 & -1 & 0 & 0 & 0 & \frac{1}{3} & \frac{1}{3} & \frac{1}{3} & 0 & 0 & 0 & -\frac{1}{3} & -\frac{1}{3} & -\frac{1}{3} \\ 0 & 0 & 1 & -1 & 0 & 0 & 0 & 0 & 0 & 0 & \frac{1}{3} & \frac{1}{3} & \frac{1}{3} & -\frac{1}{3} & -\frac{1}{3} & -\frac{1}{3} \end{bmatrix} \begin{bmatrix} 0 \\ 0 \\ 0 \\ 0 \\ 0 \\ 0 \\ 0 \\ 2.2 \\ 3.2 \\ 4.6 \\ 2.4 \\ 4.8 \\ 5.4 \\ 3.8 \\ 6.2 \\ 8.2 \end{bmatrix} = \begin{bmatrix} -2.7333 \\ -1.8666 \end{bmatrix}$$

$\mathbf{m} = \mathbf{0}$;

$$
(\mathbf{K'GK})^{-1} = \left[\begin{bmatrix} 0 & 1 & 0 & -1 & 0 & 0 & 0 & \frac{1}{3} & \frac{1}{3} & \frac{1}{3} & 0 & 0 & 0 & -\frac{1}{3} & -\frac{1}{3} & -\frac{1}{3} \\ 0 & 0 & 1 & -1 & 0 & 0 & 0 & 0 & 0 & 0 & \frac{1}{3} & \frac{1}{3} & \frac{1}{0} & -\frac{1}{3} & -\frac{1}{3} & -\frac{1}{3} \end{bmatrix} \begin{bmatrix} 0 & 0 & 0 & 0 & 0 & 0 & 0 & 0 & 0 & 0 & 0 & 0 & 0 & 0 & 0 & 0 \\ 0 & 0 & 0 & 0 & 0 & 0 & 0 & 0 & 0 & 0 & 0 & 0 & 0 & 0 & 0 & 0 \\ 0 & 0 & 0 & 0 & 0 & 0 & 0 & 0 & 0 & 0 & 0 & 0 & 0 & 0 & 0 & 0 \\ 0 & 0 & 0 & 0 & 0 & 0 & 0 & 0 & 0 & 0 & 0 & 0 & 0 & 0 & 0 & 0 \\ 0 & 0 & 0 & 0 & 0 & 0 & 0 & 0 & 0 & 0 & 0 & 0 & 0 & 0 & 0 & 0 \\ 0 & 0 & 0 & 0 & 0 & 0 & 0 & 0 & 0 & 0 & 0 & 0 & 0 & 0 & 0 & 0 \\ 0 & 0 & 0 & 0 & 0 & 0 & 0 & 0 & 0 & 0 & 0 & 0 & 0 & 0 & 0 & 0 \\ 0 & 0 & 0 & 0 & 0 & 0 & 0 & \frac{1}{5} & 0 & 0 & 0 & 0 & 0 & 0 & 0 & 0 \\ 0 & 0 & 0 & 0 & 0 & 0 & 0 & 0 & \frac{1}{5} & 0 & 0 & 0 & 0 & 0 & 0 & 0 \\ 0 & 0 & 0 & 0 & 0 & 0 & 0 & 0 & 0 & \frac{1}{5} & 0 & 0 & 0 & 0 & 0 & 0 \\ 0 & 0 & 0 & 0 & 0 & 0 & 0 & 0 & 0 & 0 & \frac{1}{5} & 0 & 0 & 0 & 0 & 0 \\ 0 & 0 & 0 & 0 & 0 & 0 & 0 & 0 & 0 & 0 & 0 & \frac{1}{5} & 0 & 0 & 0 & 0 \\ 0 & 0 & 0 & 0 & 0 & 0 & 0 & 0 & 0 & 0 & 0 & 0 & \frac{1}{5} & 0 & 0 & 0 \\ 0 & 0 & 0 & 0 & 0 & 0 & 0 & 0 & 0 & 0 & 0 & 0 & 0 & \frac{1}{5} & 0 & 0 \\ 0 & 0 & 0 & 0 & 0 & 0 & 0 & 0 & 0 & 0 & 0 & 0 & 0 & 0 & \frac{1}{5} & 0 \\ 0 & 0 & 0 & 0 & 0 & 0 & 0 & 0 & 0 & 0 & 0 & 0 & 0 & 0 & 0 & \frac{1}{5} \end{bmatrix} \begin{bmatrix} 0 & 0 \\ 1 & 0 \\ 0 & 1 \\ -1 & -1 \\ 0 & 0 \\ 0 & 0 \\ 0 & 0 \\ \frac{1}{3} & 0 \\ \frac{1}{3} & 0 \\ \frac{1}{3} & 0 \\ 0 & \frac{1}{3} \\ 0 & \frac{1}{3} \\ 0 & \frac{1}{3} \\ -\frac{1}{3} & -\frac{1}{3} \\ -\frac{1}{3} & -\frac{1}{3} \\ -\frac{1}{3} & -\frac{1}{3} \end{bmatrix} \right]^{-1}
$$

$$
= \begin{bmatrix} \frac{6}{45} & \frac{3}{45} \\ \frac{3}{45} & \frac{6}{45} \end{bmatrix}^{-1} = \begin{bmatrix} 10 & -5 \\ -5 & 10 \end{bmatrix};
$$

and, consequently,

$$
Q = [-2.7333, \ -1.8666] \begin{bmatrix} 10 & -5 \\ -5 & 10 \end{bmatrix} \begin{bmatrix} -2.7333 \\ -1.8666 \end{bmatrix} = 58.533
$$

The next step is to form the ratio

$$\frac{\dfrac{Q}{r(\mathbf{K})}}{\dfrac{\mathbf{y}'\mathbf{y} - \hat{\boldsymbol{\beta}}^{*\prime}\mathbf{X}'\mathbf{y}}{N - r(\mathbf{X})}}$$

which is distributed as F with $r(\mathbf{K})$ and $N - r(\mathbf{X})$ degrees of freedom. In this case, F is

$$\frac{\dfrac{58.533}{2}}{\dfrac{40.4}{36}}$$

which equals 26.0797. This F with 2 and 36 degrees of freedom in the numerator and denominator, respectively, is significant at the .01 level. We would conclude that the three reading programs were having differential effects on reading performance and that children exposed to program A_3 were doing the best. The researcher would probably now want to turn attention to Factor B_1, reading intensity, to determine whether the intensity levels of Factor B were having differential effects. For the unrestricted model, the null hypothesis would be

$$\beta_1 + \frac{1}{3}(\alpha\beta_{11} + \alpha\beta_{21} + \alpha\beta_{31}) - \left(\beta_3 + \frac{1}{3}(\alpha\beta_{13} + \alpha\beta_{23} + \alpha\beta_{33})\right) = 0$$

$$\beta_2 + \frac{1}{3}(\alpha\beta_{12} + \alpha\beta_{22} + \alpha\beta_{32}) - \left(\beta_3 + \frac{1}{3}(\alpha\beta_{13} + \alpha\beta_{23} + \alpha\beta_{33})\right) = 0$$

The above null hypothesis involving Factor B can be tested in the same manner as the previous test concerning Factor A. The reader can verify that

$$\mathbf{K}'\hat{\boldsymbol{\beta}}^* = \begin{bmatrix} -3.2666 \\ -1.3333 \end{bmatrix};$$

$$\mathbf{m} = \mathbf{0};$$

and

$$(\mathbf{K}'\mathbf{GK})^{-1} = \begin{bmatrix} 10 & -5 \\ -5 & 10 \end{bmatrix}$$

Consequently,

$$Q = [-3.2666, \quad -1.3333] \begin{bmatrix} 10 & -5 \\ -5 & 10 \end{bmatrix} \begin{bmatrix} -3.2666 \\ -1.3333 \end{bmatrix} = 80.93$$

and

$$F = \frac{\frac{80.93}{2}}{\frac{40.4}{36}} = 36.07$$

This is significant at the .01 level with 2 and 36 degrees of freedom in the numerator and denominator, respectively. We can therefore conclude that levels of reading intensity have differential effects, with the highest level of intensity yielding the largest effect. Once the researcher has tested these overall hypotheses of no differential effects for levels of Factors A and B separately, he or she may then be interested in testing more specific hypotheses, such as the hypothesis that $\alpha_1 - \alpha_2$ equals zero in the restricted case or

$$\alpha_1 + \frac{1}{3}(\alpha\beta_{11} + \alpha\beta_{12} + \alpha\beta_{13}) - \left(\alpha_2 + \frac{1}{3}(\alpha\beta_{21} + \alpha\beta_{22} + \alpha\beta_{23})\right) = 0.$$

As an exercise the reader can test this hypothesis and show that it is equivalent to a t test with $\overline{X}_1 - \overline{X}_2$ as the numerator.

Up to this point, we have seen that both types of program and intensity of exposure to the program have significant effects upon the reading comprehension of students. The next question to be asked of the data is whether these two factors interact with each other. Sometimes this question is asked first since a statistically significant interaction qualifies the interpretation of statistically significant main effects. This is because the magnitude of the effects of one

TABLE 7.5
Interaction Parameters for Hypothetical Reading Experiment

	Reading Program		
Intensity	A_1	A_2	A_3
B_1	$\alpha\beta_{11}$	$\alpha\beta_{21}$	$\alpha\beta_{31}$
B_2	$\alpha\beta_{12}$	$\alpha\beta_{22}$	$\alpha\beta_{32}$
B_3	$\alpha\beta_{13}$	$\alpha\beta_{23}$	$\alpha\beta_{33}$

factor varies across levels of the other factor. But since this is a more complicated hypothesis to test we have considered it last. More specifically, do the contrasts among program effects differ for the various exposure levels? The question could also be stated as follows: Do the contrasts among exposure levels differ for the various program types? There are nine interaction parameters in our model as shown in Table 7.5.

The verbal statement that the effects of A do not differ according to B can be stated statistically in terms of the following contrasts:

$$(\alpha\beta_{11} - \alpha\beta_{21}) - (\alpha\beta_{13} - \alpha\beta_{23}) = 0$$

$$(\alpha\beta_{12} - \alpha\beta_{22}) - (\alpha\beta_{13} - \alpha\beta_{23}) = 0$$

$$(\alpha\beta_{21} - \alpha\beta_{31}) - (\alpha\beta_{23} - \alpha\beta_{33}) = 0$$

$$(\alpha\beta_{22} - \alpha\beta_{32}) - (\alpha\beta_{23} - \alpha\beta_{33}) = 0$$

All of the information concerning the interaction for our experiment is contained in these four independent contrasts. Any other interaction contrasts are linear combinations of these contrasts. For example, the interaction contrast $(\alpha\beta_{11} - \alpha\beta_{31}) - (\alpha\beta_{13} - \alpha\beta_{33})$ can be expressed as the sum of contrast 1 and contrast 3. It is left as an exercise for the reader to demonstrate that these four contrasts are estimable.

We have previously seen that the **X′X** matrix has a rank of 9 and thus there are 9 degrees of freedom for regression. If we adjust for μ, the overall effect, then we have 8 degrees of freedom remaining. Of these 8 degrees of freedom, 4 have been used up in the main effect contrasts for factor A (2 degrees of freedom) and B (2 degrees of freedom). The remaining 4 degrees of freedom are accounted for by the 4 independent interaction contrasts. Let us now find the Q and its associated F test for the contribution of the interaction parameters. We have

$$\mathbf{K}'\hat{\beta}^* = \begin{bmatrix} 0 & 0 & 0 & 0 & 0 & 0 & 0 & 1 & 0 & -1 & -1 & 0 & 1 & 0 & 0 & 0 \\ 0 & 0 & 0 & 0 & 0 & 0 & 0 & 0 & 1 & -1 & 0 & -1 & 1 & 0 & 0 & 0 \\ 0 & 0 & 0 & 0 & 0 & 0 & 0 & 0 & 0 & 0 & 1 & 0 & -1 & -1 & 0 & 1 \\ 0 & 0 & 0 & 0 & 0 & 0 & 0 & 0 & 0 & 0 & 0 & 1 & -1 & 0 & -1 & 1 \end{bmatrix} \begin{bmatrix} 0 \\ 0 \\ 0 \\ 0 \\ 0 \\ 0 \\ 0 \\ 2.2 \\ 3.2 \\ 4.6 \\ 2.4 \\ 4.8 \\ 5.4 \\ 3.8 \\ 6.2 \\ 8.2 \end{bmatrix} = \begin{bmatrix} .6 \\ -.8 \\ 1.4 \\ 1.4 \end{bmatrix}$$

$$
(K'GK)^{-1} = \left[
\begin{bmatrix}
0&0&0&0&0&0&0&1&0&-1&-1&0&1&0&0&0\\
0&0&0&0&0&0&0&0&1&-1&0&-1&1&0&0&0\\
0&0&0&0&0&0&0&0&0&0&1&0&-1&-1&0&1\\
0&0&0&0&0&0&0&0&0&0&0&1&-1&0&-1&1
\end{bmatrix}
\begin{bmatrix}
0&0&0&0&0&0&0&0&0&0&0&0&0&0&0&0\\
0&0&0&0&0&0&0&0&0&0&0&0&0&0&0&0\\
0&0&0&0&0&0&0&0&0&0&0&0&0&0&0&0\\
0&0&0&0&0&0&0&0&0&0&0&0&0&0&0&0\\
0&0&0&0&0&0&0&0&0&0&0&0&0&0&0&0\\
0&0&0&0&0&0&0&0&0&0&0&0&0&0&0&0\\
0&0&0&0&0&0&0&0&0&0&0&0&0&0&0&0\\
0&0&0&0&0&0&0&\frac{1}{5}&0&0&0&0&0&0&0&0\\
0&0&0&0&0&0&0&0&\frac{1}{5}&0&0&0&0&0&0&0\\
0&0&0&0&0&0&0&0&0&\frac{1}{5}&0&0&0&0&0&0\\
0&0&0&0&0&0&0&0&0&0&\frac{1}{5}&0&0&0&0&0\\
0&0&0&0&0&0&0&0&0&0&0&\frac{1}{5}&0&0&0&0\\
0&0&0&0&0&0&0&0&0&0&0&0&\frac{1}{5}&0&0&0\\
0&0&0&0&0&0&0&0&0&0&0&0&0&\frac{1}{5}&0&0\\
0&0&0&0&0&0&0&0&0&0&0&0&0&0&\frac{1}{5}&0\\
0&0&0&0&0&0&0&0&0&0&0&0&0&0&0&\frac{1}{5}
\end{bmatrix}
\begin{bmatrix}
0&0&0&0\\
0&0&0&0\\
0&0&0&0\\
0&0&0&0\\
0&0&0&0\\
0&0&0&0\\
0&0&0&0\\
1&0&0&0\\
0&1&0&0\\
-1&-1&0&0\\
-1&0&1&0\\
0&-1&0&1\\
1&1&-1&-1\\
0&0&-1&0\\
0&0&0&-1\\
0&0&1&1
\end{bmatrix}
\right]^{-1}
$$

$$
= \begin{bmatrix}
.80 & .40 & -.40 & -.20\\
.40 & .80 & -.20 & -.40\\
-.40 & -.20 & .80 & .40\\
-.20 & -.40 & .40 & .80
\end{bmatrix}^{-1}
$$

A solution for this inverse can be obtained by any of the methods discussed previously and we find

$$
(K'GK)^{-1} = \begin{bmatrix}
2.2222 & -1.1111 & 1.1111 & -.5555\\
-1.1111 & 2.2222 & -.5555 & 1.1111\\
1.1111 & -.5555 & 2.2222 & -1.1111\\
-.5555 & 1.1111 & -1.1111 & 2.2222
\end{bmatrix}
$$

The value of Q can now be calculated as

$$[.6,\ -.8,\ 1.4,\ 1.4]\begin{bmatrix} 2.2222 & -1.1111 & 1.1111 & -.5555 \\ -1.1111 & 2.2222 & -.5555 & 1.1111 \\ 1.1111 & -.5555 & 2.2222 & -1.1111 \\ -.5555 & 1.1111 & -1.1111 & 2.2222 \end{bmatrix}\begin{bmatrix} .6 \\ -.8 \\ 1.4 \\ 1.4 \end{bmatrix} = 7.333$$

and its associated F value is

$$\frac{\frac{7.333}{4}}{\frac{4.40}{36}} = 1.634$$

This insignificant F indicates that we cannot reject the null hypothesis. We do not need interaction parameters in our model to explain the variation in reading comprehension. A main effects model with no interaction parameters will do as well in explaining the variation in reading comprehension. Both the type of reading program and the amount of exposure to the reading program were significant in explaining the variation in reading comprehension. The lack of interaction suggests that types of reading programs have the same pattern of impacts on reading comprehension for all three levels of exposure and conversely that levels of exposure have the same pattern of impacts on reading comprehension for all three types of reading programs.

If strong interactions had shown up in this analysis, then the interpretation of the main effects would have become less clear. For example, if Reading Program A_1 worked best under a low level of exposure and worst under a high level of exposure, then the significant main effect for reading programs would have to be qualified by referring to these differential effects.

7.5 ANALYSIS OF VARIANCE FOR FACTORIAL EXPERIMENTS

It might be illuminating if we summarize our results for this reading experiment in an analysis of variance table (Table 7.6). The sum of squares associated with each source of variation except for error is simply the value of its appropriate Q, and the degrees of freedom are the respective ranks of the **K** matrices. It should be noted that in balanced data sets such as this, the component sums of squares (regression sums of squares) add up to the sum of squares for the full model with all parameters (regression sum of squares due to including all parameters in the model). As we have seen previously this is not true for unbalanced data sets. The sums of squares, as they are called in analysis of variance terminology, can be computed in a much simpler manner than they were computed here. We followed the general linear model in computing Qs and testing hypotheses, but for balanced data the computations became much simplified. The reason for using the more complex computations of the general linear model is to give the reader a general method of linear model construction that is applicable to many situations including unbalanced data sets and does not depend upon specific properties of the data set. By writing out the models as we have been doing, we can easily see what parameters or contrasts involving parameters are estimable. When data sets become more complex, the advantages of using the present general approach greatly increase. For example, when data are badly unbalanced, and data in certain cells are missing entirely, the researcher will be able to appreciate the usefulness of this general approach.

Let us now return to our discussion of simplified ways to compute the Qs (sum of squares) for our balanced data set. If there are an equal number of observations in each cell, then the appropriate sum of squares can be easily computed according to the formulas presented in Table 7.7.

The reader can verify the equivalence between the Qs and the corresponding computational formulas. This two-factor model can easily be generalized to a three-factor model or, for that matter, an n-factor model. In a three-factor model with all possible interactions included in the model, we would have the following sources of variation and their associated sums of squares: A; B; C; A

TABLE 7.6
Analysis of Variance of Reading Experiment

Source of Variation	*Sum of Squares*	*Degrees of Freedom*	*Mean Square*	*F*
Factor A—type of reading program	58.533	2	29.266	26.080
Factor B—level of exposure	80.933	2	40.465	36.070
Interaction between factors A and B	7.333	4	1.833	1.634
Factor A, Factor B, and interaction between Factors A and B (regression sum of squares for full model adjusted for μ)	146.799	8	18.349	16.354
Error	40.4	36	1.122	—
Total adjusted for the overall mean	187.199	44	—	—

by B interaction; B by C interaction; A by C interaction; and A by B by C interaction. The interpretation of an A by B by C interaction is that the interaction between A and B differs across the levels of C. Higher-order interactions such as these are difficult to interpret. As an exercise, the reader should attempt to construct a model for a three-factor balanced experiment with all possible interactions. In doing this the reader should determine which functions of the parameters are estimable and develop simplified computational formulas (which are generalizations of the above) for the various sources of variation.

Returning to our reading experiment, we can see that we can predict reading comprehension scores quite readily from knowledge of the levels of Factors A and B. In fact, the coefficient of determination using Factors A and B is (58.533 + 80.933)/187.199 = .745, which means that Factors A and B account for 74.5 percent of the variation in reading comprehension. We did not include the contribution of the A by B interaction in this calculation because it turned out to be insignificant. In actual practice, we probably would not be able to predict reading comprehension to such a great extent by knowledge of only Factors A and B. Many other factors contribute to a child's reading comprehension that we have not considered in this analysis, such as aptitude, attitude toward school, and parents' socioeconomic level. However, the random assignment of children in this hypothetical experiment leads to unbiased estimates of the effects of Factors A and B, because randomization guards against the possibility that children who are assigned to level 1 of Factor A are significantly different in other respects from children assigned to the other two levels of Factor A.

TABLE 7.7
Computational Formulas for Sum of Squares of Factorial Experiment with Equal Cell Sizes

Source	*Computation Formula*	
A	$n_A \sum_{i=1}^{a} \bar{X}_i^2 - N\bar{X}_T^2$	where a is the number of levels of Factor A; n_A is the number of observations within each level of A; and $\bar{X}_T$ is the grand mean
B	$n_B \sum_{j=1}^{b} \bar{X}_j^2 - N\bar{X}_T^2$	where b is the number of levels of Factor B and n_B is the number of observations within each level of B
A × B Interaction	$n_{AB} \sum_{i=1}^{a} \sum_{j=1}^{b} \bar{X}_{ij}^2 - n_A \sum_{i=1}^{a} \bar{X}_i^2 - n_B \sum_{j=1}^{b} \bar{X}_j^2 + N\bar{X}_T^2$	where n_{AB} is the common number of observations within each cell
error	$\sum_{i=1}^{a} \sum_{j=1}^{b} \sum_{k=1}^{n_{AB}} X_{ijk}^2 - n_{AB} \sum_{i=1}^{a} \sum_{j=1}^{b} \bar{X}_{ij}^2$	where k is the subscript for observations within a cell
Total adjusted for mean	$\sum_{i=1}^{a} \sum_{j=1}^{b} \sum_{k=1}^{n_{AB}} X_{ijk}^2 - N\bar{X}_T^2$	

Another interesting thing about balanced experiments is that the sum of squares due to a particular factor remains constant no matter what other parameters are added to the model. That is, the sum of squares or Q due to Factor A in the model $\hat{y}_{ij} = \mu + \alpha_i + \beta_j + \alpha\beta_{ij}$ is the same as in the model $\hat{y}_i = \mu + \alpha_i$. However, if we include factors additional to A in the model we may be able to reduce our error sum of squares to such an extent that the precision of various contrasts involving parameters associated with Factor A is increased. This is true, however, only if the parameters associated with the additional factors reduce the error sum of squares enough to compensate for the loss of degrees of freedom for error when additional parameters are brought into the model. The inclusion of other factors in addition to the one of interest could also lead to the isolation of important interaction effects.

7.6 CREATING A FULL RANK DESIGN MATRIX

If the restrictions $\Sigma\alpha_i = 0$, $\Sigma\beta_j = 0$, $\sum_i \alpha\beta_{ij} = 0$ for all j, and $\sum_j \alpha\beta_{ij} = 0$ for all i are imposed upon the parameters, then there is a unique solution to the normal equations and the α_i's, β_j's, and $\alpha\beta_{ij}$'s are, themselves, estimable. In many cases, constraints such as these are used in computer algorithms so that the **X′X** matrix is of full rank and hence can easily be inverted. If these relationships among the parameters are merely arbitrary constraints for solving the normal equations and not actual restrictions, then the solution is merely one of an infinite number of solutions to the normal equations. In the case of arbitrary constraints involving the parameters, the estimable functions remain the same. However, if the relationships among the parameters are an actual part of the model (restrictions), then the restrictions help determine which linear functions of the parameters are estimable. We have seen in our reading experiment that the individual parameters α_i, β_j, and $\alpha\beta_{ij}$, as well as contrasts such as $\alpha_1 - \alpha_2$ and functions such as $\mu + \alpha_i$ and $\mu + \alpha_i + \beta_j$, were not estimable. If we impose the above restrictions on the model, then these linear functions of the parameters are estimable.

In general, we are not interested in estimating the individual parameters, but only in estimating contrasts among the parameters such as $\alpha_1 - \alpha_2$ or testing hypotheses such as $\alpha_1 = \alpha_2 = \ldots \alpha_r$. Let us now look at our model with the above restrictions imposed and see what it implies about the design matrix associated with the restricted model. Our previous model was

$$\hat{y}_{ij} = \mu X_1 + \alpha_1 X_2 + \alpha_2 X_3 + \alpha_3 X_4 + \beta_1 X_5 + \beta_2 X_6 + \beta_3 X_7 + \alpha\beta_{11} X_8$$
$$+ \alpha\beta_{12} X_9 + \alpha\beta_{13} X_{10} + \alpha\beta_{21} X_{11} + \alpha\beta_{22} X_{12} + \alpha\beta_{23} X_{13}$$
$$+ \alpha\beta_{31} X_{14} + \alpha\beta_{32} X_{15} + \alpha\beta_{33} X_{16}$$

where X_1 is a column vector of ones and the remaining X_i's are 1, 0 (dummy) variables.

If we impose the restrictions $\Sigma\alpha_i = 0$, $\Sigma\beta_j = 0$, $\sum_i \alpha\beta_{ij} = 0$ for all j, and $\sum_j \alpha\beta_{ij} = 0$ for all i, then $\alpha_3 = -(\alpha_1 + \alpha_2)$, $\beta_3 = -(\beta_1 + \beta_2)$, $\alpha\beta_{13} = -(\alpha\beta_{11} + \alpha\beta_{12})$, $\alpha\beta_{23} = -(\alpha\beta_{21} + \alpha\beta_{22})$, $\alpha\beta_{31} = -(\alpha\beta_{11} + \alpha\beta_{21})$, $\alpha\beta_{32} = -(\alpha\beta_{12} + \alpha\beta_{22})$, and $\alpha\beta_{33} = -(\alpha\beta_{11} + \alpha\beta_{12}) - (\alpha\beta_{21} + \alpha\beta_{22})$. Then our restricted model becomes

$$\hat{y}_{ij} = \mu X_1 + \alpha_1 X_2 + \alpha_2 X_3 - (\alpha_1 + \alpha_2) X_4 + \beta_1 X_5 + \beta_2 X_6 - (\beta_1 + \beta_2) X_7$$
$$+ \alpha\beta_{11} X_8 + \alpha\beta_{12} X_9 - (\alpha\beta_{11} + \alpha\beta_{12}) X_{10} + \alpha\beta_{21} X_{11} + \alpha\beta_{22} X_{12}$$
$$- (\alpha\beta_{21} + \alpha\beta_{22}) X_{13} - (\alpha\beta_{11} + \alpha\beta_{21}) X_{14} - (\alpha\beta_{12} + \alpha\beta_{22}) X_{15}$$
$$- (-(\alpha\beta_{11} + \alpha\beta_{12}) - (\alpha\beta_{21} + \alpha\beta_{22})) X_{16}$$

A little bit of algebraic simplification results in

$$\hat{y}_{ij} = \mu X_1 + \alpha_1 (X_2 - X_4) + \alpha_2 (X_3 - X_4) + \beta_1 (X_5 - X_7) + \beta_2 (X_6 - X_7)$$
$$+ \alpha\beta_{11} (X_8 - X_{10} - X_{14} + X_{16}) + \alpha\beta_{12} (X_9 - X_{10} - X_{15} + X_{16})$$
$$+ \alpha\beta_{21} (X_{11} - X_{13} - X_{14} + X_{16}) + \alpha\beta_{22} (X_{12} - X_{13} - X_{15} + X_{16})$$

We can see from our restricted model that we have both a reduced set of parameters and a new set of X variables. We can also see that our new X variables are simply linear combinations of the dummy variables used in the unrestricted model. For example, the X variable associated with α_1 is found by subtracting the original dummy variable 4 from dummy variable 2. The restricted model can now be written as

$$\hat{y}_{ij} = \mu X_1 + \alpha_1 X_2^* + \alpha_2 X_3^* + \beta_1 X_4^* + \beta_2 X_5^* + \alpha\beta_{11} X_6^*$$
$$+ \alpha\beta_{12} X_7^* + \alpha\beta_{21} X_8^* + \alpha\beta_{22} X_9^*$$

where

$$X_2^* = (X_2 - X_4),\ X_3^* = (X_3 - X_4),\ X_4^* = (X_5 - X_7),\ X_5^* = (X_6 - X_7)$$
$$X_6^* = (X_8 - X_{10} - X_{14} + X_{16}),\ X_7^* = (X_9 - X_{10} - X_{15} + X_{16})$$
$$X_8^* = (X_{11} - X_{13} - X_{14} + X_{16}),\ \text{and}\ X_9^* = (X_{12} - X_{13} - X_{15} + X_{16})$$

The restricted model only contains 9 parameters and their associated X* variables while the unrestricted model contained 16 parameters and their associated X variables. We will now see that our new 9×9 $\mathbf{X^{*\prime}X^*}$ matrix is of full rank (r = 9) and consequently possesses a unique inverse. The new **X*** constructed from our original dummy variables is

X_1	X_2^*	X_3^*	X_4^*	X_5^*	X_6^*	X_7^*	X_8^*	X_9^*
1	1	0	1	0	1	0	0	0
1	1	0	1	0	1	0	0	0
1	1	0	1	0	1	0	0	0
1	1	0	1	0	1	0	0	0
1	1	0	1	0	1	0	0	0
1	1	0	0	1	0	1	0	0
1	1	0	0	1	0	1	0	0
1	1	0	0	1	0	1	0	0
1	1	0	0	1	0	1	0	0
1	1	0	0	1	0	1	0	0
1	1	0	−1	−1	−1	−1	0	0
1	1	0	−1	−1	−1	−1	0	0
1	1	0	−1	−1	−1	−1	0	0
1	1	0	−1	−1	−1	−1	0	0
1	1	0	−1	−1	−1	−1	0	0
1	0	1	1	0	0	0	1	0
1	0	1	1	0	0	0	1	0
1	0	1	1	0	0	0	1	0
1	0	1	1	0	0	0	1	0
1	0	1	1	0	0	0	1	0
1	0	1	0	1	0	0	0	1
1	0	1	0	1	0	0	0	1
1	0	1	0	1	0	0	0	1
1	0	1	0	1	0	0	0	1
1	0	1	0	1	0	0	0	1
1	0	1	−1	−1	0	0	−1	−1
1	0	1	−1	−1	0	0	−1	−1
1	0	1	−1	−1	0	0	−1	−1
1	0	1	−1	−1	0	0	−1	−1
1	0	1	−1	−1	0	0	−1	−1
1	−1	−1	1	0	−1	0	−1	0
1	−1	−1	1	0	−1	0	−1	0
1	−1	−1	1	0	−1	0	−1	0
1	−1	−1	1	0	−1	0	−1	0
1	−1	−1	1	0	−1	0	−1	0
1	−1	−1	0	1	0	−1	0	−1
1	−1	−1	0	1	0	−1	0	−1
1	−1	−1	0	1	0	−1	0	−1
1	−1	−1	0	1	0	−1	0	−1
1	−1	−1	0	1	0	−1	0	−1
1	−1	−1	−1	−1	1	1	1	1
1	−1	−1	−1	−1	1	1	1	1
1	−1	−1	−1	−1	1	1	1	1
1	−1	−1	−1	−1	1	1	1	1
1	−1	−1	−1	−1	1	1	1	1

For example, the variable X_6^* was created from its relationship to the original dummy variables as

$$x_6^* = x_8 - x_{10} - x_{14} + x_{16} = \begin{bmatrix} 1\\1\\1\\1\\1\\0\\0\\0\\0\\0\\0\\0\\0\\0\\0\\0\\0\\0\\0\\0\\0\\0\\0\\0\\0\\0\\0\\0\\0\\0\\0\\0\\0\\0\\0\\0\\0\\0\\0\\0\\0\\0\\0\\0\\0 \end{bmatrix} - \begin{bmatrix} 0\\0\\0\\0\\0\\0\\0\\0\\0\\0\\1\\1\\1\\1\\1\\0\\0\\0\\0\\0\\0\\0\\0\\0\\0\\0\\0\\0\\0\\0\\0\\0\\0\\0\\0\\0\\0\\0\\0\\0\\0\\0\\0\\0\\0 \end{bmatrix} - \begin{bmatrix} 0\\0\\0\\0\\0\\0\\0\\0\\0\\0\\0\\0\\0\\0\\0\\0\\0\\0\\0\\0\\0\\0\\0\\0\\0\\0\\0\\0\\0\\0\\1\\1\\1\\1\\1\\0\\0\\0\\0\\0\\0\\0\\0\\0\\0 \end{bmatrix} + \begin{bmatrix} 0\\0\\0\\0\\0\\0\\0\\0\\0\\0\\0\\0\\0\\0\\0\\0\\0\\0\\0\\0\\0\\0\\0\\0\\0\\0\\0\\0\\0\\0\\0\\0\\0\\0\\0\\0\\0\\0\\0\\0\\1\\1\\1\\1\\1 \end{bmatrix} = \begin{bmatrix} 1\\1\\1\\1\\1\\0\\0\\0\\0\\0\\-1\\-1\\-1\\-1\\-1\\0\\0\\0\\0\\0\\0\\0\\0\\0\\0\\0\\0\\0\\0\\0\\-1\\-1\\-1\\-1\\-1\\0\\0\\0\\0\\0\\1\\1\\1\\1\\1 \end{bmatrix}$$

As an exercise, the reader should likewise create the remaining 8 variables of **X*** and then solve the normal equations for the 9 restricted parameters.

The remaining 7 parameters can be found by substituting the appropriate estimated parameters into the restrictions. The reader can verify that the full solution is

$$\hat{\boldsymbol{\beta}} = \begin{bmatrix} \hat{\mu} \\ \hat{\alpha}_1 \\ \hat{\alpha}_2 \\ \hat{\alpha}_3 \\ \hat{\beta}_1 \\ \hat{\beta}_2 \\ \hat{\beta}_3 \\ \hat{\alpha\beta}_{11} \\ \hat{\alpha\beta}_{12} \\ \hat{\alpha\beta}_{13} \\ \hat{\alpha\beta}_{21} \\ \hat{\alpha\beta}_{22} \\ \hat{\alpha\beta}_{23} \\ \hat{\alpha\beta}_{31} \\ \hat{\alpha\beta}_{32} \\ \hat{\alpha\beta}_{33} \end{bmatrix} = \begin{bmatrix} 4.5333 \\ -1.2000 \\ -.3333 \\ 1.5333 \\ -1.7333 \\ .2000 \\ 1.5333 \\ .5999 \\ -.3333 \\ -.2666 \\ -.0666 \\ .4000 \\ -.3333 \\ -.5333 \\ -.0666 \\ .5999 \end{bmatrix}$$

It is interesting to observe that for data that have equal cell sizes, these parameter estimates can be obtained directly from linear combinations of the total, row, column, and cell means.

The estimate, $\hat{\mu}$, is the overall mean. The estimates $\hat{\alpha}_1$, $\hat{\alpha}_2$ and $\hat{\alpha}_3$ are $\overline{X}_{A_1} - \overline{X}_T$, $\overline{X}_{A_2} - \overline{X}_T$, and $\overline{X}_{A_3} - \overline{X}_T$, respectively, where $\overline{X}_{A_1}$, $\overline{X}_{A_2}$, and $\overline{X}_{A_3}$ are the means for levels 1, 2, and 3 of Factor A, respectively, and $\overline{X}_T$ is the overall mean. Similarly, the estimates $\hat{\beta}_1$, $\hat{\beta}_2$, and $\hat{\beta}_3$ are $\overline{X}_{B_1} - \overline{X}_T$, $\overline{X}_{B_2} - \overline{X}_T$, and $\overline{X}_{B_3} - \overline{X}_T$, respectively. The estimates for each of the nine interaction parameters are obtained by adding the appropriate column effect (level of Factor A) and the appropriatre row effect (level of Factor B) to $\hat{\mu}$ and subtracting this sum from the corresponding cell mean. Since the model indicates that the cell mean $(\mu_{ij}) = \mu + \alpha_i + \beta_j + \alpha\beta_{ij}$, we can obtain an estimate of $\widehat{\alpha\beta}_{ij}$ by subtracting $\hat{\mu} + \hat{\alpha}_i + \hat{\beta}_j$ from the cell mean $\overline{X}_{ij}$ to obtain an estimate of $\widehat{\alpha\beta}_{ij}$. For example, the cell mean corresponding to level 1 of Factor A and level 2 of Factor B is 3.20, and $\hat{\mu} + \hat{\alpha}_1 + \hat{\beta}_2 = 4.5333 + (-1.2000) + (.2000) = 3.5333$ so that $\widehat{\alpha\beta}_{12}$ equals 3.20 – 3.5333 or –.333. In the balanced data case, the solution to the normal equations with restrictions on the parameters becomes very simplified. In the unbalanced situation, the solution to the normal equations does not reduce to such a simple form. We can use the same procedure outlined earlier in this chapter to test various hypotheses concerning the parameters. If we consider the parameters as unrestricted, then the present solution just becomes another possible solution for the 16 elements of the solution vector. If the restrictions are considered part of the model, then each parameter itself is estimable and can be tested for significance.

The reason that we have spent so much time and space in talking about the restrictions $\Sigma\alpha_i = 0$, $\Sigma\beta_j = 0$, $\sum_i \alpha\beta_{ij} = 0$ for all j, and $\sum_j \alpha\beta_{ij} = 0$ for all i is that many regression and analysis of variance computer programs solve the normal equations using some restrictions or reparameterizations. They require the researcher to specify a full rank **X*** matrix so that the program can use a standard matrix inversion routine. If we form an **X*** matrix in the manner that we have done, then each of the elements of the solution is an estimable parameter in the restricted model or an estimable function of parameters in the unrestricted model and the matrix $\hat{\sigma}^2 (\mathbf{X}^{*\prime}\mathbf{X})^{-1}$ is an estimate of the covariance matrix of these parameters or functions of parameters. For example, the estimate $\hat{\alpha}_1$ in the restricted model is an estimate of α_1, whereas in the unrestricted model it is an estimate of

$$\alpha_1 + \sum_j \alpha\beta_{1j} - \frac{1}{3}\sum_i (\alpha_i + \sum_j \alpha\beta_{ij})$$

Note that if the restrictions apply, this reduces to α_1.

7.7 AN INTERACTION MODEL WITH UNBALANCED DATA

We have seen that the major Qs of interest for the balanced data case can be obtained directly from the analysis of variance computations. In this case the regression sum of squares for the various Qs sum to the overall regression sum of squares. In the unbalanced data situation that exists in most social and behavioral science applications, this analysis of variance approach cannot be used and we must resort to solving the appropriate normal equations.

We considered in the last chapter an unbalanced data set where we considered a main effects model $y_{ijk} = \mu + \alpha_i + \beta_j + \epsilon_{ijk}$ where the α_i's represented the effects for the different levels (2) of type of community and the β_j's represented the effects for the different levels (2) of quality of school. Let us now return to this model and determine if adding interaction parameters to this main effects model improves the fit of the model. Our procedure would be to add $\alpha\beta_{ij}$ parameters to the model and test the hypothesis that $\alpha\beta_{11} - \alpha\beta_{21} = \alpha\beta_{12} - \alpha\beta_{22}$ or, equivalently, that $(\alpha\beta_{11} - \alpha\beta_{21}) - (\alpha\beta_{12} - \alpha\beta_{22}) = 0$. Since there are only two levels for each of the two factors, there is only one degree of freedom for interaction associated with this interaction contrast.

We can gain some rough preliminary insight as to whether or not interaction parameters might be useful in our present model by comparing the four cell means with the appropriate predictions based upon our previous main effects model. The cell means are again presented for convenience in Table 7.8.

TABLE 7.8
Mean Achievement by Quality of School and Type of Community

	Quality of School	
Type of Community	*Poor*	*Good*
Urban	6	7
Suburban	7.5	8.2

The predicted cell means can be obtained from our previous solution to the normal equation, which was

$$\begin{bmatrix} \hat{\mu}^* \\ \hat{\alpha}_1^* \\ \hat{\alpha}_2^* \\ \hat{\beta}_1^* \\ \hat{\beta}_2^* \end{bmatrix} = \begin{bmatrix} 0 \\ 0 \\ 1.330 \\ 6.049 \\ 6.919 \end{bmatrix}$$

Without restrictions, this is just one of an infinite number of possible solutions to the normal equations. Since we did not place any restrictions on the parameters, we cannot estimate $\mu + \alpha_1$, $\mu + \alpha_2$, $\mu + \beta_1$, or $\mu + \beta_2$, but we can estimate $\mu + \alpha_1 + \beta_1$, $\mu + \alpha_1 + \beta_2$, $\mu + \alpha_2 + \beta_1$, and $\mu + \alpha_2 + \beta_2$; the estimates of these are

$$\begin{bmatrix} \hat{\mu}^* + \hat{\alpha}_1^* + \hat{\beta}_1^* \\ \hat{\mu}^* + \hat{\alpha}_1^* + \hat{\beta}_2^* \\ \hat{\mu}^* + \hat{\alpha}_2^* + \hat{\beta}_1^* \\ \hat{\mu}^* + \hat{\alpha}_2^* + \hat{\beta}_2^* \end{bmatrix} = \begin{bmatrix} 6.049 \\ 6.919 \\ 7.379 \\ 8.249 \end{bmatrix}$$

The deviations of these predicted cell means from the observed cell means are

$$\underset{\text{predicted}}{\begin{bmatrix} 6.049 \\ 6.919 \\ 7.379 \\ 8.249 \end{bmatrix}} - \underset{\text{observed}}{\begin{bmatrix} 6.000 \\ 7.000 \\ 7.500 \\ 8.200 \end{bmatrix}} = \underset{\text{deviation}}{\begin{bmatrix} .049 \\ -.081 \\ -.121 \\ .049 \end{bmatrix}}$$

which would not seem to be large enough to indicate a significant interaction given the small sample size. However, we can test this hypothesis formally by solving the normal equations associated with the model $y_{ijk} = \mu + \alpha_i + \beta_j + \alpha\beta_{ij} + \epsilon_{ijk}$, computing the appropriate Q, and forming the appropriate F ratio. The sample data can be represented in an interaction model as

$$\mathbf{y} = \begin{bmatrix} 5 \\ 5 \\ 6 \\ 7 \\ 7 \\ 6 \\ 7 \\ 8 \\ 7 \\ 8 \\ 7 \\ 8 \\ 8 \\ 9 \\ 9 \end{bmatrix} = \mathbf{X}\beta^* + \epsilon = \begin{bmatrix} 1 & 1 & 0 & 1 & 0 & 1 & 0 & 0 & 0 \\ 1 & 1 & 0 & 1 & 0 & 1 & 0 & 0 & 0 \\ 1 & 1 & 0 & 1 & 0 & 1 & 0 & 0 & 0 \\ 1 & 1 & 0 & 1 & 0 & 1 & 0 & 0 & 0 \\ 1 & 1 & 0 & 1 & 0 & 1 & 0 & 0 & 0 \\ 1 & 1 & 0 & 0 & 1 & 0 & 1 & 0 & 0 \\ 1 & 1 & 0 & 0 & 1 & 0 & 1 & 0 & 0 \\ 1 & 1 & 0 & 0 & 1 & 0 & 1 & 0 & 0 \\ 1 & 0 & 1 & 1 & 0 & 0 & 0 & 1 & 0 \\ 1 & 0 & 1 & 1 & 0 & 0 & 0 & 1 & 0 \\ 1 & 0 & 1 & 0 & 1 & 0 & 0 & 0 & 1 \\ 1 & 0 & 1 & 0 & 1 & 0 & 0 & 0 & 1 \\ 1 & 0 & 1 & 0 & 1 & 0 & 0 & 0 & 1 \\ 1 & 0 & 1 & 0 & 1 & 0 & 0 & 0 & 1 \\ 1 & 0 & 1 & 0 & 1 & 0 & 0 & 0 & 1 \end{bmatrix} \begin{bmatrix} \mu \\ \alpha_1 \\ \alpha_2 \\ \beta_1 \\ \beta_2 \\ \alpha\beta_{11} \\ \alpha\beta_{12} \\ \alpha\beta_{21} \\ \alpha\beta_{22} \end{bmatrix} + \epsilon$$

Next, we find that

$$
\mathbf{X}'\mathbf{X} = \begin{bmatrix} 15 & 8 & 7 & 7 & 8 & 5 & 3 & 2 & 5 \\ 8 & 8 & 0 & 5 & 3 & 5 & 3 & 0 & 0 \\ 7 & 0 & 7 & 2 & 5 & 0 & 0 & 2 & 5 \\ 7 & 5 & 2 & 7 & 0 & 5 & 0 & 2 & 0 \\ 8 & 3 & 5 & 0 & 8 & 0 & 3 & 0 & 5 \\ 5 & 5 & 0 & 5 & 0 & 5 & 0 & 0 & 0 \\ 3 & 3 & 0 & 0 & 3 & 0 & 3 & 0 & 0 \\ 2 & 0 & 2 & 2 & 0 & 0 & 0 & 2 & 0 \\ 5 & 0 & 5 & 0 & 5 & 0 & 0 & 0 & 5 \end{bmatrix} \quad \text{and} \quad \mathbf{X}'\mathbf{y} = \begin{bmatrix} 107 \\ 51 \\ 56 \\ 45 \\ 62 \\ 30 \\ 21 \\ 15 \\ 41 \end{bmatrix}
$$

In order to obtain a solution $\hat{\boldsymbol{\beta}}^*$ we need to find a generalized inverse, **G** of **X′X**. Since there are only 4 free parameters in this model, or 4 cells, we know that the rank of **X′X** is 4 and hence a generalized inverse of **X′X** is

$$
\mathbf{G} = \begin{bmatrix} 0 & 0 & 0 & 0 & 0 & 0 & 0 & 0 & 0 \\ 0 & 0 & 0 & 0 & 0 & 0 & 0 & 0 & 0 \\ 0 & 0 & 0 & 0 & 0 & 0 & 0 & 0 & 0 \\ 0 & 0 & 0 & 0 & 0 & 0 & 0 & 0 & 0 \\ 0 & 0 & 0 & 0 & 0 & 0 & 0 & 0 & 0 \\ 0 & 0 & 0 & 0 & 0 & \frac{1}{5} & 0 & 0 & 0 \\ 0 & 0 & 0 & 0 & 0 & 0 & \frac{1}{3} & 0 & 0 \\ 0 & 0 & 0 & 0 & 0 & 0 & 0 & \frac{1}{2} & 0 \\ 0 & 0 & 0 & 0 & 0 & 0 & 0 & 0 & \frac{1}{5} \end{bmatrix}
$$

where we selected the 4×4 diagonal matrix in the lower right of the **X′X** matrix for inversion. Consequently,

$$\boldsymbol{\beta}^* = \begin{bmatrix} \hat{\mu}^* \\ \hat{\alpha}_1^* \\ \hat{\alpha}_2^* \\ \hat{\beta}_1^* \\ \hat{\beta}_2^* \\ \widehat{\alpha\beta}_{11}^* \\ \widehat{\alpha\beta}_{12}^* \\ \widehat{\alpha\beta}_{21}^* \\ \widehat{\alpha\beta}_{22}^* \end{bmatrix} = \begin{bmatrix} 0 & 0 & 0 & 0 & 0 & 0 & 0 & 0 & 0 \\ 0 & 0 & 0 & 0 & 0 & 0 & 0 & 0 & 0 \\ 0 & 0 & 0 & 0 & 0 & 0 & 0 & 0 & 0 \\ 0 & 0 & 0 & 0 & 0 & 0 & 0 & 0 & 0 \\ 0 & 0 & 0 & 0 & 0 & 0 & 0 & 0 & 0 \\ 0 & 0 & 0 & 0 & 0 & \frac{1}{5} & 0 & 0 & 0 \\ 0 & 0 & 0 & 0 & 0 & 0 & \frac{1}{3} & 0 & 0 \\ 0 & 0 & 0 & 0 & 0 & 0 & 0 & \frac{1}{2} & 0 \\ 0 & 0 & 0 & 0 & 0 & 0 & 0 & 0 & \frac{1}{5} \end{bmatrix} \begin{bmatrix} 107 \\ 51 \\ 56 \\ 45 \\ 62 \\ 30 \\ 21 \\ 15 \\ 41 \end{bmatrix} = \begin{bmatrix} 0 \\ 0 \\ 0 \\ 0 \\ 0 \\ 6 \\ 7 \\ 7.5 \\ 8.2 \end{bmatrix}$$

The solution is identical in form to the balanced data case with no restrictions on the parameters. That is $\hat{\mu}^*$ and all the main effects are set to zero and the interaction parameters, $\widehat{\alpha\beta}_{ij}^*$, take the values of their respective cell means. Notice that the **X′y** vector, again, corresponds to various row, column, and cell totals. Similar to the balanced case we cannot estimate the contrast $\alpha_1 - \alpha_2$ and $\beta_1 - \beta_2$, but we can estimate the contrast

$$\alpha_1 + \frac{1}{2}(\alpha\beta_{11} + \alpha\beta_{12}) - \left(\alpha_2 + \frac{1}{2}(\alpha\beta_{21} + \alpha\beta_{22})\right)$$

and the contrast

$$\beta_1 + \frac{1}{2}(\alpha\beta_{11} + \alpha\beta_{21}) - \left(\beta_2 + \frac{1}{2}(\alpha\beta_{12} + \alpha\beta_{22})\right).$$

We can also estimate the interaction contrast $(\alpha\beta_{11} - \alpha\beta_{12}) - (\alpha\beta_{21} - \alpha\beta_{22})$. Since we now have a new model we will have to reestimate $\hat{\sigma}^2$ before we can test the hypothesis $(\alpha\beta_{11} - \alpha\beta_{12}) - (\alpha\beta_{21} - \alpha\beta_{22}) = 0$.

We know that σ^2 can be estimated as

$$\hat{\sigma}^2 = \frac{\mathbf{y}'\mathbf{y} - \boldsymbol{\beta}'\mathbf{X}'\mathbf{y}}{N - r(\mathbf{X})}$$

which the reader should verify equals .8455, which is fairly close to the estimate of $\hat{\sigma}^2$ derived from the original main effects model. We can now test the interaction hypothesis that

$$(\alpha\beta_{11} - \alpha\beta_{12}) - (\alpha\beta_{21} - \alpha\beta_{22}) = 0$$

by finding $Q = [\mathbf{K}'\hat{\beta}^*]' [\mathbf{K}'\mathbf{G}\mathbf{K}]^{-1} [\mathbf{K}'\hat{\beta}^*]$. For our data, we find that

$$\mathbf{K}'\beta^* = [0 \;\; 0 \;\; 0 \;\; 0 \;\; 0 \;\; 1 \;\; -1 \;\; -1 \;\; 1] \begin{bmatrix} 0 \\ 0 \\ 0 \\ 0 \\ 0 \\ 6 \\ 7 \\ 7.5 \\ 8.2 \end{bmatrix} = -.3;$$

$$[\mathbf{K}'\mathbf{G}\mathbf{K}] = [0 \;\; 0 \;\; 0 \;\; 0 \;\; 0 \;\; 1 \;\; -1 \;\; -1 \;\; 1] \begin{bmatrix} 0&0&0&0&0&0&0&0&0 \\ 0&0&0&0&0&0&0&0&0 \\ 0&0&0&0&0&0&0&0&0 \\ 0&0&0&0&0&0&0&0&0 \\ 0&0&0&0&0&0&0&0&0 \\ 0&0&0&0&0&\frac{1}{5}&0&0&0 \\ 0&0&0&0&0&0&\frac{1}{3}&0&0 \\ 0&0&0&0&0&0&0&\frac{1}{2}&0 \\ 0&0&0&0&0&0&0&0&\frac{1}{5} \end{bmatrix} \begin{bmatrix} 0 \\ 0 \\ 0 \\ 0 \\ 0 \\ 1 \\ -1 \\ -1 \\ 1 \end{bmatrix} = 1.2333;$$

and $[\mathbf{K'GK}]^{-1} = .8108$. Substituting, we find Q = (–.3)(.8108)(–.3) = .073. Since **K** is of rank 1, F = .073/.8455 = .086 and is obviously not significant. Q can be regarded as the additional regression sum of squares due to adding interaction parameters to the original main effects model. We can easily see this by calculating the total regression sum of squares for our revised interaction model and subtracting from that the total regression sum of squares for our previously discussed main effects model. The total regression sum of squares for the main effects model was previously computed as 775.627, whereas the total regression sum of squares for our revised interaction model is

$$\beta^{*\prime}\mathbf{X}'\mathbf{y} = [0\ 0\ 0\ 0\ 0\ 6\ 7\ 7.5\ 8.2]\begin{bmatrix}107\\51\\56\\75\\62\\30\\21\\15\\41\end{bmatrix} = 775.7$$

The difference between the two regression sums of squares is .073, which is identical to the .073 calculated for the interaction Q.

7.8 USE OF COMPUTERS

SAS will generate and test for significance the adjusted regression sum of squares due to Factors A and B and their interaction. If there are more than two factors, then SAS will test for significance the sum of squares due to each factor and all possible interactions among the factors. SAS will also test any admissible hypotheses through the specification of hypothesis matrices.

The model can be respecified through restrictions or reparameterization in order to create a full rank model so that conventional regression procedures can be used. We illustrated how restrictions on the parameters led to a coding procedure called effects coding. The parameters associated with this full rank model are estimable functions of the original parameters or estimates of the original parameters themselves, if the restrictions are allowed to hold. In a model with interaction parameters, restrictions are usually adopted in order to simplify the interpretation of the regression parameters.

Effects coding, or any other coding for that matter, can easily be routinized. We begin by creating a design matrix for a main effects model using effects coding as illustrated in the previous chapter. If there are three levels for both factors A and B, then the first five columns of the full rank design matrix in section 7.7 of this chapter represent effects coding for this model. The remaining four columns, X_6 through X_9, are associated with the interaction parameters. These "interaction" columns are created by taking the element-by-element cross products of each column associated with factor A with each column associated with factor B. Returning to the full rank design matrix, it can be seen that column 6 is made up of the cross products of the elements of columns 2 and 4, column 7 is formed from the cross products of columns 2 and 5, column 8 from columns 3 and 4, and column 9 from columns 3 and 5. The restrictions imply that X_1 is associated with μ; X_2 and X_3 with α_1 and α_2, respectively; X_4 and X_5 with β_1 and β_2, respectively; and X_6, X_7, X_8, and X_9 with the parameters of $\alpha\beta_{11}$, $\alpha\beta_{12}$, $\alpha\beta_{21}$, and $\alpha\beta_{22}$, respectively.

The regression program will estimate these parameters, generate their standard errors, and test their significance. This procedure can be generalized to regression models with any number of factors and levels within factors. As discussed previously, this procedure does not test the significance of all of the factors associated with a given effect, main or interaction. In order to do this separate regressions, with and without the effects, must be run and their results compared.

Dummy variable coding can also be used to create a full rank design matrix for an interaction model. The procedure is analogous to that just described. We first create a main effects model using dummy variables as described in the previous chapter. Then the "interaction" columns are formed by taking the element-by-element cross products of each column associated with factor A with each column associated with factor B.

For example, a main effects model for two categorical independent variables, each with two levels, can be expressed, using dummy variable coding, as

$$E\begin{bmatrix} y_{11k} \\ y_{12k} \\ y_{21k} \\ y_{22k} \end{bmatrix} = \begin{bmatrix} 1 & 1 & 1 \\ 1 & 1 & 0 \\ 1 & 0 & 1 \\ 1 & 0 & 0 \end{bmatrix} \begin{bmatrix} \delta_1 \\ \delta_2 \\ \delta_3 \end{bmatrix}$$

where $E(y_{11k})$, $E(y_{12k})$, $E(y_{21k})$, and $E(y_{22k})$ are the expected values (that is, population means) of the cells 11, 12, 21, and 22, respectively. In terms of the original parameters, $\delta_1 = \mu + \alpha_2 + \beta_2$, $\delta_2 = \alpha_1 - \alpha_2$, and $\delta_3 = \beta_1 - \beta_2$.

We create an interaction dummy variable by cross-multiplying, element by element, columns 2 and 3. The resulting model is

$$E\begin{bmatrix} y_{11k} \\ y_{12k} \\ y_{21k} \\ y_{22k} \end{bmatrix} = \begin{bmatrix} 1 & 1 & 1 & 1 \\ 1 & 1 & 0 & 0 \\ 1 & 0 & 1 & 0 \\ 1 & 0 & 0 & 0 \end{bmatrix} \begin{bmatrix} \theta_1 \\ \theta_2 \\ \theta_3 \\ \theta_4 \end{bmatrix}$$

where, in terms of the original parameters, $\theta_1 = \mu + \alpha_2 + \beta_2 + \alpha\beta_{22}$, $\theta_2 = \alpha_1 - \alpha_2 + \alpha\beta_{12} - \alpha\beta_{22}$, $\theta_3 = \beta_1 - \beta_2 + \alpha\beta_{21} - \alpha\beta_{22}$, and $\theta_4 = (\alpha\beta_{11} - \alpha\beta_{12}) - (\alpha\beta_{21} - \alpha\beta_{22})$. If we make certain simplifying restrictions such as $\alpha\beta_{12}$, $\alpha\beta_{21}$, and $\alpha\beta_{22}$ are zero, then $\alpha_1 - \alpha_2$ and $\beta_1 - \beta_2$ are estimable.

Inputting this full rank design matrix along with **y** into a standard multiple regression program will result in the following output: R^2; overall significance test of the null hypothesis that $\theta_2 = \theta_3 = \theta_4 = 0$; the estimates θ_1, θ_2, θ_3, and θ_4, their associated standard errors, and their levels of significance. In this case, each main effect and the interaction has one degree of freedom so that these parameters represent overall tests of each main effect and interaction as well. We have seen earlier that this will not be the case if one or more factors contain two or more levels.

7.9 PROBLEMS

(1) Referring to problem 1 at the end of Chapter 5, test the hypothesis that the interaction parameters associated with sex and SES are zero.

(2) Verify that the estimated expected value for an observation within a particular cell is the observed cell mean itself.

(3) Plot the residuals for each of the six cells and compare with the plots from problem 1 at the end of Chapter 6.

(4) Again referring to problem 1, Chapter 6, use restrictions on the parameters and write out the equations that would yield a unique solution for the estimated parameters. Solve the equations for these parameters.

(5) Reparametrize the model in terms of estimable functions.

(6) Using the data from problem 6 at the end of Chapter 4, estimate the parameter β_4 in the model $y_i = \beta_0 + \beta_1 x_{1i} + \beta_2 x_{2i} + \beta_3 x_{3i} + \beta_4 x_{1i} x_{2i} + \epsilon_i$ and test for its significance at the .05 level.

(7) Consider the data set below and answer the following questions or address the statements.

	Treatment A		
Treatment B	*1*	*2*	*3*
	6	2	-2
1	5	5	-1
	5	1	-4
	10	1	0
2	8	4	2
	6	3	5
	2	6	3
3	8	4	2
	5	3	0

(a) Set up an analysis of variance table and test for the significance of each source of variation at the .05 level.

(b) Write out the normal equations and solve them.

(c) What hypothesis is each of the tests in problem 7a testing? If the model is reparameterized so that

$$\sum_i \alpha_i = \sum_j \beta_j = \sum_i \alpha\beta_{ij} = \sum_j \alpha\beta_{ij} = 0.$$

what hypotheses are being tested in the analysis of variance table?

(d) Determine each of the 9 estimated cell means from the solution of the normal equations.

(e) What percentage of the variation in the dependent variable do the two factors account for?

(8) Consider the data set below:

	α *Factor*		
β *Factor*	*Level 1*	*Level 2*	*Level 3*
Level 1	12, 8, 9, 14	9, 8	7
Level 2	1, 4, 6	13, 12	5, 6, 12, 7, 13

Let $R(\mu)$ be the sum of squares due to the mean, $R(\alpha|\mu)$ be the sum of squares due to α after fitting the mean, $R(\beta|\mu,\alpha)$ be the sum of squares due to β after fitting μ and α, and $R(\alpha\beta|\mu,\alpha,\beta)$ be the sum of squares due to $\alpha\beta$ after fitting μ, α, and β. (Remember from the previous chapter, $R(\beta|\mu, \alpha)$ was defined as $R(\mu,\alpha,\beta) - R(\mu,\alpha)$. The remaining sums of squares are analogously defined).

(a) Indicate the model assumed for calculating each sum of squares and the hypothesis that is being tested.

(b) Calculate each of these sums of squares and test for their significance at the .05 level.

(c) Show that the addition of these four sums of squares is equal to the sum of squares for regression unadjusted for the mean.

(9) From the same data in 8 above:

(a) Calculate the following sums of squares and test for their significance at the .05 level: $R(\beta|\mu)$; $R(\alpha|\mu\ \beta)$.

(b) Show that $R(\alpha|\mu) + R(\beta|\mu,\alpha) = R(\beta|\mu) + R(\alpha|\mu,\beta) = R(\alpha,\beta|\mu)$. Why is this a useful relationship?

8 Analysis of Covariance

8.1 INTRODUCTION

We have basically been discussing two kinds of models; the analysis of variance model and the multiple regression model. The analysis of variance model or its equivalent formulation in terms of regression with dummy variables was concerned solely with classification-type or categorical independent variables, such as sex or instructional programs, or continuous variables, such as age, that can be arbitrarily categorized. On the other hand, multiple regression analysis is concerned solely with continuous-type variables such as intelligence test scores, achievement scores, and so on.

Although we made a distinction between analysis of variance models and multiple regression models in terms of the types of independent variables, they both can be subsumed under the general linear model approach, as has been illustrated.

However, there is no reason we cannot combine mixtures of categorical and continuous variables in a model. Models with a number of categorical variables or factors and a single continuous independent variable have been referred to as analysis of covariance models. However, there is no logical reason for limiting covariance models to one continuous independent variable; we could just as well use two or more continuous independent variables along with the set of categorical variables.

This section will be concerned with statistical models that use jointly both categorical and continuous variables as independent variables. There are really no new principles involved in analyzing these types of models. All of the principles and tools that are needed for analyzing these models have been covered previously in this book.

Section 8.2 formulates the covariance model. Like any regression model, this model has an associated set of normal equations that must be solved. This is discussed in section 8.3. In section 8.4, a hypothetical data set is used to demonstrate the setting up of an analysis of covariance model, the solving of the associated normal equations, and the testing of various hypotheses. Section 8.5 discusses the use of computers for the analysis of covariance. The last section, section 8.6, demonstrates an application of a model with a mixture of categorical and continuous independent variables that has policy implications in an educational setting.

8.2 ANALYSIS OF COVARIANCE MODELS

A model with two categorical variables and one continuous independent variable can be written as

$$y_{ijk} = \mu + \alpha_i + \beta_j + \alpha\beta_{ij} + \Theta X_{ijk} + \epsilon_{ijk}$$

where y_{ijk} (the dependent variable) is the kth observation of levels i and j of factors A and B respectively; α_i is the effect (parameter) of the ith level of factor A; β_j is the effect (parameter) of the jth level of factor B; $\alpha\beta_{ij}$ is the interaction effect (parameter) for the cell defined by the ith level of A and the jth level of B; Θ is the regression weight for the continuous independent variable X; X_{ijk} is the value of the continuous covariate for the kth observation in the cell defined by the ith level of A and the jth level of B; and ϵ_{ijk} is the error associated with the ijk^{th} observation.

As in analysis of variance or multiple regression models, ϵ_{ijk} is assumed to be normally and independently distributed with mean equal to 0 and common variance σ^2. In addition, the independent variables are assumed to be fixed. An assumption of normality is needed if we are to use normal distribution theory to test various hypotheses concerning the parameters.

An example of another model with two continuous variables and three categorical variables that assumes no interactions because there is only one observation per cell is

$$y_{ijk} = \mu + \alpha_i + \beta_j + \delta_k + \Theta_1 X_{1ijk} + \Theta_2 X_{2ijk} + \epsilon_{ijk}$$

where y_{ijk} (the dependent variable) is the observation in the cell formed by the ith, j^{th}, and k^{th} levels of factors A, B, and C, respectively; α_i, β_j, and δ_k are the main effect parameters associated with factors A, B, and C, respectively; X_{1ijk} is the ijk_{th} observation on the continuous variable X_1; X_{2ijk} is the ijk^{th} observation on X_2; and Θ_1 and Θ_2 are the regression parameters associated with X_1 and X_2, respectively.

If there is only one observation per cell, then interaction contrasts are typically not estimated because there would be no degrees of freedom left for estimating the error sum of squares. For convenience, no interaction is assumed and the residual variation is attributed to error. This can easily be seen for the case of a two-factor design with three levels for each factor. There would be nine observations, one in each of the nine cells. After correcting for the overall mean, μ, there are only eight degrees of freedom remaining in the data. Two of these degrees of freedom are associated with each of the two main effects and four degrees of freedom are associated with the interaction parameters. This makes a total of eight degrees of freedom used up for regression. Hence no information remains for estimating the error variance.

8.3. SOLVING THE NORMAL EQUATIONS

In order to obtain a solution vector, $\hat{\boldsymbol{\beta}}^*$, for a model such as

$$y_{ijk} = \mu + \alpha_i + \beta_j + \alpha\beta_{ij} + \Theta X_{ijk} + \epsilon_{ijk}$$

we need first to define our **X** matrix so that we can write the model in matrix notation as

$$\mathbf{y} = \mathbf{X}\hat{\boldsymbol{\beta}} + \boldsymbol{\epsilon}$$

where **y** is the vector of observations on the continuous dependent variable; **X** is an $N \times p$ design matrix, $\boldsymbol{\beta}$ is a $p \times 1$ vector of model parameters, and $\boldsymbol{\epsilon}$ is a vector of errors. If **X** were a full rank matrix, then we could find a unique solution $\hat{\boldsymbol{\beta}}^*$ to the normal equations by utilizing the relationship $(\mathbf{X'X})^{-1}\mathbf{X'y}$. However, we have previously seen that for models we have been considering the **X** matrix is less than full rank and hence no unique solution exists for the normal equation $\mathbf{X'X}\boldsymbol{\beta} = \mathbf{X'y}$. We know, however, that we can obtain an arbitrary solution to the normal equations by finding a generalized inverse, **G**, of **X'X** and forming the matrix product **GX'y**.

8.4 AN EXAMPLE

Let us now look at an analysis of covariance model where we have two categorical variables—one having three levels, the other having two levels—and one continuous independent variable. We can easily apply the principles that we have already learned to estimate estimable functions and test various hypotheses concerning them. This can be best illustrated by working through a hypothetical example. Suppose that we have conducted a survey to determine the impact of an educational television program on children's reading skills.

TABLE 8.1
Hypothetical Data for Educational Television Survey

	Level of Exposure					
	None		*1-2 Times/Week*		*3 or More Times/Week*	
SES Level	*Posttest*	*Pretest*	*Posttest*	*Pretest*	*Posttest*	*Pretest*
Low	(1) 3	2	(1) 4	3	(1) 3	3
	(2) 3	2	(2) 5	2	(2) 6	5
	(3) 5	3	(3) 5	2	(3) 5	6
	(4) 5	4	(4) 6	3	(4) 7	7
	(5) 6	5	(5) 4	1	(5) 3	4
	(6) 3	2	(6) 5	3		
	(7) 4	3	(7) 5	4		
	(8) 6	5				
High	(1) 7	5	(1) 5	5	(1) 6	6
	(2) 6	6	(2) 4	4	(2) 8	7
	(3) 6	7	(3) 5	6	(3) 8	8
	(4) 6	5	(4) 6	4	(4) 8	9
	(5) 5	4	(5) 7	7	(5) 7	8
	(6) 7	6	(6) 8	7	(6) 6	7
			(7) 8	8	(7) 5	7
			(8) 5	4	(8) 7	5
			(9) 6	6	(9) 5	6
					(10) 8	7
					(11) 5	6
					(12) 6	7
					(13) 5	4
					(14) 4	5
					(15) 5	6

Suppose we had a random sample of 50 children and we had measures of their exposure levels to the television program, their socioeconomic statuses, and their reading skills before the program began its scheduled series of programs. In practice, of course, we would naturally want a sample larger than 50 in order to ensure a reasonable probability of detecting differences at a given level of significance when they do in fact exist in the population. After the data have been collected, let us suppose that they can be summarized as in Table 8.1.

The posttest (the dependent variable) is a measure of reading achievement obtained from the child immediately after the television series has been concluded. The pretest, the continuous independent variable or covariate, is a measure of reading aptitude that was obtained immediately prior to the scheduled television series. Cursory examination of Table 8.1 reveals that the data are fairly unbalanced. There are more high SES children than low SES children in the sample and high SES children have a greater probability than low SES children of watching the program three or more times per week.

The researcher might want to analyze these data to support the test of the hypothesis that there are no differences among the exposure parameters, that is, $\alpha_1 = \alpha_2 = \alpha_3$ where α_i is the effect of the ith exposure level. He or she would, of course, hope to be able to reject this hypothesis at a prior selected level of significance. The researcher might also be interested in determining if there is any evidence for an interaction between exposure level and socioeconomic level. The pretest score or covariate brings into the model an important determinant of reading achievement whose distributions across the six cells of this table would be expected to vary considerably. For example, we would expect low SES children to have lower pretest scores than high SES children. If these pretest scores are substantially related to the posttest scores, then we would expect high SES children to perform higher than low SES children. The pretest scores play a role in the analysis of adjusting the other estimable functions of the parameters for these initial group differences. The SES factor also plays an adjustment role in the estimation of contrasts involving the exposure factor since the data are unbalanced.

We can write the model for our hypothetical data set as

$$y_{ijk} = \mu + \alpha_i + \beta_j + \alpha\beta_{ij} + \Theta X_{ijk} + \epsilon_{ijk}$$

where y_{ijk} is the reading achievement score of the kth child in the cell defined by the ith level of TV exposure (Factor A) and the jth socioeconomic level (Factor B); μ is the overall effect; α_i is the effect for the ith level of Factor A; β_j is the effect for the jth level of Factor B; $\alpha\beta_{ij}$ is the interaction effect for the cell defined by the ith level of A and the jth level of B; Θ is the regression coefficient for the pretest score; X_{ijk} is the pretest score for the ijk^{th} child; and ϵ_{ijk} is the error associated with the ijk^{th} child.

In matrix notation, the model can be expressed as $\mathbf{y} = \mathbf{X}\boldsymbol{\beta} + \boldsymbol{\epsilon}$, which for the hypothetical data takes the following form:

$$
\mathbf{y} = \begin{bmatrix} 3\\3\\5\\5\\6\\3\\4\\6\\7\\6\\6\\6\\5\\7\\4\\5\\5\\6\\4\\5\\5\\5\\4\\5\\6\\7\\8\\8\\5\\6\\3\\6\\5\\7\\3\\6\\8\\8\\8\\7\\6\\5\\7\\5\\8\\5\\6\\5\\4\\5 \end{bmatrix}
= \begin{bmatrix}
1&1&0&0&1&0&1&0&0&0&0&0&2\\
1&1&0&0&1&0&1&0&0&0&0&0&2\\
1&1&0&0&1&0&1&0&0&0&0&0&3\\
1&1&0&0&1&0&1&0&0&0&0&0&4\\
1&1&0&0&1&0&1&0&0&0&0&0&5\\
1&1&0&0&1&0&1&0&0&0&0&0&2\\
1&1&0&0&1&0&1&0&0&0&0&0&3\\
1&1&0&0&1&0&1&0&0&0&0&0&5\\
1&1&0&0&0&1&0&1&0&0&0&0&5\\
1&1&0&0&0&1&0&1&0&0&0&0&6\\
1&1&0&0&0&1&0&1&0&0&0&0&7\\
1&1&0&0&0&1&0&1&0&0&0&0&5\\
1&1&0&0&0&1&0&1&0&0&0&0&4\\
1&1&0&0&0&1&0&1&0&0&0&0&6\\
1&0&1&0&1&0&0&0&1&0&0&0&3\\
1&0&1&0&1&0&0&0&1&0&0&0&2\\
1&0&1&0&1&0&0&0&1&0&0&0&2\\
1&0&1&0&1&0&0&0&1&0&0&0&3\\
1&0&1&0&1&0&0&0&1&0&0&0&1\\
1&0&1&0&1&0&0&0&1&0&0&0&3\\
1&0&1&0&1&0&0&0&1&0&0&0&4\\
1&0&1&0&0&1&0&0&0&1&0&0&5\\
1&0&1&0&0&1&0&0&0&1&0&0&4\\
1&0&1&0&0&1&0&0&0&1&0&0&6\\
1&0&1&0&0&1&0&0&0&1&0&0&4\\
1&0&1&0&0&1&0&0&0&1&0&0&7\\
1&0&1&0&0&1&0&0&0&1&0&0&7\\
1&0&1&0&0&1&0&0&0&1&0&0&8\\
1&0&1&0&0&1&0&0&0&1&0&0&4\\
1&0&1&0&0&1&0&0&0&1&0&0&6\\
1&0&0&1&1&0&0&0&0&0&1&0&3\\
1&0&0&1&1&0&0&0&0&0&1&0&5\\
1&0&0&1&1&0&0&0&0&0&1&0&6\\
1&0&0&1&1&0&0&0&0&0&1&0&7\\
1&0&0&1&1&0&0&0&0&0&1&0&4\\
1&0&0&1&0&1&0&0&0&0&0&1&6\\
1&0&0&1&0&1&0&0&0&0&0&1&7\\
1&0&0&1&0&1&0&0&0&0&0&1&8\\
1&0&0&1&0&1&0&0&0&0&0&1&9\\
1&0&0&1&0&1&0&0&0&0&0&1&8\\
1&0&0&1&0&1&0&0&0&0&0&1&7\\
1&0&0&1&0&1&0&0&0&0&0&1&7\\
1&0&0&1&0&1&0&0&0&0&0&1&5\\
1&0&0&1&0&1&0&0&0&0&0&1&6\\
1&0&0&1&0&1&0&0&0&0&0&1&7\\
1&0&0&1&0&1&0&0&0&0&0&1&6\\
1&0&0&1&0&1&0&0&0&0&0&1&7\\
1&0&0&1&0&1&0&0&0&0&0&1&4\\
1&0&0&1&0&1&0&0&0&0&0&1&5\\
1&0&0&1&0&1&0&0&0&0&0&1&6
\end{bmatrix}
\begin{bmatrix} \mu\\ \alpha_1\\ \alpha_2\\ \alpha_3\\ \beta_1\\ \beta_2\\ \alpha\beta_{11}\\ \alpha\beta_{12}\\ \alpha\beta_{21}\\ \alpha\beta_{22}\\ \alpha\beta_{31}\\ \alpha\beta_{32}\\ \Theta \end{bmatrix} + \epsilon
$$

In order to generate a solution, $\hat{\beta}^*$, to the normal equations

$$X'X\beta = X'y$$

we need to first compute **X′X** and **X′y**. The reader can easily verify that

$$X'y = \begin{bmatrix} 277 \\ 72 \\ 88 \\ 117 \\ 93 \\ 184 \\ 35 \\ 37 \\ 34 \\ 54 \\ 24 \\ 93 \\ 1493 \end{bmatrix}$$

and

$$X'X = \begin{bmatrix} 50 & 14 & 16 & 20 & 20 & 30 & 8 & 6 & 7 & 9 & 5 & 15 & 251 \\ 14 & 14 & 0 & 0 & 8 & 6 & 8 & 6 & 0 & 0 & 0 & 0 & 59 \\ 16 & 0 & 16 & 0 & 7 & 9 & 0 & 0 & 7 & 9 & 0 & 0 & 69 \\ 20 & 0 & 0 & 20 & 5 & 15 & 0 & 0 & 0 & 0 & 5 & 15 & 123 \\ 20 & 8 & 7 & 5 & 20 & 0 & 8 & 0 & 7 & 0 & 5 & 0 & 69 \\ 30 & 6 & 9 & 15 & 0 & 30 & 0 & 6 & 0 & 9 & 0 & 15 & 182 \\ 8 & 8 & 0 & 0 & 8 & 0 & 8 & 0 & 0 & 0 & 0 & 0 & 26 \\ 6 & 6 & 0 & 0 & 0 & 6 & 0 & 6 & 0 & 0 & 0 & 0 & 33 \\ 7 & 0 & 7 & 0 & 7 & 0 & 0 & 0 & 7 & 0 & 0 & 0 & 18 \\ 9 & 0 & 9 & 0 & 0 & 9 & 0 & 0 & 0 & 9 & 0 & 0 & 51 \\ 5 & 0 & 0 & 5 & 5 & 0 & 0 & 0 & 0 & 0 & 5 & 0 & 25 \\ 15 & 0 & 0 & 15 & 0 & 15 & 0 & 0 & 0 & 0 & 0 & 15 & 98 \\ 251 & 59 & 69 & 123 & 69 & 182 & 26 & 33 & 18 & 51 & 25 & 98 & 1441 \end{bmatrix}$$

Once again, we note that **X′X** is singular. It can be verified easily that the rank of **X′X** is 7 by examining the 7×7 matrix in the lower right-hand corner. It can easily be seen that this matrix is nonsingular; whenever we attempt to add a row and column to this matrix from **X′X**, we find that the rank still remains 7. Consequently, we can find a generalized inverse of **X′X** by replacing the 7 × 7 matrix with its inverse and changing the remaining elements of **X′X** to zero. This 7 × 7 matrix that needs to be inverted is

$$[\mathbf{X}'\mathbf{X}] = \begin{bmatrix} 8 & 0 & 0 & 0 & 0 & 0 & 26 \\ 0 & 6 & 0 & 0 & 0 & 0 & 33 \\ 0 & 0 & 7 & 0 & 0 & 0 & 18 \\ 0 & 0 & 0 & 9 & 0 & 0 & 51 \\ 0 & 0 & 0 & 0 & 5 & 0 & 25 \\ 0 & 0 & 0 & 0 & 0 & 15 & 98 \\ 26 & 33 & 18 & 51 & 25 & 98 & 1441 \end{bmatrix}$$

The diagonal elements of the upper left 6 × 6 submatrix of this matrix are the numbers of observations on the dependent variable for each of the respective cells. The first six elements of the seventh row (seventh column) correspond to the sums of the values of the covariate for each of the six cells, while the element in the seventh row and seventh column corresponds to the sum of squares of the continuous independent variable. The inverse of this matrix is

$$[\mathbf{X}'\mathbf{X}]^{-1} \begin{bmatrix} .266878 & .240102 & .112255 & .247378 & .217274 & .285212 & -.043655 \\ .240102 & .572993 & .189971 & .418639 & .369387 & .482666 & -.073877 \\ .112255 & .189971 & .231675 & .195727 & .172701 & .225662 & -.034540 \\ .247378 & .418639 & .195727 & .542436 & .380581 & .497292 & -.076116 \\ .218274 & .369387 & .172701 & .380581 & .535807 & .438787 & -.067161 \\ .285212 & .482666 & .225662 & .497292 & .438787 & .640015 & -.087757 \\ -.043655 & -.073877 & -.034540 & -.076116 & -.067161 & -.087757 & .013432 \end{bmatrix}$$

We can now obtain a solution for the normal equations for

$$\hat{\beta}^* = \begin{bmatrix} 0&0&0&0&0&0&0&0&0&0&0&0&0 \\ 0&0&0&0&0&0&0&0&0&0&0&0&0 \\ 0&0&0&0&0&0&0&0&0&0&0&0&0 \\ 0&0&0&0&0&0&0&0&0&0&0&0&0 \\ 0&0&0&0&0&0&0&0&0&0&0&0&0 \\ 0&0&0&0&0&0&0&0&0&0&0&0&0 \\ 0&0&0&0&0&0&.266878&.240102&.112255&.247378&.218274&.285212&-.043655 \\ 0&0&0&0&0&0&.240102&.572993&.189971&.418639&.369387&.482666&-.073877 \\ 0&0&0&0&0&0&.112255&.189971&.231675&.195727&.172701&.225662&-.034540 \\ 0&0&0&0&0&0&.247378&.418639&.195727&.542436&.380581&.497292&-.076116 \\ 0&0&0&0&0&0&.218274&.369387&.172701&.380581&.535807&.438787&-.067161 \\ 0&0&0&0&0&0&.285212&.482666&.225662&.497292&.438787&.640015&-.087757 \\ 0&0&0&0&0&0&-.043655&-.073877&-.034540&-.076116&-.067167&-.087757&.013432 \end{bmatrix} \begin{bmatrix} 277 \\ 72 \\ 88 \\ 117 \\ 93 \\ 184 \\ 35 \\ 37 \\ 34 \\ 54 \\ 24 \\ 93 \\ 1493 \end{bmatrix}$$

$$= \begin{bmatrix} 0 \\ 0 \\ 0 \\ 0 \\ 0 \\ 0 \\ 1.98596 \\ 2.12470 \\ 2.96723 \\ 1.83505 \\ 1.12530 \\ 1.39842 \\ .73457 \end{bmatrix}$$

The first six nonzero elements of the solution vector are the adjusted cell means of the respective cells where the adjustment is in terms of the continuous independent variable. The last element of the solution vector is the regression coefficient for the covariate.

In our previous models where we had only categorical independent variables, a solution vector for the normal equations was simply the dependent

TABLE 8.2
Cell Means for the Dependent Variable and the Covariate

	Level of Exposure		
SES Level	*None*	*1-2 Times/ Week*	*3 or More Times/ Week*
Low	$\overline{Y}_{dep}$ = 4.375	$\overline{Y}_{dep}$ = 4.857	$\overline{Y}_{dep}$ = 4.800
	$\overline{X}_{cov}$ = 3.250	$\overline{X}_{cov}$ = 2.571	$\overline{X}_{cov}$ = 5.000
	n = 8	n = 7	n = 5
High	$\overline{Y}_{dep}$ = 6.166	$\overline{Y}_{dep}$ = 6.000	$\overline{Y}_{dep}$ = 6.200
	$\overline{X}_{cov}$ = 5.500	$\overline{X}_{cov}$ = 5.666	$\overline{X}_{cov}$ = 6.533
	n = 6	n = 9	n = 15

TABLE 8.3
Adjusted Cell Means for Dependent Variable

1.985963	2.967230	1.125303
2.124696	1.835047	1.398420

variable means for the respective cells. In the covariate case, the solution vector is comprised of the cell means adjusted for values of the continuous independent variable. The regression coefficient used in this adjustment is .73457. Let us now examine Table 8.2, which presents the cell means for the dependent variable and the covariate as well as the number of observations within each cell.

Table 8.2 indicates that high SES children seem to perform better on the dependent variable than low SES children, but that they also have higher scores on the covariate or prescore. On the other hand, there is a tendency for low SES children to get some benefits out of being exposed to the TV program, while there appears to be no such benefit for high SES children. Maybe the difficulty level of the TV program was too low for the brighter high SES children and more compatible with the abilities of the low SES children. The adjusted means for the six cells corresponding to Table 8.2 are presented in Table 8.3. These are the first six nonzero elements of the solution vector and can also be computed as $\overline{Y}_{ij} - \hat{\Theta}\overline{X}_{ij}$ where $\overline{Y}_{ij}$ is the mean value of the dependent variable for the ijth cell, $\overline{X}_{ij}$ is the mean value of the covariate for the ijth cell, and $\hat{\Theta}$ is the estimated regression coefficient for the covariate. For example, the adjusted mean for cell 1,1 can be computed as 4.375 – .734569 (3.250) = 1.985963. If we compare the unadjusted cell means with the cell means adjusted for the covariate, we can easily see that the rank order of performance and relative differences between cell entries differ considerably between the two sets of cell means. Note that the absolute level of the adjusted cell means

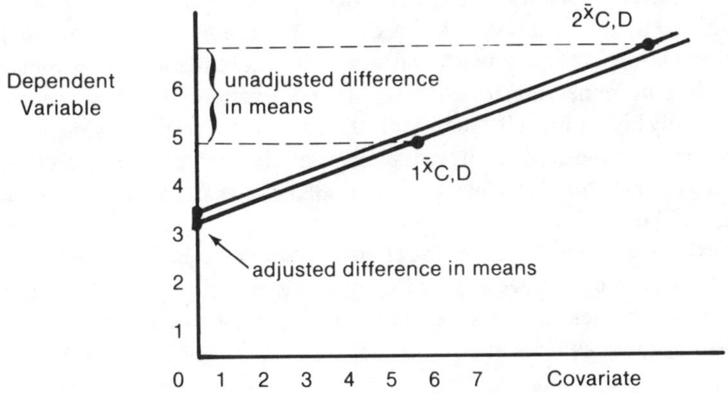

Figure 8.1 Schematic Portrayal of Covariance Adjustment of Means

differ considerably from the observed cell means. However, we know that the absolute size of individual parameters is of no importance since only differences in parameters are estimable. For the unadjusted case, the high SES children who viewed the TV program three or more times a week had the highest mean on the dependent variable. On the other hand, the adjusted mean for this cell ranked fifth out of the six adjusted means. Also, in the unadjusted case, the mean performance of the high SES group was about equal under the three viewing conditions, while in the adjusted case there was a tendency for performance to become lower as viewing exposure increased. This is a rather extreme example of how adjustments on the basis of a covariate can change the interpretation of a data set. If we look at the unadjusted results, the cell means indicate that high SES children are clearly outperforming low SES children and that TV exposure seems to benefit low SES but not high SES children. The adjusted results do not indicate any clear-cut overall advantage for the high SES children and, furthermore, both groups of children perform the worst under high TV exposure conditions. Intuitively, the covariance model is saying that higher-exposure groups are performing below the remaining exposure groups when their high scores on the covariate are considered. The situation could be pictured as in Figure 8.1.

In Figure 8.1, the point $_1\bar{x}_{C,D}$ represents the mean covariate value and mean dependent variable value for cell 1 and $_2\bar{x}_{C,D}$ is the point corresponding to the mean covariate value and mean dependent variable value for cell 2. A regression line with common slope is shown passing through each of these centroids. This slope is estimated as above. These two parallel regression lines passing so close to each other indicate that the differences in adjusted cell means are negligible. The difference in the adjusted means is the distance between the two regression lines or the difference in the intercepts of these two regression lines as indicated by the bold line on the ordinate. We can see from this figure the nature of a covariate adjustment. The mean of the dependent variable for cell 2 is considerably higher than for cell 1, but the mean value of the covariate is also substantially higher for cell 2 than for cell 1. Since the covariate happens to be highly related to the dependent variable, we could expect a higher mean score for cell 2. When this information is considered, the mean scores for both groups can be considered as nearly the same.

In order to test the null hypothesis that no parameters besides μ are needed in the regression model, we use the following familiar procedure. Like any of the previous models we have been considering we can calculate the total regression sum of squares as

$$\beta^{*}X'y = [0,0,0,0,0,0,1.985963,2.124696,2.967230,1.835047,1.125303,1.398420,.734569] \begin{bmatrix} 277 \\ 72 \\ 88 \\ 117 \\ 93 \\ 184 \\ 35 \\ 37 \\ 34 \\ 54 \\ 24 \\ 93 \\ 1493 \end{bmatrix} = 1601.87$$

and the regression sum of squares adjusted for μ as

$$\hat{\beta}^{*\prime}X'y - n\bar{Y}_T^2 = 1601.87 - 1534.58 = 67.29$$

The error sum of squares can be calculated as

$$y'y - \hat{\beta}^{*\prime}X'y = 1635 - 1601.87 = 33.13$$

and the significance of the regression sum of squares adjusted for μ can be tested by forming the ratio

$$\frac{\dfrac{67.29}{6}}{\dfrac{33.13}{43}} = 14.49$$

which is distributed as F with 6 and 43 degrees of freedom when the "regression" model is $y_{ijk} = \mu + \epsilon_{ijk}$. There are six degrees of freedom in this test because the rank of **X** is 7 and one degree of freedom was lost for adjusting the regression sum of squares for μ. Reference to an F table indicates that this F value of 14.49 is significant at the .01 level. This significant F value indicates that a model more complex than $y_{ijk} = \upsilon + \epsilon_{ijk}$ is needed to explain the variation in the dependent variable. The next steps involve the determination in which specific parameter sets are needed in the model.

It can easily be shown that Θ in our covariance model is estimable, while μ, α_i, β_j, and $\alpha\beta_{ij}$ are not estimable unless we place restrictions on the model. We showed that the estimate of Θ was .734569. We can easily see that Θ is estimable by noting that there is a vector **k** and a vector **t** such that $\mathbf{k}'\boldsymbol{\beta} = \mathbf{t}'E(\mathbf{y})$. For our example, the relationship is

$$[0,0,0,0,0,0,0,0,0,0,0,0,1]\begin{bmatrix} \mu \\ \alpha_1 \\ \alpha_2 \\ \alpha_3 \\ \beta_1 \\ \beta_2 \\ \alpha\beta_{11} \\ \alpha\beta_{12} \\ \alpha\beta_{21} \\ \alpha\beta_{22} \\ \alpha\beta_{31} \\ \alpha\beta_{32} \\ \Theta \end{bmatrix} = [0,-1,1,0,0\,.\,.\,.\,.\,.\,.\,.\,0]\begin{bmatrix} \mu+\alpha_1+\beta_1+\alpha\beta_{11}+\Theta(2) \\ \mu+\alpha_1+\beta_1+\alpha\beta_{11}+\Theta(2) \\ \mu+\alpha_1+\beta_1+\alpha\beta_{11}+\Theta(3) \\ \mu+\alpha_1+\beta_1+\alpha\beta_{11}+\Theta(4) \\ \mu+\alpha_1+\beta_1+\alpha\beta_{11}+\Theta(5) \\ \cdot\;\;\cdot\;\;\cdot\;\;\cdot\;\;\cdot \\ \cdot\;\;\cdot\;\;\cdot\;\;\cdot\;\;\cdot \\ \cdot\;\;\cdot\;\;\cdot\;\;\cdot\;\;\cdot \\ \cdot\;\;\cdot\;\;\cdot\;\;\cdot\;\;\cdot \\ \cdot\;\;\cdot\;\;\cdot\;\;\cdot\;\;\cdot \\ \cdot\;\;\cdot\;\;\cdot\;\;\cdot\;\;\cdot \\ \cdot\;\;\cdot\;\;\cdot\;\;\cdot\;\;\cdot \\ \cdot\;\;\cdot\;\;\cdot\;\;\cdot\;\;\cdot \end{bmatrix}$$

or $\Theta = 0$.

The hypothesis that $\Theta = 0$ can be tested by first computing Q_Θ, which in our example is

$$(K'\hat{\beta}^*)'(K'GK)^{-1}(K'\hat{\beta}^*)$$

$$= [0,0,0\ldots.1]\begin{bmatrix}0\\0\\.\\.\\.\\..\\.7345\end{bmatrix}\left[[0\ldots.1]\begin{bmatrix}0\ldots\ldots & .\\ \ldots\ldots & .\\ \ldots\ldots & .\\ \ldots\ldots & .\\ \ldots\ldots & .013432\end{bmatrix}\begin{bmatrix}0\\.\\.\\.\\1\end{bmatrix}\right]^{-1}[0\ldots.1]\begin{bmatrix}0\\0\\.\\.\\.7345\end{bmatrix}$$

$$= (.7345)^2(.013432)^{-1} = 40.16$$

The 40.16 is the sum of squares due to the hypothesis that $\Theta = 0$. We could also derive the sum of squares due to the hypothesis that $\Theta = 0$ by computing $R(\Theta|\mu, \alpha_i, \beta_j, \alpha\beta_{ij})$, which is the difference $R(\mu, \alpha_i, \beta_j, \alpha\beta_{ij}, \Theta) - R(\mu, \alpha_i, \beta_j, \alpha\beta_{ij})$ where the former R is the total regression sum of squares due to the full model with all of the parameters and the latter R is the regression sum of squares due to all parameters except for Θ.

Usually, the hypotheses of most interest involve the α_i's, β_j's, and $\alpha\beta_{ij}$'s. For example, in our hypothetical data set we might be interested in determining if there are any differences in responses to the three levels of exposure after adjusting for the covariate. We might also be interested in seeing if the three levels of exposure interacted with our two SES categories. The first thing that we might want to do is to test the hypothesis that the full model explains significantly more variation in the dependent variable than the reduced model $y_{ijk} = \mu + \Theta x_{ijk} + \epsilon_{ijk}$. This is equivalent to the hypothesis that α_i, β_j, and $\alpha\beta_{ij}$ contribute significantly to the model. It can be tested by finding the Q associated with the joint hypothesis that

$$\alpha_1 + \frac{1}{2}(\alpha\beta_{11} + \alpha\beta_{12}) - \left(\alpha_2 + \frac{1}{2}(\alpha\beta_{21} + \alpha\beta_{22})\right) = 0;$$

$$\alpha_2 + \frac{1}{2}(\alpha\beta_{21} + \alpha\beta_{22}) - \left(\alpha_3 + \frac{1}{2}(\alpha\beta_{31} + \alpha\beta_{32})\right) = 0;$$

$$\beta_1 + \frac{1}{3}(\alpha\beta_{11} + \alpha\beta_{21} + \alpha\beta_{31}) - \left(\beta_2 + \frac{1}{3}(\alpha\beta_{12} + \alpha\beta_{22} + \alpha\beta_{32})\right) = 0;$$

$$(\alpha\beta_{11} - \alpha\beta_{21}) - (\alpha\beta_{12} - \alpha\beta_{22}) = 0; \text{ and}$$

$$(\alpha\beta_{21} - \alpha\beta_{31}) - (\alpha\beta_{22} - \alpha\beta_{32}) = 0$$

for the unrestricted case; or

$$\alpha_1 - \alpha_2 = 0$$

$$\alpha_2 - \alpha_3 = 0$$

$$\beta_1 - \beta_2 = 0$$

$$(\alpha\beta_{11} - \alpha\beta_{21}) - (\alpha\beta_{12} - \alpha\beta_{22}) = 0$$

$$(\alpha\beta_{21} - \alpha\beta_{31}) - (\alpha\beta_{22} - \alpha\beta_{32}) = 0$$

for the restricted case in which

$$\Sigma\alpha_i = 0$$

$$\Sigma\beta_j = 0$$

$$\sum_i \alpha\beta_{ij} = 0$$

$$\sum_j \alpha\beta_{ij} = 0$$

The value of Q can be found easily by noting that

$$Q_{(\alpha_i, \beta_j, \alpha\beta_{ij})} = R(\alpha_i, \beta_j, \alpha\beta_{ij} | \mu, \Theta) = R(\mu, \alpha_i, \beta_j, \alpha\beta_{ij}, \Theta) - R(\mu, \Theta)$$

We have already calculated $R(\mu, \alpha_i, \beta_j, \alpha\beta_{ij}, \Theta)$, the regression sum of squares for the full model, as 1601.87. All that we have to do now is to calculate $R(\mu, \Theta)$, the regression sum of squares for the reduced model, and take the difference.

The design matrix for the model $y_{ijk} = \mu + \theta X_{ijk} + \epsilon_{ijk}$ can be constructed from the first and last row of the design matrix for the full model. That is,

$$\mathbf{X} = \begin{bmatrix} 1 & 2 \\ 1 & 2 \\ 1 & 3 \\ \vdots & \vdots \\ 1 & 5 \\ 1 & 6 \end{bmatrix};$$

$$\mathbf{X'X} = \begin{bmatrix} 50 & 251 \\ 251 & 1441 \end{bmatrix}; (\mathbf{X'X})^{-1} = \begin{bmatrix} .1592 & -.0277 \\ -.0277 & .0055 \end{bmatrix}; \mathbf{X'y} = \begin{bmatrix} 279 \\ 1493 \end{bmatrix}$$

and so

$$\hat{\beta} = \begin{bmatrix} \hat{\mu} \\ \hat{\Theta} \end{bmatrix} = (\mathbf{X'X})^{-1}\mathbf{X'y} = \begin{bmatrix} 2.6981 \\ .5661 \end{bmatrix}$$

The reader can verify that for this model both μ and θ are estimable. In fact, the reader should realize that this reduced model is simply a univariate regression model where μ is the intercept and θ is the regression parameter associated with the single continuous independent variable.

The regression sum of squares for the reduced model is

$$R(\mu, \Theta) = [2.6981,\ .5661] \begin{bmatrix} 277 \\ 1493 \end{bmatrix} = 1592.56$$

so that $Q_{(\alpha_i,\beta_j,\alpha\beta_{ij})} = R_{(\mu,\alpha_i,\beta_j,\alpha\beta_{ij},\Theta)} - R_{(\mu,\Theta)} = 1601.87 - 1592.56 = 9.31$, which is the regression sum of squares associated with the joint hypothesis specified above.

The reader can verify that, using the appropriate **K** and **G** for our example,

$$(\mathbf{K'}\hat{\beta}^*)' (\mathbf{K'GK})^{-1} (\mathbf{K'}\hat{\beta}^*) = 9.31$$

This hypothesis can then be tested by forming the F ratio

$$\frac{\frac{9.31}{5}}{\frac{33.13}{43}} = 2.4167$$

with 5 and 43 degrees of freedom.

This F is just significant at the .05 level and, hence, we would reject the above hypothesis. The rejection of this hypothesis indicates that the model $y_{ijk} = \mu + \Theta x_{ijk} + \epsilon_{ijk}$ is not sufficient to explain the variation in the dependent variable (y) and a model containing parameters such as α_i, β_j, and $\alpha\beta_{ij}$ better explain the variation in y. This situation is roughly illustrated by comparing Figures 8.2 and 8.3.

In Figure 8.2, the model allowing for different intercepts fits the data better than the model portrayed in Figure 8.3, where only one intercept is used. The variation of these intercepts in Figure 8.2 is explained by parameters such as α_i, β_j, and $\alpha\beta_{ij}$ and is clearly a better model than $y_{ijk} = \mu + \Theta x_{ijk} + \epsilon_{ijk}$, which, as Figure 8.3 indicates, yields a poorer fit to the hypothetical data set used in the figures. The analogous situation is true for our hypothetical example.

The researcher would probably now want to get some indication of which parameters in the full model seem to contribute significantly in explaining the variation in the dependent variable. Specifically, he or she might want to test the hypothesis that the α_i parameters associated with different levels of reading exposure satisfy the relationship

$$\alpha_1 + \frac{1}{2}(\alpha\beta_{11} + \alpha\beta_{12}) - \left(\alpha_2 + \frac{1}{2}(\alpha\beta_{21} + \alpha\beta_{22})\right) = 0$$

$$\alpha_2 + \frac{1}{2}(\alpha\beta_{21} + \alpha\beta_{22}) - \left(\alpha_3 + \frac{1}{2}(\alpha\beta_{31} + \alpha\beta_{32})\right) = 0$$

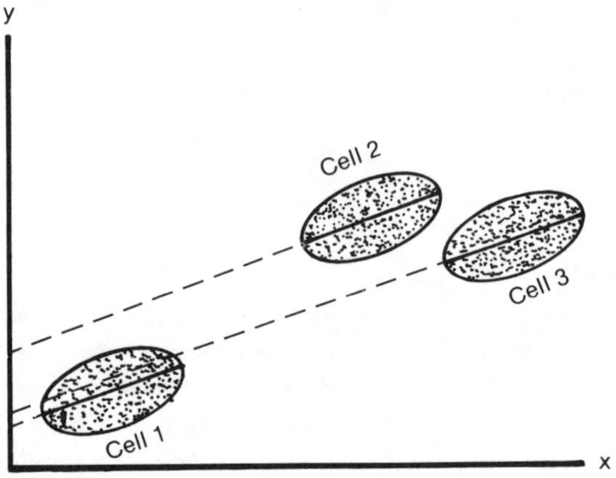

Figure 8.2 Within-Cell Regression Lines with Common Slope but Different Intercepts

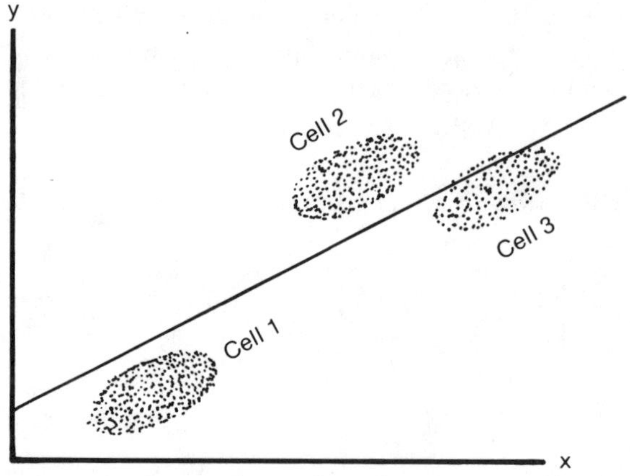

Figure 8.3 Fitting the Data from Figure 8.2 with the Model $y_{ijk} = \mu + \theta x_{ijk} + \epsilon_{ijk}$

which is really testing whether or not parameters associated with exposure levels need to be included in the model. The **K** matrix associated with this hypothesis is

$$\mathbf{K}' = \begin{bmatrix} 0 & 1 & -1 & 0 & 0 & 0 & .5 & .5 & -.5 & -.5 & 0 & 0 & 0 \\ 0 & 0 & 1 & -1 & 0 & 0 & 0 & 0 & .5 & .5 & -.5 & -.5 & 0 \end{bmatrix}$$

Using the $\hat{\boldsymbol{\beta}}^*$ and **G** that have previously been solved for, the reader should verify that $Q_{(\alpha_i)} = 7.94$ and that the appropriate F equals 5.16. This F is distributed with 2 and 43 degrees of freedom and is significant at the .05 level. As noted previously, problems in interpreting the main effect parameters are alleviated if the interaction parameters turn out to be statistically insignificant.

As an exercise the reader should calculate the Qs and associated Fs for testing the anologous hypotheses concerning SES and the SES by treatment interaction.

8.5 USE OF COMPUTERS

There are no new principles involved in the analysis of covariance as far as computer usage is concerned. As has been emphasized all along, SAS is compatible with the approach taken in this book. As has also been discussed, other regression routines may require a full rank design matrix. Dummy variable or effects coding are two principal types of coding that can be used in this situation. We simply consider the categorical variables separately from the continuous independent variables and code them into full rank form. The continuous independent variables are then added as columns to the recoded full rank design matrix representing the categorical variables. The parameters associated with the recoded variables are estimable functions of the original parameters associated with the categorical part of the model and the regression parameters associated with the continuous variables are themselves estimable.

8.6 APPLIED EXAMPLE

A good example of a model with a mixture of categorical and continuous independent variables is a model that Hanushek and Jackson (1977) developed to predict the reading achievement of third graders in a California school system. The sample consisted of 515 third graders from families with fathers in blue-collar occupations.

The intent of the analysis was to determine if teacher characteristics significantly influenced students' reading achievement. Since student reading achievement is influenced by variables other than teacher characteristics, these other types of variables needed to be included in the model for control purposes. That is, the effect of teacher characteristics on achievement should be adjusted for the effects of these other variables; otherwise, the estimated regression parameters associated with teacher characteristics will be biased.

Since sex, grade repeats, earlier reading achievement, and percentage of time devoted to class discipline were hypothesized to affect reading achievement and, at the same time, be confounded with teacher characteristics, they were included in the model along with teacher characteristics. Socioeconomic status, an important determinant of reading achievement, was controlled by the sample design since the sample was restricted to children whose fathers were blue-collar workers.

The dependent variable was third-grade reading achievement (RA_3), a continuous variable. The independent variables were as follows:

S = sex; female = 1, male = 0
GR = grade repeats; 1 or more = 1, none = 0
RA_1 = initial reading achievement
D = percentage of class time devoted to discipline
TV_2 = second-grade teacher's verbal facility
TV_3 = third-grade teacher's verbal facility
YE_2 = second-grade teacher's years since latest educational experience
YE_3 = third-grade teacher's years since latest educational experience

The first two variables in the above list are dummy variables. Each of these two-level categorical variables is represented by one dummy variable through effects coding. The remaining six variables are continuous, so that the eight variables together form a full rank design matrix. The authors estimated the regression parameters of the model with a standard multiple regression package. The estimated regression equation was

$$\begin{array}{l} A_3 = 20.8 + \underset{(1.2)}{2.81}\,S - \underset{(2.3)}{6.38}\,GR + \underset{(.04)}{.79}\,RA_1 - \underset{(.03)}{.07}\,D + \underset{(.03)}{.06}\,TV_2 + \underset{(.04)}{.09}\,TV_3 - \underset{(.24)}{.68}\,YE_2 - \underset{(.39)}{.57}\,YE_3 \end{array}$$

The standard errors of the regression parameter estimates are enclosed in parentheses below the appropriate coefficient. The R^2 was .51 and was significant at the .01 level. This is equivalent to rejecting the null hypothesis that all 8 regression parameters are jointly equal to zero. All of the coefficients were significant at the .05 level (that is, $t \geq 1.96$), except for YE_3. It should be noted that the 2.81 associated with S is the difference in effects for females and males, with females having an advantage of 2.81 points on the achievement test. Similarly, the –6.38 associated with GR is the difference in the effects of repeating one or more grades and not repeating any grades, with grade repeaters being at a disadvantage of 6.38 points.

Three of the four regression parameter estimates associated with teacher characteristics were significant at the .05 level. The authors tested the null hypothesis that the four regression parameters associated with the teacher characteristics were zero by dropping out the four teacher variables, rerunning the regression analysis, and comparing the regression sum of squares with that of the full model. The difference in the two regression sum of squares was significant at the .01 level. Hence, teachers do make a difference in respect to third-grade reading achievement for students in this particular school system. This is not to say that they make a difference in other school systems or in school systems in general.

This model was a main effects model; no interactions were included. It would be of interest to test certain interactions between teacher characteristics and student characteristics. For example, teacher's verbal facility might have more of an impact on children who are grade repeaters and who scored low on initial reading achievement. A finding such as this would certainly have policy implications. The interaction variables would be created by forming cross products between the selected pairs of variables. The interaction variables would then be added to the original eight variables for input into a regression routine. Various hypotheses concerning the interaction parameters could be tested. The initial test would be whether or not the interactions as a whole add any statistically significant explanatory power to the basic main effects model. If not, further tests of interaction hypotheses are not warranted. We should select our interactions carefully in a model with a large number of variables since there are an extremely large number of potential interactions. Theory, logic, and common sense are useful in sorting out the possibilities.

The appearance of significant interactions in a regression model certainly complicates the interpretation of the main effects. Some researchers prefer to test for interactions initially. If they are statistically significant, then they argue that statistically significant main effects should not be interpreted. A more balanced approach would be to compare the magnitude of the regression sum of squares for the interactions and the main effects. If the regression sum of squares for the main effects is quite high relative to the interaction sum of squares, then it might be more appropriate to interpret the main effects as well as the interactions.

8.7 PROBLEMS

(1) Extend the model in problem 1 of Chapter 7 by adding variable 3 (reading score) as a covariate. Is the parameter associated with the covariate significant? How do the effects of sex, SES, and their interactions change when reading is added as a covariate?

(2) Using restrictions on the parameters, write out the equations that would yield a unique solution for the estimated parameters. Solve the equations for these parameters.

(3) Reparameterize the model in terms of estimable functions.

(4) Consider the data set below, where x is the covariate and y is the dependent variable.

		α – Factor					
		Level 1		Level 2		Level 3	
		x	y	x	y	x	y
β-Factor	Level 1	2	12	2	9	3	7
		4	8	2	8	2	8
		3	9	1	8	1	4
		1	14				
		5	10				
		x	y	x	y	x	y
	Level 2	2	1	5	13	2	5
		3	4	3	12	5	6
		1	6	4	9	3	12
						4	7
						6	13

(a) Compute the normal equations and solve for a solution vector.

(b) Compute the regression sum of squares.

(c) Compute the regression sum of squares adjusted for the mean and test its significance at the .05 level.

(d) Compute the regression sum of squares due to the covariate after adjusting for the effects of the two factors and their interaction; test for its significance at the .05 level.

(e) Compute the regression sum of squares due to the two factors and their interactions after adjusting for the effects of the covariate; test for its significance at the .05 level.

(f) On the basis of the analyses up to this point, what would you conclude? Would you conduct any further tests?

(5) We can test the hypothesis that the within group regression coefficients are equal by comparing the total regression sum of squares of the above model with the total regression sum of squares of the model

$$Y_{ijk} = \mu + \alpha_i + \beta_j + \alpha\beta_{ij} + \delta_{ij}X_{ijk} + \epsilon_{ijk}$$

where δ_{ij} is the regression coefficient associated with the ij^{th} cell. Taking the difference of the regression sum of squares for the two models and testing for the significance of this difference is known as the test for the homogeneity of regression. It is a test of the hypothesis that all of the δ_{ij} are equal. Test this hypothesis.

9 Analysis Considerations and Model Extensions

9.1 INTRODUCTION

We have covered a wide range of linear statistical models applicable to a corresponding wide range of data situations. The purpose of this chapter is twofold: first, to address some of the problems in applying these statistical models on actual real-life data; second, to cover two interesting extensions of the models that have some useful applications.

The next 5 sections of this chapter discuss the treatment and interpretation of experimental versus survey data, modifications needed in statistical models for application to survey data, problems associated with nonresponse and missing data, and data editing. These are all basic considerations that arise in the analysis of real-life data.

The remainder of this chapter discusses ridge regression estimation and logistic regression analysis. Ridge regression estimation is a relatively recent effort to generate more stable estimates of regression coefficients in the case of highly multicolinear data. Logistic regression analysis is used when the dependent variable is a two-level categorical variable instead of a continuous variable.

9.2 EXPERIMENTAL VERSUS SURVEY DATA

In the social sciences, we can distinguish between two main approaches used in the investigation of social phenomena: the experimental approach and the survey or correlation approach. As the name suggests, the experimental approach involves the performance of an experiment. As with any experiment, the object is to manipulate a factor or set of factors to determine their impact on a dependent variable of interest. For example, we could vary the intensity of a reading program and examine its impact on reading achievement scores or we could implement a preschool program and examine its impact on a variety of child development measures. In both cases, an experiment is being conducted. The advantage of an experiment is that, if it is conducted properly, causal inferences can be made concerning the effects of the independent variable on the dependent variable.

The major condition that needs to be fulfilled in order for an experiment to have been properly conducted is its reliance on the principle of randomization "Randomization" means that individuals or units under investigation have been assigned by a probability mechanism such as a table of random numbers or the flip of a coin to the different levels of the factor representing the independent variable. For example, if our independent variable is made up of three levels of reading intensity, then each child must have an equal chance to be assigned to any one of the three groups. An admittedly crude but effective mechanism for randomly allocating the children to the three levels would be to put three numbers in different but identical envelopes, shuffle them, select one, and assign that child to the treatment level corresponding to the number. We could repeat this processs until we have met our sample size requirements.

Randomization assures us that children with particular characteristics that may be related to performance on the dependent variable are no more likely to be found at one level of the independent variable than another. Because child characteristics are not confounded with the levels of the independent variable(s), the estimate of the effect of the independent variable on the dependent variable is unbiased. All of the models discussed in this book can be applied to the experimental situation. Hicks (1973) provides an introduction to experimental design for the interested reader.

There has been an increasing tendency for social scientists to rely on survey data to answer questions concerning the effects of variables on outcomes important to society. For example, much interest has recently been focused upon the effects of parents' socioeconomic status on a child's school achievement and eventual status attainment in later life. Obviously, one cannot randomly assign a child at birth to a particular level of socioeconomic status, for a variety of practical and ethical reasons. The only alternative left to the researcher is to investigate the phenomenon in its natural setting. The survey approach is the investigative technique that is often applied in this setting. Basically, the survey approach involves selecting a probability sample from the target population of interest, measuring the appropriate variables on the sample members, and applying statistical models to account for the relationships among the variables. For this reason it is sometimes referred to as the "correlational approach."

Let us develop our socioeconomic status example a bit further to illustrate the survey approach. First, we must define the population to which inferences are to be made, the target population. It could be all children, white children, black children, or children from a particular region or city. The target population could even be further defined by age. Once we have defined our target population, we can select a sample from it. Since socioeconomic status is the major independent variable of interest, we might want to ensure that there are enough children at each of, say, three levels of socioeconomic status by stratifying the schools from which the children are to be selected in terms of overall student socioeconomic status from available school data.

The next step would be to collect information from the children's families and schools so that measures of socioeconomic status and school achievement can be developed. We could then use a linear regression model with socioeconomic status as the independent variable and school achievement as the dependent variable. A basic problem arises. Socioeconomic status is correlated with other variables (such as school quality) that are also related to school achievement. If we could have randomly assigned children to different socioeconomic levels, then other factors influencing school achievement would have been equally spread across the levels of socioeconomic status and hence would be unconfounded with it. With randomization we could have gotten an unbiased estimate of the effect of socioeconomic status on school achievement. The only recourse that we have is to include those other contaminating factors in the model and hope that the parameter estimates reflecting the effect of socioeconomic status on school achievement are properly adjusted. When modeling the effects of socioeconomic status, one should consider school quality, ethnic background, intelligence, and all other important variables that are confounded with socioeconomic status and related to school achievement. Even if all of these variables are entered as independent variables in our model, we cannot be certain that we have adjusted for all the important differences between socioeconomic status level. The estimated effects of socioeconomic status may still be biased. The models discussed in this book are as appropriate to survey data as they are to experimental data. The interpretation of the model results, however, differs across the two situations. In the case of experiments we can feel confident in saying x caused y. We are not so sure when modeling survey data.

Many large federal programs (for example, childhood development programs, crime and delinquency programs, educational programs, and health programs) have been evaluated through designs that creatively combine aspects of both the experimental and the survey approach since pure experimentation is often impossible. This combination is called "quasi-experimentation" and the interested reader is referred to Campbell and Stanley (1966) and Riecken and Boruch (1974) for further information.

9.3 SURVEY SAMPLE DESIGNS AND STATISTICAL MODELS

The models developed in this text as well as in comparable textbooks assume that the samples are simple random samples. A simple random sample is the simplest of the many possible forms of probability sampling procedures. The basic idea is that each individual or unit in the target population to which inferences are to be made, has the same probability of being selected into the sample. Most experiments utilize simple random sampling. Many human-subject experiments, however, select simple random samples from convenient populations such as students from a particular school or community. In these instances it is difficult to generalize the experimental findings to a more general and significant population such as the population of all students.

Many large sample surveys whose target populations are national in scope—for instance, women or minorities—are sponsored by federal agencies. Simple random sampling is often impossible in these situations since it is impossible to develop a list of, say, all college seniors, the sampling frame from which to select a simple random sample of college seniors. Instead, complex, multistage probability samples are used where the units are often selected with unequal probabilities. For example, to select a probability sample of college seniors a sampling procedure such as the following could be implemented. First, select a probability sample of geographical regions. Second, select a probability sample of colleges from all colleges located in the geographical regions selected. Third, list all of the college students in the selected colleges and select a probability sample of them. The final probability of a college senior being selected might differ among students. For example, blacks might have been sampled with a higher probability of selection than whites in order to have a sample size large enough to conduct separate analyses for black college seniors. Another complication also arises. The above sample is known as a cluster sample because "clusters" of students were selected from each college. Students within a college will be similar in many respects, including, most likely, the variables selected for study. Consequently, an intraclass correlation is said to exist among the members of a particular cluster. The observations on students are not completely independent within a school (that is, cluster) since, for example, all students within a college might be exceptionally bright. Clustering and unequal probability sampling tend to result in standard errors for statistics that are larger than those that would be obtained for a simple random sample of comparable size. The ratio of the variance of an estimator for a particular probability sample design to the variance of the same estimator for a simple random sample of the same size is known as the "design effect" (deff).

These two conditions, unequal probabilities of selection and clustering, must be taken into consideration when estimating the parameters of a linear statistical model. If we take survey data for which these conditions exist, and crank them into our linear models, then we take the considerable risk of generating both biased parameter and standard error estimates. Data from a complex survey should be handled within a linear models framework as briefly described below. First, each observational unit should be weighted by the inverse of that unit's probability of selection. For example, if blacks were selected at twice the probability rate of whites, then their sampling weights would be one-half the magnitude of the sampling weights for whites. This is reasonable since they have been overrepresented in the sample. The probability of selection for each unit of a properly designed survey can be calculated and, hence, the weights simply follow. We define the weight matrix as

$$\mathbf{W} = \begin{bmatrix} w_1 & & & & & \bigcirc \\ & w_2 & & & & \\ & & w_3 & & & \\ & & & \cdot & & \\ & & & & \cdot & \\ \bigcirc & & & & & w_N \end{bmatrix}$$

It is an $N \times N$ diagonal matrix with the N individual weights arrayed along the principal diagonal. The data can then be properly weighted for unbiased parameter estimates by incorporating **W** into the parameter estimation process as

$$\hat{\beta} = (\mathbf{X}'\mathbf{W}\,\mathbf{X})^{-1}\,\mathbf{X}'\mathbf{W}\mathbf{y}$$

which, except for **W**, is similar in form to our previous estimator.

The estimation of standard errors for the unbiased weighted estimators poses another problem because of the clustering effect. The estimated standard errors will in general be underestimated if the design effect is greater than one. If we know the design effect for simple statistics such as the mean, then we can use the appropriate design effect to adjust the estimate of the standard errors upward (see Kish and Franke, 1974). The mathematical problems involved in estimating the standard errors for complex statistics (such as regression coefficients) generated from complex samples has led to a number of other approximation methods. These include designing the sample such that independent replications are embedded within it so that a number of independent estimates of the regression parameters can be generated. These can then be averaged to generate an unbiased estimate and their variance can be calculated to generate an unbiased estimate of its standard error. Other methods such as the "jackknife" and the Taylorized deviation have also been proposed but will not be discussed here. The interested reader can refer to Moser and Kalton (1972) for a general discussion of survey sampling. An informative discussion of generating variance estimates for complex statistics from multistage sample surveys is presented by Shah (1978).

9.4. NONRESPONSE BIAS

Once a probability sample has been selected, certain individuals may elect not to respond for a variety of reasons. They may not have the time or the interest to participate in an experimental study or to complete a sample survey instrument. If the nonresponse rate is high (more than 10-20 percent) the statistical process of making inferences from the sample to the intended target population is compromised. The sample may no longer be representative of the intended target population. For example, if in a particular sample survey the response rate of men was considerably below that of women, then the sample would no longer be representative of a general population comprising roughly equal proportions of men and women.

In practice, nonresponse is often a serious problem, especially in longitudinal surveys, where the original sample members drop out over time. In many large federally sponsored surveys, it has been found that the nonresponse rates of many important target groups, such as minorities and poor people, are high. In any study, the respondents and nonrespondents should be contrasted on the distributions of those variables for which values are known for both groups. In many studies, the sex, ethnicity, education level, and other background information on nonrespondents will be available either from information in the sampling frame or from a screening questionnaire previously completed by the nonrespondent. (A screening questionnaire is a brief questionnaire administered, usually by interview, to determine if the selected sample member is, indeed, a member of the target population.)

If the nonresponse rate is high or the respondents and nonrespondents differ in significant ways, the data can be adjusted to correct for nonresponse bias. However, one can never be certain that nonresponse bias has been accounted for since the two subsamples may still differ in unsuspected and significant ways for which no measures are available. The best one can do under the circumstances is to adjust the data on the basis of available information. The variables used to adjust the data should show significant differences between the respondents and nonrespondents and at the same time be significantly related to critical survey measures (such as dependent variables).

Let us take a simple example involving a sample survey. Suppose that the objective of the survey were to assess the educational attainment of American young adults. Suppose further that blacks had a 30 percent nonresponse rate and whites a 10 percent nonresponse rate. Since blacks have a lower educational attainment level than whites, the average educational level estimated from this sample would be biased upward since blacks are underrepresented in the sample. Since it is known that blacks constitute 10 percent of the young adult population, a more appropriate estimator of the population mean would be $.10\,\overline{X}_B + .90\,\overline{X}_w$, where $\overline{X}_B$ and $\overline{X}_w$ are the black and white educational attainment means, respectively. A simple adjustment for nonresponse bias has been made.

In complex sample surveys, similar adjustments are made to adjust for nonresponse bias. In this instance, however, the individual sampling weights themselves are adjusted to reflect each respondent's appropriate representation in the sample. A weighting class procedure is often adopted for adjusting sampling weights for nonresponse. Briefly, the procedure involves the following steps. First, cross-classify all sample members, respondents and nonrespondents alike, on the important variables for which measures on both groups are available. These variables are most likely to reflect demographic and personal background variables. Second, within each of the weighting classes constructed in step one, sum the weights for all sample members (respondents and nonrespondents) and for respondents alone. Label these weight totals W_{Ti} and W_{Ri}, respectively, where i refers to the weighting class. Third, within each weighting class, form the ratio W_{Ti}/W_{Ri} and multiply each sample member's weight by this ratio. The resulting set of weights has been adjusted for nonresponse. There has been much research on nonresponse bias and many procedures have been developed to address this important problem. For more details the reader is referred to Platek, Singh, and Tremblay (1978), Bailar, Bailey, and Corby (1978), and Kish (1965).

9.5 MISSING DATA

In all of the examples presented earlier in this book, it was assumed that a complete vector of observations was available on each sample member. In actual practice this is rarely the case. For one reason or another individual data elements will be missing from certain individuals' data records. For example, some sample members may refuse to respond to questionnaire items of a sensitive nature, students may be absent on the day of an achievement test administration, and so on. If there are only a few sample vectors or records with missing data elements, then the easiest solution would be to delete the corresponding records from the data file.

In complex surveys, especially those involving a large number of measures, a significant proportion of the sample could be missing data elements here or there. If all of these incomplete records were deleted from the data file, two major problems would arise. First, the sample size would be reduced with an accompanying loss of statistical precision. Second, the problem of nonresponse bias arises if those sample members with incomplete data differ in important ways from the rest of the sample.

A number of techniques have been suggested for coping with missing data. They range from simple procedures such as substituting the overall sample mean to highly complex procedures involving iterative regression procedures. Most of the procedures involve predicting the missing data element from other data available in the data record. In order to implement this procedure, sets of regression equations have to be developed for subsets of the sample that have the appropriate data element available as well as the independent variables that are needed to estimate the parameters of the corresponding regression equation. The missing data element can then be predicted by substituting the values of other variables from the individual's data record into the regression equation. If the pattern of missing data is complex, then numerous sets of regression equations will have to be developed to meet all eventualities. More complex iterative procedures have been proposed whereby the records with predicted values are combined with the previous data and then used to develop new sets of regression equations, which in turn generate new predicted values. This procedure is continued in an iterative fashion until the predicted values for the missing data elements stabilize or converge. These final values are then substituted into the data records and the planned analysis can then proceed. For more information, the reader is referred to Dempster, Laird, and Rubin (1977), Beale and Little (1975), and Elashoff and Afifi (1966).

9.6 DATA EDITING

In practice, some individuals will have errors in their data records. In a large, complex survey, the number of errors could be considerable. These errors arise from a number of sources. Coding clerks may make errors in assigning a numerical value to a questionnaire response. The respondent or interviewer may inadvertently circle the wrong response option. The keypunch operator may hit the wrong key. Carefully designed and executed studies minimize data errors, but cannot eliminate them altogether.

Once the raw data have been entered on a computer file, they should be edited for errors via a computer editing routine. Some generalized editing software is available in the "canned" statistical computer packages such as SPSS and SAS. Sometimes the investigator will have to develop his or her special-purpose editing programs. The first step is to define the editing rules. The errors can then be listed and inspected. Rules can then be defined for correcting the errors and applied to the data records.

Edit checks may vary from simple rules to detect out-of-range responses to complex logical rules. For example, age ranges, income ranges, and so on may be defined for the target populations and values falling outside of these ranges may be considered as errors. For example, a college graduate could not have obtained his or her degree before completing high school.

Data editing is a very important step that should be taken prior to data analyses. Errors in the data base can lead to biased estimates for the parameters in the statistical models developed to summarize the data. For example, erroneous extreme values could lead to upwardly biased estimates of particular regression parameters. The reader is referred to Moser and Kalton (1972) for a more thorough discussion of data editing.

9.7 RIDGE ESTIMATION

When the independent variables are highly intercorrelated, multicolinearity may become a serious problem. As we saw previously, a consequence of multicolinearity is that the precision with which the regression coefficients are estimated is low. Hoerl and Kennard (1970) have proposed a class of estimators, called "ridge regression" estimators, that are biased but result in estimates with less total mean square error than ordinary least-squares estimators. The ridge estimator involves adding a small constant, k, to each diagonal element of $\mathbf{X'X}$ and defining the estimated regression parameter vector as

$$\hat{\beta}(k) = (\mathbf{X'X} + k\mathbf{I})^{-1}\mathbf{X'y} = (\mathbf{X'X} + k\mathbf{I})^{-1}\mathbf{X'X}\hat{\beta}$$

Since $E(\hat{\beta}(k)) = (\mathbf{X'X} + k\mathbf{I})^{-1}\mathbf{X'X}\beta$, we can see that the estimator is biased. However, there exists a value of k greater than zero such that the total mean square error of the estimator, defined as $E[(\hat{\beta}(k) - \beta)'(\hat{\beta}(k) - \beta)]$ is less than the total error of the ordinary least-squares estimator defined as $E[(\hat{\beta} - \beta)'(\hat{\beta} - \beta)]$. The procedure for finding the appropriate k to use in the ridge estimator is briefly described. Starting from zero, calculate $\hat{\beta}(k)$ for small successive values of k (.001, .002, and so on). Plot the value of each component of $\hat{\beta}(k)$ against k on a graph. This is called a ridge trace. At a certain value of k the components of $\hat{\beta}(k)$ will stabilize. If extreme multicolinearity is present the components of $\hat{\beta}(k)$ will vary dramatically at first, but they will eventually stabilize. Before accepting a value of k to be used as a final estimator, the analysis should also check the reasonableness of the regression parameter estimates in regard to sign and absolute value. In addition, the residual sum of squares should not be large relative to that generated by the ordinary least-squares estimators. Chatterjee and Price (1977) give some simple illustrations of the application of ridge regression estimation techniques.

9.8 LOGISTIC REGRESSION ANALYSIS

Quite frequently a dependent variable of interest is not continuous but takes on two values. For example, a researcher might want to predict whether or not a student enrolls in college using personal background variables as the independent variables, whether or not a patient improves under a certain treatment regimen, whether a consumer will buy a car or not, and so on.

One approach to handling this special situation is to code the two outcomes of the dependent variable as 0 and 1. For example, enrolled in college would be coded 1 and not enrolled in college coded 0. Then the binary 0,1 variable can be regressed upon the independent variables, which in the most general case can be a mixture of continuous and categorical variables.

Let $\mathbf{x}_i$ be a vector of independent variables for the ith subject, and $\boldsymbol{\beta}$ be a corresponding vector of regression parameters, then the dependent variable y_i can be expressed as $y_i = \mathbf{x}_i'\boldsymbol{\beta} + \epsilon_i$. Assuming $\mathbf{x}_i$ is fixed, $E(y_i) = \mathbf{x}_i'\boldsymbol{\beta}$. Since y_i is a 0,1 variable, $E(y_i)$ must be a probability. Let us refer to it as p_i; then we can write $p_i = \mathbf{x}_i'\boldsymbol{\beta}$. This says that for a given vector of independent variables, there is a fixed probability of the outcome coded 1 occurring. We used the fact that $E(\epsilon_i) = 0$. That this holds can be shown as follows. Suppose that $p_i = \mathbf{x}_i'\boldsymbol{\beta} = .80$, then y_i takes the value 1 with probability .80 and 0 occurs with probability .20. Consequently $\epsilon_i = y_i - \mathbf{x}_i'\boldsymbol{\beta} = 1 - .80 = .20$ with probability .80 and $0 - .80 = -.80$ with probability .20. Thus, $E(\epsilon_i) = (.20)\ .80 + (-.80)\ .20 = 0$. However, the assumption of constant variance of the ϵ_i (i.e., $E(\epsilon_i)^2 = \sigma^2$) is violated. This can easily be shown as follows:

$$E(\epsilon_i^2) = E(y_i - \mathbf{x}_i'\beta)^2 = E(y_i - p_i)^2 = E(y_i^2 - 2p_i y_i + p_i^2)$$

$$= E(y_i^2) - 2p_i E(y_i) + E(p_i^2) = p_i - 2p_i^2 + p_i^2 = p_i - p_i^2 = p_i(1 - p_i)$$

Since $E(\epsilon_i^2) = p_i(1 - p_i)$, the variance of ϵ_i is a function of the probability, p_i, associated with the vector, $\mathbf{x}_i$. That is, the variance of a 0, 1 variable depends upon the probability of occurrence of the favorable outcome, that is, one. For example, when $p_i = .20$, $E(\epsilon_i^2) = .16$ and when $p_i = .50$, $E(\epsilon_i^2) = .25$.

Even though the assumption of homoscedasticity is violated, we can still apply ordinary least squares and obtain an unbiased estimate of $\boldsymbol{\beta}$. That is, if $\mathbf{X}$ is a full rank matrix of the independent variables and $\mathbf{y}$ is a dependent variable vector of 0's and 1's, then $\hat{\boldsymbol{\beta}} = (\mathbf{X}'\mathbf{X})^{-1}\mathbf{X}'\mathbf{y}$. However, there are three problems associated with this approach. First, although $\hat{\boldsymbol{\beta}}$ is an unbiased estimator of $\boldsymbol{\beta}$, it is not an efficient estimator. Second, the classical estimator of the variance-covariance matrix of $\hat{\boldsymbol{\beta}}$, $\hat{\sigma}^2 (\mathbf{X}'\mathbf{X})^{-1}$ is biased so that tests of hypotheses concerning the elements of $\boldsymbol{\beta}$ are also biased. Third, probabilities can only take values from 0 to 1. However, it is quite possible for $p_i = \mathbf{x}_i'\boldsymbol{\beta}$ to take negative values or values greater than one for particular vectors $\mathbf{x}_i$ from a given sample.

The first two problems can be addressed by a weighted least-squares approach, which will be described briefly. First, estimate the model parameters using ordinary least squares. Second, for each observation calculate $\hat{p}_i = \mathbf{x}_i'\hat{\boldsymbol{\beta}}$. An estimate of the variance of ϵ_i for the ith sample member is then $\hat{p}_i(1 - \hat{p}_i)$. Third, reestimate the model parameters using weighted least squares where each observation is weighted by the reciprocal of its estimated variance. That is,

$$\boldsymbol{\beta} = [\mathbf{X}'\mathbf{V}^{-1}\mathbf{X}]^{-1}\mathbf{X}'\mathbf{V}^{-1}\mathbf{y}$$

where $\mathbf{V}^{-1}$ is a diagonal weighting matrix containing the reciprocals of the estimated variance,

$$\frac{1}{(\hat{p}_i)(1 - \hat{p}_i)}$$

for each observation. Observations with small variances receive more weight than observations with large variances. An iterative procedure can be used whereby the new $\hat{\boldsymbol{\beta}}$ can be used to reestimate the $\hat{p}_i(1 - \hat{p}_i)$ and these in turn can be used to generate yet another $\hat{\boldsymbol{\beta}}$. This iterative procedure can be continued until two succeeding vectors of estimated regression parameters converge in value according to some preset standard.

The third problem can be addressed by transforming the probability into a continuous variable that can take on any real valued number (that is, numbers ranging from $-\infty$ to $+\infty$). There is no problem, then, of a predicted value falling outside of a permissible range. One commonly using transformation that satisfies this property is

$$\ln \frac{p_i}{1 - p_i}$$

which is called the logistic transformation where ln represents $\log_e$.

In addition, the logistic transformation has an appealing conceptual property. Our previous formulation assumed that p_i was a linear function of the independent variables, that is, $p_i = \mathbf{x}_i'\boldsymbol{\beta}$. In many instances, this may not be realistic. The logistic transformation assumes that

$$p_i = \frac{1}{1 + e^{-\mathbf{x}_i'\boldsymbol{\beta}}}$$

a nonlinear function of $\mathbf{x}_i$. From this it can be seen that

$$\ln \frac{p_i}{1 - p_i} = \mathbf{x}_i'\boldsymbol{\beta}.$$

If we plotted p_i as a function of $\mathbf{x}_i'\boldsymbol{\beta}$, it would resemble a normal cumulative distribution function. That is, small changes in $\mathbf{x}_i'\boldsymbol{\beta}$ in the middle of the range of $\mathbf{x}_i'\boldsymbol{\beta}$ result in larger changes in probabilities than corresponding changes at the lower and upper extremes of $\mathbf{x}_i'\boldsymbol{\beta}$. For example, the probability of going to college would increase slowly until $\mathbf{x}_i'\boldsymbol{\beta}$ reached a certain threshold, then would increase at a substantially faster rate, and finally, after reaching another threshold, increase slowly again. For example, if the vector was made up of academic ability measures, then we would not expect the probability of attending college to increase very much as ability increased for low-ability individuals. It takes a certain ability level in order to succeed in college. Similarly, above a certain high ability level, more ability is not necessary to succeed in college. We would expect the strongest relationship between ability and enrollment in college in the middle range between these two thresholds.

The next step is to estimate the parameters, $\boldsymbol{\beta}$, in the logistic regression model

$$\ln \frac{p_i}{1 - p_i} = \mathbf{x}_i'\boldsymbol{\beta}$$

In the most general case we may have only one or, at best, a few 1,0 observations on the dependent variable for each $\mathbf{x}_i$. This means that we cannot use least squares to estimate the parameters of this model since no reasonable estimates of

$$\ln \frac{p_i}{1 - p_i}$$

can be generated from a sample spread so thin across the values of $\mathbf{x}_i$. The alternative is to estimate the parameters by maximum likelihood estimation. This procedure will be briefly sketched. The probability or likelihood of generating **y**, a vector of ones and zeros for the dependent variable, can be expressed as

$$\ell = \prod_{i=1}^{n} p_i^{y_i}(1 - p_i)^{(1-y_i)}$$

where p_i is the probability of the occurrence of a 1 (for example, 1 might represent enrolled in college) for the ith observation and y_i takes the value 1 if the event occurs (for example, enrolls in college) and 0 if the event does not occur (does not enroll in college). Since

$$p_i = \frac{1}{1 + e^{-x_i'\beta}},$$

the likelihood can be expressed as

$$\ell = \prod_{i=1}^{n} \left(\frac{1}{1 + e^{-x_i'\beta}}\right)^{y_i} \left(\frac{e^{-x_i'\beta}}{1 + e^{-x_i'\beta}}\right)^{1-y_i}$$

Maximum likelihood estimation involves finding an estimate of β that maximizes ℓ, the probability or likelihood of generating the sample values of $y_i = 1$ or 0 or, equivalently, the vector **y**. In other words, the idea is to find an estimate of $\hat{\beta}$ that is most likely to generate the observed vector **y**. There is no analytical solution to the problem, but there are iterative computer algorithms that yield $\hat{\beta}$. SAS and BMD have logistic regression packages. The BMD package even has a variable selection procedure.

As part of their output, these packages yield the maximum likelihood estimator $\hat{\beta}$, the standard errors of the regression coefficients, and various tests of hypotheses concerning the regression parameters. It is important to remember that the elements of $\hat{\beta}$ reflect influences of the independent variables on

$$\ln \frac{p_i}{1 - p_i}$$

and not p_i itself since we saw earlier that

$$p_i = \frac{1}{1 + e^{-x_i'\beta}}$$

a nonlinear function of $\mathbf{x}_i$. If we take the partial derivative of p_i with respect to an element x_{ij} of $\mathbf{x}_i$ where x_{ij} is the value of the jth independent variable for the ith observation or unit, we find that

$$\frac{\partial p_i}{\partial x_{ij}} = \frac{\beta_j(e^{-x_i'\beta})}{\left(1 + e^{-x_i'\beta}\right)^2}$$

The partial derivative

$$\frac{\partial p_i}{\partial x_{ij}}$$

represents the change in p due to a change in x_{ij} as the change in x_{ij} approaches zero so that it represents the influence of x_{ij} on p_i. We can see that the influence of x_{ij} on p_i depends not only on β_j but on all the values of the independent variables as well.

To help simplify the interpretation of the effect of a particular independent variable x_{ij} on p_i, some analysts arbitrarily set the elements in the vector $\mathbf{x}_i$ to their mean value in the sample, which we will denote as $\bar{\mathbf{x}}$. The influence of x_{ij} on p_i.

$$\frac{\partial p_i}{\partial x_{ij}}$$

then becomes

$$\frac{\beta_j(e^{-x'\beta})}{\left(1 + e^{-\bar{x}'\beta}\right)} = k\beta_j$$

since

$$\frac{e^{-\bar{x}'\beta}}{1 + e^{-\bar{x}'\beta}} = k$$

is a constant. This means that at the average values of the x_{ij}'s the influence of x_{ij} is proportional to β_j.

Appendix

Variable Description of Sample Data Base

Variable	Description
(1) SCVOCSC	Scaled Vocabulary Score (01-99)
(2) SCPICT	Scaled Score-Picture Numbers Total (01-99)
(3) SCRDSC	Scaled Reading Score (01-99)
(4) SCLGSC	Scaled Letter Groups Score (01-99)
(5) SCMATSC	Scaled Mathematics Score (01-99)
(6) SCMSCMT	Scaled Mosaic Comparisons Total (01-99)
(7) SEX	0 = male, 1 = female
(8) RACE	0 = white, 1 = nonwhite
(9) COLLEGE STATUS	1 = vocational, trade, or business school 2 = junior, community college 3 = four-year college/university 4 = not in school
(10) SES	Socioeconomic Status 1 = low 2 = medium 3 = high
(11) HSPGM	High School Program 0 = general, vocational-technical 1 = academic
(12) HSGRDS	High School Grades 1 = mostly A 2 = half A-B 3 = mostly C 4 = half B-C 5 = mostly C 6 = half C-D 7 = mostly D 8 = below D
(13) CREATIVE	Personal Orientation Towards Creativity scale (3-9)
(14) PRESSURE	Personal Orientation Towards Avoiding Pressure Scale (2-6)
(15) PEOPLE	Personal Orientation Towards People (2-6)
(16) PRESTIGE	Personal Orientation Towards Prestige (3-9)

APPENDIX
Sample of 300 NLS Respondents

ID	SCVOCSC	SCPICT	SCRDSC	SCLGSC	SCMATSC	SCMSCMT	SEX	RACE	COLLEGE	SES	HSPGM	HSGRDS	CREATIVE	PRESSURE	PEOPLE	PRESTIGE
1	52	48	48	63	56	57	0	0	4	2	1	5	5	4	4	4
2	66	48	68	55	56	57	1	0	2	3	1	2	4	3	5	4
3	45	45	39	45	46	52	1	0	2	3	0	6	6	4	4	7
4	58	53	54	62	58	49	0	0	2	3	1	4	5	3	4	5
5	45	65	46	59	53	54	1	0	2	2	0	4	7	5	5	6
6	51	58	46	55	50	58	1	0	4	3	1	3	5	4	5	5
7	40	50	42	55	49	41	0	0	4	1	1	3	4	3	3	5
8	46	44	45	62	51	54	0	0	1	2	0	5	4	5	3	5
9	39	56	42	40	47	37	0	0	1	2	0	3	8	4	6	7
10	60	41	64	54	62	59	1	0	3	2	1	2	5	3	4	6
11	57	49	56	54	46	49	1	0	4	2	0	2	9	5	5	6
12	34	65	44	47	49	60	0	0	4	2	0	3	9	5	6	9
13	55	66	68	60	64	49	0	0	2	2	1	3	7	5	4	5
14	51	41	61	54	47	52	1	1	4	1	1	2	8	3	6	6
15	63	61	54	59	64	62	0	0	2	2	1	3	3	4	3	6
16	49	50	56	54	58	51	1	0	4	3	0	4	7	5	3	5
17	60	61	64	62	53	54	0	0	4	2	1	3	6	5	5	6
18	66	41	50	52	50	52	0	0	3	3	1	3	6	6	6	6
19	54	38	59	61	53	49	1	0	4	2	0	2	5	5	6	5
20	54	58	56	49	49	60	1	0	1	2	0	2	5	6	5	4
21	54	45	46	43	29	48	1	1	2	1	1	5	8	6	6	6
22	36	58	64	59	60	58	1	0	2	1	1	2	7	6	3	4
23	51	43	37	36	42	53	0	0	2	2	0	5	6	4	6	5
24	51	46	54	48	53	55	0	0	3	3	1	4	7	4	6	6
25	58	49	64	48	62	50	1	0	1	2	1	5	6	4	6	8
26	69	39	66	46	65	49	0	0	2	3	1	3	6	3	3	7
27	60	64	54	51	55	41	1	0	1	1	1	3	5	3	6	5
28	43	52	50	58	55	51	1	0	3	2	1	3	5	3	6	8
29	43	59	59	64	59	64	1	1	1	1	0	2	3	3	2	4
30	39	64	39	55	51	54	1	1	1	3	0	6	3	6	4	4
31	48	59	61	59	54	51	1	0	2	2	1	3	3	5	5	5
32	51	56	57	59	60	59	1	0	3	2	1	3	6	6	3	6

33	60	66	64	55	65	48	0	0	2	3	1	2	5	4	5	7
34	60	53	44	32	50	38	0	0	3	2	1	3	5	5	4	7
35	48	63	59	59	58	60	0	0	3	3	1	2	8	4	5	4
36	57	58	37	49	55	51	0	0	2	3	0	3	6	4	4	4
37	69	66	64	64	67	53	0	0	3	3	1	1	9	4	6	8
38	36	52	38	52	39	23	1	1	4	1	0	4	6	5	6	8
39	69	39	68	56	51	51	1	0	3	2	0	2	6	5	5	4
40	57	41	42	61	49	53	0	0	3	2	0	4	8	5	6	8
41	39	46	30	42	36	41	0	1	1	2	1	4	5	5	5	9
42	42	49	56	55	55	59	0	0	3	2	1	3	7	5	6	7
43	55	49	56	50	44	53	1	0	3	3	0	2	8	4	6	3
44	60	61	61	52	65	62	1	0	3	2	0	1	8	4	5	6
45	61	49	60	46	52	52	1	0	2	3	1	4	7	4	6	7
46	49	61	66	58	67	62	0	0	2	3	1	3	6	4	5	4
47	63	50	59	52	64	58	1	1	4	2	1	1	8	4	5	5
48	48	42	49	59	55	51	1	0	4	3	1	4	7	3	6	5
49	48	49	46	57	47	61	1	1	3	1	1	3	5	5	5	6
50	49	53	58	52	44	56	1	0	4	2	1	4	5	3	4	6
51	49	50	42	51	48	53	0	1	4	2	0	7	6	4	4	7
52	54	40	49	42	53	46	0	0	4	2	0	4	8	4	6	7
53	48	45	51	48	42	56	1	0	4	2	0	4	8	6	6	5
54	57	51	59	63	64	49	0	0	3	2	1	2	4	4	3	6
55	54	64	52	58	59	54	1	1	3	3	1	3	6	5	3	4
56	39	38	42	51	53	57	0	0	2	2	1	2	3	3	3	4
57	66	66	68	55	67	49	0	0	3	3	1	1	4	3	4	5
58	66	55	64	63	58	61	1	0	4	2	1	2	5	3	4	6
59	54	41	49	58	49	60	0	0	4	2	0	4	7	6	4	8
60	69	43	56	54	53	59	1	0	2	3	0	4	9	4	6	5
61	48	44	52	46	38	35	0	1	4	2	1	2	6	5	5	6
62	60	48	64	63	58	51	0	0	2	2	1	3	4	3	4	6
63	39	52	46	49	40	43	1	0	3	2	1	3	8	4	6	9
64	51	57	46	49	55	65	0	1	4	2	0	3	5	5	3	5
65	54	41	54	59	56	52	1	0	2	2	1	2	7	4	6	5
66	66	60	68	59	62	55	0	0	3	3	1	1	8	4	5	3
67	46	65	57	52	65	58	0	1	3	1	1	1	8	4	6	9
68	42	46	40	45	42	40	1	0	1	2	0	3	4	4	6	8

(continued)

APPENDIX (Continued)

ID	*SCVOCSC*	*SCPICT*	*SCRDSC*	*SCLGSC*	*SCMATSC*	*SCMSCMT*	*SEX*	*RACE*	*COLLEGE*	*SES*	*HSPGM*	*HSGRDS*	*CREATIVE*	*PRESSURE*	*PEOPLE*	*PRESTIGE*
69	63	57	61	63	64	71	0	0	3	3	1	1	7	3	6	4
70	54	30	34	48	44	58	1	0	4	2	0	3	5	4	4	6
71	45	53	44	61	47	50	1	0	1	2	0	3	5	5	4	7
72	52	49	42	49	58	50	0	0	1	2	1	4	4	2	3	4
73	63	54	59	57	65	52	0	0	4	1	1	4	8	5	6	7
74	30	57	44	47	58	51	0	0	4	2	0	5	6	4	4	6
75	61	50	60	54	53	59	1	0	1	1	0	2	8	6	4	9
76	48	38	49	45	56	48	1	1	4	2	1	4	8	5	6	7
77	66	66	64	62	55	53	1	0	4	2	0	2	5	3	6	7
78	57	54	62	63	62	54	1	0	4	2	0	2	7	5	4	6
79	46	66	61	58	51	48	1	1	3	3	1	4	6	5	5	5
80	54	66	49	52	58	53	0	1	4	1	1	3	5	4	6	7
81	51	56	47	53	53	48	0	1	2	1	0	4	5	6	5	6
82	48	38	51	47	44	55	0	0	4	2	0	4	7	3	4	6
83	72	66	66	63	67	52	1	0	3	3	1	1	7	3	5	8
84	42	30	43	55	42	43	1	0	2	3	0	5	8	4	5	4
85	51	60	61	55	60	54	1	0	2	3	1	2	7	6	6	5
86	66	66	59	57	58	53	1	0	3	3	0	1	4	5	3	4
87	41	58	48	59	53	59	1	0	2	2	0	4	5	4	5	6
88	42	53	46	57	46	51	1	0	2	2	0	4	5	4	5	6
89	51	62	56	53	56	56	0	0	4	3	0	5	8	5	5	8
90	48	54	56	51	60	49	0	0	3	3	1	3	7	4	3	5
91	45	49	36	45	37	49	1	1	4	2	0	4	4	3	2	4
92	55	65	61	62	65	66	1	0	3	3	1	1	7	5	5	6
93	51	44	56	60	49	48	0	0	3	2	1	5	5	4	6	6
94	63	62	51	55	62	50	0	0	4	2	1	3	9	6	6	8
95	48	43	42	49	39	49	1	0	1	3	0	4	9	5	6	8
96	66	64	64	51	51	57	1	0	3	3	1	2	5	2	6	4
97	66	66	66	62	65	65	0	0	3	3	0	2	9	5	6	3
98	48	44	38	56	41	49	1	1	4	1	0	3	8	4	6	5
99	45	46	51	51	64	46	0	0	3	3	1	3	6	4	5	6
100	43	43	38	47	51	42	0	0	1	1	0	5	5	4	3	4
101	69	66	61	60	64	50	1	0	3	2	1	5	8	5	6	3
102	54	42	61	59	56	49	1	0	3	3	0	4	7	5	6	4
103	42	39	59	61	56	61	1	0	2	2	1	2	7	4	6	8
104	36	33	40	28	40	36	0	1	2	1	0	4	7	4	5	6

105	57	45	52	53	46	50	0	1	3	1	1	3	6	4	5	9
106	48	61	44	50	42	49	0	0	2	3	0	4	4	5	4	8
107	45	35	37	45	40	48	1	0	1	2	0	3	7	3	6	7
108	57	36	37	45	49	55	0	0	3	3	1	4	9	6	6	9
109	48	56	52	45	57	60	0	0	3	3	1	4	5	4	4	4
110	51	42	59	51	53	50	1	1	3	2	1	3	3	5	5	5
111	69	52	61	52	64	66	0	0	3	3	1	2	5	2	2	3
112	45	49	49	57	62	48	0	0	1	2	1	2	6	5	5	6
113	51	49	49	57	60	61	0	0	4	3	0	4	8	5	4	4
114	60	66	54	55	62	56	0	0	3	2	0	3	6	5	5	5
115	41	64	53	50	43	45	1	0	1	2	1	3	7	4	6	4
116	39	39	32	36	38	47	0	1	4	1	0	5	7	5	6	9
117	48	42	56	57	49	50	1	0	4	1	0	4	5	6	4	5
118	49	60	54	57	67	53	1	0	3	3	1	2	7	5	5	6
119	49	59	52	50	60	53	0	0	3	1	1	4	8	4	6	6
120	49	52	47	52	42	43	1	1	3	1	1	4	8	4	5	7
121	69	64	62	63	62	55	1	0	3	3	1	3	4	4	6	4
122	57	66	56	61	65	59	0	0	3	3	1	3	8	5	6	4
123	66	54	52	53	60	54	0	0	2	2	1	4	7	4	4	7
124	42	61	39	49	42	47	0	0	4	1	1	4	8	4	4	3
125	35	42	33	31	31	27	1	1	1	1	1	3	6	3	4	3
126	63	56	61	24	49	24	0	0	4	3	0	4	6	2	3	5
127	43	64	46	53	60	60	0	0	4	2	1	3	5	6	5	8
128	66	66	59	63	53	50	1	0	3	3	1	1	7	4	6	5
129	33	37	42	51	38	49	1	1	2	1	0	4	5	5	6	8
130	53	66	55	60	65	64	0	0	3	3	1	3	6	5	5	6
131	48	57	51	62	60	52	0	0	2	2	1	3	6	3	4	6
132	51	66	64	58	64	47	1	0	4	1	1	1	6	4	6	4
133	45	34	54	55	62	59	0	0	2	1	1	4	6	6	4	5
134	72	50	68	61	65	58	0	0	3	3	1	1	8	4	6	5
135	51	52	54	57	47	50	1	0	4	1	0	5	5	4	6	5
136	48	44	51	45	56	65	1	0	3	2	0	3	8	4	4	7
137	47	40	66	53	47	53	1	0	2	1	1	2	7	5	6	7
138	32	34	37	26	45	28	0	1	3	1	0	3	8	6	5	9
139	33	33	33	38	42	40	0	0	1	2	0	4	9	4	5	6
140	37	36	48	38	49	50	0	0	2	3	0	4	7	4	4	8

(continued)

APPENDIX (Continued)

ID	*SCVOCSC*	*SCPICT*	*SCRDSC*	*SCLGSC*	*SCMATSC*	*SCMSCMT*	*SEX*	*RACE*	*COLLEGE*	*SES*	*HSPGM*	*HSGRDS*	*CREATIVE*	*PRESSURE*	*PEOPLE*	*PRESTIGE*
141	40	40	37	37	37	52	1	1	4	1	1	4	9	5	6	8
142	42	60	49	57	56	45	0	0	2	2	1	4	9	6	5	8
143	63	65	68	61	58	63	1	0	3	2	1	2	8	4	6	5
144	40	60	54	53	53	50	1	0	4	2	0	4	8	5	5	5
145	36	49	42	42	42	48	1	1	4	2	1	5	7	5	6	5
146	54	60	59	55	51	63	1	0	3	2	0	1	8	4	6	5
147	61	63	49	50	51	52	0	0	4	1	0	4	7	5	3	4
148	46	57	46	53	56	63	0	0	2	3	1	4	6	6	4	8
149	66	53	66	59	67	57	0	0	3	3	1	1	7	2	6	4
150	39	66	42	48	39	40	1	1	4	1	0	4	3	4	2	3
151	57	41	56	45	64	49	0	0	2	2	1	3	7	4	3	5
152	45	51	47	46	51	55	1	0	4	2	0	2	8	6	3	5
153	45	49	59	57	55	47	0	0	2	3	1	4	8	4	4	5
154	60	64	59	63	62	52	0	0	3	2	1	3	6	5	3	6
155	66	48	68	64	60	52	1	0	3	3	1	2	8	4	6	3
156	60	64	51	57	64	78	0	0	3	3	1	2	5	4	4	7
157	66	65	68	59	67	63	1	0	3	3	1	1	7	5	6	7
158	48	47	46	45	47	50	1	0	2	3	1	3	9	5	6	5
159	61	49	44	54	45	52	1	0	3	2	1	6	6	5	6	3
160	36	45	34	33	48	41	1	1	3	1	1	2	9	6	6	9
161	55	59	52	59	62	48	0	1	3	3	1	2	8	5	4	5
162	48	42	59	45	44	53	0	0	3	2	1	3	9	6	5	8
163	66	45	54	52	53	47	1	0	2	3	1	4	5	4	6	6
164	60	43	59	57	65	57	1	0	4	1	0	2	6	4	5	5
165	51	43	37	39	35	41	1	0	1	2	0	5	7	6	6	4
166	42	40	46	56	41	67	1	0	1	2	0	3	5	5	5	5
167	39	43	55	58	58	49	0	0	4	2	0	4	6	5	4	6
168	66	40	54	57	60	52	0	0	3	3	1	5	8	4	4	4
169	36	35	37	38	40	35	0	1	4	1	0	4	5	3	4	7
170	45	57	46	50	60	52	0	1	3	1	1	2	9	4	6	9
171	39	47	44	37	46	54	0	0	3	2	1	5	3	4	6	5
172	47	37	58	42	37	38	1	0	4	2	0	5	8	6	6	5
173	66	56	68	61	67	23	0	0	3	3	1	2	5	2	6	8
174	60	66	68	60	65	56	1	0	3	3	1	1	3	6	5	6

175	48	45	31	47	39	40	0	1	4	2	0	6	5	4	6	6
176	60	57	56	57	64	56	0	0	4	1	0	4	6	4	3	4
177	60	65	46	51	46	58	0	1	4	2	1	6	9	6	6	8
178	60	37	56	60	62	59	1	0	3	2	1	2	4	2	4	3
179	66	57	61	59	58	62	1	0	3	3	1	1	8	5	6	6
180	60	44	66	59	62	52	0	0	3	2	1	3	7	5	5	6
181	69	44	64	62	64	54	0	0	3	3	1	3	9	4	6	6
182	63	62	54	63	51	49	1	0	3	3	1	2	7	5	6	6
183	51	65	51	58	60	50	0	0	4	3	0	2	6	6	4	6
184	39	53	59	43	58	44	0	0	3	2	1	3	7	4	6	6
185	39	66	61	55	59	47	1	0	2	2	1	2	6	5	5	6
186	63	64	54	59	40	93	1	0	4	2	1	3	5	4	4	5
187	51	59	42	55	51	43	0	0	2	2	0	4	6	4	4	6
188	42	35	51	36	53	32	0	1	3	2	1	5	8	5	5	7
189	54	41	42	40	35	44	1	0	4	2	0	5	8	4	6	6
190	45	64	61	62	64	53	0	1	3	2	1	5	7	4	3	6
191	45	46	32	37	29	35	1	1	4	1	0	4	7	5	6	8
192	50	49	59	49	58	41	0	0	3	2	1	2	6	4	4	8
193	45	29	35	28	37	34	1	0	1	1	0	3	7	3	6	6
194	58	56	54	57	56	55	1	0	3	2	1	1	7	5	5	7
195	39	63	46	43	44	62	0	1	3	1	1	3	5	4	6	7
196	63	64	47	56	56	56	1	0	2	2	1	2	5	6	6	6
197	48	56	44	34	45	55	0	0	2	2	1	4	9	5	6	7
198	33	47	37	49	53	36	1	1	1	1	0	4	7	3	6	7
199	52	50	64	59	64	54	0	0	2	2	1	2	6	4	3	7
200	69	58	59	60	56	55	1	0	4	3	1	2	5	2	6	6
201	57	59	59	59	58	65	1	1	2	3	0	2	4	3	4	4
202	41	55	37	59	46	58	0	1	3	1	0	3	5	3	4	4
203	52	46	52	53	53	42	0	0	4	2	1	4	8	5	6	6
204	72	65	64	50	62	51	0	0	3	3	1	1	5	3	6	8
205	54	34	45	44	42	41	0	0	3	2	1	3	6	4	5	6
206	39	46	36	38	42	47	0	1	4	1	0	5	9	6	4	6
207	45	36	42	32	38	37	1	1	1	1	0	3	8	6	6	9
208	46	58	40	57	40	61	0	1	2	1	0	6	4	3	3	4
209	69	51	68	61	64	93	1	0	3	2	1	1	7	6	6	4
210	36	43	54	22	35	38	1	0	4	2	0	4	6	5	4	6

(continued)

APPENDIX (Continued)

ID	SCVOCSC	SCPICT	SCRDSC	SCLGSC	SCMATSC	SCMSCMT	SEX	RACE	COLLEGE	SES	HSPGM	HSGRDS	CREATIVE	PRESSURE	PEOPLE	PRESTIGE
211	48	53	57	48	58	59	1	0	3	3	1	3	8	6	6	5
212	69	40	61	64	62	61	1	0	3	2	0	1	7	4	6	5
213	57	39	54	39	58	40	1	0	4	2	0	3	7	4	3	3
214	49	50	51	52	51	44	1	0	2	2	1	3	9	6	6	7
215	57	62	44	40	51	49	1	0	3	3	1	4	3	3	6	3
216	46	51	51	63	65	67	1	0	2	3	0	3	3	4	4	5
217	54	40	49	51	53	46	0	0	2	2	1	3	7	5	6	6
218	54	49	56	61	62	55	0	0	3	3	0	4	7	4	3	5
219	54	65	64	59	60	57	1	0	3	3	1	1	8	3	6	5
220	48	56	44	60	56	50	0	0	4	2	1	5	4	4	4	7
221	47	54	58	60	58	49	0	1	4	1	1	2	9	5	6	8
222	63	45	49	61	48	69	0	0	4	2	1	3	4	4	4	6
223	66	41	61	51	58	65	0	0	3	2	1	3	9	5	6	9
224	36	49	44	41	56	49	0	1	3	2	0	5	6	5	5	6
225	55	50	49	51	55	57	0	0	4	2	1	2	8	4	6	8
226	48	38	49	37	42	60	1	1	4	1	0	4	5	4	3	6
227	60	46	51	42	56	53	0	0	2	3	1	4	8	3	2	6
228	46	45	51	41	44	62	0	1	4	1	1	3	6	4	6	7
229	57	55	61	65	64	45	0	0	3	3	1	3	6	2	5	6
230	69	53	68	62	67	54	1	0	3	3	1	2	7	5	3	4
231	42	59	59	49	53	91	1	0	4	2	0	2	4	3	4	4
232	38	30	35	22	35	33	0	1	4	2	0	4	6	4	4	6
233	54	57	59	55	56	62	0	0	3	2	1	4	5	4	4	4
234	72	41	68	60	62	48	0	0	2	3	1	5	7	2	3	6
235	57	48	51	49	55	41	0	0	3	3	1	4	4	4	2	5
236	45	50	36	59	56	61	1	0	2	2	1	4	6	5	4	7
237	69	35	66	62	67	55	0	0	3	3	1	2	6	4	3	5
238	36	34	44	36	44	40	0	0	4	3	0	3	7	6	4	9
239	51	66	57	63	62	59	1	0	3	2	0	1	7	6	5	6
240	42	49	39	40	29	29	1	1	2	2	1	4	8	4	6	5
241	66	65	66	64	65	57	0	0	3	3	1	2	6	2	4	7
242	47	64	56	60	65	65	1	0	3	2	1	3	7	2	4	7
243	57	43	51	59	53	46	0	0	1	1	0	2	6	5	4	7
244	60	53	64	52	58	52	0	0	3	3	1	4	8	2	4	7

245	69	38	68	56	67	45	0	1	3	2	1	3	5	2	5	6
246	66	42	56	57	56	45	0	0	1	2	0	4	7	4	4	8
247	45	66	51	47	63	47	0	0	3	2	1	3	4	6	4	5
248	63	66	50	58	66	63	0	0	3	2	1	1	3	4	3	6
249	60	54	56	53	56	48	1	0	2	2	1	1	7	3	6	7
250	66	56	58	57	62	63	0	0	3	3	1	3	6	3	3	5
251	63	66	64	64	67	57	0	0	3	2	1	1	5	3	3	4
252	66	56	46	51	51	23	0	0	3	3	1	4	7	4	4	9
253	54	58	46	61	55	55	0	0	4	2	1	4	7	5	6	6
254	51	51	32	57	58	45	1	0	4	3	0	2	6	5	4	6
255	43	54	54	55	53	41	0	1	3	2	0	2	8	6	6	8
256	49	65	44	53	56	44	0	0	3	1	0	6	3	4	3	4
257	39	42	33	40	44	33	1	0	2	1	0	4	5	5	5	4
258	60	66	42	54	58	56	1	0	3	3	1	2	6	2	6	5
259	61	56	57	54	59	49	1	0	2	2	1	2	9	6	6	4
260	61	66	57	57	55	67	1	0	2	2	1	3	8	4	5	6
261	63	51	64	36	46	60	0	0	2	3	0	5	6	5	3	5
262	54	36	45	39	46	44	1	0	2	2	1	3	7	4	2	4
263	63	56	61	52	54	52	1	0	3	3	1	4	7	4	6	4
264	43	49	50	49	51	65	0	1	3	2	1	2	5	5	4	6
265	69	61	66	58	67	54	0	0	2	2	1	1	6	4	6	8
266	36	64	29	32	38	45	1	0	4	1	0	4	6	5	6	8
267	61	40	62	64	54	65	1	0	3	3	1	2	6	6	5	5
268	44	37	31	50	42	40	0	0	3	1	1	3	6	3	5	7
269	39	62	49	47	46	52	1	0	4	1	0	6	7	4	5	6
270	51	37	61	53	62	55	0	0	4	2	1	3	7	6	6	4
271	45	48	46	59	44	58	0	0	2	3	0	3	7	4	6	8
272	66	49	49	65	56	63	1	0	3	3	1	3	5	6	6	7
273	54	63	57	52	62	51	0	0	4	3	1	5	6	2	6	5
274	72	57	64	52	60	49	0	0	3	3	1	2	7	4	5	6
275	45	65	59	55	62	54	1	0	3	3	1	2	5	4	3	4
276	69	49	66	58	64	61	0	1	4	3	1	2	8	5	3	3
277	54	51	61	54	42	47	1	0	4	2	1	4	9	5	3	4
278	60	52	54	59	58	66	0	0	3	3	1	3	4	4	4	6
279	54	35	49	47	47	49	0	0	2	2	1	5	8	5	6	7
280	55	52	61	54	64	32	0	1	3	2	1	4	7	6	5	6

(continued)

APPENDIX (Continued)

ID	SCVOCSC	SCPICT	SCRDSC	SCLGSC	SCMATSC	SCMSCMT	SEX	RACE	COLLEGE	SES	HSPGM	HSGRDS	CREATIVE	PRESSURE	PEOPLE	PRESTIGE
281	42	36	29	61	55	48	0	0	2	1	0	4	5	4	5	5
282	47	48	49	51	55	46	1	0	4	2	0	3	3	6	6	5
283	57	59	52	52	47	54	1	0	2	2	0	3	7	4	5	8
284	48	40	46	51	55	59	0	0	4	2	1	5	9	6	6	9
285	42	47	51	47	31	59	1	0	4	1	0	4	5	2	6	5
286	63	59	56	59	49	54	1	0	2	2	1	2	3	5	6	5
287	48	54	52	61	51	40	1	0	1	2	1	4	9	4	5	5
288	58	66	59	64	64	68	1	0	3	2	1	2	5	4	6	7
289	64	61	56	57	58	49	1	0	3	3	1	4	5	4	6	4
290	48	61	51	42	40	50	0	0	4	2	0	4	5	5	3	6
291	66	65	68	60	65	54	1	0	4	3	1	2	6	5	4	3
292	52	64	64	59	64	56	0	0	3	3	1	3	8	5	4	5
293	60	53	56	55	47	52	0	0	1	2	0	4	7	3	6	6
294	51	47	54	53	42	73	0	0	1	1	0	3	7	6	6	8
295	46	37	38	47	50	46	1	0	2	2	0	3	5	4	6	6
296	69	49	59	57	55	48	0	0	4	3	0	2	6	5	2	4
297	54	64	64	42	43	57	1	0	2	3	1	4	8	6	6	7
298	54	57	59	60	64	65	1	0	2	2	1	1	6	4	6	6
299	69	63	68	64	67	61	1	0	3	3	1	1	6	4	3	4
300	48	65	64	63	65	46	1	0	3	1	1	2	8	5	4	8

References

Anderson, T. W. *An introduction to multivariate statistical analysis.* New York: John Wiley, 1958.

Bailar, B. A., Bailey, L., & Corby, C. A comparison of some adjustment and weighting procedures for survey data. In N. K. Namboodiri (Ed.), *Survey sampling and measurement.* New York: Academic, 1978.

Barnett, V. *Comparative statistical inference.* New York: John Wiley, 1973.

Barr, A. J., Goodnight, J., Sall, J., & Helwig, J. *A user's guide to SAS.* Raleigh, NC: Sparks, 1976.

Beale, E. M., & Little, R.J.A. Missing data in multivariate analysis. *Journal of the Royal Statistical Society*, 1957, *37*, 129-145.

Campbell, D. T., & Stanley, J. C. *Experimental and quasi-experimental designs for research.* Chicago: Rand McNally, 1966.

Chatterjee, S., & Price, B. *Regression analysis by example.* New York: John Wiley, 1977.

Dempster, A., Laird, N. M., & Rubin, D. B. Maximum likelihood from incomplete data via the EM algorithm. *Journal of the Royal Statistical Society*, 1977, *39*, 1-38.

Dixon, W. J. (Ed.). *BMDP: Biometrical Computer Programs.* Berkeley: University of California Press, 1975.

Draper, N. R. *Applied regression analysis.* New York: John Wiley, 1966.

Elashoff, R. M., & Afifi, A. A. Missing values in multivariate statistics, I: Review of the literature. *Journal of the American Statistical Association*, 1966, *61*, 595-604.

Freud, R. J., & Littell, R. C. *SAS for linear models: A guide to ANOVA and GLM procedures.* Cary, NC: SAS Institute, Inc., 1980.

Graybill, F. A. *Introduction to matrices with applications in statistics.* Belmont, CA: Wadsworth, 1969.

Hanushek, E. A., & Jackson, J. E. *Statistical methods for social scientists.* New York: Academic, 1977.

Harrell, T. W., & Harrell, M. S. Army general classification test scores for civilian occupations. *Educational and Psychological Measurement*, 1945, *5*, 229-239.

Hicks, C. R. *Fundamental concepts in the design of experiments.* New York: Holt, Rinehart & Winston, 1973.

Hoerl, A. E., & Kennard, R. W. Ridge regression: Applications to nonorthogonal problems. *Technometrics*, 1970, *12*, 69-82.

Hohn, F. E. *Elementary matrix algebra.* New York: Macmillan, 1973.

Johnston, J. *Econometric methods* (2nd ed.). New York: McGraw-Hill, 1972.

Kerckhoff, A. C. *Ambition and attainment.* Rose Monograph Series, 1974.

Kish, L. *Survey sampling.* New York: John Wiley, 1965.

Kish, L., & Frankel, M. R. Inference from complex samples. *Journal of the Royal Statistical Society*, 1974, *36*, 1-37.

Mendenhall, W. *Introduction to linear models and the design and analysis of experiments.* Belmont, CA: Wadsworth, 1968.

Mood, A. M., Graybill, F. A., & Boes, D. C. *Introduction to the theory of statistics* (3rd ed.). New York: McGraw-Hill, 1974.

Moser, C., & Kalton, G. *Survey methods in social investigation.* New York: Basic Books, 1972.

Nie, N. H., Hull, C. H., Jenkins, J. G., Steinbrenner, K., & Bent, D. H. *SPSS: Statistical package for the social sciences.* New York: McGraw-Hill, 1975.

Platek, R., Singh, M. P., & Tremblay, V. Adjustment for nonresponse in surveys. In N. K. Namboodiri (Ed.), *Survey sampling and measurement.* New York: Academic, 1978.

Riecken, H. W., & Boruch, R. F. (Eds.). *Social experimentation: A method for planning and evaluating social intervention.* New York: Academic, 1974.

Robinson, W. Ecological correlations and the behavior of individuals. *American Sociological Review*, 1950, *15*, 351-357.

Searle, S. R. *Matrix algebra for the biological sciences.* New York: John Wiley, 1966.

Searle, S. R. *Linear models.* New York: John Wiley, 1971.

Shah, B. V. Variance estimates for complex statistics from multistage sample surveys. In N. K. Namboodiri (Ed.), *Survey sampling and measurement.* New York: Academic, 1978.

Index

About the Author

GEORGE H. DUNTEMAN is currently Chief Scientist at the Research Triangle Institute, where he is actively involved in applied research, primarily in the social and behavioral sciences. He has previously held research appointments at the Educational Testing Service and the U.S. Army Research Institute. He has also held assistant and associate professorships at the University of Rochester and the University of Florida, respectively. Dr. Dunteman received his Ph.D from Louisiana State University in industrial/organizational psychology with a minor in industrial engineering. He also has an M.S. degree from Iowa State University with a major in industrial psychology and a minor in statistics. His B.A. degree from St. Lawrence University is in sociology. He is currently on the editorial board of Educational and Psychological Measurement *and has published widely in professional journals.*